# CHURCHILL'S 'WORLD CRISIS' AS HISTORY

ROBIN PRIOR

CROOM HELM
London & Canberra

©1983 Robin Prior
Croom Helm Ltd, Provident House, Burrell Row,
Beckenham, Kent BR3 1AT

British Library Cataloguing in Publication Data

Prior, Robin
    Churchill's world crisis as history.
    1. Churchill, Winston S. (Winston Spencer) *1874-1965*.
    World crisis 1911-1918–Criticism and
    interpretation
    I. Title
    941.082'092'4    DA566.9.C
    ISBN 0-7099-2011-3

Printed and bound in Great Britain by
Biddles Ltd, Guildford and King's Lynn

# CONTENTS

# TABLES

FOR   HEATHER

# ACKNOWLEDGEMENTS

In the course of writing this book I have accumulated many debts of gratitude to individuals and organizations which I would like to acknowledge.

For permission to quote from and use papers in their care I would like to thank; the Trustees of the British Museum (Jellicoe, Balfour, Evan-Thomas and Frewen Papers); the Public Record Office (Admiralty, War Office, Foreign Office, Cabinet, Munitions, Grey, Kitchener and Nicolson Papers); the National Maritime Museum, Greenwich (Richmond, Oliver, Limpus and D'Eyncourt Papers); Imperial War Museum (Dawnay and Godfrey Papers); Churchill College, Cambridge (Robeck, Hankey, Rawlinson, McKenna, Macliesh Papers); the Bodleian Library, Oxford (Asquith and Selborne Papers); Kings College, London (Hamilton, Robertson, Stern and Fuller Papers); the House of Lords Record Office (Bonar Law, Lloyd George and Donald Papers); the Ministry of Defence (Jackson Papers); the Australian National War Memorial (Birdwood Papers); Major C.T. Wilson (Wilson Papers); Lord Keyes (Keyes Papers); Mrs. Nutting (Beatty Papers).

I am very grateful to C & T Publications for permission to quote from the Churchill Papers, without which this work would have hardly been possible.

All quotations from The World Crisis are reproduced by the kind permission of the Hamlyn Publishing Group. Quotations from Martin Gilbert's invaluable Official life of Churchill and the Companion volumes of documents are reproduced by permission of William Heinemann Ltd.

Many people helped in the preparation of this book; I must thank Bev Arnold and Sonia Zabolocki who expertly typed the manuscript and David Watts who assisted in the compilation of the index. I am also grateful to the History Department of the University of Adelaide and its past Chairman Tony Denholm for electing me to the position of Visiting Research Fellow and thus facilitating the completion of the manuscript.

The manuscript was read in its entirety by Doctor Gordon Baker and Doctor Keith Macnider. Their comments were greatly appreciated as was their encouragement during the course of writing.

Thanks must also go to Martin Gilbert who first suggested I make use of the Churchill Archives and who took time from his busy schedule to introduce me to the riches of that collection.

Professor Trevor Wilson first suggested to me the subject of this book. He read the manuscript in its entirety and his suggestions invariably resulted in improvements in content and style. He has been to me mentor, critic and, above all, friend, and my debt to him is immense.

My wife has now lived with The World Crisis for far too long. She has borne this burden with patience and understanding. She read the whole manuscript and unerringly detected errors of logic and grammar. This book is dedicated to her, for without her it could not have been written.

It remains to be said that the responsibility for any errors of judgement or fact which remain in the book are the authors alone.

Winston Churchill wrote The World Crisis 1911-1918 between
1919 and 1926, during which time he was variously Secretary
of State for War, Colonial Secretary, out of Parliament, and
Chancellor of the Exchequer. The first volume of the book
was published in April 1923 and was an instant best-seller,
the first printing of 7,500 copies being sold out before
publication day. A further 2,500 copies were printed within
three days of publication. Volumes 2 and 3 were almost as
popular, each eventually selling over 10,000 copies. Nor did
the popularity of the book diminish over the years. In 1931
a one-volume abridgement appeared, and in 1933-4 an
illustrated edition of the whole work was issued in
fortnightly parts. In 1939 the full version with some new
material was published in two volumes, and this was reset in
four volumes in 1950. (Because the 1950 edition is the most
recent and complete version, it is the one used here.) A
paperback edition of the one-volume abridgement first
appeared in 1960 and this was reissued in a two-volume
edition which is still in print. Consequently The World
Crisis is the only general survey of the war published in the
twenties to be currently available. Over the years the book
has been translated into French, German, Italian, Swedish,
Spanish and Serbo-Croat. And rather surprisingly, given the
nature of the book, the film rights were sold to Paramount in
1960.[1]

Obviously The World Crisis has been popular over a long
period of time. But the book would clearly need to possess
some other quality than longevity to justify the intense
scrutiny to which it will be subjected here.

There are many reasons for undertaking a detailed
analysis of The World Crisis. First, the book has not only
been widely read but also influential. Popular views on such
matters as the Dardanelles, the use to which the tank was put
during the war, and the competence of the British Generals
often coincide with views expressed in The World Crisis,
suggesting a causal link between the two. Scholarly

views also have been much influenced by this work. During the period when many of the documents it contained were not generally available to historians The World Crisis was used almost as a primary source. For example Paul Guinn, writing in the mid-1960's, cites the book no less than 38 times in the course of a chapter on the Dardanelles.[2] Later, when the primary sources became available, we still find The World Crisis being extensively quoted for Churchill's comments and opinions on various phases of the war by such historians as Robert Rhodes James, Arthur Marder and George Cassar.

Secondly, the book raises many important questions fundamental to the course of the war, and a study of it provides a useful route into an inquiry about these questions.

Thirdly, The World Crisis raises all sorts of issues concerning Churchill's own role in the war, especially his influence on the navy and the part he played in the inception of the Dardanelles campaign. Given the intrinsic importance of Churchill's career, these clearly merit study.

Fourthly, although The World Crisis has been much employed as a source, it has as Robert Rhodes James remarks, "received inadequate critical analysis".[3] Only two attempts have been made in recent years to assess Churchill's historical works. Maurice Ashley, a specialist in 17th century English history and a former research assistant of Churchill's, has written a book on the subject.[4] And J.H. Plumb, an expert on 18th century history, has contributed an essay on Churchill the historian.[5] However, neither of these studies attempts a substantial analysis of any particular work of Churchill's. Ashley merely summarizes the various themes running through The World Crisis and in the main eschews critical comment.

In the nineteen-twenties a volume entitled The World Crisis: A Criticism appeared. However, this work merely consisted of five reprinted journal articles, by various authors, three of whom confine themselves to discussions of very narrow aspects of Churchill's work. Of the other chapters, one is an important critique of Churchill's treatment of the Battle of Jutland, the other a rather slight attempt to sum up Churchill's qualities as an historian.[6] The overall effect is that no real impression is gained of the strengths and weaknesses of The World Crisis.

Consequently a detailed analysis of The World Crisis is plainly overdue. In embarking on this task I have been guided in my approach by the structure of Churchill's book. The World Crisis does not deal with all phases of the war in the same detail. Two-thirds of it is concerned with the events of 1914-15 and only one-third with the remaining years of the war. The same, therefore, is true of this study. However, where appropriate a discussion of the motives which led Churchill to treat one phase of the war in detail and leave another out altogether has been included.

Some explanation is needed for the methods adopted to

analyse the various chapters. Where a subject has been examined in great detail by Churchill it has been necessary in the first half of a chapter to construct a narrative of events, based on the primary sources, so as to establish both what happened and also (where appropriate) Churchill's place therein. The second half of these chapters compares this narrative with Churchill's version of events in The World Crisis. On other occasions, where Churchill's treatment is more sketchy or episodic, it has seemed appropriate simply to summarise Churchill's main arguments and then compare them with the major documentary sources. Thus a uniform structure is not employed, but this is amply justified by the varying treatment accorded to different phases of the war by Churchill himself.

For various reasons it has not been possible to discuss all the aspects of the war dealt with in The World Crisis. Some have been excluded because of their minor importance. In this catagory can be placed such episodes as the work of the "Dunkirk Circus", the activities of the China Squadron, the marshalling of the Colonial expeditions against the German colonies. In other instances, subjects certainly of importance in themselves have been excluded because they have received summary treatment by Churchill. A noteworthy instance is the Third Battle of Ypres.

A different reason—considerations of space—has led to the exclusion from discussion of one considerable section of Churchill's work. In order to keep the present volume within manageable limits, it has been necessary to omit a consideration of Churchill's version of events prior to August 1914: that is to the sections in which Churchill relates the diplomatic manoeuvres of the Great Powers from 1870, and chronicles his own role in the development of the pre-war navy.

Some brief remarks may be made about these chapters. First, by dealing with the diplomatic origins of the war, Churchill makes it clear from the outset that his work is intended to be more than a personal memoir. Secondly, these chapters include the first (but by no means the last) sections of the book in the preparation of which he employed specialist advisers. Headlam-Morley, a Foreign Office expert, produced papers for Churchill on such subjects as the annexation of Bosnia-Herzegovina and the Agadir Crisis and sections of these were incorporated by Churchill directly into his own narrative.[7] Thirdly, two important themes which occur several times in Churchill's account of war-time naval affairs make their first appearance in the pre-war chapters. One is his lavish praise of Sir David Beatty and denigration of Sir John Jellicoe. The other is his manner of dealing with the materiel side of the pre-war navy. The romantic aspect of this subject is much emphasised. Thus we are given many pages on battleship and battlecruiser construction but nothing on mines, torpedoes, shells and armour plate. When the war-time naval chapters are discussed it will be found that this type of treatment continues and that it is the romance of battle which attracts Churchill rather than the more technical aspects of the naval war.

Finally it should be noted that The World Crisis consists of two more volumes than those discussed here. The final volumes deal with events in Europe from 1919 to 1922 (The Aftermath) and the war on the Eastern Front. The Aftermath has been omitted because, as Churchill himself said, it "is in a sense a separate publication" and only "affiliated" to the others.[8] The Eastern Front is also something of an appendage to the main work.

Much of Churchill's work, then, is not discussed here. But these omissions have a positive aspect. By placing minor and extraneous themes to one side, it is possible to focus on what for Churchill, were the fundamental aspects of the war: above all, the naval encounters which either occurred during his administration at the Admiralty or were fought with ships provided during that period; the Dardanelles operation; and the war on the Western Front from 1916 to 1918. It is to the first of these subjects that we now turn.

Chapter 1

THE ESCAPE OF THE GOEBEN

In July 1914, the naval position in the Mediterranean was
complex. While the French fleet was by far the largest in
the area, it was expected that on a declaration of war most
of its units would be involved helping to escort the French
African Army from north Africa to France. British forces in
the Mediterranean consisted of three battlecruisers and a
squadron of heavy cruisers and destroyers, all based on
Malta. Of the likely opponents of the Entente, Austria had a
powerful fleet at Pola in the Adriatic and Germany had the
Goeben, a battlecruiser, and the Breslau, a light cruiser,
also based on Pola. The Italian fleet was of considerable
size but it was expected that Italy would remain neutral in
any conflict between the Entente and the Central Powers.

Before discussing the use which the Admiralty made of the
British Squadron, one important point should be noted. In
1914 the Admiralty could communicate with ships on distant
stations by telegraph for the first time in a major war. The
actions of local commanders could now be controlled from
London. It will be seen in the following account that the
Admiralty had much to learn before they achieved the
precision and clarity of expression necessary for operating
successfully under the new conditions.

As soon as war seemed imminent, the Admiralty pondered
how best to employ the small British force in the
Mediterranean. It decided that the British commander, Sir
Berkeley Milne, should be given as his first priority the
protection of the French transports from a likely attack by
the Goeben. That is, his main concern should lie in the
westernmost sector of the Mediterranean. However, he was
also directed to maintain a watch on the Adriatic for the
Austrian fleet.

To accomplish these dual objectives, Milne assigned his
battlecruisers the former task and his cruisers and
destroyers (commanded by Admiral Troubridge) the latter. By
chance, Milne located the Goeben and Breslau west of Sicily
on the eve of the British declaration of war. However, the

1

German ships outdistanced the British battlecruisers and entered the Italian port of Messina. Intelligence sources soon alerted Milne to the Goeben's whereabouts. By this time Britain had declared war on Germany but Italy remained neutral, and given the Admiralty's desire to respect that neutrality Milne was unable to follow the Goeben to Messina.

Milne thus positioned his battlecruiser force to the west of Sicily, well placed to intercept the Goeben if it travelled westwards towards the French transports. As it happened the French had halted all troop movements because of the uncertainty surrounding the Goeben. However the Admiralty, although aware of this, neglected to inform Milne.

Meanwhile, the German commander, Admiral Souchon, had been ordered to proceed to Constantinople in anticipation of the signing of a German-Turkish Alliance. That is, he was given a purpose which did not lie within the anticipations of the British Admiralty. Souchon therefore left the Straits of Messina by the unguarded southern entrance and proceeded eastward, away from Milne's battlecruisers. However, this route led the Goeben and Breslau directly into the path of the other elements in the British force which, under Admiral Troubridge, were stationed at the entrance to the Adriatic watching for the Austrian fleet. After initially moving towards the German ships Troubridge drew back, stating at his subsequent court-martial that he considered the German ships to be a superior force with which he had been ordered not to become engaged. Whether they were in fact superior is doubtful. The British Squadron (four cruisers and eight destroyers) had a total of 56 guns against the German 22 and although the heavy guns of the Goeben outranged those in all British ships the multiplicity of targets faced by the Germans should have allowed Troubridge to score some damaging shots. Nevertheless, Troubridge's contention that he had been ordered by the Admiralty to husband his force at the outset, and that British interests would not have been served by the possible elimination of a squadron of cruisers early in the war, carries weight.

Even after Troubridge's withdrawal, with vigorous action the Goeben might still have been caught. Souchon was forced to delay his eastward movement to Constantinople, firstly to coal, and then because the alliance with Turkey had not yet been concluded. Neither Milne nor the Admiralty took advantage of these delays. Milne showed anything but vigour in pursuing Souchon, stopping unnecessarily to coal and then moving east at economical speed. Apparently Milne was still concerned that the Goeben would break back to the west and attack the French, even though he was now aware that their troop transports had not left harbour. His tactics then were not those of pursuit but those of cautious reconnaissance.

At this point a telegram was despatched from the Admiralty to Milne informing him erroneously that war had broken out between Britain and Austria-Hungary. Milne, in keeping with his war orders, turned north towards the entrance of the Adriatic to concentrate his fleet against Austria. By the time the error was discovered Souchon had entered the Dardanelles. The Goeben had escaped.[1]

How noteworthy were these events? At the time it was thought that the arrival of the German ships was the decisive factor in the Turkish decision to join the Central Powers and the Admiralty was widely held to be responsible for this undesirable event. Soon after the war however, it was discovered that Turco-German discussions on a possible alliance had begun in late July and that the alliance had been concluded while the Goeben was at Messina. Therefore the escape of the Goeben, while it provided the Turkish navy with a very useful addition, was in itself a relatively trivial incident in the naval war.

* * * * * * * * * * * * * * *

It might be expected that when Churchill came to discuss the Goeben incident in The World Crisis he would defend his actions and those of the local commanders by emphasizing the relative unimportance of the Goeben's escape. This is not the case. In his account Churchill chooses to defend the actions of the Admiralty and criticize those of Milne and Troubridge in detail. Thus he seems to accept the charge of his war-time critics that large issues were at stake. The reasons which led him to adopt this approach will be discussed later. First it is necessary to examine Churchill's detailed defence of Admiralty actions.

Churchill is concerned to refute the three main criticisms made of the Admiralty – that their instructions to Milne and Troubridge were confusing and hampered the local commanders, that the tactics adopted by Milne, despite their shortcomings were approved by the Admiralty at the time and that Staff work at the Admiralty throughout the incident was poor and contributed to the final escape of the German ships.

Churchill first draws attention to the orders issued to Milne which he quotes at length.

"It is especially important that your squadron should not be seriously engaged with Austrian ships before we know what Italy will do. Your first task should be to aid the French in the transportation of their African Army by covering and if possible bringing to action fast German ships, particularly Goeben which may interfere with that transportation. You will be notified by telegraph when you may consult with the French Admiral. Except in combination with the French as part of a general battle do not at this stage be brought to action against superior forces. The speed of your Squadrons is sufficient to enable you to choose your moment... [and] you must husband your force at the outset."[2]

Two further orders were added in the next few days; to prevent the Goeben from breaking out into the Atlantic, and to respect "rigidly" Italian neutrality.[3] To Churchill these instructions are quite clear. He wrote, "So far as the English language may serve as a vehicle of thought, the words employed appear to express the intentions we had formed."[4]

Is this claim warranted? In fact the instructions seem full of ambiguities and vague phrases. For example what did the Admiralty mean by "covering" the Goeben? This could mean "shadowing" the German ship or merely guarding the approaches to the French transports. Furthermore, the "superior force" with which Milne was not to become involved was not defined. It seems the Admiralty meant only the Austrian fleet, but this was hardly made clear. Also, the instructions definitely gave Milne as his first priority the protection of the French transports. Only in this context, and only if possible was he to bring the Goeben to action. Thus it should not have been surprising if Milne chose to concentrate on the former task rather than the latter.

Churchill's account of Milne's dispositions around Messina makes it quite clear that he did not approve of the tactics adopted by the Admiral. While not criticizing Milne directly he suggests that it might have been more appropriate either to close each end of the Straits with a battlecruiser or to signal for orders to pursue the German ships through the Straits.[5] This is less than fair to Milne. Both Churchill's suggested options were in conflict with Admiralty instructions to respect Italian neutrality rigidly. Churchill's suggested tactics also overlooked the fact that the primary task given to Milne was not the pursuit of the Goeben but the protection of the French transports. Finally, Churchill's first option supposes that Milne had some reason to suspect that the Goeben would attempt to break to the east. As far as Milne knew only neutral countries or those potentially hostile to Germany lay in that direction. On the other hand the Admiralty was aware that tension existed between Britain and Turkey over the seizure of two battleships being built for Turkey in Britain, but they neglected to inform Milne of this important fact. This point is not dealt with by Churchill in The World Crisis.

Churchill's criticisms of Milne are constructed with some skill. While merely hinting at the strategy he expected the Admiral to follow he nevertheless manages to convey the impression that he regarded Milne as utterly lacking in vigour or initiative. But it is worth noting that in an early draft of The World Crisis Churchill expressed his opinion of Milne in a much more direct way. Originally Churchill wrote of Milne's actions while the Goeben was at Messina:

"He could at any moment after he first suspected that the Goeben was at Messina have telegraphed to the Admiralty in the following sense "I believe Goeben is at Messina. Submit since she has entered Italian territorial waters I may follow her, observing that otherwise I shall be much hampered in my operations". It would not have been unreasonable to expect a Commander-in-Chief to ask the Admiralty a simple vital question like this. One would have expected him to do so, if only for his own protection. He did nothing".[6]

However, this criticism presented Churchill with the problem that soon after the event the Admiralty had approved Milne's actions, completely exonerating him from any blame attached to the escape of the Goeben. Churchill initially tried in this early draft to reconcile the two positions by claiming that when the Admiralty statement was released he had not had the time to study the circumstances of Milne's conduct. He wrote:

"I cannot but feel that this approval was couched in too sweeping terms. No doubt the Admiral acted as he thought best: no doubt he was to some extent baffled by his instructions: no doubt events happened with a surprising suddenness: no doubt in a strict and literal sense he carried out his orders. But the facts are upon record. Sir Berkeley Milne was the first British Admiral in the Great War to whom golden opportunity presented herself in vain. He was not to be the last.[7]

It is not surprising that Churchill decided to omit this section, for it laid him open to attack on several counts. First, it was highly critical of a man who, after all, was one of his own appointees. (The World Crisis does not reveal that it was Churchill who appointed Milne.) Secondly, it suggested that Milne had an obligation to request the Admiralty to reverse one of its own clear instructions, and that on the delicate issue of violating Italian neutrality. And finally it admitted that Milne could have been "to some extent baffled by his instructions", so drawing attention to the very shortcomings of the Admiralty's instructions that Churchill was claiming did not exist. So Churchill omitted his most damaging blows at Milne, possibly aware that he was wielding a two-edged sword that might be striking also at himself. But the hostile tone towards Milne was maintained.

Churchill's criticisms of Admiral Troubridge follow the same lines as those of Milne. Churchill argues that the First Cruiser Squadron was a force well able to engage the Goeben with a reasonable chance of success,[8] which, as we saw earlier, it probably was. However Churchill is not willing to admit that confusing Admiralty instructions, in this case the "superior forces" telegram and the order to "husband your forces at the outset", might have played a role in the Admiral's decision to decline battle. Nor does he admit the force of Troubridge's contention about the effect of a British defeat so early in the war. However, Churchill is not excessively hard on the local commander. He gives the impression that the incident was the one blemish in an otherwise distinguished career and he gives full acknowledgement to Troubridge's later work in the war.[9]. In this respect it is worth noting that Churchill knew Troubridge well. He had brought him to the Admiralty in 1912 as the first Chief of Staff in the new Admiralty organization, and the two men had worked together for almost two years. This fact may have served to soften Churchill's criticisms.

The modification of the criticisms of Milne and Troubridge in The World Crisis has the advantage for Churchill of giving his account the appearance of impartiality. He attempted to add to this effect by pointing to some instances where the Admiralty was at fault. These are identified as; the failure to get into touch with the French Admiralty at the beginning of the war and the failure to order Milne into the Straits of Messina as soon as it was known that the Goeben was there on August 5th.[10] However these are rather hypothetical errors. The first assumes that Milne would have acted differently if he had been aware that the French transports were still in harbour - which, judging by Milne's own account, is unlikely.[11] The second "error" postulates that it would have been possible to fight a naval action either in Messina harbour or in the narrow waters of the Straits without irrevocably alienating the Italian Government, supposing of course that Cabinet approval could have been obtained for such an act in the first place. Both were in fact very dubious assumptions.

Churchill is prepared to admit a further error on the part of the Admiralty. This was the telegram wrongly informing Milne that Britain had declared war on Austria. But it is not a large admission. For although Churchill states that this error took place at the Admiralty, he places most of the blame on an unseen and malign force, the Fates, which even then was working against British Policy in the Middle East. He wrote "At this juncture the Fates moved a blameless and punctilious Admiralty clerk to declare war upon Austria"[12]. Not only does this statement remove the source of the error from the higher echelons of the Admiralty, it even holds the clerk "blameless". Furthermore Churchill's account does not reveal that although "the mistake was repaired a few hours later"[13] a third telegram (stating situation still critical) directed Milne's attention back to the Austrian fleet requiring a fourth message to make the position clear.[14]

In a memorable passage Churchill expands on his argument concerning the Austrian telegram and proceeds to blame the whole episode of the escape of the Goeben and Breslau on the Fates.

"In all this story of the escape of the Goeben one seems
to see the influence of that sinister fatality which at a
later stage and on a far larger scale was to dog the
enterprise against the Dardanelles. The terrible "Ifs"
accumulate. If my first thoughts on July 27 of sending
the New Zealand to the Mediterranean had materialized;
if we would have opened fire on the Goeben during the
afternoon of August 4; if we had been less solicitous
for Italian neutrality; if Sir Berkeley Milne had sent
the Indomitable to coal at Malta instead of Biserta; if
the Admiralty had sent him direct instructions when on
the night of the 5th they learned where the Goeben was;
if Rear-Admiral Troubridge in the small hours of August 7
had not changed his mind; if the Dublin and her two
destroyers had intercepted the enemy during the night of
the 6th - 7th - the story of the Goeben would have ended
here."[15]

Some of these, like the failure to fire on German ships
prior to the outbreak of war and the solicitousness for
Italian neutrality, were not interventions of fate at all,
but reflected major facets of British policy.  The others
would not certainly have altered the course of events to any
large respect.  The significance of the passage lies in the
way Churchill uses these events to prepare the ground for his
discussion of the Dardanelles operation.  The latter
operation will prove, in his account, to be the war's great
lost opportunity, thwarted by "sinister fatality" and "great
ifs".  The Goeben incident is moulded by Churchill to take on
the character of a precurser to the Dardanelles.  Hence
Churchill never seeks to defend either the Admiralty in
London or the Admirals on the spot by arguing that anyway the
matter was probably a storm in a tea-cup:  that it was not
this small event of naval history, but much larger forces
outside British control, which brought Turkey into the war.
Thus, in The World Crisis Churchill assigns the
responsibility for the escape of the Goeben to Milne,
Troubridge and accidents of fate, with the Admiralty making a
minor contribution.  However as has been shown, a more
impartial assessment would place much more emphasis on the
actions of the Admiralty and how they affected the local
commanders, greatly reduce the liability of Milne and not
seek paranormal explanations for perfectly ordinary events.
Such an assessment might also note that in fact the British
naval force did achieve what it was ordered to do - even if
only because the unexpected German tactics meant that there
was no difficulty in protecting the French transports.  It
could also be noted that the British force was simply not
large enough to be certain of thwarting all of the wide range
of actions the Germans might attempt - one of which was
making a dash for Turkey.  Nevertheless Churchill has been
able to construct a convincing case and it is worth

investigating briefly how he has managed to do this. Firstly he has been aided by the fact that Milne and Troubridge were not the most brilliant of naval commanders. However much they were hampered by Admiralty instructions, there is always the feeling that they could have exercised greater initiative. Secondly Churchill has given his account a semblance of impartiality. He has tempered his criticisms of Milne and Troubridge to the extent of not placing upon them the whole blame for the fiasco and he has not attempted to conceal the fact that errors were made by the Admiralty. Where his account is deficient is in his consistent claim that the Admiralty instructions were clear, in ignoring the extent to which the decisions made by the local commanders were governed by the multiplicity and confused nature of those instructions, and in never grasping the fact that the British Mediterranean Squadron was woefully deficient for the tasks it was set in the early weeks of the war.

## Chapter 2

## CORONEL AND THE FALKLANDS

The German Far Eastern Squadron, which was to inflict on the British the humiliating defeat at Coronel, began the war off the coast of China. The force consisted of the enemy cruisers <u>Scharnhorst</u> and <u>Gneisenau</u> and attendant light cruisers. The Commander of the Squadron, Admiral von Spee, after detaching the <u>Emden</u> to raid in the Indian Ocean, decided to cruise directly to South America where he could be assured of coaling facilities and easy targets in the form of British merchant shipping. The British had two squadrons well placed to intercept von Spee. However, the China Squadron under Admiral Jerram was given such a multiplicity of tasks and split into such small units by the Admiralty that it was fortunate for Jerram that the depleted force which was searching for von Spee failed to locate him. In Australian waters the British had, in the battlecruiser <u>Australia</u>, a ship well able to sink the German Squadron single-handed. Once more Admiralty intervention ensured that this ship was not available to intercept von Spee. They insisted that the <u>Australia</u> escort colonial expeditions undertaken to capture the various German Pacific possessions despite clear evidence that von Spee was immediately to the north heading for South America. Thus when later evidence suggested that von Spee would indeed arrive off the west coast of South America the British had no modern ships available to oppose him.

Nevertheless the Admiralty began assembling a squadron under Admiral Cradock which they considered adequate to defeat the Germans. Cradock's original squadron consisted of the obsolete cruisers <u>Good Hope</u> and <u>Monmouth</u>, the modern light cruiser <u>Glasgow</u> and the armed auxiliary cruiser <u>Otranto</u>, a converted passenger liner. As it grew more likely that South America was indeed von Spee's destination, Cradock was informed that the old battleship <u>Canopus</u> and the heavy cruiser <u>Defence</u> were to be added to his force. While awaiting these reinforcements he was ordered with what ships he had to the Magellan Straits.[1]

As Cradock moved south the Admiralty signalled that as von Spee had been sighted off Samoa steaming north-west (that is away from South America) he should break up German trade on the west coast of South America and await further orders.[2] They also ordered Defence to remain in the Mediterranean but due to a staff error Cradock was not informed of this decision.[3] On September 18th Cradock advised the Admiralty that he was sending two of his ships to the west coast of South America to destroy trade, remaining in the Magellan Straits with two more to search for a lone German cruiser believed to be in the vicinity. In addition he was sending Canopus to the Plate Estuary to guard merchant shipping.[4] By assigning his battleship this lowly task it can be seen that Cradock had no great faith in its fighting ability, but never in any of his signals to the Admiralty did he make this point directly.

The next important signal from the Admiralty was received by Cradock on October 5th. It told him that von Spee was definitely approaching South American waters with his two heavy cruisers and probably three light cruisers in company.

By this time Cradock was seriously worried that his force was inadequate to defeat von Spee. He inquired if Defence was to join his command and suggested that further reinforcements might be necessary.[5] This telegram forced the Admiralty to respond. Churchill held a series of meetings with Prince Louis, the First Sea Lord, at which it was decided that Cradock should at all costs keep his squadron together and that he should merely shadow von Spee pending reinforcements if he considered his force insufficient to attack.[6] For reasons which remain obscure Prince Louis and the C.O.S., Sturdee, failed to pass these decisions on to Cradock. In addition Prince Louis and Sturdee decided to add Defence, not to Cradock's squadron, but to Admiral Stoddart's on the east coast of South America and not directly endangered by von Spee.[7]

Cradock now moved to concentrate his squadron near the Magellan Straits. During the voyage he became more concerned than ever that his squadron was inadequate. He therefore ordered Defence to join him with all haste. He also proposed to the Admiralty that as the low speed of the Canopus would hamper any search for von Spee, he would detach his battleship to convoy the squadron's colliers.[8] The Admiralty made no comment on the fact that Cradock had once more consigned his battleship to a lowly escort role but immediately informed him that Defence was to remain with Stoddart.[9] There is some doubt if Cradock ever received this message but if he did not he must have expected Defence to join him and this makes his ultimate decision to seek an action without that ship inexplicable.

In London Churchill was still clearly worried about Cradock's position and he asked for a staff appreciation of the situation. He was assured that the situation "seems safe".[10]

Cradock was now proceeding up the west coast of South America with the Good Hope, Monmouth, Glasgow, and Otranto. Canopus was some three hundred miles behind convoying colliers. On October 29th Glasgow called at the Chilean port of Coronel to collect mails, which perhaps contained the Admiralty signal directing Defence to remain on the east coast. While in port Glasgow picked up wireless signals from a German ship. At the same time von Spee learned of the presence of the British. On November 1st, late in the afternoon, the two fleets met about fifty miles east of Coronel. Cradock immediately turned towards the enemy but von Spee used his superior speed to keep out of range until the sun had set and the British ships were silhouetted against the horizon. Then he opened fire. Cradock replied but he was hopelessly outgunned and the stormy conditions made it impossible to fire many of the lower deck guns on the Monmouth and the Good Hope. The battle was all over in two hours. The Good Hope and the Monmouth were sunk with all hands. Dark and moonless conditions allowed the Glasgow and Otranto to escape. British naval supremacy in the South Atlantic had been temporarily lost.

The British response to the defeat off Coronel was to despatch two battlecruisers under Admiral Sturdee to the Falkland Islands. Although Sturdee's presence in South American waters was urgently required, his conduct of the voyage was curiously lethargic. He cruised his squadron at an economical speed, stopped frequently to examine merchant ships and appeared to be settling in for a comfortable stay at the Abrolhos coaling station when prodded into action by Captain Luce of the Glasgow. Even then Sturdee did not hurry and frequently announced his presence to the world by using his wireless.[11]

Fortunately for the British von Spee remained unaware of Sturdee's approach. Confident in the superiority of his squadron he determined to raid the Falklands, only to discover that Sturdee, quite fortuitously, had arrived just a few hours previously. A long chase developed in which the superior speed and fire power of Sturdee's battlecruisers made the conclusion almost certain and in the event four of the five German ships were sunk. The light cruiser Dresden escaped, to be hunted down in later months by the British. In London the victory was greeted with relief. Coronel had now been redeemed.

* * * * * * * * * * * * * *

Naval historians have levelled three main criticisms at the Admiralty for the defeat at Coronel; that the force provided specifically to Cradock to deal with von Spee was woefully inadequate for the task; that the Admiralty unnecessarily complicated and hampered Cradock's task by poor staff work; and that although there were ample ships in South American waters to deal with von Spee, the Admiralty failed to concentrate them in one squadron through a mistaken strategy of trying to be strong everywhere.

In _The World Crisis_ Churchill directly confronts these criticisms. He claims that the force given to Cradock was adequate for the task and that had the Admiral kept the _Canopus_ with his squadron he had good prospects for success; that the Admiralty could not be blamed for the disaster at Coronel which was entirely the responsibility of the Admiral on the spot; and that the dispositions decided upon by the Admiralty were the best possible in the circumstances. How valid are Churchill's arguments?

As Churchill readily concedes that the cruisers in Cradock's squadron were no match for the _Scharnhorst_ and _Gneisenau_, his confidence in the strength of Cradock's force rests entirely on his assessment of the battleship _Canopus_. In _The World Crisis_ he states,

> "With the _Canopus_, Admiral Cradock's squadron was safe. The _Scharnhorst_ and _Gneisenau_ would never have ventured to come within decisive range of her four 12-inch guns. ....The old battleship, with her heavy armour and artillery, was in fact a citadel around which all our cruisers in those waters could find absolute security."[12]

Now it is true that the _Canopus_ undoubtedly had the heaviest armament of any ship in the south Atlantic (four 12" and twelve x 6" guns)[13] but the ship was old (built in 1899) and ready for the scrap heap. Also there were reasons to doubt the effectiveness and range of the ship's 12" guns. Range estimates vary from the Whale Island Gunnery School figure given by Marder (14,000 yards)[14] which was about the same as the German 8.2", to 9,000 yards given by a gunnery officer who served on _Canopus_ at the time.[15] The Captain of the ship in 1914 gives the range at 10-11,000 yards.[16] However, no authority has stated that the _Canopus_ could substantially outrange the _Scharnhorst_ and _Gneisenau_. In any case it is doubtful if the _Canopus_ could have hit the German ships even at short range. The rifling on some of the 12" guns had practically worn smooth and later when the ship was firing at the Dardanelles it was common for the shells to go head over heels when they left the muzzle.[17] Furthermore the gun turrets were in the hands of reservist officers who had never before fired a shot.[18] The slow speed of the _Canopus_ was another drawback. Although her nominal speed was 18 knots, her best speed in 1914 was just over 15 knots – eight knots slower than any of the German ships.[19] A final factor was that except for the gun turrets, the _Canopus_ was no more heavily armoured than von Spee's cruisers.[20] In fact a member of the Admiralty staff, Richmond, had suggested in a paper that the battleship had grave deficiencies. This advice was ignored by Churchill and his colleagues and is not mentioned in The World Crisis.[21]

Clearly, by whichever criterion is taken, range of guns, weight of armour or experience of crew, Canopus was inferior to von Spee's heavy cruisers. Thus the picture of the Canopus as an armoured citadel, as given in The World Crisis, is most misleading. Nor would its presence necessarily have deterred von Spee from attacking as Churchill states, for in a letter written after the battle von Spee indicated that he probably would have risked an action against such a ship.[22]

What of Churchill's second point, that the Admiralty could not be held responsible in any way for the disaster at Coronel? When the telegrams which passed between the Admiralty and Cradock are examined, it becomes clear that Churchill's absolution of himself and his colleagues must be modified. At least four important mistakes were made by the Admiralty staff. Firstly, they did not make clear to Cradock that the Defence was not to join his command as a reinforcement. Secondly, Prince Louis and Sturdee on two occasions failed to pass on to Cradock the decisions reached at Admiralty meetings, even though the important second meeting had decided that Cradock should merely shadow the German squadron if he held his force to be inferior. Thirdly, the staff assured Churchill that Cradock's position was safe when this was hardly the case. Finally, the Admiralty ignored reasonably clear indications from Cradock that he regarded the Canopus as an inferior fighting unit fit only for convoy and escort duties even though their entire strategy in South American waters was based on the supposed merits of that ship.

Clearly staff work had not been brilliant. Yet Churchill is able to avoid this issue entirely by omitting from his account all the errors detailed above. However, it is also true that Churchill could, while mentioning the errors made, easily have shifted much of the blame from himself. The staff and in particular Prince Louis and Sturdee were the main offenders. Why did he choose not to discuss the matter in these terms? Two explanations seem likely. There were good reasons for Churchill to protect the reputation of Sturdee. Churchill had selected Sturdee for the command at the Falklands and his victory was important in restoring Churchill's reputation after Coronel. It would hardly be appropriate then for Churchill to criticize Sturdee for the poor staff work which contributed to that defeat. The case of Prince Louis is somewhat different. It is noteworthy that, in discussing the Goeben incident, Churchill had first made a critical reference to Prince Louis and then removed it.[23] The explanation for this attitude is the need to retain the image of Prince Louis as a first rate naval officer with whom Churchill could work, and to draw attention to the fact that here was a prominent figure driven from office by misinformed criticism. The same explanation can be applied to Churchill's suppression of Prince Louis' lapses prior to Coronel. Furthermore, if Prince Louis' errors were revealed, the real reason for his replacement at First Sea Lord might have become known; that he was, in Fisher's words, "played out"[24] and that the dispute over his Austrian parentage was just a convenient issue over which to accept his resignation. It is obvious that Churchill would not want to be responsible, even indirectly, for this disclosure.

An additional reason for Churchill choosing not to draw attention to the errors of the staff was that he saw no great need. In The World Crisis the defeat at Coronel is explained purely in terms of Cradock's mistakes. And it must be said that Churchill's case has a certain plausibility. Cradock was certainly not in the front rank of British naval commanders. Throughout this period he failed to make his doubts and anxieties about his force clear to the Admiralty, merely being content to hint at his difficulties. He also failed to communicate with the Admiralty for long periods. Finally his decision to fight von Spee without the Canopus but with the useless Otranto was the height of folly. But despite Cradock's deficiencies Churchill goes too far in assigning all the blame to the local commander and in accepting no blame on behalf of the Admiralty. In fact none of the major participants in the incident emerges with any real credit.

Churchill's third point is that the Admiralty strategy of having a squadron on each coast of South America instead of one concentrated squadron near Cape Horn was the best disposition possible against von Spee. He argues that it was not possible for the British forces to be concentrated in one squadron because von Spee had at least six courses of action open to him all of which had to be guarded against. The six alternatives, according to Churchill, were : to remain in the Pacific, to double back in the direction of Australia and New Zealand, to enter the Caribbean through the Panama Canal, to concentrate on the destruction of shipping on the west coast of South America, to slip around Cape Horn and make for either the Rio trade routes or South Africa.[25] It is hard to follow Churchill's reasoning in the light of these options. The first two alternatives clearly did not involve Cradock or Stoddart at all, and so did not affect their dispositions. In the case of von Spee passing through the Panama Canal, it would have been simpler to send the combined British-Japanese force - then off the Californian coast and working south in search of von Spee - through the Canal after them than to divert Stoddart from his station near Rio. Furthermore it is hard to see that having a squadron on either coast was a superior disposition to a concentrated force if von Spee chose to remain off Chile or to move to South Africa. In the first instance a concentrated squadron at the Magellan Straits would have been ideally placed to sweep north to locate von Spee. If the Germans headed towards South Africa, a squadron situated near Cape Horn could have reached Cape Town almost as quickly as a squadron starting from Rio. Only in the case of von Spee making for the Plate estuary was a divided squadron possibly the best. However, even if this had been von Spee's plan it was probable that because of his long voyage across the Pacific he would put into a Chilean port before rounding the Horn. Thus it was likely that Cradock would meet the German squadron before Stoddart. Yet Stoddart's squadron, in reserve on the east coast, was much stronger than Cradock's. Thus even if a divided squadron was considered best, the distribution of ships between the two detachments is difficult to defend.

We turn now to Churchill's description of the battle off the Falkland Islands. It is concise and generally reliable and need not detain us long. However it is misleading in one important area. Much of Churchill's account is taken up with a description of the despatch of the battlecruisers <u>Inflexible</u> and <u>Invincible</u> to the Falklands. Churchill relates a disagreement with a dockyard Admiral who stated that the ships could not sail before November 13th and had to be ordered to despatch them on the 11th. He goes on to say that as a result of this order

"The ships sailed accordingly and in the nick of time. They coaled on November 26 at Abrolhos, where they joined and absorbed Admiral Stoddart's squadron...and without ever coming in sight of land or using their wireless they reached Port Stanley, Falkland Islands, on the night of December 7"26

Now we know that von Spee raided the Falklands on the morning of December 8th. Thus Churchill's account gives the impression that the journey of the battlecruisers was a well ordered movement, which because of the two days gained at the dockyard culminated in the frustration of von Spee's plan by just a few hours. The reality was very different. As mentioned earlier, all urgency seemed to leave the voyage as soon as Sturdee was out of sight of land. Rather than dashing down to the Falklands as implied in <u>The World Crisis</u>, Sturdee generally behaved as though von Spee did not exist and it was by the greatest good luck and not the good management implied by Churchill that the battlecruisers arrived in time to destroy von Spee.

Chapter 3

THE NORTH SEA 1914-1915

Between the outbreak of war and January 1915 there occurred
four small naval actions in British waters, all of which
receive attention from Churchill, and two of which
(Scarborough Raid and the Dogger Bank Battle) have lengthy
chapters of their own in The World Crisis. It will be
convenient to group all these actions together and discuss
them in chronological order.

Heligoland

On August 28, 1914, a British force of destroyers, cruisers
and submarines, supported by battlecruisers and the First
Cruiser Squadron from the Grand Fleet, raided the German-held
waters of the Heligoland Bight. The plan was to intercept
the German destroyer patrols and attack any ships which
attempted to come to their rescue. The operation succeeded,
largely due to the intervention of the battlecruisers at a
crucial moment. Three German cruisers and one destroyer were
sunk while on the British side only one cruiser was damaged.
However, due to poor staff work the operation almost
miscarried. Neither Tyrwhitt (leading the destroyer
flotillas) nor Keyes (in charge of the submarines) was aware
of exactly which units of the Grand Fleet had been detailed
to support them. Luckily for the British, Tyrwhitt learnt
the nature of the supporting force before the operation
began, but for much of the time Keyes was in action, he
thought Goodenough's First Cruiser Squadron was a hostile
force. The confusion was such that the British were
fortunate not to suffer losses from their own ships. Indeed
one of the submarines tried to torpedo the Southampton,
Goodenough's flagship, which in turn tried to ram the
submarine. Neither succeeded. In the event all went well
and Churchill was able to announce the first naval victory of
the war.[1]
    Churchill's account of these events is extremely brief.
In fact in the first draft of The World Crisis no mention is

16

made of the Heligoland action.[2] However, on reflection Churchill no doubt thought it wise to balance the account of the sinking of the "three cruisers" with which the chapter ends, with a victory at the beginning.

Since Churchill concedes the major criticism of the operation, that poor staff work almost caused several mishaps, only two points need to be made about his account.

The first is that Churchill's description of the progress of the battle gives the misleading impression that the British were always in the ascendancy. He writes, "A confused, dispersed and prolonged series of combats ensued between the flotillas and light cruisers and continued until after four o'clock in the afternoon. During all this time the British light forces were rampaging about the enemy's most intimate and jealously guarded waters."[3] The end of the battle came when "the German light cruisers precipitately proceeding to the assistance of their flotillas and animated by the hopes of cutting off our own, ran into the British battle-cruisers".[4]

In fact the British light forces did not enjoy the early success that this passage implies. The light cruiser _Arethusa_, Tyrwhitt's flagship and leader of the destroyer flotillas, had been damaged in an early encounter with a German cruiser.[5] By 12.30 the crippled flagship, the other flotilla leader _Fearless_ and their destroyers were being engaged by no less than three German cruisers with another three in the near vicinity, all of which outgunned the British ships.[6] Tyrwhitt was forced to call to Beatty for aid, and it was the British battlecruisers which drove off or sank the enemy ships before any of Tyrwhitt's forces had been critically damaged.[7]

It can be seen that the action was by no means as one-sided as Churchill would have us believe and that for most of the battle the British were in the presence of superior German forces. Thus the picture given of British ships "rampaging about" the Heligoland Bight is hardly accurate.

Also Churchill's account implies that the German cruisers arrived late on the scene and then "precipitately" ran into the British battlecruisers, which Churchill also implies were already in close support of Tyrwhitt's force. As has been shown, the opposite was the case. It was Beatty's force which arrived late on the scene not the German cruisers, which at the time of Beatty's arrival had already established a clear superiority over Tyrwhitt's flotillas. Thus the action of the Germans can hardly be called "precipitate" for they were unaware that British battlecruisers were available to reinforce Tyrwhitt, and until the intervention of the heavy British ships they had a good chance to inflict considerable damage on the raiding force.

Churchill's second point is that the action "produced results of a far-reaching character upon the whole of the

naval war".[8]   To support this view Churchill quotes
Tirpitz: "Orders were issued by the Emperor...to restrict the
initiative of the Commander-in-Chief of the North Sea Fleet:
the loss of ships was to be avoided, fleet sallies and any
greater undertakings must be approved by His Majesty in
advance".[9]   However it is doubtful if the battle modified
German policy to any great extent.  The German fleet had been
effectively muzzled by the Grand Fleet since the beginning of
the war.  It was no part of German policy to make frequent
sallies into the North Sea and precipitate a battle they were
sure to lose, and the Kaiser's orders sent to the German
Commander-in-Chief Von Ingenohl at the beginning of the war
emphasized that the fleet should not be risked.[10]   It is
possible that Tirpitz, in the passage quoted by Churchill,
emphasized the new instructions in order to explain the
passivity of the High Sea Fleet and to shift the blame for
this on to the Kaiser.  The basic policy of the German Fleet
after Heligoland remained the same as it had always been: to
remain on the defensive until the mine and torpedo had worn
down the British superiority.  The Kaiser's order merely
reinforced a policy already well established.

## The Three Cruisers

Since the beginning of the war a patrol of five
obsolescent Bacchante-class cruisers had been maintained in
the southern waters of the North Sea and off the coast of
Holland.[11]   The purpose of the patrol was to aid the
Harwich force in keeping "the area south of the 54th
parallel...clear of enemy torpedo craft and minelayers".[12]
About the middle of September Churchill became concerned
about the safety of the patrol.  He minuted to Prince Louis:

> "The force available for operations in the narrow seas
> should be capable of minor action without the need of
> bringing down the Grand Fleet.  To this end it should
> have effective support either by two or three
> battlecruisers or battleships of the Second Fleet working
> from Sheerness....The Bacchantes ought not to continue on
> this beat.  The risk to such ships is not justified by
> any services they can render.  The narrow seas, being the
> nearest point to the enemy, should be kept by a small
> number of good modern ships.  The Bacchantes should go to
> the western entrance of the Channel."[13]

But, the next day Prince Louis was persuaded by the Chief of
Staff, Admiral Sturdee, that until these arrangements could
be worked out, the patrol off the coast of Holland should be
continued.[14]   Thus on September 20th Admiral Christian with
the four cruisers Euryalus (flag), Aboukir, Cressy and Hogue
arrived on "the Broad Fourteens" from the Dogger Bank.  On
the way south the flagship was detached to coal at Harwich.

The weather was too rough to transfer ship so Admiral Christian left Captain Drummond of the <u>Aboukir</u> in command with strict instructions to alter course frequently to avoid submarine attack.[15] For some reason Drummond ignored these instructions and maintained a steady course. In this position on the 23rd of September all three Cruisers were torpedoed by a German submarine. Over 1,400 lives were lost.[16]

In a public pamphlet, circulated at the time, Churchill was blamed for maintaining the <u>Bacchante</u> patrol against the advice of his naval colleagues,[17] and his account is mainly concerned with clearing himself on this point. This he is easily able to do by quoting his telegram of September 18th and showing how the War Staff failed to take immediate action upon it.[18] However in two other areas his account is open to criticism. From <u>The World Crisis</u> it appears that Churchill was the first officially to warn the staff that the patrol was in danger. This was not the case. On August 21st Keyes had written to the Director of Operations, Leveson, "For heavens sake, take those <u>Bacchantes</u> away!...I don't say those cruisers will be attacked, but the Germans must know they are about, and if they send out a suitable force, God help them."[19] A few days later the Assistant Director of Operations Division, Richmond, urged Leveson and Sturdee to remove the <u>Bacchantes</u> and replace them with modern light cruisers.[20] Further, Richmond kept up the pressure throughout September, though without effect.[21] It was the impossibility of getting any action from the Staff that led Keyes to inform Churchill of the position and resulted in his minute of September 18th.[22] Thus Churchill's warning was only the culmination of a long campaign to have the <u>Bacchantes</u> removed, and although it seems certain that Churchill would have been aware of at least Keyes' earlier attempts to warn the Staff, none of these efforts is mentioned in <u>The World Crisis</u>.

A second point which should be made is that Churchill's account implies that his warning of September 18th was against the type of disaster which eventually overtook the <u>Bacchantes</u>, that is attack by submarine. Yet a reading of that minute reveals that Churchill's proposal was to replace the old cruisers with "two or three battle-cruisers or battleships". It is obvious that the danger Churchill identified was that of attack by enemy surface craft. There is no evidence to suggest that Churchill foresaw the danger from submarines at this time. In this he was not alone for the warnings of Keyes and Richmond also seem to be directed against attacks from detachments of the High Sea Fleet.

In one respect Churchill would appear to have been too harsh on Admiral Christian, the Commander of the cruiser squadron. Churchill stated that

"One would expect senior officers in command of cruiser squadrons to judge for themselves the danger of their task, and especially of its constant repetition; and while obeying any orders they received, to represent an unsatisfactory situation plainly to the Admiralty instead of going on day after day, and week after week, until superior authority intervened or something lamentable happened."[23]

Yet Christian had done what he could to vary the patrol. Early in September he saw Sturdee and discussed the problem of the patrol being so much confined to one area.[24] A new system of sweeping patrols was suggested and these were carried out for some days. Indeed the area in which the ships were sunk had only been patrolled for five of the sixteen days, previous to the 22nd.[25] However as Christian pointed out, the patrol area was so circumscribed by mine-fields that no great variations could be employed.[26] Presumably Dutch territorial waters were also a factor. Therefore the point to be made about the patrol is not that it was carried out in a repetitious way, but that given the order to patrol the broad fourteens, some form of repetition was inevitable. Churchill's account is therefore misleading on two counts. Firstly, Christian did act to try to vary the patrols. Secondly, the patrol area laid down in Admiralty orders meant that very little variation could be made.

## The Scarborough and Hartlepool Raid

On December 16th, 1914, a German battlecruiser squadron bombarded the English coastal towns of Scarborough and Hartlepool. Because of their ability to read the German Naval Code the Admiralty had advance warning of this movement. They therefore sent Beatty's battlecruisers, a squadron of dreadnoughts, and two light cruiser squadrons from the Grand Fleet to try to force a battle with the German squadron by cutting it off from its base. In the event this force almost ran into the High Sea Fleet which was supporting the German battlecruisers from the vicinity of the Dogger Bank. However, after an indecisive and confused action had been fought between the destroyers screening the two main forces, the German Commander-in-Chief concluded that the entire Grand Fleet was present and withdrew towards Heligoland. The British force then learned of the bombardment of Scarborough and Hartlepool and turned towards the coast. However the weather deteriorated and no decisive action was fought. The British had three fleeting opportunities to engage, but these were lost because of a signalling error in the first case and poor visibility in the other two. A submarine and destroyer attack on the German ships as they returned to base failed to eventuate mainly due to the Admiralty not passing on orders quickly enough.[27]

Churchill devotes a whole chapter of The World Crisis to the "missed opportunities" of the Scarborough Raid. The first half of the chapter is an interesting account of the battle as it was seen from the Admiralty, with the small amount of information then available to them. The second half goes into the battle in detail, and is in the main accurate, following as it does the narrative given in the official history.[28] However in discussing the signalling error which resulted in contact being lost with the Germans, Churchill, as in the Goeben chapter, invokes the fates (now called Mischance) to explain the mistake.[29] What actually happened was that during the early part of the "action" the cruiser screens guarding the British and German battle cruisers met in the mist. Two of Beatty's cruisers moved to the south of the main force and opened fire. This encounter convinced Beatty that Hipper was still ahead of him, and as visibility was poor, he ordered his remaining light cruisers to maintain their scouting positions.[30] The signal officer on the Lion, Lt. Ralph Seymour, who seems to have been chosen by Beatty because he was a congenial companion with aristocratic connections rather than for any expertise in signalling,[31] incorrectly made the signal general to all the light cruisers.[32] Southampton and Birmingham, the ships engaging the enemy, therefore broke off the action and resumed their original positions and the German ships were soon lost in the thickening mist.[33]

In Churchill's account the signalling error is acknowledged but as this is put down to mischance no investigation of the error follows and the real culprits, Beatty and Seymour, escape uncensured. This method also enables Churchill to ignore completely the role of the cruiser squadron Commander, Goodenough, in this fiasco. Yet Goodenough's were the only ships in contact with the enemy and in breaking off the action he violated the first principle of naval reconnaissance, to maintain touch with the enemy at all costs and to ignore orders which might prevent this. This omission of Goodenough's error represents a moderation in Churchill's attitude. At the time he was more than ready to blame Goodenough for his actions.[34]

There are also three dubious assumptions made by Churchill in the course of his narrative. The first is that with any luck a decisive action could have been fought on December 16th and there is much wailing and gnashing of teeth as the missed opportunities are recounted one by one. However it is doubtful if these opportunities ever amounted to very much. From 11.00 a.m. onwards visibility rarely exceeded 4,000 yards. At Jutland, where the visibility was somewhat better, much larger forces than Hipper's Squadron were able to extricate themselves from the British without much difficulty. Even if the two main fleets had sighted each other in the mist, the perennial British difficulty in firing accurate opening salvos must have made the German chances of escape good.

This brings us to Churchill's second assumption. He always assumes that if the two forces had met in clear conditions the British would have won. This probably would have been the result had the combined British force met Hipper's Squadron, or had the heavily armoured 2nd Battle Squadron fought the more vulnerable and less powerfully gunned German battlecruisers. However the two best opportunities of the day were both for Beatty alone to fight Hipper. In this case British victory was much less sure for the battle was likely to be fought at close range, where the initially poor British shooting and the thinner armour protection of their ships would have put them at a distinct disadvantage.

Finally Churchill assumes that a British victory off Scarborough would have had an important effect on the naval war. He claims that the destruction of "the German battlecruiser squadron ... would fatally mutilate the whole German Navy and could never be repaired".[35] However it is doubtful if there would have been anything "fatal" in the sinking of Hipper's battlecruisers. No doubt the High Sea Fleet would have been inconvenienced without its scouting force but as there never was any intention to risk that fleet it is hard to see that it would have been a crippling blow. Probably the Germans would have made fewer raids against the English coast but these were of no strategic significance in any case. Certainly the German policy of wearing down the British superiority by mines and torpedoes would have become virtually impossible to achieve, but this might have led to a switch to U-boat warfare against merchant shipping much earlier. The fact remained that even without its battlecruisers the High Sea Fleet remained strong enough to ensure that the bulk of the British fleet would remain tied to the North Sea for the duration of the war.[36]

Only one further point need be made on Churchill's account of the Scarborough Raid. Over 500 civilians were killed or wounded in the bombardment.[37] There was an outcry against the navy for allowing such an incident to take place and partly to assuage this criticism Churchill made a speech in which he characterized the German seamen as "baby-killers".[38] However at the time it is clear that a desire to trap the German battlecruisers outweighed his undoubted sympathy with the hapless civilians. In an early draft of The World Crisis he recalled that he was taking a bath when the news that the coastal towns were being bombarded was brought to him. "I jumped out of the bath with exclamations of joy (Hartlepool, Scarborough, forgive me!)"[39] Later, he apparently decided that these sentiments might be misunderstood and substituted "I jumped out of the bath with exclamations".[40]

A month after the Scarborough raid a further battlecruiser sweep into the North Sea was sanctioned by Von Ingenohl. Once again the Admiralty, through their intelligence department, were aware of the German move and this time they correctly estimated that the German battlecruisers would be unsupported, though whether this was due to greater experience with the German codes or just good luck is not clear. On January 23rd, Beatty's five battlecruisers with the 1st Light Cruiser Squadron from Rosyth and the Harwich force were ordered to a rendezvous point in the North Sea designed to cut off the German squadron from its base.

The plan worked perfectly and just as the Harwich force was about to join Beatty's squadron, early on the morning of the 24th, the four enemy battlecruisers were sighted. Hipper immediately turned his ships 16 points and headed for home. The battle developed into a protracted chase with the British ships gradually overhauling the German Squadron. Initially British shooting was bad and few hits were made. Also the Tiger misread the fire distribution signal with the result that one of the German ships (Moltke) was left unattended and was able to score some damaging hits on the Lion. However by this time the rear German ship, the heavy cruiser, Blucher, had suffered many hits and began to drop astern. The crisis of the battle was now approaching. At this point the Lion suffered a damaging hit and listed out of the line. As the other ships swept past, Beatty thought he saw the periscope of a submarine and ordered an 8 point turn to port. This meant that the four remaining ships in the squadron were travelling at right angles across the wake of the retreating Germans, so Beatty made two more signals designed to re-direct his squadron on to the course followed by the Germans: "Course N.E." and then "Attack the rear of the enemy". These two signals were hauled down together and therefore read by the other ships as one, "Attack the rear of the enemy bearing North East". In that direction lay the crippled Blucher and Admiral Moore, Beatty's second in command, on the battlecruiser New Zealand, assumed that Beatty wanted the entire squadron to concentrate on the German heavy cruiser. Under concentrated fire from four battlecruisers and numerous light craft the Blucher sank at 12.13. Meanwhile Beatty seeing his plan going awry flew another signal "Keep nearer the enemy" but by this time the Lion was too far astern for the flags to be read. Beatty then transferred to a destroyer, caught up with the remainder of his squadron and ordered the chase resumed. It was too late, the enemy ships had escaped.[41]

Churchill's account of these events follows the same pattern as his description of the Scarborough raid. The first half of the chapter consists of an account of the battle as seen from the Admiralty; in the second half he gives a detailed investigation of the action. It is hard to avoid the conclusion that on this occasion Churchill has rather magnified the importance of the impending battle in the opening pages of the chapter. He speaks of attending a dinner the night before the expected encounter and feeling "separated from the distinguished company who gathered there, by a film of isolated knowledge and overwhelming inward preoccupation".[42] Yet it was known that only the rival battlecruisers were to clash and all that could have been expected on the British side was that two or three German ships would be sunk. However passages such as this build up the tension and convince the reader that important issues were at stake.

Only three points need to be made about Churchill's description of the battle. He mentions Beatty's 8 point turn to avoid submarines and is willing to make full allowance for the fact that the Admiral could not have known that there were actually no submarines present.[43] However he does not investigate the necessity to make the signal at all. But it is obvious that even had the submarine sighting been genuine the other ships had already passed the dangerpoint.

Churchill also mentions the two signals made by Beatty which led Moore to break off the chase and concentrate on the Blucher.[44] As in the chapter on the Scarborough raid, however, no discussion of the event follows. Seymour and Beatty once more escape uncensured. Yet in hauling down both signals at once Seymour showed his usual incompetence and surely it was possible for Beatty to make his intentions clearer than by using the obscure "Attack the rear of the enemy". (Why the rear of the enemy? Surely Beatty wanted all the enemy ships attacked.) Admittedly he had wanted to send "Engage the enemy more closely" only to find it had been deleted from the signal book,[45] but even that lacked the clarity of such simple alternatives as "Attack the enemy" or "chase". The World Crisis is silent on all these points.

Even Admiral Moore, whose decision to concentrate on the crippled Blucher, rather than chase the remaining German ships, demonstrated the lack of initiative that was to become the hallmark of subordinate British Admirals throughout the war, is allowed to escape lightly by Churchill. Although Churchill is clearly uneasy about Moore's decision, his only reproof is to state that Beatty's signals "seemed to suggest that some reason unknown to Rear-Admiral Moore had led the most daring of our naval leaders [note the flattering reference to Beatty] to break off the action".[46] However in an earlier draft of The World Crisis, Churchill in a section similar to the deleted paragraphs on Sir Berkeley Milne wrote "[To resume the chase] would have been a fine thing to do. But Rear Admiral Moore was not the first British Admiral in the Great War to whom in perplexing and uncertain circumstances the opportunity for a famous decision

presented itself in vain.  Nor was he to be the last".[47]
On reflection this paragraph was deleted, perhaps to maintain
consistency, perhaps to bring The World Crisis in line with
Churchill's attitude immediately after the battle, that the
victory should be celebrated and the lost opportunity
overlooked.[48]

Churchill concludes this section of The World Crisis by
speculating on what would have happened had Moore continued
to chase the enemy.  He first assumes that Moore would have
caught the Germans had he chased them.  This is doubtful for
Moore was almost ten miles behind Hipper when he received
Beatty's signal.  Even Churchill admits that the chase would
have been a long one.  A further assumption is that the
resulting battle would have ended in a British victory.  This
was by no means certain.  Although the British had a
superiority of four to three the better shooting of the
Germans tended to even the contest.  In this case the
sturdier construction of the German ships could have given
them a slight advantage.  In any event the result could not
be written down as a foregone conclusion.  The final
assumption was that the destruction of the German
battlecruisers would have in some way been a decisive
victory.  As stated earlier this impression is enchanced by
Churchill's dramatic build-up to the battle.  This point has
already been discussed in relation to the Scarborough Raid:
it is obvious that a British victory would have amounted only
to a minor tactical success.  Despite the impression given in
The World Crisis there were no high stakes at risk that day
at the Dogger Bank.

Chapter 4

ANTWERP

After the battle of the Marne the retreating German army had
halted on the River Aisne and from that line the Allies were
unable to dislodge them. The Western Front was now
continuous from the Swiss border to just north of Compiegne
and the eyes of the belligerents turned towards the open
flank between that point and the sea. Thus began the rapid
extension of the front northward from the Aisne as each army
tried to outflank the other.

For the Germans this movement was not without danger.
The Belgian army, which had originally stood in the path of
the invaders, had been brushed aside rather than beaten. As
the Germans marched into France, King Albert had retired with
his army into Antwerp and the Belgians now stood on the flank
of German lines of communication with the northern sector of
the Western Front. They had taken advantage of this position
and had made sorties from Antwerp on August 24th, September
9th and a smaller movement in late September. It became
obvious to the Germans that no major advance into Flanders
could take place unless Antwerp fell, and on September 28th
the bombardment of the outer forts began.

Earlier in September the Belgians had appealed to the
British and French for aid. Little had been done. Now their
requests became more urgent. An attempt was made by
Kitchener and Joffre to raise a force to aid the Belgians.
Before details could be finalised the Belgians announced that
they intended to retire from Antwerp. Churchill was sent to
the city with promises of aid if the defence could be
prolonged, and a token force of marines and elements of the
Royal Naval Division arrived in Antwerp between the 3rd and
6th October. But, on the 6th the Belgians decided that they
could delay no longer as their communications with the Allies
in Northern France were in danger and there seemed to be no
prospect of stopping the heavy howitzers which were
demolishing the Antwerp forts one by one. The evacuation of
Antwerp commenced on October 8th and the city surrendered on
the 10th. The Franco-British relieving force which had got

as far as Ghent now joined the retreating Belgian field army until the line Nieuport-Dixmude-Ypres was reached. Here the front was to stabilise until the last year of the war.[1]

\* \* \* \* \* \* \* \* \* \* \* \* \* \*

Churchill states that from the beginning of the war his attention had been directed towards Antwerp. He had been "very anxious to do everything that could be done out of our slender resources to aid the Belgian King and nation to maintain their stronghold, and such small items as the Admiralty could spare in guns and ammunition were freely sent".[2] However, Churchill claims that he was opposed to the strategy which lay behind the first Belgian appeal for help. He says the Belgians wanted "25,000 troops to co-operate with an equal number of Belgian troops for the purpose of keeping open the line Antwerp-St. Nicholas-Ghent-Bruges-Ostend".[3] He was opposed to this because

"It involves practically a flank position for a line of supply protected by forces large enough to be hit hard and perfectly powerless against any determined German attack which it is thought worth while to deliver. At any moment a punch up from Brussels by a German division or larger force would rupture the line, and drive the troops trying to hold it to be disarmed on neutral Dutch territory or into the sea."[4]

Churchill asserts that he proposed an alternative strategy; the reinforcement of the Antwerp garrison by Territorial troops and a "request" to the Dutch Government to "give a free passage up the Scheldt [which lay partly in Dutch territorial waters] to Antwerp for whatever troops and supplies were needed".[5] Churchill says he felt sure that "strong representations to the Dutch Government...[would] have induced them to grant this relief to Antwerp and the Belgian nation in their agony", but that Grey was opposed to putting pressure on the Dutch.[6] Nor did Kitchener approve of using British Territorials at Antwerp.[7] It should be noted that Churchill summarized his memorandum on Dutch neutrality instead of reprinting it because "these questions are still of some delicacy".[8]

Churchill then gives an account of the attempt by the British and French to raise a relieving force for Antwerp in response to the second Belgian appeal for help. He states that he was not involved in this process in any way and that his participation in the attempt to save Antwerp began when he was recalled by Kitchener and Grey from a visit to Dunkirk on the night of October 2nd. On proceeding to Kitchener's house he was read a telegram from the British Ambassador, Sir Francis Villiers which is quoted in The World Crisis.

"The Government have decided to leave to-morrow for
Ostend ... The King with field army will withdraw,
commencing with advanced guard to-morrow in the direction
of Ghent to protect coast-line, and eventually, it is
hoped, to co-operate with the Allied Armies....It is said
that town will hold out for five or six days, but it
seems most unlikely that when the Court and Government
are gone resistance will be so much prolonged."[9]

Churchill maintains that in the light of this message two
decisions were made by Grey, Kitchener and himself. The
first was to send a brigade of marines to Antwerp immediately
to sustain the defence. The second was that

"some one in authority who knew the general situation
should travel swiftly into the city and there ascertain
what could be done on either side. As I was already due
at Dunkirk the next morning, the task was confided to
me: Lord Kitchener expressed a decided wish that I
should go."[10]

Churchill arrived in Antwerp on October 3rd. According
to The World Crisis events developed in the following way.
He was told by the Belgian Prime Minister, M. de Broqueville,
that the field army intended to withdraw to the left bank of
the Scheldt unless help arrived. He then unfolded the
Anglo-French plan whereby a force of over 50,000 men was
promised. Following this meeting an agreement was drawn up
which stated that the Allies would decide within 3 days
whether they could launch a big operation to relieve the
fortress. If satisfactory assurances could not be given, the
Belgians would be free to abandon the defence if they thought
fit. In the meantime the British would aid the defence with
guns, marines and the naval brigades which, minus recruits,
were ordered to be sent to Antwerp by Churchill.[11]
    What follows next is a description by Churchill of what
took place in Antwerp during the next three days; how he
visited the marines in the front line; how he supervised the
arrival of the naval brigades and personally insisted that
they remain in an intermediate position until the position at
the front became clear; how the fire from the huge German
howitzers gradually demolished the outer forts and
demoralised the Belgian troops to the extent that the outer
defences had to be evacuated; how feeling himself "suddenly,
unexpectedly and deeply involved in a tremendous and
hideously critical local situation" he offered to resign his
post and take "formal military charge of the British forces
in Antwerp". And finally how, with the relieving force not
in sight the Belgians decided on October 6th that they could
wait no longer and ordered the immediate evacuation of the
field army from the city.[12]

Churchill left Antwerp that night and states that the bombardment of the city and the forts began on the 7th. After that "the enemy's attack was pressed continuously, and the enceinte of the city was considered to be untenable by the evening of the 8th."[13] Thus the retreat of the British and Belgian forces from Antwerp began.

Churchill claims that the object of prolonging the defence of Antwerp was

"to give time for the French and British Armies to rest their left upon that fortress and hold the Germans from the seaboard along a line Antwerp-Ghent-Lille. This depended not only upon the local operations but on the result of the series of out-flanking battles which marked the race for the sea. A decisive victory gained by the French in the neighbourhood of Peronne, or by the British beyond Armentieres and towards Lille, would have opened all this prospect."[14]

However, despite this failure Churchill expresses the opinion in The World Crisis that the attempt to save Antwerp was worthwhile in that the days gained at Antwerp saved the Channel Ports from German occupation. He arrived at this conclusion in the following way: had the Belgian field army left Antwerp on the 3rd or 4th

"the city would have surrendered on the 4th or 5th. No [Allied relieving forces]...would have been at Ghent to cover the Belgian retreat. But assuming that the Belgian army had made this good unaided, the same marches would have carried them and their German pursuers to the Yser by the 10th. There would have been nothing at all in front of Ypres. Sir John French could not come into action north of Armentieres till the 15th. His detrainments at St. Omer, etc., were not completed till the 19th. Sir Douglas Haig with the 1st Corps could not come into line north of Ypres till about the 21st. Had the German Siege Army been released on the 5th, and, followed by [the Reserve Corps]...advanced at once, nothing could have saved Dunkirk, and perhaps Calais and Boulogne. The loss of Dunkirk was certain and that of both Calais and Boulogne probable. Ten days were wanted, and ten days were won."[15]

* * * * * * * * * * * * * *

It is now time to test the accuracy of this account against the available documentary evidence. During this examination two factors should be kept in mind. The first is that at the time Churchill's intervention at Antwerp provoked the bitterest criticism and was surrounded by the wildest rumours. The editor of the Morning Post called the operation "a costly blunder, for which Mr. W. Churchill must be held responsible".[16] The Daily Mail asked "who is responsible for [such] a gross example of mal-organization?"[17] Sir Francis Hopwood told Lord Stamfordham, the King's secretary, that Churchill had insisted on going to Antwerp over the objections of Kitchener and Grey and had to be ordered to return by the Cabinet. Stamfordham replied, "Our friend must be quite off his head!"[18] Even Asquith who had initially supported Churchill's action was eventually to speak of the "wicked folly of it all."[19] Churchill was well aware of these criticisms and of the damage that the Antwerp venture had done to his reputation. It will be seen in the course of the narrative whether the need to answer his critics led Churchill to distort his arguments in any way.

The second factor is that some of the material used by Churchill in this chapter came from two articles on Antwerp which he wrote for the Sunday Pictorial in 1916.[20] In fact about one quarter of Churchill's entire account comes from this source.[21] It is interesting to note that this is the section in which Churchill sums up the results obtained by the Antwerp operation. Therefore, whether Churchill's conclusions are correct or not it is obvious that they were arrived at without the benefit of the perspective of time.

The general impression given by the opening paragraphs on the siege of Antwerp in The World Crisis is that Churchill was the only minister interested in aiding Antwerp at this time, that neither Kitchener nor Grey was willing to adopt any of the suggestions which he put forward and that in the event little was done during September. It is true that Churchill's plan to save Antwerp was rejected, but how realistic was that plan in the first place? We saw that the first phase of his scheme was to send Territorial troops to the city, but was it feasible to send these divisions to Antwerp when the battle in France was still undecided? Also, did not this plan violate one of the maxims of war that Churchill was fond of quoting in a naval context, namely, that forces should be concentrated for battle at the decisive point? Yet it must be said that Kitchener rejected sending Territorials to Antwerp not for the reasons given above but because he had an unreasonable fear of a German invasion of Britain. The Territorial Divisions were, therefore, kept at home to guard the east coast.

The second part of Churchill's plan was to "request" the Dutch to open the Scheldt. Churchill has been less than frank in The World Crisis in describing what his actual policy toward the Dutch was. The full texts of his memoranda reveal that he was prepared to go much further than requesting the Dutch to open the Scheldt. On the 7th September he proposed to Grey that if Holland refused, the Navy should keep the Scheldt open by force. This would have had the added advantage of blockading the Rhine. Therefore, from a naval point of view, "war with Holland would be better for us than neutrality".[22]   Earlier he had told Grey, "The Army are capable of [keeping the Scheldt open]...any time you think it necessary".[23]   However Grey was unwilling to risk adding to Britain's enemies at this crucial point and the plan was rejected.   It is little wonder then that Churchill considered these memoranda too delicate to publish in full in The World Crisis.

Nevertheless, the proposition put forward by Churchill in The World Crisis that the British should have started to construct a plan to save Antwerp in early September has considerable merit.   Kitchener not only rejected Churchill's ideas, he put nothing in their place.[24]   Thus, when the urgent Belgian appeals for help came later in the month, the British had no plan and no time to respond to the situation in a reasoned way.

Churchill's account of the meeting at which it was decided to send him to Antwerp must now be discussed.   Only one other description of that meeting written by a participant (Grey) exists.   He describes Churchill's entry into the meeting thus:   "Immediately he entered the room he said the abandonment of Antwerp must be stopped, and announced that he was going there at once to stop it."[25] Grey at first urged caution but "finally Kitchener gave an opinion in favour of his going, and then I acquiesced".[26] Thus Grey is quite certain that the idea of the Antwerp trip was initiated by Churchill.   It will be remembered that Churchill did not say with whom the idea of his going to Antwerp originated.   He gave the impression that it was the logical extension of his trip to Dunkirk.   Of course Grey's account could be wrong but the fact that Churchill evades this issue in The World Crisis suggests otherwise.   There is no doubt that because of the later criticism of his Antwerp journey he would have preferred that the public believe he had been sent to Antwerp as Kitchener's lieutenant rather than as the result of a suggestion which originated with himself.   It is also worth noting that he is careful to avoid all mention of Grey's attitude to the venture.

Although Churchill did not know it in 1914 or presumably at the time of writing Volume 1 of The World Crisis, the message from Villiers which was the immediate cause of his going to Antwerp was wrong in one of its details.   The Belgian Government had decided to leave Antwerp as stated but no final decision had been taken about the field army.[27] Villiers had been misinformed by the Belgian Prime Minister, M. de Broqueville,[28] perhaps deliberately to impress upon the British the need for haste.   Ultimately the error probably made little difference for it is doubtful if the field army would have remained once the Government had gone. However, it is also doubtful if Grey or Kitchener would have recalled Churchill from his train to Dunkirk if they had thought that the Belgian army was to remain in Antwerp. Thus, Churchill's Antwerp journey may have been caused by a misconception.

It would be strange if Churchill did not hear of this error in later years. The fact was discovered by the official historian of the British army in the war, Sir John Edmonds. Churchill and Edmonds corresponded regularly while Churchill was writing The World Crisis, but if Edmonds told Churchill of the discrepancy in the telegram, Churchill did not think it necessary to incorporate this information into the later editions of his book.

The account of Churchill's three day sojourn in Antwerp is generally accepted and contains some of the best descriptive writing in the book, depicting well the atmosphere of the besieged city. He does not succumb to the temptation of over-dramatising his own part in events. If anything, his role in inducing the Belgians to fight on is minimised. Even the controversial telegram in which he offered to resign is discussed. Churchill was not to know of course that it was received by his colleagues with a "Homeric laugh".[29]

The only controversy which emerges from this three day period is the sending of the "partially trained and ill-equipped"[30] naval brigades into the city. Churchill was much criticized for this move after the event, particularly by Asquith who told Venetia Stanley,

"I was assured that all the recruits were being left behind, and that the main body at any rate consisted of seasoned Naval Reserve men. As a matter of fact only about 1/4 were Reservists, and the rest were a callow crowd of the rawest tiros, most of whom had never fired off a rifle....It was like sending sheep to the shambles".[31]

These criticisms are hardly justified. As we saw, Churchill had asked that the naval brigades be sent minus recruits and it was the Admiralty that was at fault in not doing this. Secondly, the immediate arrival of reinforcements was part of the price demanded by the Belgians for not evacuating the city and, given Kitchener's veto on the use of Territorial troops, these were the only men who could have been sent at the time. Also, considering that only 57 men from the entire Naval Division were killed at Antwerp,[32] Asquith's "sheep to the shambles" metaphor seems hardly appropriate.

Presumably to avoid offending the Belgians Churchill has omitted some sections of telegrams sent from Antwerp during this period which dealt with the low morale of the Belgian army. For example, in his telegram to Kitchener of 3rd October the following was omitted from the text published in The World Crisis: "I must impress on you the necessity of making these worn and weary men throw their souls into it, or the whole thing will go with a run."[33] Similar passages have been omitted from two telegrams sent on October

5th.[34] There is no indication in the text that any of these excisions have been made but it cannot be said that the omissions are vital. Enough references to the poor state of Belgian morale were retained to enable a correct picture to be given. Probably Churchill had no wish to hurt the feelings of an ally by over-emphasizing this factor whereas in 1914 he needed to obtain as much help as possible.

It is never doubted in The World Crisis that the relief of Antwerp was a feasible operation or that the attempt to stave off the German besieging force was worthwhile. This optimism was of course based on the plans of Sir John French and Joffre to turn the northern German flank, fall on their lines of communication and sweep them out of Belgium and Northern France at a stroke.[35] That this plan was wildly optimistic was proved by events. However, the plan was not as unreasonable at the time as it now appears. The situation in northern France and Flanders was still fluid. There were few German troops between the Channel Ports and Antwerp. The existence of the German Reserve Corps, which the Allies ran into at Ypres, was unknown. In short, at the time there seemed to be a reasonable prospect that the plan would succeed. In any case, although this point is not put forward by Churchill, it was perhaps inevitable that the British should attempt to save Antwerp. The comprehensive violation of Belgian neutrality was the most important factor in bringing Britain into the war. Yet so far the aid given to Belgium had been slight. It was inconceivable that when the Belgian appeal for aid came, Britain could have remained unmoved. Whether it was worthwhile or not, the attempt to save Antwerp had to be made.

The rather vague plans of the Allied High Commands were really more concerned with the wholesale defeat of the German Army than with the relief of Antwerp. By contrast, Churchill in The World Crisis put forward a definite strategic objective which he thought could have been accomplished by the Allies if they outflanked the German forces in the North. As noted earlier, his plan was to anchor the left of the Allied line on Antwerp and establish the front along the line Antwerp-Ghent-Lille. Leaving aside the fact that none of the Allied commanders mentioned this line as a possible objective, Churchill's plan is open to grave strategic objections. In fact, these objections are similar to those raised by Churchill himself to the Belgian proposal to supply Antwerp through Ostend and Ghent which was mentioned previously. A glance at a map shows that the line proposed by Churchill could have been ruptured in much the same way (a punch up from the south) with much the same dangers (internment in Holland or isolation from the Allied armies to the west) as that proposed by the Belgians.

A second objection to the plan was that it would have involved the Allies in holding a front line 50 miles longer than that which eventually solidified at a time when the shortage of troops was acute. Finally, was a city the size of Antwerp an ideal place on which to rest the front? The civilian population of 400,000 would have required evacuation and the city, under constant bombardment, would have become a death trap for troops, an Ypres on a large scale.

Churchill's wish to incorporate Antwerp into the front line invites comparison with Verdun, the most famous fortress city of the war. Churchill seemed to envisage for Antwerp a role similar to that played by Verdun. However, his remarks on the French strategy at Verdun were in marked contrast with his projected plan for Antwerp. In his discussion of Verdun Churchill wrote much good sense about the need for strategic withdrawal and shortening the line. "Ground should have been sacrificed" he wrote," ... with the sole object of exacting the highest price from the enemy at every stage".[36] Instead the French had been "fastened to fixed positions by sentiment, and battered to pieces there by artillery".[37] Yet "strategic withdrawal" played no part in Churchill's plan for Antwerp. In this case it was going to be a matter of holding on at all costs because "Antwerp was ... the sole stronghold of the Belgian nation".[38] Yet what was this but sentiment? And the fate of the defenders of Antwerp must surely have been to be "battered to pieces by artillery". What was the difference between Verdun and Antwerp that made Churchill recommend such different solutions? One suspects that the only difference was that Churchill was personally involved with the defence of one and not with the other.

In The World Crisis the most important conclusion drawn by Churchill from the siege of Antwerp is that "Antwerp saved the Channel Ports". By this he means that the five or six days delay in the fall of the city, which was achieved by British intervention, enabled a line to be formed across northern Belgium which prevented the German breakthrough to the Channel. This assertion is difficult to prove depending as it does on the complex movements of three separate forces, the German Reserve Corps advancing from Germany, the B.E.F. arriving in Flanders from the Aisne, and the retreating Belgian Field Army and Anglo-French relieving forces. It was noted earlier that the Germans had decided that no major advance could be made through northern Belgium until Antwerp had fallen. When the city capitulated on the 10th four reserve Corps, whose task it was to outflank the Allied line and reach Calais, began their forward movement. On the 13th they were detraining south west of Brussels. On the 14th they began an advance to the line Eecloo-Deynze-Wortegem. Protecting their right was the Antwerp besieging force, the III Reserve Corps. By the 17th the new Corps were 6 miles east of a line Courtrai-Thielt-Oostcamp and by the 18th they had reached the line Courtrai-Thourout, 2 miles from Ypres.[39] The battle for Ypres began the next day.

Assuming that Antwerp had fallen on the 4th or 5th October, the new Corps would have arrived before Ypres on the

12th or 13th. What forces would have been available to oppose them? The 7th Division and the 3rd Cavalry Division were only sent to Belgium to save Antwerp and would otherwise have remained in England. Likewise, the French Territorial Division and the Marine Brigade were sent to Flanders specifically to aid in the relief of Antwerp. The Belgian Field Army, had it escaped, would have been well to the north of Ypres and fully occupied by the German III Reserve Corps. From October 1st the B.E.F. was transferring from the Aisne to Flanders.[40] By October 11th the II Corps was at Bethune, the Cavalry Corps between Hazebrouk and Merville and the III Corps detraining near St. Omer.[41] All of these positions were well to the south and west of Ypres and obviously the B.E.F. would have been in no position to stop the German Reserve Corps reaching at least Dunkirk. By the 18th the gap in the line had been filled. Thus it is probably reasonable to say, as Churchill does, that the days gained at Antwerp enabled the battle of Ypres to be fought and the Channel Ports saved.

However, what Churchill does not make clear in The World Crisis is that the saving of the Channel Ports was not the object of the Antwerp enterprise but only an accidental by-product. After all, it was Churchill himself who defined the object of sending a relieving force to Antwerp as an attempt to gain "time for the French and British Armies to rest their left upon that fortress".[42] But at the end of his account Churchill gives the impression that the main object was to delay the German advance until the B.E.F. arrived in Flanders from the Aisne. In fact the existence of the German Reserve Corps, with which the British collided at Ypres, was only vaguely known to the Allied Commanders. Thus they could hardly have made plans to delay it by sending a relieving force to Antwerp. And it is clear that Churchill could not have foreseen this result. In an earlier draft of The World Crisis he admitted this. He wrote, "It is by the results and as a whole that the episode will be judged; and these, though I do not by any means claim to have foreseen them or controlled them, were certainly advantageous to the Allied cause".[43] Later he decided to claim slightly more prescience for himself and wrote, "I do not by any means claim fully to have foreseen them or controlled them".[44] Finally he dropped the whole section underlined above and wrote, "It is by the results and as a whole that the episode will be judged; and these as will be shown were certainly advantageous to the Allied cause".[45]

Thus to justify further his attempt to save Antwerp Churchill has concentrated on the results achieved rather than on the aims of the original attempt and has claimed rather more foresight for himself than was evident at the time. However, in emphasizing the part Antwerp played in the first battle of Ypres, Churchill is going no further than writers such as Liddell-Hart, Crutwell and Edmonds,[46] although it is possible that their accounts were influenced by The World Crisis. In the case of Edmonds this is known to be true. While Churchill was writing the chapter on Antwerp he consulted Edmonds. In return Edmonds wrote, "I shall be grateful for a copy of the proof of the Antwerp Chapter, that I may bring the "Official History", which I am now writing into line with it."[47] As for that part of his account which deals with his own role in the siege, Churchill is really remarkably accurate and restrained, especially considering both the opportunities which existed for self-aggrandisement and the pressure Churchill was under from his critics to justify his intervention. In short, in this chapter of The World Crisis the participant, the journalist and the historian have combined to produce a lively and, in the main, accurate record of the event.

Chapter 5

STRATEGIC OPTIONS 1914

Most of the second volume of The World Crisis deals with the
genesis, execution and demise of the Dardanelles project.
Because of his close involvement with that operation and the
effect that it was to have on his political career, this
volume is perhaps the most important written by Churchill and
therefore the volume most worthy of detailed discussion.
Churchill obviously recognized the importance of the subject
and the chance that it offered to vindicate his policies. He
therefore set about, in three carefully written chapters, to
prepare the ground for the line to be followed in the
remainder of the volume. The first chapter "The Deadlock In
The West" sets the scene for the other two, "The Search For A
Naval Offensive" and "The Beginning Of The Year", as well as
for the remaining Dardanelles chapters. It deserves close
attention.
    Churchill's main theme in this chapter is that a
strategic, diplomatic and mechanical deadlock existed in the
West and that this led to a search for separate theatres of
action outside France and Flanders. He opens the chapter by
asserting that the failure to develop any of these
alternative theatres had catastrophic results.

> "The year 1915 was fated to be disastrous to the cause of
> the Allies and to the whole world. By the mistakes of
> this year the opportunity was lost of confining the
> conflagration within limits which though enormous were
> not uncontrolled....Thereafter events passed very largely
> outside the scope of conscious choice....But in January,
> 1915, the terrific affair was still not unmanageable. It
> could have been grasped in human hands and brought to
> rest in righteous and fruitful victory before the world
> was exhausted".[1]

    Churchill also claims that there existed a mechanical as
well as a strategic deadlock, on land and sea, a deadlock
which could have been broken had those in authority adopted

the obvious solutions. Those who perceived these solutions

> "were a class apart, outside the currents of orthodox
> opinion, and for them was reserved the long and thankless
> struggle to convert authority and to procure action.
> Eventually they succeeded. On sea authority intervened
> at an early stage: on land the process was more
> painful. The Monitor and the 'bulged' or 'blistered
> ship' were the beginning of the torpedo-proof fleet, the
> Tank was the beginning of the bullet-proof army".[2]

Finally Churchill postulates a diplomatic deadlock. He
claims that this deadlock could easily have been broken by
diplomatic manoeuvres which could have brought additional
allies to the side of the Entente. The Balkans are suggested
as the most fruitful field for these manoeuvres.[3]
    Churchill then turns to an explanation of why it was
essential to break the deadlock on the Western Front.
Russia, he states, was failing, and it was vitally necessary
for the allied cause that Russia be supplied with arms and
material aid[4]. Moreover, a moral debt was owed by the West
to Russia. At the beginning of the war the Russians launched
an offensive into Germany before their mobilization was
complete, thus rescuing the allies at the Marne by forcing
the Germans to withdraw two army corps at a critical time.[5]
    Churchill puts forward two ways in which help could have
been sent to Russia. These involved operations on the
"flanks" of the Central Powers and are characterised by
Churchill as operations of manoeuvre which he contrasts with
the operations of slaughter which were carried out on the
Western Front.

> "The line of the Central Powers from the North Sea to the
> Aegean and stretching loosely beyond even to the Suez
> Canal, was, after all, in principle not different from
> the line of a small army entrenched across an isthmus,
> with each flank resting upon water. As long as France
> was treated as a self-contained theatre, a complete
> deadlock existed, and the Front of the German invaders
> could neither be pierced nor turned. But once the view
> was extended to the whole scene of the war, and that vast
> war conceived as if it were a single battle, and once the
> sea power of Britain was brought into play, turning
> movements of a most far-reaching character were open to
> the Allies".[6]

These turning movements are identified by Churchill as the
mobilization of the northern neutrals coupled with British
domination of the Baltic, and the mobilization of the Balkan
neutrals coupled with British action at the Dardanelles.[7]
This then is how Churchill sets the scene for his discussion
of the Dardanelles operation. Several observations about

this section should now be made.

It should be noted that Churchill's opening paragraph assumes that the strategic deadlock could have been broken in 1915 by the Dardanelles operation or perhaps by some action on the northern flank. In the case of the Dardanelles it is intended to show in subsequent chapters that even had the operation at Gallipoli succeeded it is by no means certain that larger results would have followed. In the case of the northern project it will be suggested that such an operation was almost impossible to carry out and rested on many major fallacies. However, in this section Churchill has planted a seed in the mind of the reader that the poor execution of the Dardanelles campaign was a disaster of unprecedented magnitude for the Allies.

As for Churchill's mechanical expedients with which to break the deadlock, the tank is dealt with in a separate chapter, but it is hard to avoid the conclusion that Churchill has overstated the case for monitors and blistered ships. He is obviously anxious to make the point that in the navy it was his authority that enabled those expedients to be adopted quickly, whereas on land the military authorities took years to be convinced of the utility of the tank. But, it could also be said that the tank developed into an effective weapon of war, while no real use was ever found for the monitors and blistered ships. Nor were these craft "torpedo-proof" as Churchill seems to imply. The British Navy was to spend another quarter of a century on experiments with "blistering" and torpedo-proofing only to find that their ships were as vulnerable to underwater explosions as ever. The "torpedo-proof" fleet was a myth, a product of Churchill's imagination.

It is not intended to discuss in detail here Churchill's contention that attempts to break the diplomatic deadlock by bringing new allies into the field were thrown away. Churchill's Balkan policies are discussed later. It is merely worth noting at this point that Churchill believes that Germany could have been brought down by the accession to the allied cause of several small peasant states on the periphery of the conflict.

Churchill's point that it was necessary to break the strategic deadlock in the West because of Russia's desperate need for help is no doubt valid. However, the fact remains that even if communication had been established with Russia during this period, Britain and France would have had no surplus war material with which to supply their ally. This was the period of the great shortages of munitions in the West. In these circumstances it is hard to see how any shells could have been diverted to Russia, always assuming that the shipping to get them there was available. Churchill's second point, that the allies owed a moral debt to Russia is also fairly dubious. There was no question of the Russians attacking before their mobilization was complete. The two armies which invaded East Prussia were fully mobilized and indeed had been the first Russian armies to complete this procedure. Nor was the action of these armies in launching an early attack a matter of quixotic self-sacrifice. It was commonsense to attack in the east while the Germans were fully occupied with the allies in the west.[8]

A glance at a map of Europe reveals how dubious is Churchill's contention that the Western Front could have been turned had it been regarded as a line no different from that of a "small army entrenched across an isthmus". An army holding a small isthmus has very definite and defensible flanks. The only flank which bore any relation to this situation in 1914-15 was the German right flank in Flanders which could theoretically have been turned by an allied landing on the north Belgian coast. Churchill's stategy in the north, a landing on the Pomeranian coast, could hardly be called a turning movement at all. The landing point was so far from the main armies that the concept of "out-flanking" was not relevant. Moreover, to counter this movement it would only have been necessary for the Germans to send troops northwards from their central reserve.

The situation in Southern Europe, far from being "even more remarkable" as characterized by Churchill, was even less promising. At least a landing on the North German coast directly threatened the main enemy. In the south a group of small neutral states stood between the allies and Austria-Hungary, the weaker member of the Central Powers. It is difficult to see how this area could be regarded as a flank. The main fronts were hundreds of miles distant and a landing anywhere in the area would hardly have affected the situation on either of them. In any case, with interior lines, it would have been a relatively simple matter for the Central Powers to convert this "flank" into another front.

Thus all the assertions upon which Churchill builds up his case for the Dardanelles enterprise can be challenged and be shown to rest on arguments of dubious validity.

* * * * * * * * * * * * * *

Having postulated the need to break the "deadlock in the West" Churchill proceeds to discuss alternative ways of achieving this. He lists a number of operations under consideration in 1914, namely, some form of action against Turkey, the capture of an island off the German coast followed by naval operations in the Baltic, and an advance along the Belgian coast towards Zeebrugge. Churchill's discussion of these options forms an essential preliminary to his Dardanelles chapters and his treatment of them needs careful consideration.

The first alternative discussed is the proposal for action against Turkey. Churchill first examines the events which led to Anglo-Turkish estrangement. Of these events, the arrival of the Goeben and Breslau have already been dealt with. It is Britain's seizure of two Turkish battleships being built in Britain which warrants further attention because of the suggestion that this act may have influenced Turkey's decision to join the Central Powers. In The World Crisis Churchill refutes this suggestion. He claims that when the ships were seized Turkey had already made the decision to join Germany. He then goes on to make larger claims. He states "The requisitioning of these ships, so far from making Turkey an enemy, nearly made her an Ally".[9] This startling claim is justified on the grounds that the ships were to be Turkey's means of controlling the Black Sea in a projected war with Russia. Withholding the ships thwarted this plan (called the Pan-Turk War Plan by Churchill) and forced Turkey, for the time, to remain neutral.[10]

Churchill then discusses the first possibility for action against Turkey, the Greek offer of aid of August 19th. Briefly stated, this offer involved the use of a Greek army of three divisions in conjunction with the British fleet should Britain be contemplating action against Turkey. Churchill suggests that the rejection of this plan was one of the great lost opportunities of the war.

"A combination of the Greek armies and fleet with the British Mediterranean squadron offered a means of settling the difficulties of the Dardanelles in a most prompt and effective manner. The Gallipoli Peninsula was then only weakly occupied by Turkish Troops, and the Greek General Staff were known to be ready with well-thought-out plans for its seizure".[11]

He goes on to deal with the conferences held in London between the naval and military authorities to consider the Greek offer. He quotes his letter of September 1st to the C.I.G.S. which arranged the first meeting and continues,

"The Director of Military Operations, General Callwell, replied on the 3rd, on behalf of the General Staff, that the operation of seizing the Gallipoli peninsula would be an extremely difficult one. Sixty thousand men would be required, thirty thousand of whom should be landed in the first instance, should gain as much ground as possible, should prepare landing stages, and hold their own for a week while the transports returned to Greece for the second thirty thousand. On this basis the operation was considered feasible".[12]

For various reasons the Greek offer was later withdrawn but the strong impression given by Churchill is that the combined operation which would have resulted from the acceptance of the offer was militarily feasible.

Turkey's entry into the war is next considered by Churchill. He describes the Turkish attack on the Russian Black Sea ports and the bombardment of the Dardanelles forts by Britain which followed on November 3rd. He explains the reasons behind this action.

"A British squadron had for months been waiting outside the Dardanelles. War had been declared with Turkey. It was natural that fire should be opened upon the enemy as it would be on the fronts of hostile armies. It was necessary to know accurately the effective ranges of the Turkish guns and the conditions under which the entrance to the blockaded port could be approached.[13]

He adds that the Turkish decision to strengthen the defences at the Dardanelles was not caused by this bombardment but by a longer term plan which had been implemented at the very beginning of the war.[14]

The next section of The World Crisis of relevance to the Dardanelles comes many pages later. Churchill mentions that at the War Council of November 25th he suggested that transports be collected in Egypt for the purpose of landing 40,000 men at the Dardanelles at short notice and that this was later vetoed by Kitchener. About Kitchener's decision Churchill comments,

"I do not censure the War Office decision not to act at this time. Action would have been a master stroke, but no one could be blamed for not attempting it.[15]

However, he restates his opinion that action at the Dardanelles along the lines proposed was both desirable and feasible and that a further opportunity to solve the Turkish question had been lost.

Churchill's treatment of the Borkum-Baltic option is quite brief. As detailed by Churchill the plan involved launching a combined operation to capture an island off the German coast (various alternatives were put forward but the island most mentioned is Borkum). An attempt by the Germans to recapture the island, necessary because otherwise it could have been used as a base for submarines and torpedo-craft, was expected to provoke the decisive naval battle. After this, the victorious British fleet would be free to enter the Baltic, establish control of that sea and be in a position to land a large force of Russian troops on the Pomeranian coast. This would establish a direct threat to Berlin and force the withdrawal of a substantial number of German troops from the Western Front to counter it, thus materially shortening the war.[16]

Churchill was strongly in favour of this operation but in The World Crisis he laments that he could find no Admiral willing to undertake it. He castigates the Admirals for their timidity and accuses them of resting content with the distant blockade and complains that when he reproached them from time to time for their inactivity "they replied by using all the perfectly correct arguments about not jeopardizing the Grand Fleet".[17] He argues that this negative approach was not sufficient and that it was the Admirals' business

"to invent or discover some offensive plan which without engaging the Grand Fleet at a disadvantage either forced the Germans to give battle or helped the allied armies in some notable way and took some of the pressure off them. A civilian Minister could never compel them to such a course. He could suggest, encourage and sustain. But if they remained immovable, like George II at the Battle of Dettingen, 'sans peur et sans avis' nothing could be done".[18]

It is clear that Churchill considered his Borkum project as falling into the catagory of a desirable offensive plan.

The plan to advance along the Belgian coast with the navy providing artillery support for the army also receives brief treatment in The World Crisis. From his first paragraph on the subject Churchill seems determined to minimize its importance.

"About the third week in November, 1914, Sir John French wished to make an advance... along the sea coast from Nieuport towards Ostend and Zeebrugge. This project was a limited and local operation not at all to be confused with the great strategic alternatives [of Borkum and the Dardanelles]".[19]

He goes on to quote from a series of his letters to Sir John French designed to show that he (Churchill) nevertheless supported the plan. He ends this section by showing how the plan foundered on the opposition of Joffre, a decision which he claimed was a heavy blow to the navy, and ended another promising operation.[20]

Has Churchill given a fair summary of these plans in The World Crisis?

\* \* \* \* \* \* \* \* \* \* \* \* \* \* \*

Consideration must first be given to Churchill's discussion of operations against Turkey. In relation to Turkey's entry into the war, Churchill's claim that Turkey had decided to join the Central Powers before the requisitioning of the battleships on July 28th can readily be accepted. It is now known that negotiations for a German-Turkish alliance began on July 24th.[21] As for his statement that the seizure of the ships thwarted the

"Pan-Turk War Plan", it has to be said that modern scholarship has not been able to establish the existence of this plan. In fact it appears that the decision to bombard the Russian Ports was forced on Enver, the Turkish Minister of War, by the failure of some of his colleagues to support the Turko-German alliance, rather than being the culmination of a previously arranged plan.[22] If this version of events is correct then Churchill has somewhat overstated his case.

Of course it is now known that in seizing the Turkish battleships Churchill acted better than he could have known at the time, for on August 1st Turkey had decided to direct one of the seized ships to a German North Sea port where it would have made a dangerous addition to the High Sea Fleet.[23]

Churchill's version of the Greek offer of aid against Turkey on August 19th must be discussed in some detail as it is the first of many "lost opportunities" which are to feature constantly in his account of the Dardanelles operation. Churchill always assumes that the Greek offer would have led to the immediate use of the Greek army in combination with a British squadron at the Dardanelles. This is a dubious assumption. In the first place, at the time the offer was made, Britain and Turkey were not at war and Churchill offers no explanation as to how this inconvenient problem could have been overcome. Secondly, it is not mentioned in The World Crisis that the Greek offer was almost certainly conditional on Bulgaria entering the war on the allied side. The Greek General Staff considered this to be essential to remove the threat of Bulgarian intervention on the Greek northern frontier while the bulk of the Greek army was supporting the British fleet at the Dardanelles.[24] Churchill's description of the Greek plan as "well-thought-out" is also hardly accurate. The only "plan" which the Greeks had available was for a landing on an undefended beach before Turkey had mobilized.[25] When the Greek offer was made on August 19th this condition did not apply. In fact the offer had been made by Venizelos, the Greek Prime Minister, on his own initiative and without consulting the General Staff, who in these circumstances would have hardly agreed to its implementation.[26]

If the above factors are taken into account the Admiralty-War Office conference on the possible use of the Greek army at the Dardanelles, which is discussed at length by Churchill, is invested with a rather theoretical quality. Nevertheless, Churchill's account of this episode must be examined for in some ways it is quite misleading. According to The World Crisis there was one conference at which the War Office representative stated that the proposed operation was feasible though difficult. In fact there were two conferences and at the first the D.M.O. (Callwell) stated that "considering the strength of the Turkish Garrison & the large force already mobilised in European Turkey, he did not regard it as a feasible military operation".[27] Why has Churchill omitted all reference to this meeting, and thus Callwell's change of mind, from his account? The reasons must remain speculative but it is known that in the interval between the two meetings Churchill urged the Greek "plan" on the Cabinet[28] and it is hard to avoid the conclusion that at the second meeting he put strong pressure on Callwell to produce a more favourable answer.

Churchill's defence of his decision to bombard the Dardanelles forts on November 3rd is also misleading in several details. Churchill states that at the time of the bombardment war had been declared between Britain and Turkey. This was not the case. The formal declaration only came two days later on the 5th. In addition Churchill omits from his account two memoranda received by him from Admiral Slade and Admiral Limpus (the latter described in The World Crisis as "the Admiral who of all others knew the Turks, and knew the Dardanelles")[29] that the operation offered little prospect of success and would only serve to alert the Turks if more serious operations were contemplated later.[30] As for Churchill's assertion that the bombardment was necessary to test the range and calibre of the Turkish guns, it has been stated by one well-placed authority that these details were already known and published in a naval intelligence handbook.[31]

What of Churchill's statement that the bombardment did not affect the Turkish decision to strengthen the Dardanelles defences? There is evidence to support this statement. In August, coastal defence experts, mines and ammunition were despatched to the Straits from Germany[32] and the Turks later testified that the main increases had been decided on before the war.[33] Furthermore, the Straits were such a vital factor in the defence of Turkey it is reasonable to suppose that they would have received a high priority in wartime. What Churchill's account does neglect is that the risk that the Turks would accelerate the defences was hardly commensurate with the meagre results likely to be achieved by the bombardment. Churchill also makes no comment on the fact that the bombardment increased the confidence of the defence by demonstrating that naval shells had little effect on modern earthwork forts.[34] This information is contained in a file of correspondence between the German commander of the Straits defences and the Kaiser that Churchill is known to have consulted in writing The World Crisis.[35]

Churchill was highly critical of the War Office for not preparing an amphibious assault against the Gallipoli Peninsula in late November 1914 and declared that a golden opportunity was lost as a result of this inaction. Was this the case? If the War Office had acted immediately following the War Council of November 25th, as Churchill suggests they should have, six weeks at least would have been necessary to collect the transports and work out a plan. This would have placed the landing in early January. At that time of year weather conditions at the Dardanelles are hardly conducive to combined operations. In January 1915 gale force winds were experienced on 28 days.[36] Furthermore the only troops available were the untrained Anzacs and a Territorial Division. This factor combined with the bad weather could have turned the operation into a disaster rather than the "master-stroke" anticipated in The World Crisis.[37]

Churchill's section on the proposal to capture a German island, dominate the Baltic and aid a Russian landing on the German coast provides an example of the extremely theoretical treatment of military operations which is characteristic of his writing. He states that the operation would have achieved the desired result. But the complexities of the plan and the difficulties in carrying it out are never discussed. These difficulties were formidable. The waters around the German islands under consideration for attack were mined and further protected by submarines and torpedo-boat flotillas. The bombarding force would have been open to attack by the entire High Sea Fleet. There were the additional problems of hitting unlocated shore batteries from moving ships and of landing troops under the fire of machine guns and artillery. If an island had been captured, supplying the garrison and supporting flotillas could have been a precarious affair, involving a constant stream of slow merchant ships passing through submarine and mine infested waters. But not one of these factors is mentioned by Churchill.

The domination of the Baltic and the landing of a Russian force on the German coast, the dangers of which are so lightly dismissed by Churchill, presented an even greater hazard. Even if the entire High Sea Fleet had been destroyed in an attempt to recapture the island, the dreadnoughts of the Grand Fleet would have encountered mines, with which the Baltic was sown, and the submarines and torpedo-craft permanently located in that sea. Moreover, landing Russian troops presupposed that the Russians had troops available, that these troops were skilled in combined operations, that logistic support in the form of artillery and stores was available in sufficient quantity, that the language problem could have been overcome, and that the Russians would have been willing to risk such a highly trained, well supplied force on a hazardous operation well away from their main theatre. In fact not one of these conditions applied throughout the war. Churchill's account, while not confronting these issues, implies the contrary. Neither does he deal with the possibility that with their highly efficient railway system, the Germans could have countered a successful landing by moving reserves northwards at a faster rate than the attacking army could be reinforced from the sea.

When the difficulties of the Borkum-Baltic scheme are outlined it can be seen that Churchill's strictures against the Admirals for failing to undertake the project are grossly unfair. The Admirals refused to consider Churchill's schemes seriously, not because they "rested content" with the situation at sea, but because his schemes were basically unsound. All Churchill's northern projects involved risking the Grand Fleet in mine and torpedo infested waters. No likely gain warranted these risks and it was decidedly <u>not</u> the business of the Admirals to invent operations of this kind.

To a certain extent Churchill seems to have played down in <u>The World Crisis</u> his interest in the Borkum-Baltic project. He had been a consistent advocate of the scheme since the beginning of the war when he had first ordered plans to be drawn up. In the following months he pursued these plans with Jellicoe, Sir Arthur Wilson, Fisher and others.[38] Yet in <u>The World Crisis</u> only a section of a short chapter is devoted to a discussion of the project. Moreover, several paragraphs which would have made Churchill's attitude to the operation much clearer were omitted while the chapter was in draft form. The relevant section of the first of these deletions reads,

"Up till the end of the year my mind turned on the whole to intervening on the Northern rather than on the Southern flank... it was to the Baltic that my thoughts were principally turned".[39]

The second omission included the following,

"Up till the end of 1914 I was working at the Borkum-Baltic plan, encountering some opposition, much apathy, but also enjoying a great deal of support, especially from Fisher....Anyhow it had been clear from the beginning that many months would be required before any decision other than preparation and study need be taken as far as the Northern Borkum movement was concerned. Meanwhile the naval operation at the Dardanelles, which was a far smaller and less formidable business, would either fail or succeed. If it failed, then very likely I should be made the scapegoat and the responsibility for further events would be passed to others. If it succeeded, we should gain the prestige, which alone would enable so terrific and deadly a business as the storming of Borkum... to be carried out... even while the Dardanelles was on I always regarded it as [long] as I was in power only as an interim operation, and all the plans for the Borkum-Baltic project were going forward".[40]

These two paragraphs give a unique insight into Churchill's thinking on the relative merits of the Borkum plan and the Dardanelles operation. They reveal that even after the naval attack on Gallipoli had begun, Churchill still regarded the "northern theatre" as the one in which the really decisive operation would take place. The Dardanelles was merely to be a preliminary to the main offensive. This is a strikingly different line from that eventually taken in The World Crisis, where the importance of Borkum is played down in relation to the Dardanelles.

Why did Churchill in the published version of these events wish to convey the opposite impression to that revealed by the deleted paragraphs? The answer may lie in how the two operations were viewed at the time when Churchill was writing The World Crisis or in how he wished them to be viewed in the future. The Borkum operation was never supported by any substantial body of naval opinion, either during or after the war. Even Keyes, the most aggressive of naval commanders, rejected the scheme as impractical.[41] By contrast, the Dardanelles plan was always regarded by a section of military and public opinion as a brilliant strategic concept which had unfortunately failed due to a lack of political and military support. Liddell Hart is an example of this school of thought. For obvious reasons Churchill was in sympathy with this line of reasoning and there is no doubt that he wished to propagate the view that the Dardanelles plan had been the one imaginative strategic conception of the war. However he could hardly do this if it was revealed that he saw the Dardanelles attack as a mere preliminary to a larger event and one that was undertaken partly as a stop-gap operation. All references to the true state of his thinking were therefore removed from The World Crisis and, as will be shown, the consistent line adopted throughout the book was that the Dardanelles and not Borkum was the key to a shorter and less costly war.

Churchill's emendations also provide an answer to a question that has often puzzled historians. It has never been known why preparations and discussions about the Borkum plan continued well after the Dardanelles operations had begun. The answer is now obvious.

Several points need to be made about Churchill's account of the Zeebrugge plan. Firstly, it will be remembered that in The World Crisis Churchill was at some pains to minimize the importance of the operation and emphasize that it was not in the same category as Borkum or the Dardanelles. However, the plan did involve the use of the entire British and perhaps Belgian armies in France and Flanders, a squadron of battleships and monitors and a combined operation to land 10,000 men at Zeebrugge. Thus if the number of troops involved is taken as a measurement, the plan was a far larger affair than either of Churchill's southern or northern alternatives. Of course Churchill did not regard the Zeebrugge attack as a war-winning plan in the same way as the other great strategic alternatives. But this reasoning merely highlights the strategic fallacy behind the Borkum and Dardanelles plans. For if a successful attack with a large number of troops in the main theatre could not win the war, how was this feat to be achieved by greatly reduced numbers at the periphery?

In any case it is not certain that Churchill regarded the Zeebrugge operation as of minor importance at the time. On December 9th Churchill wrote to French about Zeebrugge: "A good & brilliant operation is in sight, conducent immediately to the safety of this country & the general success of the war".[42] Later Churchill told French that he had tried to convince his colleagues of the advantages of the coastal operation. "I argued in the War Council strongly against deserting the decisive theatre & the most formidable antagonist to win cheaper laurels in easier fields".[43] Such statements hardly imply that Churchill was discussing a subsidiary operation. It is noteworthy that both letters were originally selected for inclusion in The World Crisis but were eventually omitted, one suspects because they would have weakened Churchill's argument about the subsidiary nature of Zeebrugge.[44]

A final point that should be made about Zeebrugge is that in The World Crisis Churchill definitely attributes the origin of the plan to French. This is in fact doubtful. As early as November Churchill expressed concern at the development of the submarine bases at Ostend and Zeebrugge and he ordered plans to be prepared for the bombardment of the two Belgian ports.[45] Shortly after these plans were drawn up the scope of the operation was broadened to include an advance by the army along the Belgian coast, for we find Sir John French warning Churchill of the difficulties which the extensive inundations and canals would cause.[46] From this reply it is obvious that it was Churchill who first mentioned the operation to French. Perhaps this fact was obscured by Churchill to conceal that he had been the originator of yet another alternative operation.

Two general comments seem necessary about these chapters of The World Crisis. The first is that, broadly speaking, Churchill deals with the origins of the Dardanelles, Borkum and Zeebrugge plans in three separate chapters. This gives the impression that the operations were discussed at different times and in different circumstances. This was not the case. Discussions concerning the three operations often took place simultaneously.

Secondly, by playing down Borkum and Zeebrugge Churchill has enhanced the importance of the Dardanelles plan during this period and given the impression subsequently adopted by historians that "His eyes had been on the Dardanelles from the moment that Turkish intervertion on the German side appeared probable".[47] In fact, of the three plans, Borkum seemed the most important to Churchill at this time. However, for reasons which have been explained, Churchill did not want to be remembered as the author of the Borkum plan, while he was quite content to be known as the driving force behind the Dardanelles campaign. Therefore, in studying this section of The World Crisis, the reader needs to bear in mind Churchill's overriding concern to emphasize the Dardanelles operation at the expense of the others.

It should now be obvious that Churchill's chapter on the deadlock in the west has given a misleading impression of the motive behind the search for a new offensive. This search began long before the solidification of the Western Front and the major impulse behind the search was Churchill's restlessness and dissatisfaction with the progress of the naval war. Indeed, our discussion has revealed that investigations into extraneous operations involving the navy began in the earliest days of the war. However, such is the force with which "The Deadlock In the West" has been written, and so attractive are the arguments used, that combined with the fact that these three operations are treated separately, the impression is left on the mind of the reader that all three operations were considered because of the paralysis of the Western Front. As a result the operations themselves have an appeal, an urgency, and an inevitability which in fact they did not possess at the time. It is after this preparation that Churchill's readers are introduced to a discussion of the Dardanelles operation proper.

Chapter 6

THE DARDANELLES I - THE DECISION

At the end of 1914 scepticism of the strategic possibilities offered by the Western Front led Hankey, Lloyd George, Churchill and Fisher to commit alternative strategies to paper. Hankey suggested that Germany could be struck most effectively through Turkey and he recommended that eight divisions be earmarked for use in co-operation with Bulgaria and Greece to capture Constantinople. This paper was not notable for its precision. Hankey spoke vaguely of "weaving a circle round Turkey", left unargued the novel proposition that Germany could be defeated by attacks on weaker allies, failed to fill in the military details of how Constantinople was to be captured and did not specify how the desirable result of Balkan unity, a sine qua non for his plans, was to be brought about.

Lloyd George's paper also rested on the remarkable idea that Germany was "propped up" by such countries as Austria-Hungary and Turkey and could be destroyed by knocking away these props. He suggested an attack on Austria-Hungary in conjunction with the Greeks, Roumanians and Serbians by landing 600,000 British troops on the Dalmatian coast, though he made no suggestions as to how such a force was to be transported and supplied. A second option of a landing in Syria to cut off Turkish expeditions against Egypt was also put forward.[1]

Churchill merely restated his German island, now identified as Borkum, scheme and added details of how it was to be captured.[2] However, after reading Hankey's paper, he wrote to Asquith that regarding future strategy he and Hankey were "substantially in agreement and our conclusions are not incompatible. I wanted Gallipoli attacked on the Turkish declaration of war."[3] Thus Churchill was apparently advocating both the Borkum scheme and an attack on Turkey. It should be noted, however, that Hankey had not mentioned an attack on the Gallipoli Peninsula. This was a Churchillian contribution.

Fisher had also read Hankey's paper and he expanded Hankey's ideas into a full scale invasion of Turkey with British landings on the Asiatic coast, coupled with a Greek attack on the Gallipoli Peninsula and a simultaneous forcing of the Dardanelles by the British Fleet.[4] Fisher was concerned that Churchill's German island strategy would blind him to the possibilities in Turkey and he undertook to convince the First Lord of the merits of Hankey's scheme.[5] As Churchill's note to Asquith indicates, the First Lord was by no means opposed to an attack on Turkey, though he perhaps regarded it as secondary to his northern schemes. All Fisher needed to do then was to change his chief's priorities.

It was at this moment that the Russian plea for help arrived. Grey was informed that the Russian position in the Caucasus was threatened by the Turks. "Grand Duke ... asked if it would be possible for Lord Kitchener to arrange for a demonstration of some kind against the Turk elsewhere."[6] The next day Kitchener asked Churchill if he considered anything could be done to help Russia.[7] Kitchener's own view was that "I do not see that we can do anything that will seriously help the Russians in the Caucasus....We have no troops to land anywhere....The only place that a demonstration might have some effect in stopping reinforcements going East would be the Dardanelles....We shall not be ready for anything big for some months."[8] Before Churchill could consider his own position Fisher passed on to him his "Turkey Plan". His advocacy of it was enthusiastic, even violent. "I consider the attack on Turkey Holds the Field! - but Only if it's Immediate!" After detailing the military operations which he considered should take place Fisher came to the role of the Royal Navy, "Sturdee forces the Dardanelles at the same time with Majestic class & Canopus class! God Bless him!"[9] Both Kitchener and Fisher had mentioned the Dardanelles as a possible sphere of action, although the two operations were very different, Kitchener's a mere naval demonstration, Fisher's a wildly impractical combination amounting to a separate war.

With Fisher's and Kitchener's proposals fresh in his mind Churchill attended a meeting of the Admiralty War Group (Churchill, Fisher, Wilson, Oliver, Bartoleme and Greene (Secretary)). The Russian plea for help was discussed but exactly what passed at the meeting is not known. However, shortly after its conclusion Churchill sent the following telegram with the apparent concurrence of Fisher and Oliver[10] to Admiral Carden, commanding the allied squadron off the Dardanelles,

"Do you consider the forcing of the Dardanelles by ships alone a practicable operation. It is assumed older Battleships fitted with minebumpers would be used preceded by Colliers or other merchant craft as bumpers and sweepers. Importance of results would justify severe loss. Let me know your views."11

The nature of the operation mentioned in the telegram is interesting. It was neither a demonstration as requested by the Russians nor a large combined operation as recommended by Fisher, and it had nothing in common with the suggestions made by Hankey and Lloyd George. The operation suggested to Carden by Churchill was nothing less than an attempt to use the navy alone to force one of the belligerents out of the war. It is hard to avoid the conclusion that this message was deliberately framed to encourage a positive response for if severe losses were justified what commander would admit that the operation should not be attempted? Churchill later stated that the telegram was cast in such a way to indicate "that action, if possible, would be very desirable [and]... that we should have been very glad if he had had a good plan."12

Some historians have held that the wording of the telegram shows that Churchill was determined to attack Turkey at all costs and that this had been his policy since the beginning of the war.13 However, it has been shown that in the early months of the war action at Gallipoli was by no means an "idee fixe" for Churchill but just one of a series of options. That this remained his position is indicated by the fact that on the same day the telegram was sent to Carden he advised Fisher that plans for Sylt (probably Borkum) should be ready for the operation to commence on either March 1st or April 15th, and the next day he made the same point to Jellicoe.14

However, Admiralty opinion was by no means convinced of the efficacy of the Borkum operation. Richmond regarded Churchill's scheme as "quite mad" and Fisher urged acceptance of Hankey's plan, the advantages of which he considered "overwhelming".15 Churchill remained cautious. "I think we had better hear what others have to say about the Turkish plans" he wrote "before taking a decided line. I wd. not grudge 100,000 men because of the great political effects in the Balkan peninsula: but Germany is the foe, & it is bad war to seek cheaper victories & easier antagonists."16 Thus we have Churchill favouring action in the main theatre and Fisher advocating an attack on the periphery, the exact opposite of what is usually thought to be their respective strategies. In fact at this time Fisher had gone completely cold on the Borkum project. His naval secretary, Captain Crease, told Richmond not to worry over the operation because "the 1st Sea Lord didn't intend to have the Borkum business done ... Crease said they can go on getting their plans as much as they like, but Jacky is simply not going to do them in the end."17

Carden's reply to Churchill's telegram arrived on the 5th: "I do not consider Dardanelles can be rushed. They might be forced by extended operations with large number of ships".[18] This was at best a grudging admission that under certain circumstances the operation might be attempted. However, Carden had not said that the operation was absolutely impossible and for Churchill this was enough. He was determined to obtain a plan from Carden and he telegraphed back, "Your view is agreed with by high authorities here. Please telegraph in detail what you think could be done by extended operations, what force would be needed and how you consider it should be used."[19] According to Churchill the "high authorities" mentioned were Jackson and Oliver with whom he had talks about the idea of a naval attack at the Dardanelles.[20] But Carden naturally assumed that Fisher was included.[21] What Fisher's response to Carden's telegram was is not known. He had however, recently expressed an opinion against naval bombardments which were not accompanied by military operations[22] and it is hard to believe that Fisher could have shown much enthusiasm for a purely naval bombardment at the Dardanelles. In fact, Jackson's support is also in some doubt. It appears that at about this time Jackson had a conversation with Churchill concerning a naval attack at the Dardanelles. While deprecating a rush at the Straits Jackson seemed to agree with a step-by-step approach. However, he apparently also stated that troops would be needed to complete the naval attack and to occupy Constantinople.[23]

Certainly a memorandum written by Jackson on the 5th, but not seen by Churchill until after the "high authorities" telegram had been sent, confirms that Jackson had grave doubts concerning Carden's plan. Jackson considered a rush at the Straits was certain to fail and, although he thought a methodical approach would yield better results, he warned that such a method would require the expenditure of a large amount of ammunition, would mean a great amount of wear on the guns, and would also entail some losses. He concluded that "to arrive off Constantinople with depleted magazines and [crippled ships] ... would be a fatal error,"[24] and it therefore appears that any support that Jackson gave to the Carden proposal was of a highly qualified nature.

Oliver's opinion at this time is unknown although later he became a supporter of the plan. But it seems unlikely that any naval authority had expressed marked enthusiasm for a naval attack on the Dardanelles. Yet by not questioning anyone too deeply on what their actual opinions were, Churchill was rapidly creating a situation where he could claim that a substantial body of naval opinion supported the concept.

In fact, by this time the original raison d'etre of the naval attack had disappeared for, on January 3rd the British liaison officer with the Russian Army, General Hanbury-Williams, told Kitchener that the immediate danger of a Russian reverse in the Caucasus had passed[25] and on the

6th Reuter published news of a big Russian victory over the Turks in that region.26

The events of the next few days were to show that Churchill was by no means single-minded in his advocacy of an attack on the Dardanelles at this stage. At a War Council meeting on the 7th he spoke in favour of an attack on Zeebrugge as advocated by Sir John French. When this plan was vetoed by Kitchener, Churchill switched discussion to the capture of a German island and, with Fisher's support (had he reversed his apparent decision of January 5th "not to do" the operation or was he trying to humour Churchill in the knowledge that the plan would probably break down at the planning stage?) obtained the War Council's approval for the Admiralty to proceed with the detailed planning of the attack.27

At a further meeting on the 8th Churchill produced yet another alternative plan. He asked if Holland could not be induced to enter the war. This would far outweigh the advantages of action in the Mediterranean and would provide Britain with an island base near Germany without fighting.28 No solutions were offered to the not inconsiderable problem of how to convince the Dutch that the German Army, which surrounded them on three sides, could be offset by naval operations.

Perhaps to divert Churchill's attention from the Dardanelles and Borkum Fisher now enthusiastically took up the "Holland Plan", telling Churchill that its successful prosecution would mean "The End of The War!"29 Churchill needed little encouragement. He now spoke of "bringing in" Holland as the "greatest hope" in the northern theatre and cautioned, "It is not until all the northern possibilities are exhausted that I wd look to the S of Europe as a field for the profitable employment of our expanding milty forces. But plans shd be worked out for every contingency."30

At this point Carden's plan arrived. It provided for a step-by-step reduction of the Dardanelles forts beginning at the entrance and working up the Straits. He considered that the expenditure of ammunition would be large and that the forces required would include 12 battleships, 3 battlecruisers, a cruiser and destroyer force, submarines and 12 minesweepers including Fleet sweepers. With this force he thought "might do it all in a month about".31

Churchill claimed later to be much impressed with this plan. He described Carden's message as "The most important telegram. Here was the Admiral, who had been for weeks sitting off the Dardanelles, who presumably had been turning this thing over in his mind ... who produces a plan and a detailed plan and a novel plan, and this plan found immediate acceptance by the Chief of the Staff, and by Sir Henry Jackson."32 Both Oliver and (with qualifications) Jackson testified that they thought Carden's plan worthy of a try at this stage.33 But was the plan as impressive as Churchill stated?

On examination, Carden's "plan" is seen to be hardly a plan at all but merely a statement of the order in which the Dardanelles defences were to be reduced. The details of how this was to be achieved were sketchy and the problem of the Turkish guns and the minefields protecting them was hardly mentioned. Yet the Admiralty War Staff accepted the basis of the plan without question. Why they did this is hard to explain. There is some evidence to suggest that opinion at the Admiralty, and in particular Jackson's opinion, had undergone a recent change on the question of whether ships could fight forts.[34] Oliver had stated that he had been impressed by how easily the Germans had demolished the Antwerp forts.[35] Significantly, Godfrey, the member of Carden's staff largely responsible for the plan, was also influenced by the Antwerp analogy.[36]

But the proposition that ships could fight forts was not as simple as it appeared. In Carden's plan the ships were to attack the forts outside the range of the Turkish guns. In this situation a very efficient spotting force was required, for the long ranges involved meant that the fall of shot could not be seen from the ships. It also required a large amount of ammunition for the percentage of hits that could be expected on the guns at those distances was no more than 2 or 3%.[37] Moreover ships fighting forts was not the crucial problem at the Dardanelles. For the ships to dominate the forts and ensure their destruction it would have been necessary for Carden to attack from close range. This required that the minefields protecting the forts be swept and to enable this to be done either a force capable of sweeping in the face of heavy fire from the batteries protecting the minefields was needed, or some method devised of destroying the batteries so that the minefields could be swept at leisure. A vital question then was whether the ships could destroy these batteries as well as the forts. There is no evidence that these additional factors were considered by the Staff.

Did the Staff or Churchill perhaps feel that the plan carried particular weight as coming from Carden? It seems hardly likely. Carden had not been Churchill's original choice to command the squadron at the Dardanelles. He had wanted to appoint Admiral Limpus, the former head of the British naval mission to Turkey, a man familiar with the Dardanelles defences and possessing intimate knowledge of the Turkish Navy.[38] This appointment had been vetoed by the Foreign Office on the advice of the British ambassador to Turkey on the extraordinary grounds that the appointment would offend the Turks.[39] Churchill protested at this move but was over-ruled.[40] Thus Carden, the Superintendent of the Malta dockyard, got the job. Yet there is no evidence to suggest that Carden's career had in any way been exceptional and as late as December 23rd Churchill had written, "As for

Carden - he has never even commanded a cruiser Sqn & I am not aware of anything that he has done wh is in any way remarkable."[41]

On January 13th. Churchill decided to put Carden's plan before the War Council. It is probable that he did so because no other operation seemed possible at this stage. Jellicoe's last communication on Borkum had been decidedly pessimistic.[42] Zeebrugge had been shelved by the War Council. No one knew how to bring in Holland.

The War Council met on the 13th. The Zeebrugge operation was reintroduced by French but after a lengthy discussion it was again decided to postpone it.[43] Churchill then unveiled Carden's plan. He said it was based on the fact that the old guns of the Dardanelles forts were outranged by the guns of the warships.

"The Admiralty were studying the question and believed that a plan could be made for systematically reducing all the forts within a few weeks. Once the forts were reduced the minefields would be cleared and the Fleet would proceed up to Constantinople and destroy the Goeben. They would have nothing to fear from field guns or rifles, which would be merely an inconvenience."[44]

It is noticeable that Churchill did not go into the details of what would happen after the Goeben was sunk. Would Constantinople surrender? Would the Gallipoli Peninsula be evacuated by the Turks? Would troops be needed to occupy those positions?

These questions were not considered. In their enthusiasm for the Churchill-Carden plan, offering as it did the prospect of a victory without the enormous casualties being suffered on the Western Front, no one on the War Council had stopped to consider that even if the Fleet was successful troops would be needed in reasonably large numbers to garrison the captured territory. However, if the substance of the Jackson-Churchill conversation of January 4th or 5th is correct, then Churchill must have been aware of this need and it seems possible that he deliberately concealed this fact from his colleagues in order to get the operation accepted. For the mere mention of troops must have raised questions as to their availability, and Kitchener's opinion that there were no troops to land anywhere was well known. The failure of the War Council to investigate this point was to lead them into a much larger operation than they would have been willing to contemplate at the time.

But so far from being sceptical of the Churchill plan the War Council enthusiastically endorsed it and gave the Admiralty permission to prepare for its implementation. At the same meeting they also set up a sub-committee to consider alternative theatres in which British troops could be used in the event of the stalemate on the Western Front being prolonged into the spring.[45] Significantly no one suggested that they be used in combination with the Fleet at the Dardanelles.

At the Admiralty, planning for the naval attack now got under way. Fisher suggested to Oliver that the Queen Elizabeth, the most powerful battleship in the world, should test her 15" guns at the Dardanelles.[46] Churchill ordered that the fleet for the bombardment be collected at once. He also instructed an officer of the War Staff to analyse Carden's proposals "in order to show exactly what guns the ships will have to face at each point."[47] He had clearly decided that the operation was to go forward for he added, "this officer is to assume that the principle is settled, and all that is necessary is to estimate the force required".[48]

After Carden's plan had been received by the Admiralty, Churchill had asked Jackson to make a study of it and report his conclusions. Jackson reported to Oliver on January 15th. Of Carden's proposals he wrote, "Concur generally in his plans. Our previous appreciations of the situation differed only in small details."[49] Echoing Carden, he warned that a large amount of ammunition would be required (3,000 rounds per gun) and suggested that the first phase of the operation "be approved at once, as the experience gained would be useful".[50] This was a particularly ambiguous document. Although Jackson "concurred generally" in Carden's plans and gave details of how the first two stages were to be carried out, he only definitely recommended that the first stage be attempted. Perhaps Jackson realized at this early stage that the operation would be a difficult one and he was trying to hedge his bets in case of failure.

What views were held by other members of the Admiralty War Group towards the Carden-Churchill plan? Unfortunately few members of the War Group committed to paper their opinions of the plan during this period. The historian therefore often has to fall back on their evidence given to the Dardanelles Commission, held after the operation had failed. Obviously no member of the Admiralty would have wanted to be identified too closely with the inception of the operation. Their evidence is therefore often so contradictory as to defy analysis. A case in point is that of Churchill's naval secretary, Commander de Bartoleme. He testified that he was not generally in favour of making the naval attack without military co-operation but that he thought the Carden plan worth trying and that it stood a good chance of success.[51] It is hardly possible to work out from this evidence what advice he gave to Churchill at the time.

Oliver, the C.O.S., seems to have been the one authority at the Admiralty who was consistently in favour of the naval attack. In his unpublished autobiography he stated that he thought Churchill was right to go ahead with the operation.[52] At some time during January he apparently expressed a wish to command the squadron at the Dardanelles.[53] Oliver was strongly opposed to operations against Borkum or in the Baltic[54] and may have seized on the Dardanelles plan as a less dangerous alternative. Finally he made no attempt to conceal from the Dardanelles Commissioners that he approved generally of Carden's proposals.[55]

Sir Arthur Wilson's opinion is harder to establish. He concurred in Jackson's first appreciation of January 5th in which Jackson seemed to favour a methodical bombardment.[56] However, Wilson's work at the Admiralty had almost exclusively been involved with the preparation of plans to bombard and capture certain German islands, particularly Heligoland. All these plans involved the use of troops and this perhaps indicated Wilson's preference. However, he also told the Dardanelles Commission that he thought an attack on the outer forts worth trying provided it was broken off if resistance proved too great.[57] It is quite possible then, that he expressed no firm view against at least the first phase of Carden's plan.

What of Churchill's view? It is necessary to modify the assumption that the wording of his first telegram to Carden showed that he had already made up his mind to attack the Dardanelles using ships alone. In early January he was cautious about an attack on Turkey and reluctant to abandon his schemes for action in the north. His opinion seemed to change after the arrival of Carden's plan on January 11th. Whether Churchill considered that Carden's plan was novel enough to change the situation, or whether by that time he was convinced that none of the other alternative operations would get past the planning stage, is not known. What is evident is that by January 15th Churchill seemed to have a new-found determination that the Dardanelles operation would take place.

The most important figure in relation to naval operations at the Admiralty was Fisher, who was responsible for planning and authorizing all operations undertaken by the navy. If he disagreed with an operation, all other opinions would count for little, for theoretically only he could give the necessary orders to the Fleet. The problem of divining Fisher's opinion of the naval attack during this period is even more difficult than is the case for the other Admirals, for it is known that Fisher's evidence to the Dardanelles Commission was concocted with Churchill to produce the least damaging effect on their respective reputations.[58] Occasionally, under cross-examination Fisher was drawn away from his prepared story and some of his statements have a ring of truth but obviously his evidence has to be treated with caution. What Fisher's early view of a purely naval operation at the Dardanelles was is not known. Presumably he could not have expressed violent disagreement with Churchill's first enquiries to Carden or they would not have taken place. Perhaps he felt that as with Churchill's Borkum investigations the plan would be found to be practically impossible. To the Dardanelles Commission Fisher stated that in these early days he stood rather aloof from the question leaving the matter in the hands of Jackson and Oliver.[59] Certainly there is hardly a written comment by Fisher on the Dardanelles in the first ten days of January. But it was noticed that on January 9th he took up Churchill's "Holland Plan" with alacrity and this may have been an indication that he was uneasy with a naval operation at Gallipoli. However, a few days later he made no comment on a memorandum by Churchill which pointed out that Carden's proposals could be implemented without weakening the Fleet in Home Waters,[60] a significant omission considering that this was to be Fisher's main criticism of the operation later on. Furthermore, it was Fisher who first suggested adding the <u>Queen Elizabeth</u> to Carden's force, hardly the act of an opponent of the scheme. Under cross-examination at the Dardanelles Commission Fisher admitted: "I really thought that we might get through, through the possible ineptitude of the Turks... the way I looked at it was that you could cut your loss at any moment".[61] Here then was another half-hearted opinion that the operation might work.

An attempt should now be made to sum up Admiralty opinion on the Dardanelles. Taken overall, it can be seen that the quality of advice given to Churchill by his professional colleagues was lamentably poor. Not one of them was prepared to state unequivocally that a purely naval operation against land fortifications was unsound. This criticism particularly applies to Fisher who had the stature, the experience and countless opportunities to make his views known to Churchill in the clearest terms. Also his relationship with Churchill was much closer than was usual between a First Sea Lord and his political chief. However, Fisher failed, in this period, to express a clear opinion about the operation. In short, although it is reasonably clear that Fisher and most of Churchill's advisers were ambivalent about the naval attack, by not speaking out plainly about the difficulties of the operation they enabled Churchill, the only real enthusiast for the plan, to say to the War Council on January 13th that the Admiralty believed that Carden's proposals could lead to success.

For his part, Churchill should have realized the ambivalence of the support given to the naval attack by his advisers. Jackson's memoranda are particularly good examples of hedging on vital issues. Whether Churchill needed a success to salvage his flagging reputation, whether his inability to contemplate a further period of inactivity at sea led him to ride roughshod over the doubts of his naval advisers, or whether in his enthusiasm for the Carden plan he grasped only those positive aspects of their advice is not clear. What is evident is that he should have proceeded with much more caution and taken more care to find out exactly what views his advisers, and particularly Fisher, held.

The remaining two weeks of January were characterized at the Admiralty by the continuing preparations for the naval attack and by an increasing reluctance on the part of Fisher that the attack should take place at all. On the 14th Churchill wrote to Carden telling him that his plan had been accepted by the War Council,[62] and he then set about informing Britain's allies about the forthcoming attack. The French were asked to contribute a squadron of battleships to the bombarding force.[63]

Meanwhile Fisher was becoming alarmed at the growing scope of the operation. On January 19th he wrote to Jellicoe condemning the naval attack on the grounds that it was taking ships which were vitally necessary in home waters. He concluded, "I don't agree with one single step taken".[64] Two days later he told Jellicoe, "I just abominate the Dardanelles operation, unless a great change is made and it is settled to be made a military operation, with 200,000 men in conjunction with the Fleet."[65]

It is difficult to know what should be made of these outbursts. Rather than disagreeing with "every single step taken" Fisher had personally approved of the number of battleships to be allotted to Carden, had himself suggested the addition of the Queen Elizabeth, and had countersigned most of the orders and requisitions for materials which passed between the Admiralty and Carden. Obviously something had happened between the 13th and the 19th to make Fisher violently opposed to the naval attack. Perhaps the lurking doubts he always seemed to have about it came to the surface as the scope of the operation became apparent. Perhaps, in agreeing to the initial proposal, he thought that somehow troops would be made available but by mid-January he had become convinced that this would not be the case. The violent change in Fisher's stand certainly shows signs of mental instability, the result of the enormous pressure which the Admiralty was placing on a man of 74 years.

It is possible that if Fisher had written to Churchill in terms similar to those he used to Jellicoe the naval attack would have stopped there. However, he chose to approach the subject in correspondence to the First Lord in a much more oblique manner. He wrote to Churchill on the 20th complaining of the weakness of the Grand Fleet in destroyers[66] and later the same day he asked that the destroyer flotilla at the Dardanelles be returned home.[67] Churchill tried to persuade Fisher that various changes in the distribution of destroyers in Home Waters would solve the problem[68] but Fisher was not convinced and matters came to a head on the 25th when Fisher announced that he would not attend the War Council scheduled for the 28th and submitted a paper on the naval situation for Churchill to circulate to his colleagues.[69] The key passages of this paper suggested that the only justification for coastal bombardments was to force a decision at sea and no operation that did not contribute to this end (which obviously the Dardanelles operation did not) should be undertaken. He considered that "Even the older ships should not be risked, for they cannot be lost without losing men, and they form our only reserve behind the Grand Fleet." The paper concluded, "Being already in possession of all that a powerful fleet can give a country, we should continue quietly to enjoy the advantage without dissipating our strength in operations that cannot improve the position."[70] Fisher had now made it clear that he was opposed to the Dardanelles operation but once again he made his objections more in terms of the strength of the Grand Fleet than by producing a reasoned critique of the naval attack. Churchill refused to circulate the paper. Instead he wrote a reply easily proving that the margin of the Grand Fleet over the High Sea Fleet had greatly widened since the beginning of the war.[71] He also suggested that the two papers be shown to Asquith in the presence of himself and Fisher before the War Council meeting of the 28th.[72]

Churchill also reminded Fisher that he had assented to the operation "& so far as I am concerned there can be no withdrawal without good reason".[73] Assuming that Churchill was determined to embark on some operation, he had compelling reasons for holding Fisher to his earlier "concurrence" for it was by now even less likely that either the Borkum or Zeebrugge operations would be attempted or Holland intervene. Concerning Borkum, Churchill had received two more papers deprecating his plan from Jellicoe and Richmond.[74] In relation to Zeebrugge, Kitchener had learned from the French Minister of War, Millerand, that Joffre was opposed to the idea[75] and then French told Churchill that if the attack took place at all it would have to be on a greatly reduced scale.[76]

Asquith met with Churchill and Fisher on the morning of the 28th. According to Churchill, Asquith said of the two operations to which Fisher was opposed, he (Asquith) thought Zeebrugge was not worth an argument but that "the Dardanelles was very important and on the whole he thought it was an operation that should be undertaken. Lord Fisher said 'well it is very important, very important and with great political advantages' and so on, and then we got up and went down to the War Council."[77] Asquith believed that Fisher had withdrawn his opposition to the naval attack at this meeting but Churchill's evidence says nothing about a firm decision being reached by Fisher on this point.[78]

Given that Fisher's paper was not circulated beforehand, Churchill is often criticized for deliberately misleading the Council. The details of this meeting are therefore important. At the War Council Churchill informed the members that he had been in touch with the French and the Russians and that preparations were in hand to begin the naval attack in mid-February. "He asked if the War Council attached importance to this operation, which undoubtedly involved some risks?" At this point Fisher interjected. He said "that he had understood that this question would not be raised to-day. The Prime Minister was well aware of his own views in regard to it." Here was a clear indication to the War Council that Fisher was not happy with the naval attack. Yet none of the members asked him to explain his views more fully. In reply to Fisher Asquith then said that the operation could hardly be left in abeyance in view of the preparations which had been made.[79] Fisher then left the table, followed by Kitchener. Fisher told Kitchener that he intended to resign but Kitchener said that his duty to the country was to continue in office and with some reluctance Fisher returned to the council table.[80] According to Fisher "everybody" noticed this incident, "there was a pause in the proceedings - a collapse of everything". However Balfour, Haldane, and Asquith all testified that they had not noticed the incident at all.[81]

When the formal discussion resumed Kitchener, Balfour and Grey all spoke out strongly for the operation, Balfour and Grey in particular claiming that the operation would have a decisive effect on the Balkan states and would influence favourably the situation in Russia. Churchill then closed proceedings by stating that the ultimate aim of the navy was still to gain access to the Baltic but that the necessary preliminary step, the capture of a German island, would have to be postponed until the special craft being prepared for the operation had been completed.[82] Although this announcement could have been made as a sop to Fisher, the construction of the special craft would indicate that Churchill had by no means given up the Borkum operation.

The vital question to be asked in relation to this meeting is, did Churchill, by not circulating Fisher's paper of the 25th, mislead his fellow council members? Of the civilian members who attended the meeting Asquith, Churchill and Kitchener obviously knew that the First Sea Lord was unhappy with the naval plan. Hankey also knew, for he had helped Fisher draft his paper of January 25th.[83] Of the remainder, Crewe, Lloyd George, and Balfour all told the Dardanelles Commission that they were aware that Fisher had reservations about the operation.[84] This leaves Grey and Haldane, both senior members of the Government. Both men were close to Asquith and it is hard to believe that no hint of Fisher's opinions could have reached them. Grey had good reason for disregarding such doubts. He had been convinced since the beginning of the war that to win over the Balkan neutrals the allies had to become militarily active in the area.[85] About this time he wrote to Churchill, "The sooner they [Carden's plan] can be put in execution the better as some striking offensive is necessary to counteract the effect, that the presence of German troops ... is having in the Balkans."[86]  It is interesting that Grey thought that a group of old battleships could offset the presence of the German Army, but it is obvious that someone so anxious for action to back up a failing diplomacy would not be likely to quibble because of the vague doubts of the First Sea Lord.

In any case Grey and Haldane were only two out of ten. Eight members of the War Council knew of Fisher's views and chose to ignore them.  Why they did this is not clear. Perhaps they thought that Fisher did not object to the operation as such but preferred action elsewhere.  This was certainly the view of Lloyd George who said that he regarded the Dardanelles operation as much less risky than the northern schemes supposedly espoused by Fisher.[87]  Other members of the War Council were no doubt reassured by Churchill about Fisher's contention that the operation would weaken the Grand Fleet.  All of them may have been so attracted to a project which offered large gains cheaply that they allowed their enthusiasm to overcome any doubts they might have had concerning Fisher's view of the plan. Balfour, at least, seemed to fall into this category.  After the War Council meeting he read Fisher's paper of the 25th. He then proceeded to lecture the First Sea Lord on the political and economic advantages of the plan which he thought would be "enormous" while he considered that the "risk to the ships does not seem great".[88]

Churchill had noticed that Fisher had left the council table and after the meeting had adjourned for lunch he spoke to Fisher alone in his room.  Churchill told the Dardanelles Commission that he strongly urged Fisher to undertake the operation and that Fisher "definitely consented to do so.  I state this positively.  (Well, I state everything positively, but I state this super-positively)."[89]  Churchill may have been "super-positive" but it is obvious that Fisher only accepted the naval attack under great pressure and with extreme reluctance, for the next day he wrote to Churchill, "Not a grain of wheat will come from the Black Sea unless there is military occupation of the Dardanelles!  And it will be the wonder of the ages that no troops were sent to cooperate with the Fleet with half a million ... soldiers in England!"[90]

The main topic of discussion for the next two weeks was whether any of those half million soldiers should be used in theatres outside the Western Front.  The consensus seemed to be that sooner or later troops would have to be sent to aid Serbia in the event of an Austro-German attack.  The Greek port of Salonica was usually favoured as the point of disembarkation although Greece was still neutral and had not requested troops.  Such ideas were put forward by Lloyd George, Churchill, and Callwell.[91]

Hankey, however, had arrived at the seemingly obvious conclusion that British troops should be used to support the naval attack at the Dardanelles.  He prepared a paper on the subject for Asquith which made this point very strongly but it had no observable effect.[92]

Indeed at a War Council on February 9th no mention was made of sending troops to the Dardanelles. Instead a decision was made to send one British and one French division to Salonica in the event of the Serbs being attacked. Presumably this was to be conditional on Greek co-operation. Kitchener announced that the 29th, the last of the regular divisions, would be sent.[93]

At about this time naval opinion began to harden against the naval plan. On the 13th Jackson had submitted a memorandum on the operation to Churchill. It was largely a technical document but the conclusions were less ambiguous than those contained in Jackson's earlier papers. Jackson recommended that a fleet of transports be on hand to proceed through the Straits as soon as the forts were silenced. However, he considered that unarmoured ships would not be able to pass the Straits until the Peninsula was in allied hands.[94] He concluded that in this event it would be impossible to keep the Fleet in the Marmora supplied and ended by saying, "The naval bombardment is not recommended as a sound military operation, unless a strong military force is ready to assist in the operation."[95] These views were reinforced by a paper from Richmond. He stated that in his judgement, "the bombardment of the Dardanelles, even if all the forts were destroyed, can be nothing but a local success, which without an army to carry it on can have no further effect."[96]

On the 16th an informal meeting of the War Council, attended by Asquith, Lloyd George, Churchill, Fisher, Grey, and Kitchener, was held. Hankey was not present, and unfortunately for the historian, no minutes were kept. One of the conclusions of the meeting was that the 29th Division which had already been earmarked for the east was now to be available to support the naval attack at the Dardanelles if necessary.[97] Why had the destination of the 29th Division been changed? No firm conclusion can be reached. Perhaps it was merely looked on as a useful precaution to have troops in the area. Perhaps Churchill now decided to inform his colleagues of Jackson's opinion that troops would be needed for occupation duties even if the fleet operation was successful. Why it was thought that regulars were needed for these duties is another question. Probably the 29th Division was chosen for no better reason than that it was already destined for the east.

Whatever the reason the War Council had now gone a step further than on January 13th or 28th. They had now sanctioned a naval operation with military support "if necessary". This decision was no doubt made easier by the fact that at the time it could not have seemed a very serious step to take. The naval attack was scheduled for February 19th. It was obvious that any troops sent could not arrive until two or three weeks after that date. There was therefore no reason to suspect that they would be used as an integral part of the naval attack. By the time they arrived the fleet would be through and the troops merely used for occupation duties. However the first step had now been taken along the road to a combined operation.

On February 19th the War Council discovered that their deliberations of three days previously had gone for nothing, for Kitchener had changed his mind about the 29th Division. He announced that as the Turks were retreating from the Suez Canal, he considered the garrison troops in Egypt sufficient for local defence. This meant that the Australian and New Zealand troops (39,000 strong) were available to support the operation at the Dardanelles. Therefore he was holding back the 29th Division, which in any case should be kept in readiness to intervene in France in view of the Russian reverses in the east and the likely transfer of German troops to the west.[98] This brought an immediate reply from Churchill. He said:

"it would be a great disappointment to the Admiralty if the 29th Division was not sent out. The attack on the Dardanelles was a very heavy naval undertaking. It was difficult to overrate the military advantages which success would bring....In his opinion, it would be a thrifty disposition on our part to have 50,000 men in this region....which could be concentrated....in three days. He was sending out the ten trained battalions of the Naval Division. Neither these, however, nor the Australians and New Zealanders, could be called first-rate troops at present, and they required a stiffening of regulars....We should never forgive ourselves if this promising operation failed owing to insufficient military force at the critical moment."[99]

A long discussion on the use of the 29th Division followed. Asquith read out extracts from a 1906 C.I.D. report on the Dardanelles, "tending", as the minutes state, "to show that military co-operation was essential to success".[100] In fact the report had gone further than this and had deprecated even a combined operation but whether this section was also read out by Asquith is not known.[101] Kitchener was unmoved. He refused to budge and the most the committee could extract from him was that transports should be prepared to take the 29th Division to the east if required.[102]

At first glance the position adopted by Churchill at this meeting is puzzling. He had stated clearly that he wanted 50,000 men within easy reach of the Dardanelles. But Kitchener had not vetoed this move or even disagreed with it and had offered the 39,000 Anzacs as part of the contingent. To this figure could be added the 10,000 men of the Naval

Division, making a total of 49,000 men, almost exactly the number specified by Churchill. Yet he considered this force inadequate and proceeded to argue about its composition, insisting that the crack 29th Division be included in it. But on the only occasions when Churchill specified the tasks troops would be required to carry out at the Dardanelles he stated that they were merely needed to occupy the Gallipoli Peninsula _after_ it had been evacuated, to occupy Constantinople if a revolution took place and to clear the shores of the Straits of riflemen and field guns.[103] Now none of these operations involved much heavy fighting and suggested that troops would only be needed to follow up a naval success. However Churchill had also told the War Council that the whole operation might _fail_ owing to insufficient military force. This remark, which went unchallenged by his colleagues, in fact disclosed Churchill's real purpose in insisting that the 29th Division be included in the Gallipoli force. What had brought about this change of mind?

Obviously Churchill had been affected more than he was willing to admit by the arguments of Fisher, Jackson and Richmond in favour of using troops at the Dardanelles and he had been shaken in his view that the navy could succeed alone. Thus troops might be needed, not to follow up, but to _ensure_ a naval success. This would involve fighting on the Gallipoli Peninsula for which a "stiffening of regulars" would be indispensable. Moreover if the 29th Division was sent, there would be almost 70,000 men available for use. If the naval attack failed they could be thrown in at once. But it was inconceivable that a force consisting wholly of partly trained troops would be used in such a way. Therefore the despatch of the 29th Division was crucial. However Churchill could not use this line of argument openly. Thus far he had assured the War Council that the navy alone could achieve success. He could hardly now say that the operation was not feasible unless troops were used. Nor could he stop the naval attack which began on February 19th. All he could do was to proceed by stealth. He could press for troops, ostensibly to "reap the fruits" of a naval victory, and hope that if a division of regulars was sent and there were 70,000 men in the area and the naval attack faltered, the logic of the situation would compel their use.

* * * * * * * * * * * * *

The opening of the naval attack on the Dardanelles is a convenient point at which to break off the narrative of events and examine Churchill's treatment of this period in The World Crisis. Over half Churchill's account is taken up with the quotation of letters, memoranda, minutes and telegrams. This documentation is important to Churchill. In the preface he claimed that he "made no important statement of fact relating to naval operations or Admiralty business", on which he did not possess unimpeachable documentary proof.[104]  Now, in these chapters, in which he seeks to justify his role in the origins of the Dardanelles campaign, he attempts to convince the reader that this claim has been made good.

Churchill begins his narrative of these events with a discussion of the papers on the war written at the turn of the year by Hankey, Lloyd George and Fisher.  He states that he forwarded Hankey's paper to Asquith with a covering note which said in part, "We are substantially in agreement, and our conclusions are not incompatible.  I wanted Gallipoli attacked on the declaration of war."[105]  Churchill makes two separate points here, both of which must be examined. The first is the degree of agreement between Hankey and Churchill.  The second is Churchill's claim that he had wanted Gallipoli attacked on the declaration of war.  To deal with the second point first, Churchill had originally said in his letter to Hankey, "I wanted Gallipoli attacked on the Turkish declaration of war".  Leaving aside the fact that it was Britain that declared war on Turkey, the version published in The World Crisis clearly gives the impression that Churchill had wanted Gallipoli attacked in August when Britain entered the war, rather than in November when Turkey entered.  Churchill's reasons for doing this are rather obscure.  It should probably be seen as a continuation of previous attempts in The World Crisis to convince the reader that he had held a consistent policy about attacking Turkey from the very beginning of the war.  The naval attack could then be presented as the culmination of that consistent policy.  However, it will be remembered that an attack on Gallipoli was only one, and by no means the most important, of several options which Churchill investigated in the first five months of the war.  Moreover, most of the early plans to attack Turkey involved landing an army (usually Greek) on Gallipoli and had nothing in common with a purely naval plan.

To return to Churchill's first claim, that he and Hankey were "substantially in agreement", it is necessary to examine the content of Hankey's paper.  As was noted earlier, Hankey had not mentioned an attack on Gallipoli but had only spoken generally of "weaving a web round Turkey".  The attack on Gallipoli was a purely Churchillian gloss.  Also, Hankey's plan was basically for a land attack, involving 90,000 British troops and the armies of two other countries.  That is, Hankey's and Churchill's plans were more remarkable for their differences than for their similarities.  The reader is not able to draw this conclusion for himself though, for not even a summary of Hankey's paper is included in The World Crisis.

It would also appear that at the time not even Churchill saw great areas of agreement between himself and Hankey, for it will be recalled that the very day after Hankey's paper was written and again two days later, Churchill wrote to Asquith advocating that the best strategy for Britain was the capture of a German island in the North Sea. Once again, however, the evidence is concealed; neither letter to Asquith is published in The World Crisis.

Churchill next discusses the Russian appeal for help of January 1st. Nowhere in The World Crisis is it mentioned that this reason (or excuse) for the naval attack soon disappeared with the defeat of the Turks in the Caucasus in early January. Indeed, Churchill gives as one of the reasons for holding Fisher to his acceptance of the Carden plan, the fact that the operation "would give the Grand Duke the help he so sorely needed".[106] Yet if it was known from such a public source as Reuters that the Turks had suffered a defeat, it is hard to believe that Churchill would not have been aware of it. On the other hand it is obviously convenient for Churchill if his readers continue to believe that the naval attack was pushed through to help a hard pressed ally, for this gave the plan an urgency that it would otherwise not have possessed.

Churchill goes on to indicate the effect that the coincidence of the Russian appeal with the papers of Hankey, Lloyd George and Fisher had upon him.

"This series of weighty representations had the effect of making me move. I thought I saw a great convergence of opinion in the direction of that attack upon the Dardanelles which I had always so greatly desired. The arguments in its favour were overwhelming. And now the highest authorities, political, naval and military, were apparently ready to put their shoulders to the wheel. All Mr Lloyd George's advocacy and influence seemed about to be cast in the direction of Turkey and the Balkans....I knew from my talks with Mr Balfour that he too was profoundly impressed by the advantages which might be reaped by successful action in this South-Eastern theatre. Lastly, the Foreign Office and Sir Edward Grey were, of course, keenly interested. Here was a great consensus of opinion. Here it seemed at last was a sufficient impulse and unity for action. But was there a practicable scheme? This I determined to find out."[107]

It cannot be said that this passage is remarkable for its accuracy. In the first place the passage implies that the Balkans and Turkey were identical for the purpose of military operations. This was not the case. They were in fact alternative spheres of operation and were regarded as such by the proponents of the various plans discussed by Churchill. Our earlier investigation of the contributions of Hankey, Lloyd George and Fisher revealed no "consensus" and no "convergence of opinion" on an attack upon the Dardanelles.

Hankey thought that Turkey should be attacked but had not specified where or how: Lloyd George favoured an attack on Austria-Hungary through Dalmatia and to say that all his "advocacy and influence" were cast in the "direction of Turkey and the Balkans" is hardly evidence that he favoured an attack on Gallipoli. Fisher, on the other hand had outlined a vast plan encompassing most of the countries of South-Eastern Europe and the Near East. Balfour, so far from favouring action in South-Eastern Europe had told Hankey on January 2nd that he did not see any solution to Britain's problems in that direction. It is possible that Grey did want action in the Balkans for he always believed that diplomacy in war time was futile unless backed by armed force, but it is very unlikely that he would have advocated any particular operation. In fact the only person who had even mentioned Gallipoli was Fisher and it formed only a minor part of his plan. Thus in The World Crisis Churchill has again conveyed an impression of unity and agreement which did not in fact exist, this time between members of the War Council. Once again he reinforces the idea, already introduced, that he had always greatly desired an attack on the Dardanelles. And once again Churchill ignores in The World Crisis the fact that he continued to advocate alternative operations in the face of the apparently "over-whelming" advantages of the Carden plan.

It was stated earlier that it was possibly the realization that other operations would not get past the planning stage rather than any supposed convergence of opinion on the Dardanelles which led Churchill to telegraph Carden on January 3rd. This controversial and crucial message is quoted in The World Crisis but Churchill does not comment on it.[108] In our earlier investigation it was suggested that the telegram had been deliberately worded to produce a favourable response and that Churchill seemed to admit as much to the Dardanelles Commission. It might have been expected that this important point would have been discussed or rebutted in The World Crisis but this is not the case.

It is at this point, however, that Churchill makes his only reference to the importance still attached to the Zeebrugge and Borkum projects during this period. He explains that the telegram to Carden did not commit him "even to the general principle of an attack upon Turkey," and he "was still thinking a great deal of the Northern theatre, of Borkum and of the Baltic."[109] He also says that Zeebrugge was still under consideration and quotes a part of his letter to Fisher of January 4th in which he remarked that he would prefer to "hear what others have to say about the Turkish plans before taking a decided line."[110] With the introduction of these issues, otherwise so carefully excluded from this section of The World Crisis, Churchill is able to lessen the importance of his telegram to Carden and hence the importance of its strong wording. The risk that these references to Zeebrugge and to Borkum might contradict the impression given of the supremacy of the Dardanelles plan is fairly small given that this is their only mention in a chapter entirely devoted to the genesis of the Dardanelles plan.

Churchill has also omitted a key sentence from his letter to Fisher, quoted above. The sentence reads, "Germany is the foe & it is bad war to seek cheaper victories and easier antagonists".[111] By omitting this sentence Churchill again is seeking to conceal the fact that he had been very sceptical about the efficacy of action against Turkey in early January. This deletion also saves him from explaining why this scepticism disappeared within the next few weeks.

Churchill next deals with Carden's reply to the telegram of January 3rd. "On January 5 the answer from Admiral Carden arrived. It was remarkable."[112] Even to a vivid imagination it is hard to see how this reply (the Dardanelles cannot be rushed, they might be forced, large numbers of ships will be needed) could be described as remarkable. As noticed earlier, it was at best a grudging admission that under certain circumstances the operation might be possible. Considering the wording of Churchill's original telegram the reply is surprisingly restrained. The only way in which it could have been considered remarkable by Churchill is that it did not say that the operation was impossible.

Churchill does not discuss in The World Crisis what particular competence Carden had in naval strategy which might have made a favourable reply from him "remarkable". It will be remembered that several memoranda written by Churchill about this time indicated that he had quite a low opinion of Carden. However, there is no mention of this in The World Crisis and the reader is left with the impression that, both on this occasion and at the time of the arrival of Carden's detailed plan on January 11th, Churchill regarded Carden as quite capable of producing a plan that would substantially shorten the war. Furthermore, if Carden was the ideal man, what of Churchill's earlier view that, by bowing to Foreign Office pressure on the question of Limpus's appointment, the Admiralty lost "the Admiral who of all others knew the Turks, and knew the Dardanelles with all its possibilities."[113]

According to The World Crisis, the "high authorities" whom Churchill claimed agreed with Carden's views were Jackson and Oliver.[114] The introduction of these personalities to Churchill's narrative makes it necessary to investigate Churchill's analysis of the opinions held by various members of the Admiralty about the Carden plan.

The three important papers written by Sir Henry Jackson about the Dardanelles question on January 5th and 25th and February 13th are discussed at length in The World Crisis. In view of the importance Churchill places on the opinions of

Jackson it is surprising to find that his first paper of January 5th is not published. It was shown earlier that this document did not throw a great deal of light on what Jackson's opinions actually were. However, the paper certainly did not underrate the difficulties facing the fleet and perhaps this is the reason that it was omitted by Churchill. Churchill's conversation with Jackson about this paper is, however, included. He states that on January 5th,

> "I had a conversation with Sir Henry Jackson, who had that day completed a memorandum upon the ... [Dardanelles] (which I read some days later). Sir Henry Jackson deprecated any attempt to rush the Straits, but he spoke of the considerable effects of the brief bombardment of November 3, and he was attracted by the idea of a step-by-step reduction of the fortresses; though troops would be needed to follow up and complete the naval attack and especially to occupy Constantinople."115

Other aspects of this important conversation will be discussed later. All that needs to be noted now is that, as reported by Churchill, Jackson clearly makes the use of troops an integral part of the projected operation and it is therefore hardly accurate for Churchill to claim him as a "high authority" supporting the concept of a purely naval plan in his telegram of January 6th.

Jackson's second memorandum of January 15th is quoted in full in The World Crisis. Churchill claims that this document reveals that at this time Jackson fully supported the Carden plan and, although he considers that Jackson did not have "accountable responsibility", "he is certainly responsible for the opinions which he expressed in so much detail".116 No one could argue with this statement. However, the vital question is not whether Jackson should be held responsible for his opinions but exactly what those opinions were. Churchill never confronts this issue. The ambiguities of the memorandum and the alternative interpretations which could be placed upon it were noted earlier. They are, however, totally ignored by Churchill in The World Crisis as they apparently were at the time.

Jackson's third memorandum of February 13th presents Churchill with a more difficult problem. It will be recalled that this memorandum was a fairly straightforward condemnation of the Carden plan raising few problems of interpretation. It concluded that the naval attack was not recommended as a sound military operation unless a strong force was at hand to assist or follow up any success gained by the Fleet. Churchill could have regarded this, the clearest statement of Jackson's opinions, as the culmination of Jackson's views on the Dardanelles. Instead he concentrates on the only "ambiguity" which the paper contained, namely the alternative uses of troops in either assisting or following up the naval attack. Churchill points out that these two alternatives relate to fundamentally different operations and on these grounds he dismisses the entire paper as the product of "mixed" thinking.[117] However, Jackson's position is quite clear. He wanted troops at the Dardanelles. Preferably they could land on the Peninsula and assist the fleet in destroying the forts. If this was not possible they should at least be ready to follow up a naval success and occupy the Peninsula after it was evacuated by the Turks and provide a garrison for Constantinople. This is not "mixed" thinking but a reasonable statement of alternatives.

Of the opinion of Admiral Oliver towards Carden's plan, Churchill says very little. He states that on the 5th of January Oliver viewed the plan "with favour" and later, after Carden's plan had arrived, that the "Chief of the Staff seemed favourable to it."[118] From Oliver's testimony to the Dardanelles Commission and the other evidence quoted earlier, this would seem to be a reasonable summary of his opinion at the time. Of all Churchill's naval advisers, Oliver seemed most consistent in his endorsement of the Carden plan. Certainly it has been suggested earlier that his enthusiasm for the plan may have sprung from his dislike of Churchill's German Island schemes, which he considered too risky. But it is hardly to be expected that Churchill would have been aware of such an attitude.

Churchill next sums up the opinions of the three naval personalities so far considered, Carden, Oliver and Jackson. "So here we had the Chief of the Staff, the Admiral studying this particular theatre, and the Admiral in command, all apparently in general accord in principle. This coincidence of opinion in officers so widely separated and so differently circumstanced impressed me very much."[119] As the previous narrative has demonstrated this is hardly a fair summary of the opinions of these officers. Under great pressure Carden had only said that the operation <u>might</u> succeed. Jackson, according to Churchill's own account, had suggested that troops be used. Only Oliver seems to have endorsed Carden's plan although it is not possible to say with what enthusiasm. Thus there was no "coincidence of opinion" and the only thing that could have impressed Churchill was that none of the authorities concerned had said that the operation was impossible. In addition, although Churchill claimed that the officers were "widely separated" and "differently circumstanced", they were all open to his influence and it is perhaps this fact which may have resulted in what little "agreement in principle" there was.

We now come to what must be a crucial section of the Dardanelles chapters of <u>The World Crisis</u>, Churchill's discussion of the attitude which Fisher held towards the naval attack. It was shown earlier that Fisher's attitude was complicated and not always easy to define. How does Churchill handle this difficult task? Fisher's first letter of January 3rd, outlining the "Turkey Plan", is quoted in full in The World Crisis. Churchill describes this letter as being of

"great importance [because] it reveals Lord Fisher's position fully and clearly. The turbulence of its style in no way affects the shrewdness and profundity of its vision. I do not think that Lord Fisher ever took any action or expressed any opinions which were irreconcilable with the general principles of these first thoughts. He was always in favour of a great scheme against the Turks and to rally the Balkans. He always believed that Bulgaria was the key to the situation in this quarter. He was always prepared to risk the old battleships as part of a large naval, military and diplomatic combination. In all this we were, as his letter shows, in entire agreement. That these large schemes were not carried into effect was not his fault nor mine."[120]

It is hard to see how Churchill could justify the statement that the failure to adopt Fisher's "larger schemes" was no fault of his, for by immediately suggesting a "smaller" plan to Carden and then enthusiastically endorsing it he virtually ensured that larger combined operations of the type suggested by Fisher passed out of contention.

In an earlier version of The World Crisis, after the last sentence quoted above, Churchill added "That, in their default, less satisfactory and smaller expedients were adopted is largely due to me."[121] He then deleted this sentence. Probably his reason for doing so was that the line taken in The World Crisis is that in advocating the Dardanelles operation Churchill was following the advice given by his naval colleagues. Thus he would want to avoid the impression given by the deleted sentence that he had been the principal agent responsible for the adoption of the naval attack. Nor would Churchill want to propagate the view that the naval attack was in some way a "less satisfactory" or "smaller" expedient.

Turning to Churchill's comments on Fisher's letter, it seems reasonable to assume that Churchill's main purpose is to convince the reader that Fisher was always in favour of the Carden plan. This he attempts to do by stating that Fisher was always in favour of a large scheme against the Turks and was always willing to risk the old battleships as part of it. Now this may well have been true, but it is not correct to deduce from this that Fisher was an enthusiast for the naval attack. It is quite obvious that Fisher's "large naval, military and diplomatic combination" bore no resemblance to an attempt to force the Dardanelles by ships alone. In other words what Churchill says about Fisher's "first thoughts" may be correct, but Churchill has no warrant for claiming from this that Fisher supported a naval attack.

Churchill goes on to say that in this early period Fisher "seemed favourable" to the Carden plan.[122] It is difficult to establish whether or not this assertion is justified. It has already been noted that Fisher expressed no opinion on the Carden plan in writing during this period. On January 6th however, Churchill apparently did not feel able to name Fisher as a "high authority" supporting the naval attack. On the other hand, Fisher let Churchill's correspondence with Carden proceed without comment, so giving Churchill grounds for his statement that Fisher "seemed favourable" to the plan. (It might be thought that the addition by Fisher of the Queen Elizabeth would confirm Churchill's statement. However Churchill says in The World Crisis that it was the Staff who proposed that the ship be sent and he seems unaware of the part played by Fisher in this decision.)[123] In the circumstances no final judgement can be made on Churchill's statement but it is quite possible that Fisher's reluctance to state his position allowed Churchill to write as he did.

It is clear from The World Crisis that Churchill is aware that Fisher's attitude to the operation changed about January 20th.[124] He seems at a loss to explain this apparently sudden reversal of opinion and the only explanation put forward is that Fisher's dislike of the project arose because reluctance to undertake the Zeebrugge operation led him to condemn all naval attacks on hostile coasts.[125] This argument is not convincing. Although Fisher had mentioned both Zeebrugge and the Dardanelles in his paper of January 25th, there is no evidence to suggest that Zeebrugge was the cause of his dislike of the Dardanelles operation. Fisher's letters to Jellicoe, quoted earlier, which contain his first outbursts against the project, do not mention Zeebrugge and seem to be based on the shortcomings of Carden's plan, or on the fact that the operation was taking vital ships away from home waters. However, although Churchill's theory is unconvincing, his failure to follow the workings of Fisher's mind should be treated sympathetically. It was noted earlier that whenever Churchill confronted Fisher about his objections to the naval attack Fisher shifted his ground, and it is little wonder that eight years later Churchill is still unable to explain the mental processes of the old Admiral during this period.

Churchill is on much stronger ground in saying that Fisher's "arguments did not take the form of criticizing the details of either operation in question. He did not, for instance, deal with the gunnery aspects of the Dardanelles, or with any purely technical aspect."[126] It was demonstrated earlier that Fisher used a much less direct line of argument against the Dardanelles with Churchill than was expressed, for example, in his letters to Jellicoe. To this extent the First Sea Lord was at fault.

The events leading up to the War Council of January 28th are discussed in detail in The World Crisis and the full texts of Fisher's memorandum of January 25th and Churchill's reply are printed.[127] Churchill also comments on the meeting between Asquith, Fisher and himself on the 28th. He says that both Zeebrugge and the Dardanelles operations were discussed and that Asquith decided in favour of the latter with which conclusion "Lord Fisher seemed on the whole content".[128] This version of events generally agrees with the only other account of the meeting, that given by Asquith to Venetia Stanley. However, in The World Crisis Churchill does not attempt to expand further on Fisher's attitude, even though there is quite a difference between being "on the whole content" and being a supporter of an operation.

The final aspect of Churchill's treatment of Fisher in this section of The World Crisis concerns the results of the meetings of January 28th. Churchill states that during the interval between the first and second meetings he determined to find the reason behind Fisher's action in leaving the Council table. He says he called Fisher to his room and in the course of the discussion, "I strongly urged him not to turn back from the Dardanelles operation; and in the end, after a long and very friendly discussion... he definitely consented to undertake it."[129] Churchill continues, "I am in no way concealing the great and continuous pressure which I put upon the old Admiral....Was it wrong to put this pressure upon the First Sea Lord? I cannot think so. War is a business of terrible pressures, and persons who take part in it must fail if they are not strong enough to withstand them."[130] Nowhere in The World Crisis is the doubtful propriety or even utility of forcing colleagues to accede to a plan against their better judgment admitted although, given the circumstances of Fisher's resignation, it would be expected that Churchill by the time he wrote his book would have been aware of its dangers. However a draft of this chapter in the Churchill Papers tells a very different story. Originally this chapter was headed by two lines of poetry from Hudibras by Samuel Butler

"A man convinced against his will
Is of the same opinion still"[131]

This was an obvious reference to the incident described above. Churchill continued in the draft -

"Here it was that I consider I made my greatest mistake. I thought that with the assent of the First Sea Lord I shd have sufficient power to carry the plan through. But much more than this was needed. His active aid, his devising energy, his positive authority, his willpower were all vital to success. If the Admirals on the spot had felt the real drive of Lord Fisher behind them, a different spirit wd have animated their proceedings."[132]

The first part of the paragraph is important. The couplet from Butler and the next three lines of the deleted section are the only occasions on which Churchill admits his mistake in pressuring Fisher to agree to the naval attack "against his will", for Churchill's downfall came, not when the Admirals at the Dardanelles changed their minds, but when Fisher reverted to his "own opinion" about the Carden plan and resigned. This was indeed Churchill's greatest mistake. But only in the unpublished version of The World Crisis does he admit it.

Only one other naval authority is mentioned in connection with the genesis of the naval attack, Sir Arthur Wilson. Churchill says of Wilson's attitude to Carden's plans, "he was not committed like others by anything he had written at the time - indeed he had another policy".[133] It is difficult to discern from this whether Wilson was in agreement with the naval attack or not. However, the Churchill Papers show that Churchill originally wrote, "indeed on general grounds he had not been in favour of the policy".[134] This was a much clearer statement of Wilson's position but less favourable to Churchill's case.

As well as discussing the opinion of individuals towards the naval attack, Churchill makes several statements in the course of these chapters on the general attitude of his naval advisers towards the Carden plan. It has already been noticed that Churchill has attempted to convey the impression that there was a convergence of opinion among his War Council colleagues and Fisher towards an attack on the Dardanelles. Also, he has claimed, on the flimsiest of evidence, that Carden, Jackson and Oliver were all united behind the idea of a piecemeal reduction of the Straits defences. He now continues this process into his discussion of the reception that the Carden plan received at the Admiralty. He states that Carden's plan

"produced a great impression upon everyone who saw it... Both the First Sea Lord and the Chief of the Staff seemed favourable to it. No one at any time threw the slightest doubt upon its technical soundness. No one, for instance, of the four or five great naval authorities each with his technical staff who were privy said, 'This is absurd. Ships cannot fight forts', or criticized its details. On the contrary they all treated it as an extremely interesting and hopeful proposal; and there grew up in the secret circles of the Admiralty a perfectly clear opinion favourable to the operation."[135]

There is a certain amount of truth in this statement, although it is interesting to note that the first sentence originally read, "The plan produced a great impression upon my mind,"[136] which is probably more accurate than the published version. However it does seem reasonable for Churchill to claim that no one at the Admiralty spoke out strongly against the scheme. It will be remembered that this was the conclusion reached in the first half of this chapter and it will be shown later that the instructions sent to Carden from the Admiralty did not deviate significantly from the propositions contained in the original plan. Nevertheless, Churchill overstates his case in saying that "a perfectly clear opinion" had grown up at the Admiralty in favour of the operation. Jackson's opinion, as we have seen, was anything but clear. It also seems unlikely that Fisher had expressed a "clear" opinion at this stage. Thus, although Churchill is correct in stating that no one had said that the operation was impossible, this is hardly proof that there was a strong body of opinion in favour of it.

Churchill, however, persists with this line of half truth, saying at the end of the chapter that no one had spoken out against the plan, which was more or less true, and then saying that all were in agreement with it, which was not true.[137] And in the next chapter we find, "Up to about January 20 there seemed to be unanimous agreement in favour of the naval enterprise against the Dardanelles .... all the Admirals concerned appeared in complete accord."[138] By this time these sentiments were even less accurate than Churchill's previous statements to this effect. For by now Churchill had received and read Jackson's extremely equivocal memorandum of January 15th and it was on the 19th that Fisher informed Jellicoe that he had not agreed with a single step taken concerning the operation. Thus once more Churchill has tried to create an impression of unity at the Admiralty which in reality did not exist.

How does The World Crisis deal with Churchill's own role in these events? Churchill discusses the origin of the Carden plan in the following terms:

"It will be seen that the genesis of this plan and its elaboration were purely naval and professional in their character. It was Admiral Carden and his staff gunnery officers who proposed the gradual method of piecemeal reduction by long-range bombardment. It was Sir Henry Jackson and the Admiralty staff who embraced this idea and studied and approved its detail. Right or wrong, it was a Service plan ... At no point did lay or civilian interference mingle with or mar the integrity of a professional conception."[139]

There is another series of half truths here. Churchill is certainly correct in stating that he did not interfere with the technical elaboration of Carden's plan. Nor does he seem to have played a part in drafting the Admiralty instructions which were sent to Carden. However, to state that the genesis of the plan was purely "naval and professional" in character is quite misleading. It was shown earlier that the genesis of the plan lay with Churchill. It was he who first broached with Carden the subject of forcing the Dardanelles by ships alone, and he did it in such a way as to make sure that Carden replied favourably. Churchill then actively discouraged his advisers from expressing an opinion on the overall conception of the naval attack by instructing that the Staff Officer who was to analyse Carden's proposals was "to assume that the principle is settled".[140] The responsibility for the general concept of the plan lay with Churchill, that of filling in the technical details with his naval advisers. Only in the latter sense can the plan be described as a service plan.

How does Churchill deal with the state of his thinking on alternative operations in the first weeks of January? There is only one mention of the Borkum plan, which it will be remembered Churchill was still pushing strongly during this period. Moreover there is no mention at all of his plan for bringing in Holland although it seemed important enough at the time for Churchill to recommend it to the War Council on two separate occasions. Nor is it made altogether clear that discussions about Zeebrugge continued throughout this period.

The World Crisis would seem to be more reliable on Churchill's attitude after the arrival of the Carden plan. It will be remembered that he had originally written that the plan had "produced a great impression on my mind" and it is of the period immediately after the arrival of the plan that he wrote: "I had now become deeply interested in the enterprise, and nothing but new facts and reasons, the merit of which might convince me, would turn me from pressing it forward."[141] However, it was suggested earlier that it was perhaps not the intrinsic merits of Carden's plan which made such an impression on Churchill as the difficulty in getting an operation underway anywhere else. In any case he is probably correct in identifying the period after January 11th as the time in which he became the enthusiastic advocate of the Dardanelles enterprise.

It was noted that part of the "novelty" in the Carden plan lay in its assumption that ships could fight forts. This issue is discussed at length in The World Crisis. Churchill strongly defends Carden's assumption on this point. He states, "No general or absolute rule can be laid down about fighting between ships and forts. It depends on the ship; it depends on the fort. If, for instance, the ship has a gun which can smash the fort, and the fort has no gun which can reach the ship, it is hard to prove that the ship is at a great disadvantage."[142] This statement is true as far as it goes but Churchill does not say with what frequency and effect the ship could expect to hit the fort at these ranges, a critical question, as it happened, at the Dardanelles. Nor does he discuss the point that at these ranges effective spotting and a large amount of ammunition, neither of which were supplied to Carden, are essential to success.

Of course the problem at the Dardanelles was not really that of ships versus forts. It was ships versus <u>minefields</u> which were protected by forts, fixed artillery defences and movable batteries. Yet Churchill does not discuss these additional factors and, therefore, he does not come to grips with the real issues. Indeed he defends himself by saying, "There was no fallacy in the technical arguments of the Admiralty so far as the gunnery was concerned. The difficulties which frustrated the plan lay in the absence of good conditions of observation at the long ranges, or of the opportunity of coming to close quarters."[143] But this is exactly the point which was made earlier against the naval plan. The gunnery calculations were irrelevant. The fallacy in the plan lay in not taking the additional factors into account.

To support his argument Churchill quotes a long memorandum by Sir Arthur Wilson on ships versus forts.[144] This paper is also largely irrelevant to the main issues because it does not mention mines, mobile guns, and methods of observation. However, it is a good example of Churchill's selective use of evidence. At one time or another Jellicoe, Fisher, Jackson and Richmond all expressed the opinion that ships could not fight forts. They are not quoted. Nor does Churchill quote Wilson extensively on other aspects of the operation.

Churchill's attitude to the use of troops and the role he played in this matter must now be examined. It was suggested earlier that even if Churchill had not foreseen the necessity for troops at least to follow up a naval success, he must nevertheless have been aware of their need after seeing Jackson's memorandum of January 5th. Yet this issue was not raised at the War Council on January 13th and <u>The World Crisis</u> offers no explanation for this omission. Not surprisingly there is no suggestion in <u>The World Crisis</u> that this was the result of deliberate deception on Churchill's part. The theory that Churchill first gained the War Council's agreement to the naval attack before pointing out the need for follow-up or occupation troops cannot definitely be proved, but in the light of the available evidence must remain the most likely explanation.

A second phase in the use of troops starts in February, when, as has been shown, Churchill seemed to change his mind about their need and likely role. At this stage the obvious need for troops had been recognized by the War Council and all the troops claimed by Churchill to be necessary for occupation and mopping up duties had been granted by the

Council. These troops comprised the Royal Naval Division and the Anzacs, which together constituted a force adequate in both skill and numbers to their apparent tasks. Churchill, however, glosses over this fact in The World Crisis and concentrates instead on the withholding of the 29th Division by Kitchener.[145] As was shown earlier it was Churchill's persistent attempts to regain this division which provided such strong evidence that his attitude towards a purely naval attack had changed and that he foresaw the duties of the troops as involving far more than mere occupation and mopping up. Churchill, however, states that in early February "I still adhered to the integrity of the naval plan".[146] He can therefore hardly admit to his change of mind, nor can he reveal that Kitchener's main reason for withdrawing the 29th Division was that such a division was hardly necessary for the humble duties proposed by Churchill. Instead he falls back on the argument that Kitchener's decision was forced by pressure from G.H.Q. in France.[147]

Following Churchill's statement that he still adhered to the integrity of the naval plan, there is a passage, which, if it is a true representation of Churchill's thinking at the time, shows the vague and uncertain foundations on which the naval plan was based. It reads,

"I had of course thought long and earnestly about what would follow if the naval attack succeeded and a British fleet entered the Marmora. I expected that if, and when, the Turkish forts began to fall, the Greeks would join us, and that the whole of their armies would be at our disposal thenceforward. I hoped that the apparition of a British fleet off Constantinople and the flight or destruction of the Goeben and the Breslau would be followed by political reactions of a far-reaching character, as the result of which the Turkish Government would negotiate or withdraw to Asia. I trusted that good diplomacy following hot-foot on a great war event, would induce Bulgaria to march on Adrianople. Lastly, I was sure that Russia, whatever her need elsewhere, would not remain indifferent to the fate of Constantinople and that further reinforcements would be forthcoming from her. It was on these quasi-political factors that I counted in our own military penury, for the means of exploiting and consolidating any success which might fall to the Fleet."[148]

This passage is remarkable for several reasons. Firstly, Churchill's expectations of assistance from the Greeks, Bulgarians and Russians display an extreme degree of optimism. Certainly in the case of the Greeks Britain's previous negotiations would give no cause for such extravagant hopes. Secondly, and even more remarkably, this section implies that the successful passage of the Straits by the Fleet would in itself have no direct effect upon the Turkish Government but would merely be the means by which the Greeks, Bulgarians and Russians were encouraged to march on Turkey. Far from exploiting and consolidating a naval success these armies would be the sole means of obtaining a worthwhile result. The most likely explanation for this paragraph in The World Crisis is that it reflects not so much Churchill's belief that these foreign armies would be supplied, a result which even he must have considered unlikely, but his fears that a purely naval attack would achieve no decisive results. However, given his role in initiating a purely naval attack he is forced to defend the absence of British troops from this plan by suggesting that outside military help would have been available. His realization that such help would not eventuate was no doubt the reason for Churchill's persistent efforts to obtain British troops. None of this however is admitted in The World Crisis.

Churchill's belief that troops were essential to the Dardanelles operation combined with his need to disguise his real attitude no doubt largely explain his treatment of Kitchener in this section of The World Crisis. He introduces a lengthy section on Kitchener by saying, "The workings of Lord Kitchener's mind constituted at this period a feature almost as puzzling as the great war problem itself."[149] His main point is that Kitchener "was torn between two perfectly clear-cut views of the war."[150] According to Churchill these were the views put forward by G.H.Q. in France that the war could only be won by killing Germans on the Western Front, and the other put forward by the War Council that the campaign for 1915 should take place in South Eastern Europe. (It is worth noting in passing that the War Council did not hold this view. They agreed to the initial enterprise at the Dardanelles solely because they were assured that it could be effected without diminishing the war effort in the west.) Churchill claims that it was possible to reconcile these policies by developing an offensive in the Balkans and then subsequently attacking on the Western Front in the autumn of 1916. However, he concludes, Kitchener failed to choose between them and "succumbed to conflicting forces and competing policies".[151]

It would appear that far from failing to make a choice between "east" and "west" Kitchener had made a choice to which he adhered throughout this period. He had chosen, as he was bound to do, the Western Front. It was in this theatre that the bulk of the British Army was deployed. It was here that a major defeat would mean the loss of the war. Therefore it was obvious that the security of this front would have to be provided for as the first priority. Kitchener accepted this and it was this fact that lay behind his statements in January that there were no troops available for extraneous operations. Not that he was averse to action in other areas, but the troops used for these operations would have to be surplus to British needs in France. There is no need to look for a conspiracy on the part of G.H.Q. in France to explain this choice. It was dictated by the logic of the situation. But in The World Crisis Churchill cannot see this and he is led to condemn as vacillation what was a perfectly consistent policy.

In contrast to the treatment given to the naval officers and Kitchener, The World Crisis is generally reliable on the attitude of the civilian members of the War Council to the operation as expressed at the five important meetings of January 13th and 28th and February 9th, 16th and 19th. These meetings are all discussed and long quotations given from the minutes of the first two.[152] Churchill claims that "the collective opinion of the War Council" was strongly in favour of the naval attack.[153] This view would seem to be justified for it was demonstrated earlier that none of the civilian members of the War Council spoke against the Carden plan and that some members (Balfour and Grey) spoke in sweeping terms of the results that could be expected from it. Nor were the members really misled by Churchill on naval opinion towards the attack, for it has been seen that most of them were well aware of the doubts and hesitations of Fisher but made no attempt to question the First Sea Lord closely about his opinions. However, it was also noticed that the War Council only approved of the various stages of the plan because it was presented to them by Churchill in a piecemeal way and this fact should not be lost sight of when the attitude of the War Council is discussed.

Two rather general points remain to be discussed. It was suggested earlier that it was remarkable no one suggested that the naval attack be delayed until troops were available to support it. Churchill discusses this point in The World Crisis but rejects it. He claims that if the naval attack had been delayed no operation at all would have been the result for "nothing less than the ocular demonstration and practical proof of the strategic meaning of the Dardanelles, and the effects of attacking it on every Balkan and Mediterranean Power, would have lighted up men's minds sufficiently to make a large abstraction of troops from the main theatre a possibility".[154] This is a quite defensible opinion. It is possible that G.H.Q. in France would have resisted the diversion of four or five divisions at one blow. However, this passage also reinforces the view that Churchill led the War Council into a larger operation than they at first anticipated, for the suggestion that the naval attack was a necessary prerequisite for obtaining troops to be used against Turkey bears a strong resemblance to the view put forward earlier that Churchill first committed the War Council to the operation by suggesting that ships alone were necessary and only later pointed out that after all troops would be needed.

Churchill goes on to conclude that it was better to have had the type of muddled operation that eventuated at the Dardanelles than no operation at all. The positive effects of the operation are stated to be : the Italian entry into the war, the delay in the accession of Bulgaria to the Central Powers, the destruction of "the flower of the Turkish Army, which ... would certainly have fought us or our allies somewhere else", and the prevention of a disaster to the Russians in the Caucasus.[155] It only need be noted here that all these statements are extremely contentious. For example, the Italian entry into the war was to prove of dubious benefit to the allies; the obvious impotence of the force at Gallipoli may have hastened Bulgaria's adherence to the Central Powers; the Turkish Army need <u>not</u> have been fought elsewhere except perhaps on the line of the Suez Canal, a defensive operation that would have proved far less costly to Britain than the Gallipoli campaign; the Russians, as shown earlier, had defeated the Turks in the Caucasus before the naval attack got under way. Churchill recognizes none of this in <u>The World Crisis</u>. The advantages he claims are clearly designed to condition the reader at this early stage in the narrative into accepting the immense value of the campaign. To this end Churchill strengthened his original concluding sentence which read, "The pity was that we did not persevere", to the more dramatic, "Not to persevere - that was the crime."[156]

## Chapter 7

THE DARDANELLES II – THE NAVAL DEBACLE

By early February the operations orders for the naval attack had been drafted at the Admiralty. On the 5th they were sent to Carden. Regarding ships and seaplanes most of Carden's requirements had been met (12 battleships, 4 light cruisers, 16 destroyers, 6 seaplanes, 21 minesweepers). However he was sent none of the fast fleet sweepers he had requested.

The orders had several peculiar features. A major premise on which Carden's plan had been based was that a large amount of ammunition would be required to silence the forts. Yet Carden was exhorted in the orders to use ammunition sparingly lest "wasteful expenditure" resulted in the "operations having to be abandoned". This instruction (drawn up by Oliver) was an extraordinary reversal of policy but Churchill made no comment. Nor did Jackson, although he had agreed with Carden on the need for an ample supply of ammunition. Later in the instructions Carden was also warned that he should not hurry operations "to the extent of taking large risks and courting heavy losses" thus overturning a second premise on which the plan had been based (importance of result would justify severe loss). But despite these modifications Churchill still felt able to write "Excellent" on the orders.[1]

On February 19th. at 9.51 a.m. a combined British and French squadron opened fire on the entrance forts at the Dardanelles. Ten battleships took part in the opening attack, six ships firing and four supporting. They were joined by one other and Queen Elizabeth late in the afternoon.[2] Their targets were four forts, two on the Asian coast (Kum Kale and Orkanie) and two near Cape Hellas (Sedd-el-Bahr and Hellas). Between them these forts mounted 17 larger guns (between 8.2" and 11") and 11 smaller guns and howitzers.[3]

From the beginning some of the problems that were to plague the operation became obvious. The opening salvoes were fired when the ships were under way. This was found to be too inaccurate and the ships were ordered to anchor.[4]

Two seaplanes ordered to spot for the Inflexible, proved totally ineffectual due to problems with their radio equipment.[5] It was soon found that smothering the forts with fire produced only poor results. Orkanie and Hellas were hit on many occasions but when the ships closed in all guns in the forts opened fire.[6] It was then realized that it was necessary to hit each gun to put it out of action and as Keyes said, at a range of 13,000 yards this was a "matter of chance".[7] It was also a matter of having a large amount of ammunition for calculation showed that only two shells in a hundred could be expected to hit a gun. Yet in line with Admiralty instructions, Carden had issued an order that "Strict economy of ammunition must be practised on all occasions".[8] That this instruction was obeyed is obvious from the tables of firing from the first day. The Triumph fired only 14 shells from its main armament and the Inflexible only 18.[9] The bombardment was, therefore, by no means heavy and at 5.20 it was broken off.[10] The results were, to say the least, disappointing.

Carden had intended to resume the attack the next day but then another factor to which very little attention had been paid – the weather – intervened. A strong gale blew up from the south west and it was to be six days before firing could be resumed.[11]

During this interval a desperate debate on the provision of troops for the operation continued, Fisher, Lloyd George and Churchill all urging that troops be sent. At the War Council of February 24th Churchill renewed pressure on Kitchener to release the 29th Division. He argued that 100,000 troops were available to be concentrated at the Dardanelles and added, "we were now absolutely committed to seeing through the attack on the Dardanelles".[12] Although many of the Council members had only agreed to the attack on the grounds that it could be broken off in the event of a failure, no one challenged this statement. Kitchener, however, for the first time queried Churchill's commitment to the naval attack. He asked "If Mr. Churchill now contemplated a land attack. Mr. Churchill said he did not; but it was quite conceivable that the naval attack might be temporarily held up by mines, and some local military operation required."[13] This statement also went unchallenged, even though its first half is hardly compatible with the second – for if the naval attack was held up by mines, the only effective help that could be rendered by the military was the occupation of the peninsula. Thus Churchill was indeed contemplating a land attack but, because of his constant advocacy of a purely naval operation, could not say so directly. This "indirect approach" enabled Kitchener to strike at the weak point of Churchill's argument. If Churchill still thought the naval attack would succeed, for what purpose were 100,000 troops including regulars required? Kitchener pointed out that if the naval attack succeeded, all that was contemplated for the troops was a cruise in the Sea of Marmora for which purpose the Naval Division and the Anzacs were quite good enough. Once again Churchill had no real answer and had to fall back on the usual arguments of using the troops to influence the situation in the Balkans. On one issue however Churchill had obtained a commitment from Kitchener. In the course of the discussion Kitchener had said that "if the fleet would not get through the Straits unaided, the army ought to see the business through. The effect of a defeat in the Orient would be very serious. There could be no going back."[14] However, the only positive conclusion reached by the War Council was to instruct General Birdwood, the Anzac Commander-in-Chief, to contact Carden to obtain his thoughts on what military aid he considered necessary to assist the navy.[15]

The naval attack was resumed on the 25th. Although the weather had moderated, it was still too rough to get any planes into the air for spotting.[16] However events proceeded more smoothly than on the 19th. The Queen Elizabeth dismantled one of the guns at Hellas and the fort was soon entirely out of action. By 3.00 a.m. the forts had virtually ceased firing and an area up to the entrance of the Straits was swept, though no mines were found.[17] Nevertheless, one of the ships had been hit 6 times and had to withdraw to Lemnos for repairs[18] and Carden had found it necessary to censure another ship for using too much ammunition.[19] In summing up the day's operations Carden told Churchill that the forts "at the entrance of Dardanelles ... are reduced".[20] The next day this claim was found to be inaccurate. Landing parties at Orkanie and Sedd-el-Bahr found most of the guns intact and they blew up 5 of the major pieces.[21]

While these operations were in progress Churchill had suffered another series of reverses over the 29th Division. At the War Council on the 26th Churchill stated that "At the previous meeting Lord Kitchener had asked him what was the use to be made of any large number of troops at Constantinople. His reply was that they were required to occupy Constantinople and to compel a surrender of all Turkish forces remaining in Europe after the fleet had obtained command of the Sea of Marmora."[22] They could then be used to dominate the Balkans. The point had obviously long since passed when any members of the War Council were prepared to point out to Churchill that he had promised these objectives using the fleet alone. It could also have been pointed out that even the numbers recommended by Churchill (100,000) would not be sufficient to "compel" any Turkish surrender (there being at least 400,000 Turkish troops in the area of the fleet's operations) unless the Turks felt disposed to capitulate. Nor was the force large enough to influence events in the Balkans.[23]

Certainly Kitchener was not moved by Churchill's arguments - he said he felt sure "from his knowledge of Constantinople and the East, that the whole situation in Constantinople would change the moment the fleet had secured a passage through the Dardanelles"[24] - which after all had been the argument Churchill had been using himself until recently. A long discussion on the use of the 29th Division followed but Kitchener refused to budge and Churchill was driven to say that "If a disaster occurred in Turkey owing to insufficiency of troops, he must disclaim all responsibility"[25], an extraordinary remark from the man who had convinced the War Council that no troops at all would be needed.

At this point the mood at the Admiralty seemed to change and a new confidence in Carden's attack was noticeable amongst the naval personnel. That this euphoria was hardly justified by the experience of the bombarding squadron should be obvious from the previous narrative. On the other hand it was known that the outer forts had been rendered ineffective in less than a week (though not by bombardment, but perhaps this was not made altogether clear by Carden) and that the bombardment had made a great impression in Bulgaria and Italy[26] and had resulted in new proposals of help from Greece.[27] For whatever reason, it was thought that Carden might get through. The new feeling of optimism was recorded by Lady Richmond. "Winston has now become tremendously keen about the whole business, & behaves as though it was all his own idea.... H [that is Richmond] is enchanted at the success of the Bombardment up to now."[28] Richmond asked to be sent out to Carden in some capacity but was told by Oliver that "it wd be all over before he cd get there"[29]

Even Fisher, who the week before had written, "Diplomacy and the Cabinet have forced upon us the Dardanelles business. So damnable in taking away the Queen Elizabeth"[30], could now write, "we seem to be getting on nicely in the Dardanelles."[31] In the van of the enthusiasts was, of course, Churchill. On the 28th he outlined to Grey a draft armistice to be concluded with Turkey. He thought Britain "cannot be content with anything less than the surrender of everything Turkish in Europe."[32] At the same time he called for a report on the reduction of the Bosphorus defences [33] and asked Carden for an estimate of the number of days needed to arrive in the Marmora.[34]

The mood spread to the other members of the War Council. Hankey wrote a detailed paper entitled "After The Dardanelles; The Next Steps" which discussed what peace terms might be offered to Turkey.[35] This question was discussed by the War Council on March 3rd. The success of the fleet now seemed to be regarded as a foregone conclusion. Churchill re-iterated that they must seek the surrender of Turkey in Europe. "All must pass into our hands, and we ought to accept nothing less". He suggested that the Turkish army ought to be hired as mercenaries. Grey suggested that Bulgaria and perhaps Italy be invited to join the Allies but Asquith said "it was by no means improbable that Bulgaria was already on the move". The future of Constantinople was also discussed, the general opinion being that Britain and France would not oppose its cession to Russia provided they received compensation in Asia Minor and Syria.[36]

Even the importance of the 29th Division had receded. Carden had told Churchill that he expected to be in the Marmora in 14 days.[37] Churchill now informed Kitchener of this fact and stated that 40,000 troops (now apparently regarded as sufficient) should be available for "land operations on Turkish soil" by March 20th. He said he still regarded the provision of the 29th. Division as "grave and urgent" but added "I wish to make it clear that the naval operations in the Dardanelles cannot be delayed for troop movements, as we must get into the Marmora as soon as possible in the normal course".[38]

On the same day he wrote to Grey that the Greeks should be told that "the Admiralty believe it in their power to force the Dardanelles without military assistance".[39]

However he did not send this letter, for the prospect of Greek participation was rapidly diminishing. On the 3rd Buchanan told Grey that the Russians had informed him that on no account would they allow Greek soldiers to aid the British.[40] This veto was later modified, the Russians allowing the Greeks to operate in areas (excluding Constantinople) designated by the Allied commanders.[41] In the meantime however, the pro-Allied Venizelos government had resigned,[42] to be replaced by a more neutralist administration and all chances of Greek aid were at an end. It was once thought that the Russian veto was the direct cause of the "loss" of the Greek divisions. Churchill certainly took this line at the time and was very critical of the Russians for their attitude.[43] It is now known however that the Greek General Staff were absolutley opposed to sending any force to the Dardanelles, as they had been in August, because of the uncertain attitude of Bulgaria,[44] that the King was in total agreement with this policy, and that this position had been arrived at before the details of the Russian veto were known.[45] Therefore the second Greek offer was as illusory as the first, having once more been made by Venizelos on his own initiative without consultation with the military authorities.

In other areas in the Balkans the British were finding that the naval attack had not made the complex diplomatic situation any less intractable. Regarding Bulgaria, on March 4th. Bax-Ironside reported that the position of the pro-German Cabinet had not been shaken by the naval attack and that they were determined to remain neutral.[46] The Prime Minister remained convinced that the fleet would not get through.[47] Much the same view was expressed by the

King of Roumania.[48]  Indeed, in some ways the Dardanelles operation had made the situation more complicated. The rumour soon spread that Britain and France had offered Constantinople and the Straits to Russia. This immediately aroused the hostility of the small Balkan States who were more content with Turkish control of the Straits than with the prospect of a great power controlling the vital waterway. To counter the Allied offer it was suggested by Bulgaria that Greece and Roumania join her in opposing Russian aspirations in the area.[49]  These moves obviously made the task of trying to induce the Balkan States into the war on the same side as Russia more difficult. Allied action at the Dardanelles was starting to create as many problems as it was supposed to solve.

Nor were operations inside the Straits adding conviction to Allied diplomacy. Only if the ships anchored could they hit the forts but they were kept moving by the fire of the mobile howitzers which could not be located. They were further hampered by the restriction on ammunition which meant that few shells per day could be fired.[50]  Ominously the Triumph, which had taken part in the bombardment of the German forts of Tsingtao, reported that "an opinion was formed that no more progress can be made without the assistance of land forces, to supplement and make good the work done by the Fleet."[51]

On March 4th there was another setback. Companies of marines were landed to complete the destruction of the forts of Kum Kale and Sedd-el-Bahr. Both parties were stopped by heavy fire from large numbers of Turks. Only two machine guns were destroyed at a cost of 41 casualties at Kum Kale alone.[52]  This was indeed a gloomy sign for if the guns could only be destroyed by landing parties and the landing parties could not land, then clearly new factors would have to be introduced or the landing of much larger numbers of men attempted.

One possible solution was tried on the 5th when the Queen Elizabeth bombarded the forts at the Narrows across the peninsula from a point off Gaba Tepe. This too proved a failure. Firstly, the ranges involved were enormous (16,000 yards).[53]  Then it was found that the spotting force was totally inadequate. Hardly any hits were inflicted on the forts. The attempt was broken off. Carden was driven to admit that a force of aeroplanes was needed to replace the seaplanes he had originally asked for. An enquiry to the War Office elicited the response that none was available.[54]

The direct attack from ships inside the Straits resumed on the 7th and 8th. No success was obtained. The fact now had to be faced that the long range bombardment had failed utterly. Because of the need to conserve ammunition only four or five ships had been used at any one time and they had only been permitted to fire between 10 and 40 shells each. With an expected hitting rate of 2% and a total of 37 large guns to hit at the Narrows alone, [55] it would obviously be a long time before the fleet got through. Furthermore, the aerial spotting had not proved effective and there was no prospect of an early improvement in the efficiency of the force. The obvious answer was that the forts would have to be attacked at closer range but to do this the minefields, which were keeping the battleships at a distance, would have to be swept. Thus a new phase of the operation began.

In fact minesweeping operations had been proceeding inside the Straits since March 1st. Very little progress had been made. The ships provided were North Sea trawlers manned by civilian crews. But even if the crews had been experienced they faced formidable difficulties. The minefields (10 main lines - 387 mines)[56] were protected by 48 guns and 5 searchlights, all trained on the sweeping area.[57]. In addition, it was found that with their sweeps out the trawlers could hardly make headway against the 4 knot current flowing down the Dardanelles; in other words, they were practically stationary targets for the minefield defences. Various expedients were tried to overcome these difficulties, including sweeping at night and sweeping under the protection of a battleship. On March 9th a mass attack was attempted using every available sweeper with a powerful escort of warships. All attempts failed. Stalemate had been reached.

By now almost everybody at the Dardanelles had come to the conclusion that military aid would be essential if the fleet were to get through. Not surprisingly the military had been the first to arrive at this conclusion. On March 5th General Birdwood, who had been in touch with Carden, told Kitchener that he doubted if the navy could force the passage unassisted.[58] De Robeck, second in command to Carden, had reached the conclusion that the forts could be dominated but not destroyed and that in this case even if warships passed into the Marmora, the passage would be barred to the unarmoured supply ships necessary to maintain them there.

> "The situation is therefore reduced to a point at which strong military co operation is considered essential in order to clear at least one side of the straits of the enemy and their movable batteries. I am not prepared to suggest the proper place for landing or to indicate the method the military should employ but I would point out from my almost daily personal observations that the enemy are continuously making new entrenchments and improving their position at the southern end of the straits and a landing at Morto Bay and Seddul Bahr with a view to attacking the ridge of which Achi Babi is the commanding point would be extremely costly".[59]

This must be deemed an extremely interesting statement in the light of further developments.

Even Carden was coming around to this view. On the 10th he admitted that "The methodical reduction of the forts is not feasible without expenditure of ammunition out of all proportion to that available.... Our experience shows gunfire alone will not render forts innocuous most of the guns must be destroyed individually by demolition".[60] The implication behind all these statements was that the military would have to land to destroy the guns; but, although there is evidence that Carden had privately arrived at this position,[61] he was apparently not yet willing to recommend to Churchill that the naval attack be postponed until troops were ready.

At home the War Council were still parcelling out the Turkish Empire. It was considered that if Russia was to have Constantinople, the Opposition should be involved in the decision and Asquith invited Bonar Law and Lansdowne to a War Council held to consider the question.[62] It was mutually agreed at the meeting that Constantinople should be offered to Russia subject to French and British desiderata in the rest of the Turkish Empire being met.63

Kitchener also announced that as the position on the Western Front was "sufficiently secure" he was now prepared to release the 29th Division.[64] Exactly how the security of the Western Front had increased since February 26th is not clear. Nor did Kitchener elucidate on the role that he expected these regular troops to play in the East. Perhaps he too was affected by the general atmosphere of optimism and considered that the 29th Division might form the nucleus of a large British army which would operate in the Balkans after the Turkish surrender. In any case he now estimated that there were 130,000 troops available for use "against Constantinople".[65]

With such a large force being assembled it was considered that a senior General should be appointed to command. Kitchener chose General Sir Ian Hamilton, his C.O.S. during the Boer War. On his appointment Kitchener assured Hamilton that he would not be sent out until he had studied the situation thoroughly. This promise was soon forgotten. Hamilton was rushed out within a few days of taking command, supplied with only the sketchiest details of the terrain over which he would operate and of the Turkish defence. In fact these oversights only became important in retrospect. Hamilton's instructions stated that military force was only to be used "in the event of the Fleet failing to get through after every effort has been exhausted".[66] As the fleet was thought to be doing well this eventuality seemed unlikely to arise. Hamilton was warned however, that "Having entered on the project of forcing the Straits, there can be no idea of abandoning the scheme. It will require time, patience, and methodical plans of co-operation between the naval and military commanders".[67]

Hamilton and a few staff officers dug out from the War

Office left for France on the rather inappropriately named HMS Foresight and travelled from Marseilles to the Dardanelles in the Pheaton, arriving just in time to witness the culmination of the naval effort on March 18th.

The origins of that attack, as with so much concerning the Dardanelles, lay with Churchill. Although on the 9th he wrote confidently to Jellicoe that affairs at the Dardanelles were going so well that the Grand Fleet should begin preparations for the attack on Borkum,[68] he was clearly becoming worried by Carden's lack of progress. As early as the 5th he had asked Carden to report on minesweeping operations and whether any ships had "yet opened fire on the forts at the narrows". He originally concluded the letter, "This is what I am anxious to know",[69] but then perhaps to conceal his anxiety from the Admiral, crossed out the last line. However, he was convinced that Carden was not pressing the attack with enough vigour and on the 11th he informed the commander that he would be supported by the Admiralty if he considered that the time had come to push for a decision.[70] Carden responded by saying that he too considered the time right for vigorous action. This however can hardly have been his real view, for he added, "In my opinion military operations on large scale should be commenced immediately in order to secure my communication line immediately Fleet enters Sea of Marmora".[71]

Whether Fisher agreed with the decision to make a major naval attack on March 18th is not known. After his brief period of optimism his attitude to the operation hardened again and he was soon writing to Churchill, "The more I consider the Dardanelles – the less I like it!"[72] However, on the 12th, that is after Churchill's letter to Carden suggesting the attack, Fisher commented, "Carden to press on! and Kitchener to occupy the deserted forts at extremity of Gallipoli and mount howitzers there!"[73] and on the 14th he offered to go to Gallipoli and take command of the naval forces himself.[74] This, however, should be looked on as a vote of no confidence in Carden rather than a sign of any renewed enthusiasm for the naval attack for he told Jellicoe next day that "Things are going badly at the Dardanelles!"[75]

The only other member of the Admiralty to express an opinion on the operation at this time was Jackson. On the 11th he prepared a paper for Oliver saying that he deprecated an attempt to rush the Straits but advocated a landing on the Gallipoli Peninsula in force. He thought that this was the only way to eliminate the enemy's artillery which was essential to make the waterway safe for troop transports.[76] This is a typical Jackson production. No one had suggested rushing the Straits. The proposed large scale attack was not in this category at all, being merely an extension of the step by step approach. However, it did show that Jackson was convinced that troops would be needed to make the passageway safe for the troops which would be later needed at Constantinople. This was a direct repudiation of the Carden plan but by the introduction of the irrelevant concept of a "rush" at the Straits, Jackson virtually ensured that his paper would not receive from Churchill the consideration that his main argument deserved.

Meanwhile planning for the big attack was getting underway. The plan envisaged using virtually all the available battleships in an attempt to silence the guns of the forts and the minefields defences simultaneously – while the forts were silenced a passage would be swept through the minefields up to Sari Siglar Bay. From there the fleet would destroy the Narrows forts at close range and attack the two forts near Nagara Point. The squadron for the Marmora was to consist of the Lord Nelson(flag), Agamemnon, and all other available ships, except the Queen Elizabeth, one or two French battleships and some cruisers and destroyers.[77]

Two days before the attack Carden collapsed from a stomach complaint brought on by nervous exhaustion.[78] He was put in hospital at Malta, from where it was expected that he would return to the Dardanelles, but he never did. The command was now given to de Robeck, Carden's deputy. He was a much more forceful character than his former chief and seemed to inspire confidence even in those like Keyes who opposed his strategy. Fisher thought him better than Carden,[79] and Birdwood thought him "a real fine fellow – worth a dozen of Carden at least".[80] What Churchill's contemporary opinion of him was is not known. Certainly on March 19th Churchill had no hesitation in appointing de Robeck to the command, asking him if he considered "after separate and independent judgement that the immediate operations proposed are wise and practicable. If not, do not hesitate to say so".[81] This placed de Robeck in a difficult position. It will be remembered that he had recommended to Carden as early as March 9th that military operations should be undertaken and that the fleet would not be able to maintain itself in the Marmora unless this was done. Although Hamilton had now arrived at the Dardanelles, it was obvious that a landing in force could not be made for some time, for the 29th Division had only just sailed from England. Cancellation of the naval attack, which was due to begin in a few hours, would mean that no action at all would be taken for several weeks. De Robeck later stated that it was for this reason, involving as it did considerations of prestige and political necessity, that he decided to continue with the attack.[82] However, pressure from London and the advanced stage of the planning must also have played a part. In any event the attack was now to be directed by a commander who had grave doubts that, even if it succeeded, any substantial results would be obtained.

The great naval attack on the Narrows began at 10.45 a.m. on March 18th. Almost every available battleship was used inside the Straits and a heavy fire was maintained on the forts and the intermediate defences. By noon the forts had fallen silent. Hope of victory ran high. Then at 1.30 p.m. one of the French ships, Bouvet, blew up and sank with the loss of 600 lives. Later Irresistible, Inflexible and Ocean hit mines and Suffren and Gaulious were so badly damaged by gunfire that they were forced to withdraw. By 5.00 p.m. one third of de Robeck's fleet was either sunk or out of action.

Meanwhile a concerted attempt to sweep the minefield had failed. The main force, manned once more by civilian crews, did not even reach the main minefield and the operation was broken off without any mines having been cleared.[83]

With six of his battleships out of action (3 sunk and 3 damaged) and the causes of the casualties still unknown, de Robeck had little alternative but to withdraw. What damage had been inflicted on the forts could only be guessed at. (In fact only 1 heavy gun had been destroyed and four others put out of action temporarily).[84] But Keyes for one realized that the minefield was the real problem and no headway at all had been made against that.[85] De Robeck's immediate reaction seemed to be that the naval attempt was at an end, not a surprising decision given his earlier attitude and the loss of a third of his force. He asked Wemyss, the Commander of the Mudros base, to see him on the 19th and told him "We have had [a] disastrous day".[86] At this meeting Wemyss later claimed he and de Robeck had come to the conclusion that "combined action must be postponed until plans had been developed and perfected".[87] Furthermore, de Robeck had been told by his own staff that ammunition for the fleet was short and that the state of wear on many of the old guns was critical.[88] On the other hand de Robeck had told Hamilton on the 19th that although "I was sad to lose ships & my heart aches when one thinks of it....We are all getting ready for another 'go' & not in the least beaten or down-hearted".[89]

That the War Council was prepared to authorize another attack was confirmed on the 19th.[90] In a splended burst of irrelevancy the Council spent most of the meeting discussing "The Partition of Turkey in Asia" and on the 20th Churchill informed de Robeck that his losses would be replaced and that "It appears important not to let the forts be repaired or to encourage enemy by an apparent suspension of the operations".[91]

In fact the suspension of operations was inevitable. The weather had changed on the 19th and a strong gale blew until the 25th.[92] Also, de Robeck realized that no further action was possible until the minesweeping force was reorganized, although he then stated that he would press on with the naval attack.[93] Even Keyes, an incurable optimist, realized that nothing could be done until the destroyers were fitted out with sweeps and he estimated that this would take until about the 4th of April.[94] A further factor was that the Inflexible, de Robeck's only dreadnought, was damaged and there was no ship (Queen Elizabeth was not to be risked) capable of dealing with the Goeben.[95]

On March 23rd a conference of the naval and military leaders was held on the Queen Elizabeth. At that meeting de Robeck decided to abandon the naval attack. No minutes of the meeting were kept and it was once thought that de Robeck had been influenced by Hamilton in reaching a decision. But this was strongly denied by Hamilton.[96] And as has been shown already, de Robeck had come to the conclusion as early as March 9th that the military would have to land, and therefore he cannot have been wholehearted in his decision to press on with the March 18th attack. His view on the 22nd then really represented no change of mind at all and it is doubtful if his statements made after the 18th about giving the naval attack "another go" amounted to more than an attempt to put a brave face on what amounted to a lost battle.

Hamilton, of course, was in favour of a military attack, having arrived at the conclusion that the navy could not achieve success alone. In addition, just before the meeting with de Robeck, Hamilton had received a telegram from Kitchener which stated "You know my views - that the passage of the Dardanelles must be forced, and that if large military operations on the Gallipoli peninsula by your troops are necessary to clear the way, these operations must be undertaken".[97] The Dardanelles Commissioners thought, and Hamilton agreed with them, that this was a "peremptory" order to take the Peninsula.[98]

In London Churchill was opposed to the shelving of the naval attack. After receiving de Robeck's letter stating his intention to wait for the army,[99] Churchill set about writing a reply ordering de Robeck to continue the attack.[100] The telegram was never sent. The Admiralty War Group insisted that the Admiral on the spot was in the best position to judge. Churchill then drafted another letter to de Robeck. He pointed out that enemy submarines were expected to arrive at any minute, that the army faced heavy losses (at least 5,000) if they landed and that "the possibilities of a check in the land operations [were] far more serious than the loss of a few old surplus ships....These must be balanced against the risks and hopes of a purely naval undertaking. You must not underrate the supreme moral effect of a British fleet... entering the Sea of Marmora".[101] He considered this effect would be the evacuation of the Gallipoli Peninsula and the probable surrender of Constantinople. This attitude is consistent with Churchill's renewed faith in the naval attack, which as has been shown took place about the beginning of March, but it is hardly compatible with his appeals to Kitchener to release the 29th Division.

De Robeck replied on March 27th after telling Limpus that "he was not going to be hurried by W.C.".[102]

"The original approved plan for forcing the Dardanelles by ships was drawn up on the assumption that gunfire alone was capable of destroying forts. This assumption has been conclusively proved to be wrong....The utmost that can be expected of ships is to dominate the forts to such an extent that gun crews cannot fight the guns....To destroy forts therefore it is necessary to land demolishing parties".[103]

He concluded that the only way to do this was to capture the Peninsula which would have the added advantage of ensuring that the Straits remained open when the fleet passed through.[104] Churchill had to accept this decision, replying to de Robeck that "the reasons you give make it clear that a combined operation is now indispensable. Time also has passed, the troops are available & the date is not distant".[105]

Thus ended the naval attempt to force the Dardanelles and the historian is left with one of the most intriguing questions of the war; could the fleet have got through if the attack had been renewed?

There are several factors to be considered. The first is the alleged Turkish shortage of ammunition. It has been held by many authorities that the naval attack was broken off when Turkish supplies of ammunition for the forts were so low that a renewed attempt by the Fleet must have succeeded. The table below gives a summary of various estimates of the ammunition supply available on March 19th.

Certain features of the table should be noted. The estimates by Enver Bey and the Turkish G.H.Q. were both given to the Mitchell Committee and have enough similarities to suggest that they had a common source. Enver's were much more detailed[106] while the G.H.Q. grouped the figures more under type of gun[107] and this could account for any discrepancies. The figures from the Official German account quoted by Dewar and Aspinall-Oglander are different. Perhaps differences in translation account for this. James has quoted from the same passage as Aspinall-Oglander but, while mentioning that the high explosive shells were practically used up, has omitted the sentence which includes the details of the rounds per gun that remained.[108] The figures given by Captain Serri are significantly lower than most of the other estimates but are based on one battery. Mitchell thought his evidence was largely hearsay.[109] Within broad areas the other estimates are really remarkably similar considering the inevitable errors in counting numbers of shells and the undoubted crudities in Turkish statistics of the time. Thus there seem to have been 50-60 rounds for the heavier guns and 70-80, 120 and at least 250 for the three smaller categories in descending order. What is more speculative is how many attacks on the scale of March 18th this amount of shells could have repulsed. There are no

Table 7.1      ESTIMATES OF TURKISH AMMUNITION SUPPLY 19/3/15

| Source | Forts' Ammunition Supply |
|---|---|
| German Official Account quoted by R.R. James | H.E. Shells "nearly used up" |
| German Official Account quoted by Aspinall-Oglander | 35.5 cm(heavy) - 50 rounds per gun<br>23 cm    -    30-50 rounds per gun<br>+ H.E. shells "almost all gone" |
| German Official Account quoted by K.G.B. Dewar | 35.5 cm (heavy) - 46 rounds per gun<br>20"              - 62 rounds per gun |
| Turkish War Office quoted by Corbett | Heavy - 70 rounds per gun<br>Light - 130 rounds per gun<br>+ stocks of old ammunition |
| Turkish G.H.Q. | 35.5 cm - 52 rounds per gun<br>21-18 cm - 82 rounds per gun<br>15 cm - 128 rounds per gun<br>10-12 cm - no figures<br>smaller calibres - 258 rounds per gun |
| Enver Bey | 35.5 cm - 52 rounds per gun<br>21-28 cm - 110 rounds per gun<br>15 cm - 131 rounds per gun<br>15 cm (How)-120 rounds per gun<br>10-12 cm - 19 rounds per gun<br>smaller calibres - 312 rounds per gun |
| Djevad | 35.5 cm - 11 rounds per gun<br>24 cm - 79 rounds per gun<br>15 cm - 74 rounds per gun<br>15 cm (How)-116 rounds per gun |
| Austro-Hungarian Military Attache | 2/3 of stocks on 18/3/15 remaining |
| Capt. Serri | 35.5 cm - 36 rounds per gun<br>24 cm - 29 rounds per gun<br>(based on one fort) |

Source : James, Gallipoli, p.64; Aspinall-Oglander, Gallipoli VI, P.105N; Dewar, The Dardanelles Campaign, Naval Review, 1957;

Corbett, Naval operations V2, P.223-4; Turkish G.H.Q. and Enver Bey in "Answers given to the Mitchell Committee" Adm 116/1714; Djevad, Serri, Mitchell Committee Report, P.436-8; Austro-Hungarian Attache in Germains, Tragedy of Winston Churchill, P.195N.

reliable estimates of what was fired by the forts on March 18th although the Austrian Military Attache said that forts Hamidie and Rumili Medjidieh on the European side fired from the heavy guns, 95 shells (12 per gun). Hamidie on the Asian side fired 75 (8 per gun).[110] This would have allowed several more large scale attacks before the forts ran out. The Attache concluded that at least two more attacks could be sustained, a conclusion also reached by the Mitchell Committee[111] and Djevad.[112] Turkish G.H.Q. were more optimistic saying that "many attacks could have been repulsed".[113] Most authorities also agree, however, that there were further reserves of older ammunition which were not counted in the returns given above and which could have been used.[114] It would seem reasonable to conclude that at least two attacks on the scale of March 18th could have been repulsed by the Turks using their modern ammunition and a further indefinite number using old shells. Thus in all probability the immediate resumption of the naval attack, as desired by Churchill, would have had no dramatic effect and, if similar casualties had been suffered, very little of the British fleet would have remained at the end. Moreover, the quality of the ammunition used would not seem to be a vital factor. Providing the forts kept firing some kind of shells, the ships would have to keep underway which would make their fire less accurate. This was a much more important factor than the forts needing modern ammunition to sink the ships, for it is admitted by all sides that no vital hits were made on the fleet by the forts. Still more important, the question of the ammunition supply for the forts would seem to be largely irrelevant to the chances of the fleet. It was the minefield that was the crucial factor. The mines prevented the fleet from rushing the Straits and kept the ships from engaging the forts at close range, the only position from which they were likely to be destroyed without the aid of landing parties. As far as the batteries protecting the minefields were concerned no authority has suggested that they were running low on ammunition. Thus any attempt at sweeping would yet again have had to be made under fire.

Turning to the minefields themselves, hardly any of the mines had been swept. Moorehead claims however that "many of... [the mines] were old and... had broken from their moorings and drifted away".[115] This is open to question. The Mitchell Committee investigated the state of the minefield because of the impression "that the Turkish personnel would be ineffective, and also... the doubt whether any mines could remain at their correct depths in such strong, and probably variable current".[116] They found that "Both these impressions have proved to be without foundation".[117] Would the reorganized sweeping forces have made any impression on the minefields? In a recent study of this problem Marder has suggested that they would. He points to the fact that 16 destroyers had been fitted as sweepers by April 14th and by the 18th they could sweep at 14 knots which he thinks would have been too fast for the poor ranging equipment of the Turkish batteries.[118] Marder also pointed out that the draft of the destroyers (10' 6") was less than the depth of the mines so that no casualties could be expected from that source.[119] However, the destroyers would have had to face the full weight of the minefield defences, and even Marder concludes that the Fleet had only a 50-50 chance of success (or to put it another way a one in two chance of failure).[120]

Another factor which seems to have been ignored by historians is the depleted state of the Anglo-French Fleet after March 18th. De Robeck had only two dreadnoughts at his disposal, the Queen Elizabeth and the Inflexible. The Queen Elizabeth, apart from having turbine trouble on the 18th, was not to be sent through the Straits. The Inflexible had been mined and had to be sent to Malta where it took two months to repair.[121] Thus even allowing for the time taken to reorganize the sweeping force, the British would have had no ship capable of fighting the Goeben.[122]

An even more speculative question now must be asked. What would have happened had the Fleet got through? In the first place would the British Fleet have been able to maintain itself in the Marmora? With the Forts still in Turkish hands and at least some of the guns working, it would have been difficult to send through a continuous stream of supply ships. Thus a quick victory by the Fleet was required but it is by no means certain that it would have eventuated. The Turks had made plans to attack the Fleet with all the ships they had as it passed Nagara Point. They hoped that the British would approach in a single line which would enable them to be attacked one at a time.[123] If the British had entered the Marmora without a dreadnought the Goeben might have been able to effect some losses before weight of numbers told. Nor would the Turkish Fleet have been the last of de Robeck's problems. Batteries had been placed on the Princes Islands, which the Fleet must pass on its way to Constantinople.[124] Furthermore, the Turkish capital was defended by 5 batteries of guns capable of inflicting damage on the Fleet.[125] Of course, the British were relying on a pro-allied coup d'etat or revolution in Constantinople as soon as the Fleet appeared in the Marmora. The only evidence that this might have occurred comes from the account of the American Ambassador to Turkey, Hans Morganthau. However, apart from mere assertions,[126] the only hard evidence he produces is contained in the following quotation:

"[By March] the exodus from the capital had begun; Turkish women and children were being moved into the interior; all the banks had been compelled to send their gold into Asia Minor; the archives of the Sublime Porte had already been [sent away]; and practically all the ambassadors and their suites, as well as most of the government officials, had made their preparations to leave".[127]

These facts are no proof that the government was about to capitulate. Many of them could be taken as evidence that resistance was going to be continued from the interior. Similar scenes would have been observed in Paris in August and September 1914 and yet no one has suggested that the French were on the point of surrendering. Their moves, as with the Turks, were merely sensible precautions taken in the face of an advancing enemy. One suspects that with the Turks these scenes were taken to be indicative of the panic that could be expected of a non-European race.

Much the same type of evidence as used by Morganthau was put forward by naval intelligence as proof that the Turks would surrender.[128] At the same time any evidence which would contradict this view is usually ignored. The fact that trenches were being dug in Constantinople and the artillery defences of the city increased would not seem to indicate an abject intention to surrender.[129] Moreover, Constantinople was in military hands and there is no evidence to suggest that the army leaders would not have remained loyal to Enver Pasha. Thus it seems highly doubtful that the desired political upheaval would have taken place, and this might have left de Robeck with little choice but to return back down the Straits.

Even the hope that the passage of the Fleet would have forced the evacuation of the Gallipoli Peninsula seems doubtful. Sea communication with the garrison would have been completely cut and road communications could have been controlled by warships during the day. However, it is doubtful if road traffic could have been completely cut during the night and it is possible that a diversion inland, out of sight of the guns of the fleet, could have been made.[130] Therefore if the Turks had kept their heads, and later fighting would suggest that this would have been the case, not even this "success" could have been claimed by the British.

* * * * * * * * * * * * * *

The events from the opening of the naval bombardment on February 19th to the failure of the attack in late March occupy over 80 pages of The World Crisis, over $2^{1/2}$ pages for every day covered. For convenience five main topics dealt with in The World Crisis will be discussed in roughly the order in which they occur in the book. The first four of these are; the continuing controversy surrounding the provision of troops for the operation, the naval attack, its effect on opinion abroad and at the Admiralty, and the aftermath of the failure of March 18th. The fifth topic deals with a long retrospective chapter entitled "The Case For Perseverance and Decision" in which Churchill attempts to establish a case for continuing the naval attack after March 18th.

Concerning the use of troops in the operation, the main point Churchill is anxious to establish is that Kitchener's failure to release the 29th. Division during February was a decisive "turning-point in the struggle", and eventually led to disaster.[131] To make his case Churchill states that he argued strenuously for the despatch of the 29th. Division at the War Councils of February 24th and 26th, and disclaimed responsibility for the consequences of any military operation that might arise.[132] What Churchill has not done is to give the other side of the story. For, as has been shown, at the same time that he was advancing these arguments he was also stating that the naval attack would still succeed. It has also been noted that the reasons Churchill put forward for needing the 29th Division in the east (mopping-up, occupation duties) were not of the kind that Kitchener was likely to find persuasive, for these tasks could have been performed by troops already in the east. However these issues are not discussed in The World Crisis.

In fact the whole issue concerning the date of despatch of the 29th Division is of much less importance than Churchill's narrative supposes, for because of the weather it would have been virtually impossible to land the troops at Gallipoli in March or early April. However, by concentrating on the need for troops instead of on factors surrounding their use, Churchill is able to ignore this point without the omission becoming obvious and readers of The World Crisis never realize that the amount of space devoted to the tussle between Kitchener and Churchill over the 29th Division is hardly in keeping with any practical advantages that might have accrued to the British had Churchill been successful.

Kitchener continues to come under attack from Churchill in The World Crisis even after the 29th Division was released.

"But even after decision was at last taken to send an army including the 29th Division, the use to which that army was to be put remained a Secret of the Sphinx. When Lord Kitchener had decided in his heart that if the Navy failed to force the Dardanelles, he would storm the Gallipoli Peninsula, he ought to have declared it to his colleagues".[133]

This form of attack on Kitchener is hard to justify. When Kitchener released the 29th Division on March 10th he had no intention of "storming" the Gallipoli Peninsula. Such an operation had never been seriously considered by the War Council. The troops were to be sent in Churchill's own phrase "to reap the fruits" of the naval attack. On the

102

other hand Kitchener <u>had</u> said that if all else failed the army should see the fleet through. Thus, his policy was quite clear involving no "Secrets of the Sphinx" and had been declared to his colleagues many times. In fact Kitchener's decision to storm the Gallipoli Peninsula was only made after the naval failure of March 18th and therefore could hardly have been revealed before then.

For convenience Churchill's description of the naval attack will be divided into five sections (the opening bombardment, the fall of the outer forts, operations inside the Straits from March 3rd to 11th, the crisis surrounding the replacement of Carden by de Robeck, and the great attack of March 18th and its aftermath) and discussed in order.

It has been seen that the opening bombardment of February 19th was indecisive and something of a disappointment to those on the spot. Nevertheless Churchill feels able to say that "a favourable impression had been sustained" as a result of the first day's firing,[134] though he does not say by whom. A few pages later Churchill sums up the lessons learned from the opening bombardment.

"The results of this inconclusive bombardment seemed to show, first, that it was necessary for ships to anchor before accurate shooting could be made; secondly, that direct fire was better than indirect fire; and, thirdly, that it was not sufficient to hit the forts with the naval shells-actual hits must be made on the guns or their mountings. This last fact was important".[135]

This would seem to be a fair summary of the day's events and it is hard to see how the results listed tie in with Churchill's earlier statement that the events made a "favourable impression".

Also the revelation that the ships had to hit each gun was not just "important", as Churchill states, but disastrous. For in the plan as modified by the Admiralty Staff nothing like the amount of ammunition required for the fleet to achieve this feat had been allowed. In other words, the basis on which the plan had been prepared was found to be false on the first day.

Furthermore, it has been shown that the fact that the ships had to anchor to fire accurately pointed to a future problem when firing commenced inside the Straits. For if the ships had to anchor in that narrow waterway they would provide easy targets for the mobile batteries which lined either bank, and if this fire proved effective enough to keep the ships underway, then the accuracy of the ships' fire at long range would be greatly reduced. Thus, although Churchill sums up the day's firing in a reasonable manner, he does not mention these important conclusions which highlight some of the fallacies on which the naval attack was based.

The events which encompassed the fall of the outer forts

103

are now considered by Churchill. Of the attack by the fleet on the 25th he says, "The effect of the bombardment was remarkable. It proved conclusively the great accuracy of naval fire, provided good observation could be obtained",[136] and, "The bombardment clearly proved the power of the ships anchored at about 12,000 yards, if good observation at right angles to the range was available, to destroy the Turkish guns without undue expenditure of ammunition."[137] Although the 25th was one of the most successful day's firing ever carried out by the fleet (four guns were disabled), the previous discussion of the problems encountered would suggest that Churchill's summary is too optimistic. That the accuracy of the day's bombardment was never repeated would indicate that a certain amount of luck was involved. Furthermore, Churchill's statement about good observation being necessary for success begs an important question. In the bombardment of the outer forts "observation at right angles to the range" could be provided by warships spotting for the ships carrying out the bombardment. Once inside the Straits, however, this service would have to be provided by seaplanes which had already been found to be ineffective. As for Churchill's contention that the day's firing showed that it was possible to destroy the guns without "undue expenditure of ammunition", this was not the case. It was shown earlier that the Mitchell Committee Report, which Churchill read before writing The World Crisis, held it to be almost an "iron law" of gunnery that at extreme ranges only two shells in a hundred would hit a gun and this would have required more ammunition than was available to the fleet. In fact the bombardment of the outer forts "proved" very little about the problems to be faced later. The manoeuvring area available to the ships was virtually unlimited, good observation was possible, no minefields were encountered and there were few heavy guns to face. None of these factors applied inside the Straits and it is hardly appropriate for Churchill to draw positive conclusions from this phase of the attack.

The small section on the landing parties in The World Crisis is not consistent with Churchill's optimistic approach to the opening bombardment. From the figures given by Churchill it is possible to work out that it was the landing parties and not the firing of the ships which destroyed most of the guns.[138] However, this fact is not pointed out to the reader and as a result the conclusion is not drawn that landing parties might also be essential inside the Straits where they would be more likely to meet stiff resistance from Turkish troops.

Churchill next describes the operations inside the Straits from March 3rd to the 11th. It will be remembered that no great results were obtained by the fleet during this period. Churchill ascribes this lack of success to : periods of unsuitable weather; inefficiency of the seaplane spotting service; the mobile howitzers which forced the ships to keep moving; the inadequacy of the minesweeping force coupled with the efficiency of the minefield defences.[139] The failure of the indirect bombardment by the <u>Queen Elizabeth</u> is put down to the Admiralty restriction on ammunition and the inadequacies of the spotting force. Churchill states that both of these problems were eventually remedied "but meanwhile the method had itself been precipitately condemned and was never resumed".[140] Several observations should be made on these remarks. Firstly, it should be said that Churchill has given a quite adequate summary of the reasons for the failure of operations inside the Straits. Only the lack of ammunition, which seems to have been the reason for Carden committing only a few ships at a time in the Straits, seems to have been omitted. It is rather the conclusion drawn from these facts that is open to objection. Churchill states that "it was clear that a much more vehement effort must be made"[141] and then quotes his telegram of March 11th authorizing Carden to make a more vigorous attack.[142] It was shown earlier that this message committed Carden to an attack using the same methods which had failed, but on a larger scale. There was to be no improvement in the aerial spotting force, no attempt to eliminate the mobile howitzers. The lifting of the restriction on the use of ammunition was the only new development. Yet, as has been shown, many of the naval and military authorities at the Dardanelles concluded that the original methods had failed, and they reached the conclusion that military support was essential if progress was to be made. In fact, it has been shown that Churchill was one of the few who had not drawn this conclusion and in <u>The World Crisis</u> he follows exactly the same line.

What of Churchill's statement that the indirect bombardment was abandoned just as the causes which led to this action, shortage of ammunition and the inefficient spotting force, were being remedied? It is true, as he states, that the restriction on the use of the <u>Queen Elizabeth's</u> ammunition was lifted, but the indirect bombardment was not broken off <u>primarily</u> from a need to conserve ammunition but because of poor weather and the failure of the seaplane spotting force. The weather was a factor which no one had previously taken into account and at this time of the year many days' bombardment from long range would have been lost, even allowing for efficient spotting. However, the major factor which crippled the indirect bombardment was the poor performance of the seaplanes, and this force was not re-organized until the end of March, that is, <u>after</u> the decision had been taken to land the military, a fact which made <u>any</u> indirect naval bombardment redundant.

The next events to be described in <u>The World Crisis</u> are the collapse of Carden on March 16th and the appointment of de Robeck to the command. Churchill is critical of the ability of the new commander,

> "One could not feel that his training and experience up to this period had led him to think deeply on the larger apsects of strategy and tactics. His character, personality, and zeal inspired confidence in all"[143]

By thus stating that de Robeck was not a deep thinker on matters of naval strategy and tactics Churchill is predisposing the reader to question the Admiral's decision to call off the naval attack on March 23rd. Yet it may be wondered if any great strategic insight was needed on March 23rd to see that the naval attack had failed.

Churchill's account of the great attack of March 18th need not detain us. It is generally accurate and is told with Churchill's usual skill.[144] More important and controversial are Churchill's claims concerning the effect of the naval attack on opinion at home and abroad. In relation to Admiralty opinion he states that at the beginning of March,

> "The greatest satisfaction[at the progress of the naval attack] was expressed at the Admiralty, and I found myself in these days surrounded by smiling faces.... If the Dardanelles Commisioners could only have taken the expert evidence on the feasibility of ships attacking forts in the first week of March, 1915, instead of in the spring of 1917, they would have been impressed by the robust character of naval opinion on these questions. They would also have been struck by the number of persons who were in favour of the Dardanelles operations and claimed to have contributed to their initiation."[145]

This seems to be a fair summary of the change in opinion which became general at the Admiralty in early March. It has been shown that Oliver, Richmond, and even Fisher, expressed confidence in the naval attack at this time. However, Churchill is less accurate in examining his own position. He does not mention that his own opinion concerning Carden's plan had also undergone a recent change and that after several weeks of doubt he too had a new found optimism that the navy would get through alone. Instead he claims that he continued urgently to push for troops[146] and as proof publishes his letter to Kitchener of March 4th in which he said that the need for the 29th Division was "grave and urgent".[147] However it was shown earlier that the main thrust of that letter was that the Straits could be forced by ships alone and would be in the Marmora before large contingents of troops could be assembled and that "naval operations in the Dardanelles cannot be delayed for troop movements". The view was then put forward that anyone reading this letter could be forgiven for thinking that the provision of troops had now become a secondary consideration for Churchill and it is clear that the fall of the outer forts, rather than acting on Churchill as a spur for military action as claimed in The World Crisis, pursuaded him that after all the navy could achieve success.

Churchill is aware that Admiralty opinion and more specifically Fisher's opinion underwent a reversal when the naval attack began to falter in mid-March. He states, however, that his own confidence in the operation was unaffected by this set-back. This was the time for those

"who did not share these clear-cut conclusions, who had doubts-had always had doubts about the feasibility of the operation, about the margin of the Grand fleet, about the utility of operations in the Eastern theatre! [to come forward].... Here surely was the time for Lord Fisher. He could say with pefect propriety and consistency, 'We have given the Carden plan a good trial. I never liked it much. It has not come off...now let us break off altogether or turn to something else.'...But what happened? So far from wishing to break off the operation, the First Sea Lord was never at any time so resolute in its support. He assented willingly and cordially to the new decision which was now taken to change the gradual tentative limited-liability advance into a hard, determined and necessarily hazardous attack....He even offered to go out and hoist his flag and take command at the Dardanelles himself."[148]

This long and important quotation will now be discussed in detail. Without doubt there is something to be said for Churchill's view that Fisher could have intervened in mid-March to stop the operation. A more determined and courageous First Sea Lord could certainly have done so. However, Fisher's difficulties should not be underestimated. His paper of January 25th had made it clear that he did not like the operation and that he would have preferred action elsewhere, but it had been ignored. Now that the operation was underway, to object was much more difficult.

Churchill also exaggerates the amount of support given by Fisher to the operation at the time. It was noted earlier that Fisher had told Churchill as recently as March 4th that the more he considered the Dardanelles the less he liked it, and that on the 15th he had told Jellicoe that things were going badly there. These opinions could hardly be described as evidence of "resolute support". Churchill also exaggerates the differences between the naval attack up to March 8th and the operation on March 18th. It is hardly accurate to describe the first method as gradual and tentative with limited liability and the other as something different and more hazardous. Exactly the same method was used on March 18th as on previous occasions. All that was different was the scale of the attack. It is also dubious judgment on Churchill's part to see Fisher's offer to take command at the Dardanelles as evidence that Fisher supported the operation. As suggested earlier it is far more likely that by this time Fisher was convinced of Carden's incompetence and that the offer was made in desperation to try to salvage something from the ruins.

The only other high official whose opinion is considered in this section of The World Crisis is Jackson. His memorandum of March 11th, which deprecated a rush at the Straits, but recommended a landing in force on the Gallipoli Peninsula is quoted in full by Churchill who states that it "reveals a certain confusion of thought".[149] There is certainly something to be said for this point of view. No one had suggested a rush at the Straits. However by concentrating on this aspect of Jackson's paper Churchill is able to ignore the quite clear recommendation of a military landing. He thus conveniently obscures the fact that here was plain advice from a "high authority", previously held up as a supporter of the purely naval attack, that the navy could not achieve success alone.

The effect which the naval bombardment had on the Balkan states is now investigated by Churchill. He claims the effect was "electrical". "The attitude of Bulgaria changed with lightning swiftness....The attitude of Roumania also became one of extreme and friendly vigilance....On March 2 our Minister at Bucharest telegraphed that the Roumanian Prime Minister had said that his conviction that Italy 'would move soon' had become stronger."[150] There is no doubt that Churchill is justified in the view that the opening of the naval bombardment had an effect on the Balkan states. It was shown earlier that several countries immediately expressed more sympathy to the allied cause. But the impression given by The World Crisis is that there were a group of states awaiting the first opportunity to declare for the Entente. This was by no means the case. No commitments of any kind were received by the allies during the period of the naval attack. Moreover, in stressing that the situation changed with lightning swiftness Churchill has ignored the fact that it could change back again at the same speed. The opinions of the Bulgarian and Roumanian authorities which were quoted in the first part of this chapter suggest that the situation was extremely volatile but that the Balkan states were very cautious in their approach. Churchill also ignores the fact that these states were far more likely to be influenced by events on the Russian front than by the activities of a handful of obsolete battleships at the Dardanelles. Thus changes in Balkan attitudes cannot always, or even often, be put down to what was happening at Gallipoli. Churchill is prepared to admit that the cession of Constantinople to Russia "was bound to cause unfavourable reactions in Greece, Bulgaria and Roumania"[151] but he does not follow this statement through and investigate the form which those unfavourable reactions took. Nor does he seem to be aware of the possibility that the news of the Russian acquisition might have been regarded in the Balkans as being more important to their destinies than the naval operations at the Dardanelles.

It is, however, the reaction of Greece to the operation on which Churchill concentrates. He recounts how the Greek offer of troops was made and the hopeful prospects which it opened up. He then continues:

"But now a terrible fatality intervened [note once more the intervention of the fates]. Russia - failing, reeling backward under the German hammer, with her munitions running short, cut off from her allies - Russia was the Power which ruptured irretrievably this brilliant and decisive combination. On March 3 the Russian Foreign Minister informed our Ambassador that:- 'The Russian Government could not consent to Greece participating in operations in the Dardanelles, as it would be sure to lead to complications.'"[152]

It should be noted that this passage once more contains the assertion that a victory at the Dardanelles could have saved Russia and somehow enabled Britain and France to augment her depleted supplies of munitions from their own non-existent surplus. However, the main point to observe is that Churchill considers that it was the Russian veto which caused the Greeks to withdraw their offer of troops. Yet it was shown earlier that it was the opposition of the Greek General Staff and the King that led to the offer being withdrawn. Churchill, however, quotes a letter from the British Military Attache in Athens which makes it appear that the Greek General Staff approved of the offer of troops,[153] but this quotation does not make it clear that the Staff would have only supported the offer in the event of Bulgaria declaring for the allies and attacking Turkey. Furthermore Churchill does not explain that although the Russians modified their position a week later and agreed to limited Greek participation, this had no effect on the Army or the King. It may be thought that, as the chronology of the incident is complicated and as Churchill did not have access to Greek records, he might be excused his error. However it is revealed by the Churchill Papers that although this may have applied to the first edition of The World Crisis it should not be applied to later editions. Just after the publication of Churchill's second volume, he received a letter from Venizelos. Concerning the withdrawal of the Greek offer Venizelos said, "Neither King Constantine nor the Chiefs of the parties summoned to the two Crown Councils held under the presidency of the King in February of 1915, took the opportunity to invoke the Russian objections to the action of Greece in favour of the opinion held by some of them that it was in the interest of Greece to take no part in the Dardanelles attack."[154] Thus, Churchill was aware that the Greek decision came about through internal political considerations rather than from the Russian veto. Yet he chose not to correct the account given in The World Crisis in later editions. The reason for this must remain speculative and could be as simple as an unwillingness to spend further time on the book. However, the fact remains that the version of events supplied to Churchill by Venizelos would have dealt a serious blow to the chain of "fatalistic causation" which Churchill was building up to explain the British defeat at the Dardanelles. It suited this theory to have the Greeks quixotically rebuffed by Russia, who thus ensured their own doom, rather than to put the decision down to cold political calculation by the Greek authorities.

Churchill's version of events surrounding Admiral de Robeck's "change of plan" must now be discussed. Churchill first speculates on what led de Robeck to call off the naval attack. Naturally he is unaware that de Robeck well before March 18th had expressed the opinion that troops would be needed. He concludes that it was the shock of losing so many ships that broke the Admiral's resolve to continue:

"to an Admiral of this standing and upbringing, these old ships were sacred. They had been the finest ships afloat in the days when he as a young officer had first set foot upon their decks. The discredit and even disgrace of casting away a ship was ingrained deeply by years of mental training and outlook. The spectacle of this noble structure on which so many loyalties centred, which was the floating foothold of daily life, foundering miserably beneath the waves, appeared as an event shocking and unnatural in its character. Whereas a layman or soldier might have rejoiced that so important an action as that of March 18 could have been fought with a loss of less than thirty British lives [so much for the 600 Frenchman lost on Bouvet] and two or three worthless ships, [one third of de Robeck's force was sunk or out of action] and that so many valuable conclusions had been attained [what were they?] at such a slender cost, Admiral de Robeck was saddened and consternated to the foundations of his being".[155]

This passage has been quoted at length because it is one of the most fatuous pieces of writing in The World Crisis. It will be remembered that de Robeck's reasons for breaking off the naval attack were cogently and logically set down in his telegram to Churchill of March 27th and that they had nothing to do with feelings of sentiment towards old battleships. It was also noted that Churchill's comment on this telegram was "the reasons you give make it clear that a combined operation is indispensible". In fact de Robeck's telegram is included in The World Crisis directly after the long passage quoted above but Churchill's contemporary response is omitted and he merely says that the telegram "consolidated all the oppositions to action."[156]

Concerning his response to de Robeck's decision Churchill states that his major worry was the difficulty of the impending military attack.

"I feared the perils of the long delay; I feared still more the immense and incalculable extension of the enterprise involved in making a military attack on a large scale. The mere process of landing an army after giving the enemy at least three weeks' additional notice seemed to me to be a most terrible and formidable hazard. It appeared to me at the time a far graver matter in every way than the naval attack."[157]

If this was really Churchill's attitude at the time it was short-lived. Looking ahead, we find him telling the War Council on April 6th that he "anticipated no difficulty in effecting a landing",[158] and soon after this he told Balfour, "You must not be unduly apprehensive of the Military operation".[159] Nor is Churchill's description of his attitude in The World Crisis consistent with his message to de Robeck that a military attack was "indispensible". It is thus hard to avoid the conclusion that Churchill's apprehensions about a military attack in The World Crisis owe a great deal to hindsight.

In an earlier version of The World Crisis, Churchill had commented on de Robeck's telegram: "I read this telegram with consternation. It was plain to me from the beginning that some absolutely confused decision had been come to on the spot between the naval and military authorities and that a dangerous compromise had resulted."[160] Churchill later deleted this section. It certainly implied that he placed the blame for breaking off the naval attack partly on Hamilton as well as de Robeck and he may have wanted to avoid this criicism of his friend. Furthermore, correspondence with Hamilton while The World Crisis was being written reveals that Hamilton informed Churchill that this decision had been de Robeck's alone,[161] an opinion that Churchill was probably only too glad to accept.

In discussing the meeting of the Admiralty War Group which upheld de Robeck's decision to cancel the naval attack, Churchill merely comments adversely on the "infirm relaxation of purpose".[162] Initially he had gone much further than this in his criticism of his Admiralty colleagues. In a draft chapter he had written:

"the Admirals seemed entirely happy that the army was going to pull the chestnuts out of the fire...they seemed to think that a military attack on the Peninsula in the prevailing conditions was a small thing compared to breaking their old ships up to fight the Turkish forts in the Straits...everybody pulled long faces at the petty losses of March 18 and appeared quite cheerful about the awful impending slaughter of April 25."[163]

This deleted passage is important for indicating the depth of Churchill's feelings against those who thwarted a further naval attack.

The consequences of de Robeck's decision to break off the naval attack are now summed up by Churchill.

"It was a far-reaching decision. It put aside altogether the policy of the Government and of the Admiralty, with which, up to this, the Admiral had declared himself in full accord. The plans which had emanated from the Fleet, on which both Admiral and Admiralty had been agreed, were cast to the winds. It withdrew the Fleet from the struggle, and laid the responsibilities of the Navy upon the Army. It committed the Army in the most unfavourable conditions to an enterprise of extreme hazard and of first magnitude."[164]

This statement makes far too much of de Robeck's decision and assigns to him a responsibility more properly borne by others. All de Robeck had decided was that the navy could not get through the Straits unaided. It was not he who "committed the Army to an enterprise of extreme hazard". This decision was made by Kitchener, Hamilton and - though it was by default - the War Council and the Cabinet. The onus was on these authorities to veto the military landing if they thought the risk too great. Churchill, for instance, could have at any time registered a protest about landing an army under such "unfavourable conditions" but as we saw this was far from being his attitude at the time. De Robeck did not "put aside" the policy of the Government and the Admiralty as Churchill claims in The World Crisis. Those bodies put aside that policy themselves and no dissenting voice was raised against the landing of the army.

We must now deal at some length with a speculative chapter in The World Crisis called "The Case for Perseverence and Decision" in which Churchill makes the case for a continuance of the naval attack after March 18th.

Churchill states that the defences within the Straits consisted of four factors; forts, mobile howitzers, minefield batteries, and minefields.

"All [were] well combined but all mutually dependent. The minefields blocked the passage of the Straits and kept the Fleet beyond their limits. The minefield batteries prevented the sweeping of the minefields. The forts protected the minefield batteries by keeping battleships at a distance with their long guns. The mobile howitzers kept the battleships on the move and increased the difficulty of overcoming the forts. So long as all four factors stood together, the defences constituted a formidable obstruction. But not one could stand by itself, and if one were broken down, its fall entailed the collapse of the others."[165]

There are several dubious assumptions here. For example let us imagine that the mobile howitzers had been eliminated. This would have enabled the battleships to anchor within the Straits and consequently the accuracy of their fire would have improved. But was this a vital factor? In the two weeks firing on the intermediate defences and at the forts at the Narrows only a handful of guns had been put out of action. No doubt this performance could have been bettered had the ships been able to anchor. However the main minefield still would have kept the ships at a range long enough to make hitting the guns at the forts a very protracted procedure. It is open to question whether the fleet had the necessary ammunition to engage in this kind of operation or whether the continual firing would have not worn down the old guns to such an extent that their accuracy was destroyed. To take another factor, suppose the forts at the Narrows had not existed or had been abandoned. Churchill assumes that this would have enabled the Fleet to close up to the edge of the minefield and destroy the minefield batteries which would have then enabled the sweeping to begin. But would the Fleet have been able to destroy these batteries? Many of them were concealed from direct view. Would the low trajectory guns of the ships have been able to range on these small targets? Obviously these questions are a matter of some debate but it would not seem to follow that the fall of one sector of the Straits defences automatically meant the fall of the others. Of course Churchill's passage in The World Crisis is rather irrelevant to the actual operation for the British Fleet proved unable to destroy any of the four components of the Turkish defence.

Churchill now turns his attention to the forts.

"The forts by themselves could not withstand the Fleet. They were vulnerable to indirect fire from over the Peninsula. They could be dominated and greatly injured by direct fire from inside the Straits below the minefields. Lastly, they could be forced to exhaust their ammunition in conflict with the Fleet. The amount of ammunition possessed by the Turks is therefore cardinal."[166]

All of these assumptions can be challenged although it is probably true but rather irrelevant to say that the forts alone could not have withstood the Fleet. It was never proved that the forts were vulnerable to indirect fire. Several shells from the Queen Elizabeth hit the forts but no irreparable damage was done. Secondly it was proved conclusively that the Fleet could not greatly injure the forts from inside the Straits and it is incredible that Churchill can make a statement to the contrary. In addition it is by no means certain that the forts could have been forced to exhaust their ammunition by the ships. This assumes that the Fleet had a supply of ammunition large enough to subject the forts to a long and steady bombardment and that this would have always provoked a reply by the forts. In fact the ammunition supply for the Fleet was strictly limited. Also it would not have been necessary for all the Turkish guns in the forts to respond to an attack by the Fleet. On many occasions the forts fell silent only to resume firing when the ships closed in. Thus it was possible for the Turks to conserve their ammunition in ways that were not open to the Fleet.

Concerning the "cardinal" question of the Turkish ammunition supply, Churchill quotes figures which are an amalgam of those given by Enver Bey and Djevad to the Mitchell Committee,[167] although the fact that they came from the report of that committee is not stated. Also quoted are the much lower totals given by Captain Serri[168] but it is not mentioned that the Mitchell Committee suggested that his evidence was unreliable and based on hearsay. The main figures used by Churchill are, however, as reliable as any likely to be obtained but he then goes on to say "that for the heavy guns which alone could injure the armoured ships, they had not twenty rounds a piece."[169] Now to reach this total Churchill cannot be using the figures of Enver or Djevad for they reveal that the 14" guns had 40-47 rounds per gun remaining and the 9.4" 79. He is perhaps using figures from the German official account which, as we have seen, quoted approximately 20 rounds H.E. per heavy gun. In fact this evidence is contradicted by a note by the Mitchell Committee which says that most of the forts had 20 H.E. and 20 Armour Piercing left per heavy gun and as A.P. was also effective against armoured ships this doubles the total effective shells per gun remaining to the Turks.[170] Further doubt is thrown on the German figures by the fact that their estimate for the 9.4" guns is between 30 and 50 shells per gun and the figures given to the Mitchell Committee were almost double at around 79 shells per gun. In The World Crisis both sets are quoted by Churchill [171] but he does not comment on the discrepancy. Perhaps if he had noticed it he would have been less confident that the figure of 20 rounds per gun included all the shells capable of inflicting damage on the Fleet and more wary of trying to build a case on such shaky foundations.

The conclusions drawn from the Turkish ammunition figures by Churchill are as ambiguous as his arithmetical calculations. He states that "We knew at the time from secret sources, the credit of which was unquestionable, that the Turkish Army was short of ammunition. We had only to resume a gradual naval advance and bombardment to discover the wonderful truth that they had, in fact, scarcely any more ammunition".[172] It is not clear if Churchill intended his first statement to apply to the Turkish Army as a whole. If he did then the alleged shortage did not materialize during the Gallipoli campaign. Churchill's next statement that the forts had "scarcely any more ammunition" is contradicted by the figures which he quotes on the previous pages and by the conclusion drawn from the figures by the Turks, which Churchill seems to accept, that two more attacks on the scale of March 18th could have been sustained. Perhaps Churchill regards a supply of ammunition for two more attacks as being "scarcely any more". However, it should be pointed out that the guns of the Fleet would have been considerably worn after two more such attacks and the number of ships available for the Marmora substantially reduced. In fact, as Churchill admits, after exhausting their modern ammunition the Turks would have switched to the older shells and by this means could have engaged the Fleet in an indefinite number of attacks.

This point brings us to the crux of the debate about Turkish ammunition. It was suggested earlier that the ammunition question was not as crucial as Churchill thought it to be. For, as has been shown, provided the forts were firing some kind of shells the British would have been forced to engage them at long range and whether the shell could destroy the ships was hardly relevant as hits were made so infrequently. At long range it had been proved that the ships could destroy neither the forts nor the minefield defences. Churchill never addresses himself to this problem. Furthermore, his whole argument about ammunition rests on the assumption that once the forts were silenced the minefield defences could have been destroyed and the minefields swept, an assumption, as our previous discussion showed, which was hardly warranted by the previous performance of the Fleet.

Churchill next attempts to prove that there was no shortge of ammunition for the Fleet. He does this by quoting figures which prove that the stocks of 12" shell held by the Admiralty remained at the same levels from the beginning of the war until March 1915 (56,000 rounds) and from then on greatly increased deliveries were received. Similar statistics are quoted for the smaller calibres.[173] However, these are total figures for the entire Fleet and the magazines which held these stocks were all in Britain. A much more relevant question, which Churchill does not answer, is the extent to which these stocks were available to Carden and de Robeck. They were clearly low on supplies throughout the naval operation as the continuous requests to the ships to limit their expenditure of shells shows. A further point to be made is that it is questionable whether the old guns could have engaged in repeated heavy bombardments without cracking or requiring reboring. Even Churchill admits that this was a "limiting factor".[174]

Two more facets of the defence, torpedo tubes and floating mines, are then examined by Churchill. He claims that "No factor exercised a more deterrent effect upon the attackers than the possibility and alleged existence of large numbers of torpedo - tubes on each side of the Straits,"[175] and he then goes on to prove that the tubes were of negligible importance. Now it is true that in the letter explaining why the naval attack had been broken off, de Robeck mentioned that torpedo-tubes increased the difficulties for the Fleet. But to say that this factor was among the greatest deterrents to further action is a wild exaggeration. Even the most casual reading of the Admiral's message reveals that the vital factors were the unswept minefields and the inability of the Fleet to destroy the defences protecting them. Moreover the information to Churchill in 1923 concerning the torpedo-tubes was hardly available to de Robeck eight years earlier.

Exactly the same point can be made about Churchill's paragraph on floating mines. He states that the Turks had only forty of these available and half of them had been released by March 18th.[176] De Robeck could not possibly have known this at the time. The damage caused to the ships on March 18th. mainly occurred in an area supposedly free from mines. That the Turks had floated mines down the Straits seemed to be the most likely explanation. Floating mines had to be taken into calculation by the Admiral on the spot and Churchill does little to strengthen his case by pointing out with knowledge gained after the war that they could have been ignored.

In one paragraph of this chapter Churchill does admit that "the force of minesweepers provided by the Admiralty was ... inadequate both in numbers and efficiency".[177] However, the Churchill Papers reveal that he was originally in a much more chastened mood. In a retrospective section, at first included in the chapter on Suvla Bay[178], and which looked back over the whole operation, Churchill gave three reasons for the failure of the naval attack. These were: the inadequate amount of ammunition available to the Fleet, the inadequate spotting force and the inefficiency of the minesweepers. He then went on to say, "These three serious defects in detail brought to temporary failure a conception in itself sound. For all of them in spite of their technical character, I must accept to the full a general responsibility."[179] This last sentence was then crossed through and eventually the whole section was omitted. The paragraph is interesting because it is the only occasion on which Churchill admits responsibility for anything other than the quality of the minesweepers. Furthermore in the chapter under discussion so far from admitting that the ammunition supply was inadequate he has gone to considerable lengths to prove that it was sufficient. Finally, although the defects admitted were of a technical nature, in a sense Churchill was correct to take responsibility for them. For by rushing through the operation he ensured that adequate time to consider technical problems was not available. However it is clear that he had no intention of admitting this in The World Crisis.

Churchill endeavours to strengthen his opinion that the Fleet could have forced the Straits after March 18th. by quoting the views of a number of Turkish and German officers. With the exceptions of Enver Pasha and Major Endres all the officers quoted in The World Crisis were interviewed by the post-war Mitchell Committee, although Churchill does not acknowledge this fact. One general comment on the worth of these informants is in order. They were representatives of the losing side facing a series of questions from the victors. That there would be a certain urge to please their interrogators and supply the type of answers that was thought to be wanted would seem a reasonable conclusion. However, no caution or any qualification about their evidence appears in The World Crisis and Churchill obviously expects the reader to take their comments at face value.

Of the seven Mitchell Committee informants quoted by Churchill five, Souchon, Balzer, Serri, the Dardanos signal officer, and the Lieutenant on the Hamidieh all expected that the allied Fleet would get through. One, Salahidden, thought that the ships could get through if the mines were disposed of (a fairly fundamental qualification) and another, Djevad, did not expect the Fleet to succeed.[180] However, the Mitchell Committee interviewed 10 officers and they divided: five in favour of the Fleet getting through, four against, and Salahidden doubtful.[181] Thus three officers who took a pessimistic view of the Fleet's chances are not quoted by Churchill. One of these officers, Major Zati, Chief of Staff to G.O.C. Dardanelles, was described by the Mitchell Committee as an officer who "did not appear to possess any great knowledge or ability".[182] Another, Commander Hilmi Bey, a Turkish Navy gunnery officer, was said by Mitchell to be "Friendly and anxious to please. Some detailed knowledge of gunnery, but not much weight should be attached to his general opinions".[183] Thus far Churchill could be excused for deciding to omit the testimony of these informants. The exclusion of Enver Bey is a more serious omission. Enver thought that the British would be held up by the minefields and the Mitchell Committee suggested that "Some weight must ... be attached to his opinions, owing to the opportunities of the position he held on the Naval Staff [C.O.S. to Souchon] particularly as regards the capacities of the

Turkish Fleet."[184]   It seems reasonable to conclude then
that any truly impartial survey of these men should include
Enver Bey on the negative side.

More serious defects in Churchill's account are found
when the remainder of his list is examined. Thus Churchill
describes Col. Salahidden, whom he places on the positive
side, as a "very capable Turkish soldier".[185] This is a
quotation from the Mitchell Committee Report but Churchill
has omitted the remainder of the sentence which reads "and in
general, though not always, his statements were
reliable".[186] Furthermore the signal officer at Fort
Dardanos (Lt. Hussan-Ed-Din), who is quoted in The World
Crisis, is described thus in the Report: "Although willing
to impart information, this officer did not appear to be very
capable or reliable".[187] This qualification was not
printed by Churchill. In addition Mitchell pointed out that
the First Lieutenant of the Hamidieh whom Churchill also
quotes had as his "main object" the desire to please "and no
weight can be given to his opinions".[188] No mention is
made of this statement in The World Crisis. Thus although
Churchill has omitted those informants thought to be
unreliable who took a negative view of the chances of the
fleet, he has included all those with a positive outlook no
matter how untrustworthy they seem to be. Moreover, one of
the more reliable informants whose views coincide with
Churchill's, Lt-Commander Balzer, was located in Berlin
during the entire naval attack. His contribution must be
regarded then as entirely theoretical.

The major contribution by an "expert authority" comes
from Major Endres, who was C.O.S. of the First Turkish Army
and answered a set of questions on Gallipoli sent to him by
Churchill.[189] How reliable is his testimony? Before
including Endres' answers in The World Crisis Churchill put
this question to Sir John Edmonds, the official British
historian of the war. Edmonds replied, "I should say that he
has a good knowledge of Turkey & the Turkish Army but as he
was not with Limans army would have no special knowledge of
Gallipoli".[190] This is a very important qualification and
would seem to reduce the value of Endres' contribution.
However this did not prevent Churchill giving Endres' answers
to his questionnaire great prominence in The World Crisis or
using them to help him prove his case.

There is one topic which is noticeable by its absence in
Churchill's retrospective chapter, namely, what would have
been the result had the fleet succeeded after March 18th and
proceeded to Constantinople. This topic is not dealt with at
all. Rather Churchill relies on an unwritten assumption that
success in forcing the Straits was tantamount to victory –
that is either the Turks would surrender when the fleet
appeared before Constantinople, or they would be brought to
heel by the threat of a sustained bombardment. However, it
was suggested earlier that although the evidence of what the

Turks might have done had the fleet got through is contradictory, it is by no means certain that victory was inevitable. By not discussing this issue, Churchill concentrates the mind of the reader on the events at the Straits, where it is implied the most important and final aspect of the campaign was taking place.

Chapter 8

## THE DARDANELLES III - MILITARY FAILURE

The 29th Division commenced sailing from England on March 16th. Originally it had been intended to disembark the troops on the Greek island of Lemnos, near the Dardanelles, but the inadequacies of the island as a base (few landing facilities and little water) forced a diversion to Alexandria. Upon arrival there it was found that the division had been loaded onto the transports in a way which made landing on open beaches impossible. All the ships therefore had to be unpacked and reloaded. This caused some delay but given the circumstances in which the division was despatched a delay was inevitable. In March, when the transports were being packed, the responsible War Office and Admiralty authorities in England knew of no plan to land the 29th Division on open beaches. In fact, at that stage, there was no plan. The naval attack was proceeding and it was thought likely that the army would only be required for "a cruise in the Sea of Marmora" to use Kitchener's phrase. Therefore the 29th Division was not tactically loaded onto the transports. Even had it been known that such a landing was contemplated it is doubtful if much could have been accomplished without a detailed plan. As Braithwaite (C.O.S. to Hamilton) said,

"I do not think anybody could stow the ships properly, except the people who knew how the men were going to be taken off the ships .... We took the different beaches, and saw how many men we could get on to them, and from that we worked it backwards on to the boats, on to the lighters, on to the ships, and into the holds."[1]

In other words, the transports could only be properly stowed after Hamilton's plan had been formulated in detail.

This debate over the delays in landing the division raises a related question over the delay in its despatch from Britain. Had the 29th Division been sent earlier (that is when Kitchener first decided to release it on February 16th)

could it have landed on the Peninsula in mid-March? The crucial factor was the weather. Between February and April 25th the weather was particularly unsettled with long periods of gale force winds and rough seas.[2] Whether the navy would have agreed to land the army in these conditions is conjectural, as is the question of whether the army could have been sustained on the Peninsula during long periods of bad weather. Of course had the 29th Division sailed a month earlier (mid-February instead of mid-March) there is no reason to suppose that its transports would have been packed any differently. Thus there would probably have been a two week delay to repack them which would have meant that the earliest the army could have landed was early April, a period of very bad weather indeed. Obviously in discussing a question of this kind no final conclusion can be reached but it is clearly imprudent to assume that the only factor affecting the landing of the 29th Division was its date of dispatch from England. A complementary question is how much the Turkish defences were strengthened between mid-March and April 25th. It is usually stated that the appointment of Liman von Sandars to the command of the Turkish 5th Army on March 24th was the crucial factor and that the measures undertaken on his instructions were responsible for the establishment of an adequate defence. No doubt Liman brought new energy to the defence but the major landing places had been trenched and wired well before he took command,[3] and this factor alone meant that any landing in March would have been a considerable undertaking.

Consideration now has to be given to the task facing Hamilton. It was estimated, fairly accurately, that there were 40,000 Turks on the Peninsula and 30,000 nearby in reserve.[4] In addition many of the Turkish Armies' 22 divisions could reinforce the Gallipoli garrison in the event of a protracted struggle. As Hamilton had only 70,000 men available (the Anzac Corps, the Royal Naval Division, a French division and the 29th Division) the essence of success was a quick victory. No consideration was ever given by Hamilton or the home authorities to the question of whether such a victory could be obtained with the force available. Indeed, no formal meeting of the War Council was ever held to consider the feasibility of a military landing. Nevertheless, Hamilton remained outwardly confident of success despite the pessimism of two of his divisional commanders.[5] He may have thought in the light of Kitchener's directive that he had little choice but to attempt a landing. His sanguine temperament no doubt made the task of converting this necessity into a virtue relatively easy.

Hamilton's main problem was where to land. The Asiatic coast was forbidden him by Kitchener but the lack of suitable landing places and the rough nature of the ground probably excluded it anyway. Bulair, the obvious place at the neck of the Peninsula, was too heavily defended. Much of the coast to the south was lined with cliffs. In the end the choice lay between Hellas and Gaba Tepe. Hamilton chose to make the main landing at Hellas because of the assistance which could be given by the fleet. However, Hellas had considerable disadvantages. It was much further from the ultimate objective, the Narrows forts, than Gaba Tepe. The only landing places were very narrow and would inhibit rapid deployment, so necessary for success. Hamilton also knew at the time that the Hellas beaches were heavily defended with a "complete system of trenches and entanglements, supported by guns in concealed positions".[6] He was also aware that naval gunfire was ineffective against wire and trenches.[7]

Landing his whole force at Gaba Tepe (where Hamilton intended to make his secondary assault with the Anzacs) would have placed it within striking distance of the Narrows. However, the route across the Peninsula was dominated by high ground to the north and south and therefore open to attack from both directions. Probably Hamilton would not have had sufficient men to throw out defensive flanks, advance across the Peninsula and capture the Narrows forts. The inescapable fact is that wherever Hamilton landed, his force was not adequate for the task in hand.

As Hamilton finalized his plans, Fisher's doubts about the operation surfaced once more. Previously, as has been observed, Fisher based his opposition to naval involvement at the Dardanelles on the ground that it weakened the Grand Fleet. However, during February and March he had pushed for troops to be sent to the East to convert the attack into a combined operation. Now his opinion began to harden against the operation as a whole. In a series of memoranda to Churchill he suggested that fundamental questions about the sufficiency of Hamilton's force were not being asked. He felt unable to rely on the judgement of Hamilton and de Robeck and requested that Churchill circulate his memoranda to the War Council with a view to stimulating an independent survey of the situation by that body.[8] Churchill refused. Perhaps the final chance for a reappraisal of the operation was lost.

On April 7th the Junior Sea Lords (Hamilton, Tudor, Lambert) seemingly strengthened Fisher's anti-Dardanelles stand. They presented him with a memorandum which stated that they wished to be reassured that extraneous operations such as the Dardanelles were not endangering the superiority of the Grand Fleet and that naval strategy was still being decided by the First Sea Lord.[9] Here, it might be thought, was a chance for Fisher to form a united front against Churchill and demand that he take some action on Fisher's papers questioning the Dardanelles strategy. It seems certain that this option was not considered by the First Sea Lord. He was of the firm opinion that the Junior Sea Lords should not be involved in matters of strategy and it was he who had removed the Second Sea Lord from the Admiralty War Group. He merely wrote the Sea Lords a mildly worded reply, assuring them that the Grand Fleet was safe but stating that no more material of any kind could be sent to de Robeck.[10]

A clearer indication of Fisher's position is contained in a memorandum which he wrote for Churchill later on April 7th. He argued that as Italy was about to join the Allies, the Dardanelles attack should be postponed until after that country had definitely come in, as failure might prejudice her conduct.[11] Churchill would not hear of an alternative strategy. Indeed he had been furious with Richmond, the originator of Fisher's scheme, for submitting his paper in the first place.[12] Thus ended Fisher's attempt to stop the Dardanelles operation. From this point his communications to Churchill on the subject became less frequent and although he remained pessimistic, all he could do, as he told Jellicoe, was hope that the defenders made "a mess of it".[13]

Originally scheduled for April 23rd the military landing was delayed by the weather until the 25th. In the south the 29th Division was to land at the foot of the Peninsula while the French created a diversion at Kum Kale, from where they would later be evacuated and join the main advance inland. In the north the Anzacs would land north of Gaba Tepe while the R.N.D. feinted a landing at Bulair.

At Hellas a covering force of 6,000 men was to land at five beaches, followed by the main body when the landing places were secure. The three main landings were to take place at the foot of the Peninsula at beaches V, W and X. These troops were immediately to advance up the Peninsula and link up with the flank landings at Y and S, whereupon the whole force would move on Achi Baba, a ridge dominating the southern end of the Peninsula.

The landings were covered by a naval bombardment which in the event was a considerable failure. Visibility was poor,[14] the airspotting arrangements broke down,[15] the number of shells used had to be limited,[16] and in any case it was known that the armour piercing shells used by the navy were ineffective against wire entanglements and trenches.[17] There were local difficulties. Because of a change in orders,[18] only one ship covered the major landing at V beach and for the entire day this ship (Albion) fired only 12 shells from its main armament.[19]

If Hamilton's plan was to work, quick successes were needed at V, W and X. But at V and W the landing places formed amphitheatres which gave the Turkish defenders (only some 200 at each place)[20] perfect shooting. The men were shot down in heaps often before they had reached the beach. The expedient of landing troops from a British collier (River Clyde) only provided the Turks with a better target as the men issued from several sally ports cut in the sides. It is hard to see why the massacres at V and W were not anticipated. The restricted nature of the beaches could clearly be seen from the sea and Hamilton was aware that ship's fire could not destroy the trenches and wire. Yet it was here that he chose to land the bulk of the covering force whose success was vital to the whole operation.

Ironically, on the flanks, where the landings did succeed, the troops had no orders to advance independently across the Peninsula or to intervene if the southern landings were held up. Their leaders had no knowledge of the number of Turks likely to be in their immediate area although the troops at Y alone outnumbered the entire Turkish force south of Achi Baba. The troops at Y and S, therefore, dug in according to orders and remained inactive for the whole day.[21] Y was evacuated on the 26th after a heavy night attack, and S was eventually joined to the main body on the 27th.

An opportunity to convert the flank landings into something more important came on the 25th when Hamilton suggested to the divisional commander, Hunter-Weston, that troops be diverted from V and W to Y.[22] Hunter-Weston refused on the grounds that this would disrupt the naval landing arrangements.[23] He continued to reinforce failure by sending additional men to V and W throughout the day and Hamilton declined to overrule him, reasoning that the man on the spot knew best. In fact, Hunter-Weston, offshore on the Euryalus, had little more local knowledge than Hamilton, and at the time Hamilton's request was made had not grasped that the situation at V was desperate.

Much has been made of the "lost opportunities" at Y and S. In retrospect they seem largely theoretical. To strike out into the unknown, against orders, could hardly be expected of junior officers in 1915. The higher command could have exploited the situation but this would have involved shifting the entire centre of gravity of the operation while it was in progress, a considerable undertaking given the primitive state of communications.

Another theoretical opportunity existed at X. Here the covering force and the main body had landed with few casualties. These troops also remained inactive for most of the day.[24] Their commander could not commit them to the battle without divisional sanction as they consisted largely of the divisional reserve. But Hunter-Weston, still in Euryalus, was unaware of the success at X and the commander of the covering force, who might have coordinated their movements, was dead. When the Brigadier in local command at X went to see for himself the position at W, the neighbouring beach, he was wounded.[25] Deprived of their senior officers, the men dug in on the edge of the beach and waited.

Thus at S, X and Y the troops were ashore and well established. At W the position gradually improved throughout the day and a foothold was secured. At V nightfall gave the survivors of the day the opportunity to scramble ashore though they were barely able to advance beyond the edge of the slope overlooking the beach.

From the 26th to the 28th various efforts were made to coordinate an advance inland. All ultimately failed. There seem to be two main factors involved in these failures. The most obvious was the exhaustion of the troops, who by the evening of the 26th had been without sleep and proper food for 48 hours. Also, the most exhausted troops were usually found where the enemy's resistance had been strongest but in the prevailing doctrine of the day it was at these points that new attacks had to be made. Thus on the 26th while the weary survivors at V beach spent most of the day taking Sedd-el-Bahr village and the hill that overlooked it,[26] virtually no fighting took place on the front of the fresher troops at X.[27]

Fatigue was also a factor on the 27th. The troops on the right of the line (the survivors of W and V) were by then thought to be incapable of further effort. Before an advance could be made it was necessary to replace them with the relatively fresh French troops. But shortage of small craft and congestion on the beaches meant delay in landing the French and the advance did not begin until the afternoon.[28] Thus although no Turkish opposition was experienced when this forward movement got underway, it was only possible to reach a line Gully Beach-S beach before nightfall.[29]

From the 28th onwards a new factor had to be taken into account. This was the increasing strength of the Turks in the area. On the 25th the landing had been opposed by no more than 800 men with another 1,000 in local reserve.[30] By April 27th there were at least 6,000 Turks south of Achi Baba though few were in contact with the British.[31] On April 28th (the date of the First Battle of Krithia) this number had increased to between 8,000 and 10,000.[32] The British and the French entered this battle with no more than 14,000 men,[33] and thus did not possess the necessary superiority to ensure success. However, other factors on the British side make it doubtful if an advance could have been made, had only half the number of Turks been present. The troops on the left of the line were worn out, the strain of the last three days having finally taken its toll.[34] In other sections of the line ammunition had begun to run out[35] and to move supplies from the beach meant men had to be taken out of the firing line. The only reserves at hand were the exhausted 86th Brigade which had just been replaced by the French and although a small party of these men got within 3/4 mile of Krithia, the Turkish line was in no sense broken.[36]

It has often been said that if a new division had been available to throw into the battle after the landings, a victory could have been obtained. This proposition, however, begs the important question of whether it would have been possible to land the additional division before corresponding

Turkish reinforcements were brought up. We have already seen that due to the crowding on the beaches and the lack of small craft, the French were unable to land before the 27th. Even a small body like the Zion Mule Corps took three days to disembark at V beach.[37] Moreover, the unloading of the stores and material of the 29th Division was not completed until 10 days after the landing.[38] Given this situation it is doubtful if the necessary small craft would have been available to land an extra division,[39] or if they had, that the congestion on the beaches would have allowed the unloading of their supplies. Furthermore, if a third division had landed and advanced inland say for three or four miles, it is possible that they would have outrun their logistic support. With the troops virtually on the edge of the coast it was just possible to manhandle ammunition to the front line. If these troops had been 2 miles inland it has been calculated that only $1/4$ the ammunition asked for could have been supplied.[40] Thus a rapid advance could have been followed by an equally rapid retreat. In these circumstances the best that Hamilton could have hoped for was to capture Krithia or Achi Baba. Of course proponents of the plan would argue that this would have been sufficient, that the possession of Achi Baba would have enabled Hamilton to bring the Narrows forts under direct artillery and howitzer fire and that with the increased accuracy obtainable from shore based guns, he could have knocked the forts out. These assumptions are hardly justified. As many observers have pointed out there is "Not the slightest observation over Chanak or the Narrows [from Achi Baba]".[41] The view is completely obscured by a nearby spur and the Kilid Bahr Plateau.[42] Thus no assistance to the fleet could have been provided by the occupation of Achi Baba. The capture of this hill would certainly have provided relief to the troops at the foot of the Peninsula because of the excellent artillery observation point it offered to the south, but considering the campaign as a whole it was only one step along the road. The most formidable obstacle, the Kilid Bahr Plateau, was yet to come and this precipitous feature was two miles beyond Achi Baba.

The Anzac landing, although relatively lightly opposed, also failed to achieve any of its objectives. What caused this failure? It is well known that the landing took place one mile to the north of the designated beach. Because of the restricted size of Anzac Cove the landing was made on a much narrower front than had been intended and this made deployment of troops inland more difficult. The compression of the landing zone also caused units to become mixed. Some authorities have held that the troops lost cohesion because they found themselves faced with unfamiliar country. But the maps of the area were so poor, and as few of the men had any idea where they were landing anyway, this factor has probably been exaggerated.[43] The difficulty of the country rather than its unfamiliarity is probably a more important factor. Thus the tangled and tortuous ravines and spurs with which the men were now faced made merely reaching the first ridge an achievement, and although the landing was opposed only by two companies of Turkish troops,[44] no coherent move inland could be organised. A few parties of men did manage to advance to the second ridge and beyond but they remained isolated and tended to advance in different directions because of the rough going.

These are important considerations in assessing the reasons for the failure of the plan, but it is doubtful if the scheme as outlined by Hamilton ever had a chance of success. It was really absurdly ambitious to expect a force of two divisions to capture a succession of difficult positions along a ridge 4 or 5 miles long, advance 4 miles across the Peninsula, capture more difficult positions and beat off any counter attacks after this had been done. Walking over the ground after the war, Bean found the objectives almost impossible to attain even with the help of a Turkish guide.[45]

There were to be no further opportunities to break through from Anzac. By the evening of the 26th the preponderance of troops in the allies' favour had fallen to less than 2 to 1.[46] Moreover the Turks had always been able to reach the high ground ahead of the attackers and it soon became clear that no further advance was possible.

A few days later a renewed attempt was made to break out from Hellas. The only result was to decimate the southern force, 6,500 casualties being suffered in three days.[47] This experience only made Hunter-Weston more determined than ever to break through and a mixed brigade of Australian and New Zealand troops was brought to Hellas to spearhead a new attack on May 8th. The assault was a fiasco. The troops were thrown in without proper orders and with less than two hours notice. Some had little idea of where the Turkish front line was situated.[48] After the war it became clear that the advance had not even reached the main enemy trench but had been stopped by a line of skirmishers 100 yards in front of it.[49] Hamilton's force, for the moment, had shot its bolt.

The landings immediately demonstrated that one of the assumptions on which the decision to launch a combined operation had been made, namely that troops would restore the prestige lost in southern Europe by the fleet, was false. In the event the news of the landings caused hardly a stir in the Balkans. Indeed the actions of two states, Roumania and Bulgaria, indicated that the cause of the Entente had become less attractive at this time. In late April and early May they raised their price for entering the war by increasing their territorial demands to completely unrealistic dimensions.[50] It is clear that the event which precipitated this action was the series of defeats inflicted on Russia by the German armies.[51] If the British expected these setbacks to be offset by an army of 70,000 men that was manifestly finding the Turks difficult to defeat they were deluded. The attention of the Balkan States continued to be focused on the Eastern Front.

In Britain the news of the landings was greeted with mixed feelings. It was felt that to effect a lodgement ashore in enemy territory was a great achievement. On the other hand the heavy casualties caused concern. Churchill's initial reaction to the landings was to write to Kitchener suggesting that 20,000 men be despatched to Hamilton immediately.[52] This letter was not sent but in any case Hamilton had not yet asked for reinforcements. A feature of the campaign was to be Hamilton's reluctance to request additional troops. When finally his request did arrive on April 28th it was expressed in such terms as hardly suggested an urgent need. Why Hamilton adopted this approach, which after the war he himself described as mealymouthed, is not clear.[53] Perhaps his experience as Kitchener's staff officer in South Africa led him to be too deferential.

In any event Hamilton received Kitchener's permission to take the 42nd Division and an Indian brigade from Egypt and with these fresh troops he began to plan for his next attack. It was clear however, that this operation could not take place for some time and in the interval attention turned once more to the navy.

In late March, when Churchill had acquiesced in de Robeck's decision to call off the naval attack, he had asked de Robeck what he proposed to do if the army was checked.[54] De Robeck replied that if it were thought that by forcing the Narrows the navy could assist the army, the attempt would be made. At the same time he made it clear that he considered the fleet could best assist the army "from below Chanak with communications intact [rather than] from above cut off from its base".[55] Now the situation outlined by Churchill had arisen and de Robeck immediately came under pressure from Keyes and the French Admiral, Guepratte, to renew the attack on the Narrows.[56] De Robeck refused to comply but he was induced to write to the Admiralty setting out the issues. These he saw as (1) Could forcing the Straits ensure the success of the operation? (2) Would a reverse jeopardize the position of the army? He reiterated his own opinion that the answer to the first point was no and to the second yes.[57] It is hard to disagree with this judgement. Practically the whole fleet was now needed to support the army with fire power. In addition, the ammunition supply of the fleet had not improved. On May 1st it was found that the entire fleet had only 400 rounds of 12" shell and a similar amount of 7.5".[58] It is extremely doubtful if these limited supplies would have been enough to allow extensive operations against the Turkish forts, the Turkish Navy and perhaps Constantinople, as well as supporting the army. Eventually, under pressure from Fisher, and confronted with the logic of de Robeck's case, Churchill had to submit. There was to be no further naval attempt to force the Straits.

On May 14th the War Council held its first formal meeting since March 19th. Kitchener opened proceedings by attacking the Admiralty for withdrawing the Queen Elizabeth from the Dardanelles, claiming, almost certainly incorrectly, that he had first been convinced that the operation might succeed by Churchill's statement of the power of the ship's 15" guns.[59] Churchill replied by saying that "If we had known three months ago that an army of from 80,000 to 100,000 men would now be available for the attack on the Dardanelles, the naval attack would never have been undertaken".[60] This remarkable statement ignored the fact that a force of 80-100,000 men was only provided because the naval attack had failed and that in March it was extremely unlikely that either Kitchener or the War Council would have sanctioned the removal of a large number of troops from the main theatre. Clearly this was a day for recriminations, for when Fisher was asked for his view "He reminded the War Council that he had been no party to the Dardanelles operations",[61] a scarcely accurate but, from Churchill's standpoint, a truly ominous contribution.

Churchill had noted Fisher's intervention with concern, and later in the day had a long discussion with him on the Dardanelles and what reinforcements de Robeck should be sent. The meeting seemed to end satisfactorily. As was his habit, Churchill then embodied in a minute what he thought had been agreed, for Fisher's approval in the morning. Later he made a pencilled amendment to this minute, adding a further two E class submarines for de Robeck.[62] According to Crease it was this addition plus the fact that Churchill had increased the number of monitors to be sent to the Dardanelles which caused Fisher to resign the next morning.[63] After reading Fisher's resignation letter, which indicated that the Admiral had left for Scotland,[64] Churchill informed Asquith, who wrote out a note ordering Fisher to return to his post.[65] Churchill composed a reply to Fisher. He suggested that they meet to discuss a proposition that he wanted, with the consent of Asquith, to put before him. Fisher refused to agree and a further exchange of letters did nothing to alter the situation.[66]

Later in the day the Junior Sea Lords intervened in the crisis. They wrote to Churchill and Fisher stating that they considered Fisher's resignation had been largely caused by the First Lord's continual interference in operational matters, but suggested that these difficulties should be "capable of adjustment by mutual ... concession" in the national interest, a strong hint that Fisher should return to his post and Churchill mend his ways.[67] It was clear from the tone of the letter that the Sea Lords saw it as their duty to remain in office until the crisis had been resolved. A copy of the letter was sent to Asquith.[68] After receiving the Sea Lords' letter, Churchill apparently drove to Asquith's country house and informed him that he could reconstitute the Board with Sir Arthur Wilson taking Fisher's place and the Junior Sea Lords remaining in their respective offices. However, it is by no means certain that this accurately represented the Junior Sea Lords' position. According to one version of events, on May 17th Hamilton (2nd Sea Lord) had asked Captain Hall (D.N.I.) to inform Asquith via Lord Reading that if Fisher had definitely resigned the Sea Lords considered Churchill should also go.[69] Presumably they adjudged Fisher the only man likely to keep Churchill's activities within reasonable bounds. Thus their support for Churchill was conditional on Fisher returning to office. This version does have support from another source. Hankey recorded in his diary on May 20th (that is when the Sea Lords knew that Fisher would not be returning) that "senior Admiralty officials favoured a Balfour-Wilson or a Balfour-Jackson administration".[70] In short, when it was clear that Fisher would not return the Sea Lords immediately withdrew support from Churchill.

Any chance Churchill had of remaining at the Admiralty was ended on the 17th. On that day Asquith capitulated to Bonar Law's demand for a coalition government,[71] and it was highly unlikely that Conservatives would serve in a government in which Churchill continued to direct the naval war. Sir Henry Wilson had already warned Bonar Law that Churchill was largely responsible for holding up reinforcements for France.[72] Fisher then informed the Conservative leader that the reason for his resignation had been his inability to work with Churchill.[73] In the course of the day Bonar Law made it known to Lloyd George that Churchill could not remain at the Admiralty,[74] and Churchill was informed of this decision by Asquith. Churchill's fall had been accomplished in a remarkably short time and he obviously had difficulty in adjusting to the new situation. Not realizing that his credit was exhausted and his influence nil, he wrote to Asquith with various suggestions for the new government.

> "I am sure L.G. will not do for W.O. Balfour with L.G. doing Munitions as well as Treasury wd be a far sounder arrangement. So far as I am concerned if you find it necessary to make a change here [had he not realized he was to go?] I shd be glad - assuming it was thought fitting - to be offered a position in the new government. But I will not take any office except a military department, & if that is not convenient I hope I may be found employment in the field."[75]

Meanwhile a dramatic event had taken place at sea. The German Fleet had left harbour. Churchill returned to the Admiralty and the Grand Fleet was ordered out. Would a victory at sea have been enough to restore Churchill's flagging fortunes? He must have contemplated this question as the two fleets drew closer together. But it was not to be. Before Jellicoe could intercept the High Sea Fleet, Scheer reversed course and returned to base.

On the 18th Churchill at last began to realize that his position was desperate. For the second time in three days he had been attacked editorially in the Times.[76] He now wrote to Asquith, saying that if the Colonial Office was still open to him (he had apparently refused it on the 17th), he "shd not be right to refuse it".[77] He still considered there was a chance that he could remain at the Admiralty and he concluded, "Above all things I shd like to stay here - & complete my work .... If Balfour were to go to the War Office the two departments wd work with perfect smoothness".[78] The suggestion that Kitchener, whom the Conservatives considered indispensable, be sacked to enable Churchill, whom they considered a menace, to remain, was received in silence by Asquith.

Although by the 18th it had been decided that Churchill should leave the Admiralty, Fisher's position was still undetermined. In a letter to him on the 17th Asquith hinted that he might not be excluded from office.[79] On the same day Bonar Law advised him to "keep yourself free until the new Gvt is formed".[80] These messages apparently gave Fisher the false impression that his position was relatively secure and that he could dictate terms. Perhaps advised by Lord Esher,[81] Fisher sent Asquith what amounted to an ultimatum. He demanded that Churchill and Wilson be excluded from the Admiralty and that he be given complete control of the war at sea, the sole right to distribute the fleet and a veto on all naval appointments.[82] This amazing document was seen by many as proof that Fisher had gone mad[83] and certainly ended any prospects he had of returning to the Admiralty.[84]

Churchill was also living in a dream world. On the 19th Sir A. Wilson told Asquith that, while he had consented to serve under Churchill, he would not take office under any other First Lord.[85] Churchill, considering his position had been greatly strengthened, immediately wrote to Asquith saying that he was now confident that he could get a Board as "The Three Naval Lords are also ready to serve under me".[86] However, it seems certain that Asquith now knew that opinion at the Admiralty favoured the removal of both Churchill and Fisher. Also Wilson was not the asset that Churchill imagined. Jellicoe had told Hamilton that Wilson's strategic ideas were so ludicrous that "we all doubted his sanity",[87] and Fisher warned Bonar Law that, if Wilson were appointed First Sea Lord, Jellicoe would resign.[88]

Churchill's position deteriorated further when Lord Emmot, the Under Secretary of State for the Colonies, told Asquith that Churchill's appointment to the Colonial Office would cause a revolt among the permanent officials,[89] and W.M.R. Pringle, a back bench Liberal M.P., informed the Prime Minister that a group of his supporters in the Commons regarded Churchill's presence in the Government "as a public danger".[90]

Churchill seemed oblivious to the fact that he had hardly a supporter left at Whitehall. More incredible, he still believed that he had a role to play concerning the composition of the new government and patronage to bestow. Late on the 19th he sent Lambert, the Civil Lord at the Admiralty, to Fisher offering him "any terms he liked, including a seat in the Cabinet, if he would stay with him at the Admiralty".[91] This remarkable offer, which was hardly Churchill's to make, was turned down by Fisher who immediately informed Bonar Law of Churchill's action.[92]

Perhaps the suddenness of his fall had induced in Churchill a state resembling shock for even on the 21st he believed he could remain at the Admiralty. In expressing this hope he told Asquith "It is no clinging to office or to this particular office or my own interest or advancement wh moves me. I am clinging to my task & to my duty. I am straining to make good the formidable undertaking in wh we are engaged; & wh I know - with Arthur Wilson - I can alone discharge".[93] These hopes were finally dashed by Bonar Law. In a desperate attempt to win over the Conservatives Churchill had sent a folder of documents to Bonar Law which he claimed told the true story of Antwerp, Coronel and the Three Cruisers.[94] Bonar Law now replied thanking Churchill but saying that his removal from the Admiralty was inevitable.[95]

Finally, Churchill accepted defeat. In a mood of contrition he wrote to Asquith "I am very sorry for yr troubles, and sorry to have been the cause of a situation wh has enabled others to bring them upon you - I will accept any office - the lowest if you like - that you care to offer me".[96] For the first time since Fisher's resignation Asquith replied to Churchill. He told him that it was settled that he was not to remain at the Admiralty and continued "Every one has to make sacrifices: no one more than I, who have to part company with valued and faithful colleagues."[97] Churchill may have mused that any sacrifices made by Asquith were, at that moment, extremely difficult to detect; certainly he felt much bitterness towards his former chief for his lack of support during and after the crisis.[98] However, there was little Asquith could have done to save him. The Conservatives were implacable in their desire to remove Churchill from the Admiralty and it has been shown that even a section of the Liberal Party looked upon Churchill's fall with equanimity.

132

Churchill never realized how hostile opinion was towards him or what a liability to his party he had become. In the circumstances he was fortunate in being offered a Cabinet post, even if the lowly office of the Chancellor of the Duchy of Lancaster, and still more fortunate in retaining his seat on the War Council or, as it was now to become, the Dardanelles Committee.

* * * * * * * * * * * * * *

For convenience Churchill's account of these events may be divided into six sections; the various controversies in late March surrounding the 29th Division, the planning of the military attack and Fisher's reaction to it, the landings at Anzac and Hellas and the further battles in the South during April, the effect of the landings on opinion in the Balkans, Churchill's attempt to have the naval attack reviewed, and the political crisis in Britain.

Two important issues relate to the 29th Division. Churchill places great emphasis on the two week delay in the departure of the division from England and also strongly criticizes the way in which the transports were packed when it was sent. For the latter situation he blames Kitchener who "had allowed the division to be embarked otherwise than in order for battle".[99] However, it should be pointed out that when the 29th Division left England (even with the delay) there was no suggestion that it would be involved in immediate fighting. Indeed, it will be remembered that Churchill strenuously denied this possibility, maintaining that the 29th Division would only be used to "reap the fruits" of the naval attack. There was thus no perceived need to despatch the division in battle order. Further, even if the need had been foreseen, the transports could not have been packed suitably without detailed landing plans, including which contingents were designated for which beaches. These plans, it was shown earlier, could only have been drawn up on the spot by Hamilton and could not have been available in England.

A similar case can be made against Churchill's criticism of the two-week delay in despatching the 29th Division from England. Churchill contends that if despatched on time and in battle order the 29th Division would have arrived at the Dardanelles in mid-March and could then have "gone into action within a few days of its arrival".[100] Once again Churchill discreetly ignores the fact that such immediate use of the 29th Division was not contemplated at the time of its departure from England. The delay in its arrival at the Dardanelles did not, therefore, affect the plans in force at the time. Furthermore, it has been shown that it was extremely doubtful whether the division could have been used immediately had it arrived in mid-March. The weather in March and April was very unsettled and in fact a strong gale was in force between March 19th and the end of the month.

Churchill's contention also assumes that the landing of the 29th Division could have been improvised within a few days. In view of the complexity of combined operations, this assumption is doubtful.

To Churchill, however, the delayed departure of the 29th Division and the faulty packing of its transports form yet another link in that chain of causation which he builds up throughout The World Crisis to explain the defeat at the Dardanelles. They become two more accidents of fate along the path of "Destiny".[101]

In an earlier section of The World Crisis Churchill implies that it would have been worth taking the risk of landing the 29th Division in uncertain conditions because of the virtually undefended state of the Peninsula in March. To support this case he quotes lengthy extracts from the memoirs of Liman von Sandars to show how the Turkish defences were strengthened during April.[102] However, as mentioned earlier, Liman has rather overstated his case, for even prior to his assumption of command all the landing beaches chosen by Hamilton were wired and overlooked by trenches. This fact makes a critical difference to Churchill's case, for if the beaches were defended an improvised plan would have run into serious difficulties, and given that the uncertain weather would have made reinforcement and resupply of the force ashore hazardous, could have converted the enterprise into a risk not worth taking.

On the planning of the military attack The World Crisis is virtually silent. In fact there is nothing at all on Hamilton's plan in the narrative chapters and it is to the retrospective chapter "The Case for Perseverance and Decision" that we have to turn to obtain some clue of Churchill's thinking on the subject. Why this should be so will be investigated shortly, but first the points made in this retrospective chapter should be examined.

The subject discussed in the most detail by Churchill is the adequacy of Hamilton's force for the task in hand. He writes,

> "at the period which this story has now reached [April 1915] at least 40,000 Turks were known to have been assembled, and to have made and be making whatever preparations were possible; and to overwhelm these with certainty before they could be reinforced might well have required an army of a hundred thousand men. Without such numbers the enterprise passed out of the sphere of sound preparation and reasonable certainty, and depended for its success upon good fortune and a great feat of arms."[103]

Few would disagree with this analysis. However the reader gains no inkling from this passage that Churchill himself was at the time reassuring Balfour that "the military could do it" and telling the War Council that he saw no difficulty in effecting a landing. Therefore the passage in The World Crisis will be taken as a stricture only against Kitchener.

Churchill goes further than merely criticizing the size of the original force. He states that adequate reinforcements should have been on hand to be used as required.

> "To descend upon the Peninsula in the greatest possible numbers and the shortest possible time; to grapple with the local Turkish forces; to fight them day and night with superior numbers till they were utterly exhausted, to thrust in fresh troops and renew the battle unceasingly, to grip and racket the weaker enemy till the life was shaken out of his smaller organism - in that process lay victory."[104]

There are two dubious assumptions here. The first is that British and French troops could be fed into the battle faster by sea than the Turkish forces could be reinforced by land. It was shown earlier that to land the 29th Division and all its stores took more than a week. To land further divisions could have taken even longer as the crowding on the beaches became more acute. Moreover, British divisions had to be sent from France, a journey of at least ten days, and unless six or seven divisions had been sent at once (probably an impossibility due to the shortage of shipping) it is hard to see how a preponderance of troops could have been built up over the Turks, who could reinforce by a shorter sea journey from Constantinople or by ferry across the Straits. This brings us to Churchill's second assumption, that the Turkish Army was the "weaker" and "smaller organism". In the context of Gallipoli this was not true. The Turks had an army of over 500,000 men, a large proportion of which could be concentrated on the Peninsula. The troops that could be spared for the Dardanelles by the British and French were never likely to approach that number, let alone reach the superiority needed in the prevailing conditions to obtain victory. Thus it was not a matter of throwing troops in until the Turks were overwhelmed by weight of numbers, as Churchill implies, for such a situation could never be attained.

The section on troop strengths ends Churchill's discussion of the planning of the military attack. He thus leaves the many controversies surrounding Hamilton's plan untouched. For example, Churchill does not deal with the question of whether Hamilton chose the correct place to land, why he chose Hellas knowing that the help offered by the navy was likely to be small, why the main landing was made against the most heavily defended beach, or why Hamilton did not query the size of his force. The World Crisis is silent on all these questions. It is very uncharacteristic for Churchill to avoid areas of controversy associated with battles. It is plain why he did so in this instance. Throughout the writing of The World Crisis Churchill was in touch with Hamilton and Aspinall, the two men most involved with the planning of the April 25th landings. Aspinall had supplied Churchill with information concerning Hamilton's appointment and the way in which the staff had been assembled for the operation[105] and, as will be shown, he was able to pass on a great deal of material on Gallipoli which he was collecting for the official history. Hamilton and Churchill were old friends and they collaborated over their evidence to the Dardanelles Commission.[106] It is also clear from the Churchill Papers that Hamilton read other Dardanelles chapters of The World Crisis in proof.[107] The reason for Churchill's reticence now becomes clear. To criticize the April 25th plan it would have been necessary for Churchill to criticize two friends who had been very useful to him in the past and whose general view of the Dardanelles operation - that it had been ruined by Kitchener - was identical to his own.[108] Churchill was obviously not prepared to do this and apparently decided to avoid the issue altogether. What he actually thought of the plan is therefore not known but given the way it is treated in The World Crisis the reader is invited to make the assumption that the plan was sound and that it was the blunders made by Kitchener that caused it to go awry.

It should come as no surprise to those who have read the preceding chapters that in The World Crisis Churchill once more misrepresents the attitude of Fisher towards the military attack. After March 18, Churchill claims,

> "the attitude of the First Sea Lord had become one of quasi-detachment. He was greatly relieved that the burden had now been assumed by the Army. He approved every operational telegram which I or the Chief of the Staff drafted for him. In the end he assented to whatever steps were considered necessary for the proper support of the Army. But while he welcomed every sign of the despatch of troops, he grudged every form of additional naval aid".[109]

Thus we have a picture of Fisher, approving of the combined operation, but attempting to reduce to a minimum the material supplied to the Navy to enable it to carry out its part, a basically irrational approach. It would be a mistake to exaggerate Fisher's rationality during this period but the evidence brought forward earlier would suggest that his approach to the military landing was far sounder than that of Churchill and significantly different from that outlined in The World Crisis. It will be remembered that Fisher was not at all "relieved that the burden had now been assumed by the

Army". He had little faith in Hamilton's judgement (amply justified in the circumstances) and suggested on several occasions that the War Council reconsider the whole operation. This can hardly be characterized as an attitude of "quasi-detachment". In fact Fisher was asking many of the important questions which Churchill and Kitchener seemed to be avoiding. (What are the prospects of success with the force available? Were siege operations likely to develop on Gallipoli? Should not the War Council form an independent judgement on these points?) These questions show that Fisher had little confidence in the military attack and, although Churchill is correct in stating that Fisher did all he could to limit the role of the Navy at the Dardanelles, it is hardly accurate to say that he looked forward with relief to the landings on the Peninsula.

To prove Fisher's adherence to the Dardanelles enterprise Churchill quotes Fisher's reply of April 8th to the enquiry of the Junior Sea Lords whether the Dardanelles operation was endangering the Grand Fleet.[110] It will be remembered that Fisher's mild reply, to the effect that he was satisfied with the position, was probably designed to silence the Sea Lords, with whom he had no intention of sharing matters of strategy. Thus it would seem that Churchill has chosen this incident carefully to illustrate his case, whereas a franker statement of Fisher's view would include Fisher's memorandum of the same date (8th) in which he suggested that the entire attack be diverted to Haifa in case failure jeopardized the entry of Italy into the war. This document finds no place in The World Crisis.

This chapter of The World Crisis contains other interesting material on Fisher. Of the First Sea Lord's physical and mental state in what was to be his last week in office, Churchill wrote,

"that Lord Fisher was under considerable strain. His seventy-four years lay heavy upon him. During my absence in Paris upon the negotiations for the Anglo-Italian Naval Convention, he had shown great nervous exhaustion. He had evinced unconcealed distress and anxiety at being left alone in sole charge of the Admiralty. There is no doubt that the old Admiral was worried almost out of his wits by the immense pressure of the times and by the course events had taken".[111]

Thus we have a picture of Fisher on the verge of collapse. Further, the Churchill Papers contain an earlier draft portraying an even more alarming situation, that of the First Sea Lord being incapable of performing his duties. In the section quoted above Churchill had originally included, "The Chief of the Staff had found difficulty in securing from him the necessary signatures for such action as had to be taken. On more than one occasion his Confidential Secretary (Captain

Crease) had written the essential initials himself".[112]
Thus the man whom Churchill had chosen for the highest naval
post in the land is revealed as a shattered wreck, incapable
of carrying out the simplest functions of his high office.
No doubt Churchill decided to conceal the full truth about
Fisher's state to protect the reputation of the old Admiral,
but it must be admitted that this also had the effect of
concealing the magnitude of Churchill's mistake in
re-installing him at the Admiralty and later pleading with
him to come back.

We must now turn to an examination of Churchill's account
of the landings of April 25th. Churchill describes
operations at Hellas in his usual vivid and compelling
prose. Of the landing at V beach he says,

> "As the Irish troops rushed from the hold of the River
> Clyde, or as the boats reached the submerged barbed wire,
> an annihilating fire burst upon them from all parts of
> the small amphitheatre. The boats were checked by the
> wire or by the destruction of their rowers. The
> lighters, swayed by the current, were with difficulty
> placed and kept in position. In a few minutes more than
> half of those who had exposed themselves were shot down.
> The boats, the lighters, the gangways, the water, and the
> edge of the beach were heaped or crowded with dead and
> dying".[113]

Yet despite this decription Churchill makes no mention of the
fact that such slaughter was caused in part by the failure of
the naval bombardment. Nor does Churchill mention the fact
that Hamilton seemed to be aware that naval shells could not
destroy wire and trenches but did nothing to alter his plan.

A further point is that the account of the landings is
purely descriptive. There is no analysis of what went wrong
or why. For example, after describing the carnage on V beach
Churchill does not question the reason which led Hamilton to
make his "most important"[114] landing at this point. Nor
does he comment on the use made of the contingents landed at
S and Y beaches.[115] It was suggested earlier that rather
too much has been made of these "lost opportunities" but one
would not expect Churchill to avoid altogether such a
controversy. Similarly at X beach Churchill records that the
landing was made with relative ease[116] but does not draw
attention to the fact that these troops remained virtually
inactive for 3 days, while the exhausted survivors of W and V
beaches made costly frontal attacks on Sedd-el-Bahr.

One explanation for Churchill's treatment of the landings
at Hellas is that he perhaps felt a full disclosure would be
embarrassing to Hamilton. It has been shown that Hamilton
was open to criticism in his handling of the V beach landing
and over the failure to overrule Hunter-Weston and direct
troops to Y beach. After the war Hamilton followed closely

the writing of this section of The World Crisis and Churchill even asked him to contribute a piece on V beach.[117] Whether this was incorporated into the book is not known, for no copy of Hamilton's contribution seems to have survived.

Perhaps another explanation is that, under the influence of Hamilton and Aspinall, Churchill did not realize the deficiencies and areas of controversy surrounding the landing. Hamilton certainly regarded the feat of establishing a beachhead as proof that his plan had succeeded. In this atmosphere, and relying as he did on Hamilton and Aspinall to provide much of the documentation, it is perhaps not surprising that Churchill's account reads like one of Hamilton's despatches.

Churchill next turns his attention to the Anzac landing. To explain the failure of the troops to advance he concentrates on the rapid deployment of the Turkish reserves by Mustapha Kemel.[118] There is no doubt that this is an incident full of drama - the future nationalist leader emerging at this early date as the saviour of his country. However, Churchill has probably made too much of this incident. Kemel's 57th Regiment only came into action late on the 25th. Certainly it played a major part in parrying further progress along the Sari Bair ridge. However, it was suggested earlier that by this time the plan had already failed. The difficult nature of the ground, the confusion caused by landing in the wrong place and the ambitious nature of the original objectives had already played their part. The fact is that from the dawn landing until 4.30 p.m. on the 25th the Anzac troops were faced with very few Turkish defenders but they were still unable to make substantial advances and it was only at the end of this period that Kemel and his men became a serious factor in the defence.

Only the briefest account is given in The World Crisis of the events from April 26th to the 28th at Hellas[119] and Churchill does not investigate the local factors which affected the rate and progress of the advances. This could be justified on the grounds that no matter what plan had been made by Hamilton on the 26th, he did not have troops, either in fighting condition or in enough quantity, to carry it through to victory. Churchill's solution to Hamilton's dilemma is simple.

"If, during the 28th and 29th, two or three fresh divisions of French, British, or Indian troops could have been thrown in, the Turkish defence must have been broken and the decisive positions would have fallen into our hands [but] .... Where was the extra Army Corps that was needed? It existed. It was destined for the struggle. It was doomed to suffer fearful losses in that struggle. But now when its presence would have given certain victory, it stood idle in Egypt or England."[120]

Like so much of Churchill's writing about Gallipoli this assertion ignores logistic factors. (These, it has been noted, are often basic to military strategy, but are often ignored by military historians because they make little appeal to the imagination.[121] This seems to be the case with Churchill.) As has been shown, it is doubtful if one division could have landed in time for the battles at the end of April and early May. It is certain that this feat would have been impossible for the two or three divisions specified by Churchill. Furthermore, although in time the Navy <u>might</u> have been able to collect enough small craft to land these divisions, it would have been necessary to land them in relays, thus doubling or trebling the time taken for their deployment. And once the divisions were ashore it is by no means certain that the Navy with the small craft available would have been able to supply a total of 6 or 7 divisions in the early stages of the campaign, or if a rapid advance commenced whether ammunition could have been supplied in sufficient quantities to a front line miles from the beaches.

It is revealed in the Churchill Papers that <u>The World Crisis</u> originally included a note of criticism of Hamilton at this point. In place of the section underlined above Churchill had initially written, "Unhappily we too had exhausted our reserves, and no preparation had been made before the attack to use at this moment the large numbers of troops which already stood idle in Egypt."[122] It is indeed a fair criticism of Hamilton to suggest that he was in error in not having a force on hand to follow up in the event of a stalemate. (Whether the reinforcement would have proved decisive is another matter; reserves are usually regarded as essential to any battle.) This criticism of Hamilton was then removed and the passage above substituted. The differences between the two passages should be noticed for they are good examples of Churchill's skilful use of language. The phrase in the final version, "it stood idle in Egypt or England" carries none of the criticism of Hamilton implied by the earlier "no preparation had been made". In fact the inclusion of England would possibly indicate that the home authorities (i.e. Kitchener) were partly to blame. Thus both these amendments direct attention away from Hamilton.

A final point that should be made on the passage quoted is that Churchill claims that in the event of success, the "decisive positions would have fallen into our hands". By this he can only mean Achi Baba, for even the most optimistic observer could not have supposed that the Straits could be reached in one bound from the line reached on the 28th. Yet it has been shown that the Achi Baba position was not the key to the Peninsula. It was not even a good observation point from which to direct the fire of the fleet for no view over the Narrows was to be had from the summit. In fact the capture of Achi Baba would have only been the beginning of the assault on the Kilid Bahr Plateau, an even more formidable undertaking.

Concerning the question of reinforcements for Hamilton's force, Churchill reproaches Kitchener for his slow response in releasing additional troops. However, as has been shown, there is another side to this question and that is Hamilton's reluctance to ask for the troops available in Egypt and the qualifications and hesitations contained in Hamilton's requests when they were made. In fact this point should have been obvious to Churchill as he had consulted the Hamilton-Kitchener correspondence before writing this section of The World Crisis.

The opening pages of the next chapter of The World Crisis are devoted to a description of the effect of the landing on opinion abroad.

> "In spite of the fact that the Army was brought to a standstill, the great event of the landing continued to produce its impression throughout Europe. Italy, Greece, Roumania, Bulgaria assumed that now that large allied forces were definitely ashore, they could and would be reinforced from the sea until the Turkish resistance was overcome. The Italian momentum towards war proceeded unchecked: and the Balkan States continued in an attitude of strained expectancy".[123]

As far as Italy is concerned, Churchill is probably correct. Certainly the date of the signing of the Treaty of London, which brought Italy into the war, is suggestive. It is hard to see that Churchill's claim in relation to the other Balkan States is justified. It will be remembered that the actions of these countries suggested that they remained unimpressed by British activity at the Dardanelles. In any case their enthusiasm must have been short-lived because of the stalemate on the Peninsula and it is certain that this situation, despite Churchill's assurances in The World Crisis, impressed no one.

Churchill next turns to a discussion of the problem of whether to renew the naval attack. In our earlier discussion of de Robeck's telegram of May 10th concerning the renewal of this attack, it was suggested that it was fairly clear that the Admiral deprecated a further attempt by the fleet. In The World Crisis, Churchill contends that in this telegram de Robeck "intimated unmistakably his readiness to make the attempt if the Admiralty gave the order".[124] This seems to be a very optimistic view of de Robeck's message. Certainly the question of what the Admiral would do if ordered is left open, but the phrasing of the telegram was probably constructed to prevent that situation ever arising. In other words, de Robeck made it clear that he would have to be ordered to renew the attack against his better judgement and was no doubt confident that the Admiralty War Group would uphold him as they had after March 22nd. In fact there is evidence that Churchill realized that, in the form it was received, de Robeck's telegram prevented further action. In a draft of The World Crisis he wrote "The telegram drafted by Keyes was considerably modified and neutralized before it was sent".[125] However, in keeping with the line he pursued at the time, that the telegram did offer the prospect of a renewal of the naval attack, he later deleted this passage and substituted "The telegram bears the imprint of several hands and of opposite opinions".[126] This version also had the added advantage of concealing that the "opposite opinions" and "other hands" belonged to Keyes. Furthermore, by the time he came to write The World Crisis, Churchill seemed to agree that de Robeck had been right. In a first draft of the chapter he concluded by saying that "the arguments against decisive naval action were conclusive".[127] However, as he realized, his position at the time had been that some sort of naval attempt should have been made, so he deleted "conclusive" and substituted the less prohibitive "very weighty".[128] (An additional factor, never discussed or commented on by Churchill, is that the shortage of ammunition in the fleet might have made any order to de Robeck to renew the naval attack impossible to fulfill.)

Churchill devotes an entire chapter of The World Crisis to the May political crisis in Britain. He opens his account with a discussion of the War Council of May 14th. Churchill describes the mood of the Committee as "sulphurous"[129] which, considering the acrimonious debate between Kitchener, Churchill and Fisher concerning the withdrawal of the Queen Elizabeth and the failure of the army at Gallipoli to advance, seems a reasonable conclusion. After correctly summarizing Kitchener's statement he moves on to his own reply, making the point that "if it had been known three months before that an army of from 80,000 to 100,000 men would be available in May for an attack on the Dardanelles, the attack by the Navy alone would never have been undertaken".[130] He does not elaborate on this statement, thus giving the impression that such an army could have been provided and that Kitchener was to blame that it was not. However, as has been suggested, in February there had been no proposal from Churchill that the naval attack should be delayed until troops were available. His statement in The World Crisis also ignores the fact that in February he had given repeated assurances that an army would not be required.

The resignation of Fisher is dealt with differently in some important ways in the earlier editions of The World Crisis than the Odhams edition used here and they should briefly be noted. Originally Churchill believed that it was a telegram assigning four cruisers to work with the Italian Fleet marked "First Sea Lord to see after action" that had been "the spark that fired the train".[131] Later after correspondence with Crease he realized that it was the additions made to the list of ships for the Dardanelles on a minute of May 14th that was the real cause. Churchill incorporated most of the new information into the later editions of The World Crisis, one of the few occasions in which he substantially revised a section of his work. Although The World Crisis may initially have been misleading on some of the details associated with Fisher's resignation, from the first Churchill accurately represented the reason behind the resignation of the First Sea Lord. In the first edition of the book Churchill states that what had caused Fisher's resignation was the fact that he "was compelled by arguments and pressures he had never been able to resist, but had never ceased to resent, to become responsible for operations to which he had taken an intense dislike".[132]

Turning to Churchill's handling of the resignation crisis, little need be said of his account of events of the 15th of May which is quite accurate and covers all the important incidents. For May 16th he prints the inconclusive exchange of letters between himself and Fisher. He then turns his attention to the Junior Sea Lords. Initially he had intended to publish his letter to them of May 17th repudiating their criticism that movements of the Fleet had been taken out of the hands of the First Sea Lord, their reply reaffirming their criticism, and his further letter maintaining his original view.[133] It cannot be said that these omissions are very important but it should be noticed that Churchill apparently never intended to publish the Sea Lords' original letter criticizing his actions and largely blaming him for Fisher's resignation.

On the question of whether the Sea Lords would resign with Fisher Churchill states that Sir Arthur Wilson "had informed them that it was their duty to remain at their posts"[134] and that he later informed Asquith that "the other Members of the Board would remain".[135] It was stated earlier, however, that the Sea Lords seem to have made their own acceptance of Churchill conditional upon the return of Fisher. At this stage, therefore, it is probable that they were merely indicating that they would remain until Fisher's position was resolved one way or another. Therefore the two statements made by Churchill are somewhat misleading although they are carefully worded to avoid the statement that the Sea Lords' stay would be permanent.

Churchill's movements for the remainder of the 16th and for most of the 17th as detailed in The World Crisis are difficult to verify. But there seems no reason to doubt his account of the meeting with Asquith at the Wharf later on the 16th, or of his meetings with Lloyd George and Asquith the next day. There has been some controversy over his claim that he rejected the Colonial Office when it was offered to him by Asquith.[136] Beaverbrook states that he accepted it.[137] However, it will be remembered that Churchill wrote to Asquith on the 18th accepting the Colonial Office if it was still open to him, a clear indication that he had already rejected it. Where Churchill's version of events is open to question is concerning his statement that after meeting Asquith "I saw at once that it was decided I should leave the Admiralty".138 It has been shown earlier that this did not seem to be the case and that for some time after this Churchill clung to the hope that he would remain in charge of the navy. Even a letter to Asquith published in The World Crisis indicates that he did not consider that Asquith's decision was final.139 However, that letter has not been quoted in full. It was noted that the gratuitious advice offered by Churchill to Asquith in the letter ("L.G. will not do for W.O." etc.) was a measure of how little Churchill had realized that his own fortunes had undergone a disastrous reversal. In The World Crisis this section of the letter is omitted,140 thus in part preserving the impression that Churchill had accepted his fate, but perhaps more importantly concealing from Lloyd George the fact that Churchill thought him unsuitable to be War Minister.

For the 17th Churchill also includes a full account of the preliminary moves of the impending sea battle, the dramatic effect being heightened by the publication of the most important telegrams which passed between the Admiralty and Jellicoe.141 Indeed, considering the inconsequential nature of the event rather too much has been published but Churchill achieves the effect of contrasting the real business of running the war with the rather sordid trading for office which was proceeding around him.

In fact Churchill was not as far removed from this latter process as his account would have us believe and from this point his narrative of his own part in the fall of the government becomes much less reliable. The general line he takes is that by the 18th he had accepted with dignity his removal from office and that from then on he remained rather aloof from political manoeuvring.142 It was indicated in the first part of this chapter that this was by no means the case and that in a series of letters to Asquith and the Conservative leaders Churchill desperately tried to cling to office. Initially, as the Churchill Papers reveal, a much franker version of these events was to have been given in The World Crisis but then some of the more revealing letters were omitted. We have already seen that Churchill removed his exchange of letters with the Sea Lords and an important section of his letter to Asquith of May 17th. Now, in his account of events of the 18th, he omits altogether a further letter to the Prime Minister asking to be kept on in office, though it was his original intention to include it.143 Then, regarding the 19th, in his discussion of Wilson's letter to Asquith indicating that he would serve under no other First Lord, Churchill originally wrote that this information was not made public but "I could not, however, forbear writing to Mr. Asquith the letter which I do not hesitate to print below".[144] This letter, it will be remembered, stated that Churchill was confident that he could continue in office supported by Wilson and the other members of the Board. In the outcome Churchill did hesitate to print it and it was not included in the published version of The World Crisis. Also excluded were Asquith's letter to Churchill of the 20th saying that it was settled that Churchill should leave the Admiralty and a further letter from the Prime Minister saying how delighted he was that Churchill had accepted the situation.[145] The inclusion of these letters would have helped to clarify Churchill's reactions to the crisis. However it should be noted that he never intended to print his letter of the 21st to Asquith which claimed that only he and Wilson were capable of effectively running the Admiralty or his further letter of the same day accepting office, "even the lowest". These letters are quite crucial, and without them it is hard to gauge the extent of Churchill's attempt to cling to the Admiralty or his chastened mood when that office was denied him.

There are other omissions from this section. None of Churchill's correspondence with the Conservative leadership is published and indeed Bonar Law's name does not occur anywhere in the chapter. Churchill does include an oblique attack on the makers of the coalition from all parties by stating that it is in the House of Commons that governments should be made and that the House had a right to be consulted on this occasion.[146] However, the Churchill Papers disclose that it had originally been his intention to include an attack on Bonar Law. No doubt in the intervening years Churchill had discovered the role played by the Conservative leader in excluding him from the Admiralty. So he penned a rebuke (in the form of a footnote) which was to have read:

> "Three times" said Mr. Bonar Law speaking at Glasgow during the recent election [the 1922 General Election] "have I taken the responsibility of breaking up a Government". It is quite true & it is also true that in each case the House of Commons was not consulted, that the action took place behind closed doors & in secret negotiations & that the weapon was throughout the strong partisanship of the Conservative party wh never rested till it had driven from power every Liberal Ministry. Let us hope that the results of the latest of these palace revolutions will be less disastrous to the state than those wh attended the first".[147]

Thus is laid bare Churchill's real opinion of the formation and composition of the first wartime coalition. Why was this section deleted? As will be seen in a later chapter Beaverbrook was successful in getting Churchill to moderate criticisms of Bonar Law in the third volume of The World

Crisis and he may have played a similar role here although written evidence is lacking. However, it is likely that the footnote was removed to maintain the rather aloof and dignified tone adopted by Churchill towards domestic politics and clashes of personality. The impression he seems to be anxious to convey is that he was above the sordid party battle. Perhaps he also hoped that this approach would give his book a more detached and scholarly appearance. A more obvious reason for the deletion is that Churchill probably was not anxious that the harsh indictment of the Conservative Party should become public. During the time that elapsed between the writing of this section (probably in 1922) and the publication of the second volume of The World Crisis in 1923, Churchill had moved much closer to the Conservatives. He was to rejoin the party in 1924. Clearly a statement condemning the party as irresponsibly partisan, would not have furthered his cause.

Churchill also attempts to take a detached view of the role of Asquith in the crisis. He does make the point that the Prime Minister supported all the actions taken at the Dardanelles but that Churchill well understood his difficulties during the crisis and "there never was and never has been the slightest personal recrimination upon the subject".[148] In fact, as Martin Gilbert shows, Churchill resented Asquith's role in the crisis very much and was very bitter over what he saw as Asquith's failure to support his Dardanelles policy. Before the end of the year he was referring to "That odious Asquith, & his pack of incompetents and intriguers".[149]

The last major omission from this section is Churchill's amazing offer on the 19th of a cabinet post to Fisher. This is of course further evidence of the frantic attempts by Churchill to remain at the Admiralty and his silence on this point is hardly surprising.

In The World Crisis Sir Arthur Wilson's decision, made on May 17th to serve only under Churchill as First Lord is represented as a possible turning point in his fortunes had the news been made public by Asquith. He writes,

> "I knew well the profound impression which Sir Arthur Wilson's action, had it been made public, would have produced upon the Naval Service. It would instantly have restored the confidence which press attacks, impossible to answer, had undermined. In no other way could the persistent accusations of rash, ignorant interference by the civilian Minister in the naval conduct of the war be decisively repelled".[150]

No statement could be at such variance with the facts, although it is probably true that Churchill was never aware of the depth of feeling against Wilson in the Service. It will be remembered that Jellicoe, the only man who really

counted regarding opinion afloat, considered Wilson a
menace. The knowledge that Wilson was prepared to serve
under no one but Churchill therefore weakened Churchill's
position rather than strengthened it, and although it is
possible that publication of Wilson's letter might have
raised Churchill's standing with the public this would have
counted for nothing in the prevailing political atmosphere.

In relation to these chapters of The World Crisis two
descriptions by Churchill of conditions on the Western Front
should be noticed. The earlier passage is a description of
trenches in Belgium visited by Churchill on the 18th of March.

"Corpses entangled in the wire were covered with seaweed
and washed by the tides as they mouldered. Others in
groups of ten or twelve lay at the foot of the sandhills
blasted in their charge, but with the sense and aspect of
attack still eloquent in their attitude and order. These
dead had lain there for months".[151]

The second passage occurs in the same chapter as his account
of the April 25th landings and the subsequent fighting.
Churchill includes a brief sketch of a casualty clearing
station in Belgium which he visited about this time. "More
than 1,000 men suffering from every form of horrible injury,
seared, torn, pierced, choking, dying, were being sorted
according to their miseries".[152] He goes on to describe
the activities of a burial party, a room full of men who were
beyond help and "the terrible spectacle of a man being
trepanned".[153] The juxtaposition of these passages with
descriptions of the Gallipoli battles can hardly be an
unconscious exercise. Perhaps to offset his vivid
description of the V beach landing Churchill is reminding his
readers that great as was the carnage at Hellas it was as
nothing to what was happening in France. The passages,
however, also illuminate a facet of Churchill more to his
credit. The vividness with which he is able to recall these
terrible scenes is an indication of the deep impression which
war, as fought in 1915, made upon him, and of the horror with
which he regarded it. His frequent visits to France in 1914
had made him aware, perhaps more than any other Cabinet
Minister, of the type of war that was being fought and it is
possible that the wish to avoid the sordid nature of trench
warfare and return to a cleaner war of movement and action
may have played a part in his search for a theatre of war
away from the Western Front.

Chapter 9

THE DARDANELLES IV - THE TERRIBLE IF'S

After the failure of the Second Battle of Krithia the effective strength of Hamilton's force had been reduced from 70,000 to under 45,000 men.[1]  The immediate problem was reinforcements.  Yet apart from a weak Territorial division from Egypt no reinforcements were despatched to Hamilton until June.  It is often said that it was the collapse of the Liberal Government in England which caused this delay. Certainly this event did not make decisions on the conduct of the war any easier.  But it is doubtful if this was the only factor delaying troop movements to the East.  At least as important as the political crisis was the attitude of Hamilton himself.  During this entire period (early May to early June) no direct request for reinforcements was received from the Commander-in-Chief.  In May he informed Kitchener that ultimately two Army Corps would be needed to achieve victory but at the same time suggested that further advances along the Peninsula would be necessary before additional troops could be deployed.[2]  Not surprisingly, as no advances were being made, Kitchener failed to respond. Eventually, under some pressure from his staff, Hamilton requested additional troops but then suggested that only one division be sent as an interim measure and that the question of more substantial reinforcements be delayed until the result of a new push to be made in early June was clear.[3]

Hamilton's "push", the Third Battle of Krithia, was launched on June 4th.  Approximately 30,000 British and French troops attacked an almost equal number of Turks.  On the flanks the attack failed, but in the centre the Manchester Territorials captured the two Turkish lines that were their objectives and even managed to place three companies beyond the second line.[4]  The crucial question then was: where would the divisional reserve of 10,000 men be placed?  Hunter-Weston did not hesitate.  The reserves were sent to the flanks to try to redeem the failures there.[5]  The Manchesters finally had to withdraw because of lack of support.[6]  This was yet another example of

Hunter-Weston's ineptitude. But was it also another of the "missed opportunities" of Gallipoli? It seems certain that a local success could have been scored, for there were no more continuous trench lines in the vicinity of the Manchesters and the Turks were in considerable disarray. However, even if all the reserves had been used in the centre it is doubtful if they would have been in sufficient numbers to cause more than local retirements. In any case they must soon have met the Turkish reserves (two divisions) which began to appear on the scene at about 4 p.m. on the 4th.[7] In these circumstances a "success" might at the most have pushed the Turks back to Krithia village, but this was hardly a position of great importance. Indeed, even if Achi Baba had been captured (as was shown earlier) this too would not have inconvenienced the Turks to any great extent.

There is also the perennial question to be considered of what would have happened had the allies had another fresh division available. The question is so speculative that to attempt an answer is difficult. All that can be said is that Hamilton, even with an extra division, would not have had a superiority of 2 to 1, and it was always difficult to obtain a decisive result in these circumstances. The fact remains, however, that no one had pressed for an extra division to be present. The reinforcements desired by Churchill after April 25th were sent and indeed took a leading part in the battle. Hamilton's request of May 17th was of a long term nature and bore no relation to the June battle. Thus the need for a reserve division in early June had not been foreseen by anyone.

On the 7th of June the Dardanelles Committee (the old War Council) met for the first time under the coalition. In addition to Asquith, Kitchener, Balfour, Churchill and Crewe, it was attended by Landsdowne, Curzon, Bonar Law and Selborne. The Government were in receipt of a letter from Hamilton written the previous day stating that he considered the reinforcements originally asked for, two army corps, sufficient to force a decision.[8] It was quickly decided to accede to Hamilton's request. Three divisions of the new armies (the 10th, 11th and 13th) were to be sent "with a view to an assault in the second week of July",[9] and as one division (the 52nd) had already been sent the two army corps were complete.

Later, largely at Churchill's insistence, two more divisions, the 53rd and 54th, were added to Hamilton's force to provide a useful reinforcement in case of failure. The two divisions were, however, only at half-strength when they were despatched.[10]

Churchill now began to contemplate the use to which the new divisions should be put. He considered that a landing on the Bulair Isthmus would produce the best chance of success. It would cut the Turkish supply lines by land and if submarines could be placed in the Marmora the Turkish army on

Gallipoli would be starved out.[11] A similar idea had also been put forward by Ashmead-Bartlett, a newspaper correspondent recently returned from the Dardanelles.[12] As a result of these submissions Kitchener asked Hamilton if he considered such an operation possible.[13] Hamilton replied that he did not. All the available landing places on the Isthmus were commanded by trenches which it had been proved the guns of the fleet could not destroy. Furthermore, the navy could not keep three separate forces supplied and there was a great danger from submarines in the exposed anchorages. Even if possible from a naval point of view, Hamilton argued that the force landed would have to be extremely large as it would be open to attack on two fronts. Finally, even if Bulair was cut, the Turks could be supplied to a certain extent from the Asiatic shore.[14] In fact the only place a landing could be effected safely in the area was the Gulf of Enos but de Robeck had informed Hamilton that such a landing could not be maintained because of the lack of small craft.[15]

While these operations were being discussed the fleet confined itself to supporting the army, despite the efforts of Keyes to have the naval attack reinvestigated.[16] In fact, despite many attempts to improve efficiency, the navy was found to be inadequate for even the former task. The ships found it impossible to locate and silence the Turkish artillery with any consistency at Hellas and Anzac.[17] Nor could the Asiatic batteries which continually shelled the southern beaches be eliminated.[18] The aerial spotting force had improved but it was still too small to be of any real value and one ship reported that only on one occasion was an aeroplane provided to aid its fire.[19] Furthermore, as time went on, the wear on the guns became serious. On the Vengeance a 12" gun was discovered to be completely smooth bore and towards the end some guns had a firing pattern of 1,000 yards diameter.[20]

Was Keyes correct in stating that the fleet should have renewed the attack on the Narrows? It has sometimes been suggested that June or July was the ideal time for a renewed attack because many of the guns defending the Straits had been removed by the Turks for the use of the army. Indeed in July, von Usedom, the German commander of the Straits defences, compiled a list of 82 guns which had been removed for this purpose.[21] From this list it is clear that 2/3 of the guns from the intermediate defences had been removed and the mobile batteries on either side of the Straits, which had so harassed the fleet, had been practically dismantled. However, it is also clear from the Mitchell Committee Report that new guns were continually being installed, although often in different positions from those removed. From April until November 52 guns were added in this way, mainly around In Tepe, opposite Helles.[22] These changes resulted in the defence of the Straits being shifted towards the entrance and thus losing to some extent its integrated and mutually supporting features. Nevertheless, the guns remained a formidable barrier and the performance of the fleet in this period suggests that they would have enjoyed no more success in silencing them than in the earlier phase of the operation. Of course the minefields and the batteries protecting them remained intact throughout the period and would no doubt have proved the major obstacle to a renewed naval attack.[23]

Planning for Hamilton's big attack began in May and the scope of the operation was enlarged as more reinforcements became available. As finally developed the plan called for the capture of the Sari Bair Ridge from Anzac. For this operation Birdwood was to be reinforced by the 13th Division, a brigade of the 10th Division and an Indian brigade. Once the ridge had been taken an advance across the Peninsula to the Straits was to be made. A landing was also to be made immediately to the north of the Anzac perimeter at Suvla Bay. General Stopford, a retired officer of no distinction, was given the command on the ludicrous grounds that he was the only General available (none could be spared from the Western Front) who was senior to Mahon, one of the divisional commanders.[24] Stopford's instructions were, to a certain extent, puzzling. Initially he was told that after securing some intermediate features his objective was to capture the main ridge overlooking the bay by "coup de Main".[25] Later Stopford was informed that his first objective was to secure Suvla Bay as a base for all the forces operating in the northern zone and if possible[26] assist the Anzac attack to take the main ridge.[27] Much has been made of this change of plan. It is said that it directed Stopford's attention towards securing the area around the landing beaches and away from the necessity to capture the ridge overlooking the bay. This theory hardly stands up to investigation. It was quite obvious, even to Stopford, that the area near the shore could not be secure until the dominating ridge had been taken and he emphasized this point in his operations orders.[28] As will be shown later, the thwarting of Hamilton's plan was the result of more complex factors than Stopford's interpretation of his orders.

The main attack was launched from Anzac on the night of the 6th of August. The plan was for two columns of troops to seize the foothills which commanded the routes to the summit of the ridge. Then two more columns would pass through them, the left one splitting in two and making for Hill 971 and Hill Q, the right advancing directly up Rhododendron Ridge to Chunuk Bair.[29] Sari Bair was meant to be in British hands by dawn.

A diversion at Lone Pine began on the 6th. It was designed to draw Turkish reserves away from the main battle. Unfortunately for Birdwood it also attracted Turkish reserves to the northern theatre and by the time they had arrived it was clear that Lone Pine was not part of the main attack. These reserves were then used against the main advance.[30]

The covering columns succeeded in driving the Turks from the foothills and all their objectives were eventually taken. However, the poor physical state of many of the Anzac veterans and the difficulties of a night march in tortuous and largely unreconnoitred country delayed the capture of the key positions for some two hours.[31] This meant that the assaulting columns began late. More delays were then caused by the lack of space to deploy troops in the assembly areas and one battalion took over an hour to leave its dugouts and form up in marching order.[32] The left column, which had the furthest to go, never really had a chance. The 4th Australian brigade (Monash) leading the left fork of that column soon become lost. At dawn it was nowhere near its objective and although it had suffered few casualties,[33] the men were exhausted and a rest was ordered. The centre column (Hill Q) lost cohesion and direction in the difficult country. One group diverged to the left and joined up with Monash, another eventually joined the column on Rhododendron Ridge to the right. Only the 6th Ghurkas took the correct route and at dawn they were only a thousand yards from Hill Q.[34]

The right column (Chunuk Bair) had made better progress although the greater part of it also lost its way and eventually returned to the start line. However, Brigadier Johnson with a small force pushed to within 55 yards of Chunuk Bair which at this time was undefended. Johnson then paused, according to John North to have breakfast,[35] according to Aspinall-Oglander to await the advance of the other columns.[36] Finally, Godley (C in C, A & N.Z. Division) ordered an advance. Less than one hundred men of the three hundred who set out even reached the pinnacle beneath the summit.[37] The first attempt on the ridge had failed. Was this another of the lost opportunities of Gallipoli? It seems unlikely. The fact that the summit of Chunuk Bair was unoccupied during the period of Johnson's pause is hardly relevant. Chunuk Bair was enfiladed from Hill Q on the left and possibly from Battleship Hill on the right. Some of the fire that drove back Johnson's attack certainly came from Hill Q.[38] Thus Chunuk Bair was untenable unless other sections of the ridge were also taken.

The remainder of the 7th was spent in resting and reorganizing for a renewed attempt on the 8th. The plan was that columns of reserve troops under General Cox would reinforce Monash on the left and in the centre attempt to take Hill Q. On the right Johnson would again endeavour to take Chunuk Bair.[39]

On the left no progress was made, the difficult country and the increasing numbers of Turkish reinforcements beating Monash back.[40] In the centre, Cox's column all lost their way and failed to reach the Ghurkas still holding out just below the summit of Hill Q.[41] On the right, however, the New Zealanders occupied Chunuk Bair with little loss, the Turkish defenders having drifted away during the night. Throughout the day they managed to beat off a succession of counter-attacks and by evening were still holding out though in much reduced numbers.[42]

During the night of the 8th another plan was developed. On the left the attempt to take Hill 971 was abandoned. In the centre Cox was to renew his attempt to take Hill Q and on the right more reinforcements under General Baldwin were to support the New Zealanders on Chunuk Bair.[43]

In the event neither Baldwin's nor the majority of Cox's troops had arrived by the time the assault was scheduled to go in. Allanson, commanding the Ghurkas and a small number of reinforcements which had reached him on the 8th, (about 350-450 men all told)[44] decided to assault Hill Q alone. The summit was reached without loss. As Allanson recalled, "We dashed down towards Maidos, but had only got about 300 feet down when I saw a flash in the bay and suddenly our own Navy put six 12" monitor shells into us".[45] About one-third of Allanson's force was wiped out by the shells and the rest retired to their original positions.[46] Hill Q was never retaken.

The navy, which was apparently responsible for the shelling,[47] has been much blamed for preventing the capture of the ridge. However, this overstates the importance of Allanson's force. With the numbers he had available, Allanson stood no chance of fighting off Turkish counter-attacks which must have developed and reinforcements for his small group were nowhere in sight. The army was not shelled off the ridge by these few shells for it had never really occupied the ridge in the first place. As Hamilton later said, "It is perfectly clear to me that the "Army" did not lose, and could not lose, grip ... [of Sari Bair] owing to the fact of a few misdirected shells".[48]

On the right, no reinforcements reached the New Zealanders on the 9th. As a result Col. Malone, now in charge of the force holding the summit, withdrew most of his men to a trench on the forward slope, leaving about 100 men to dig in beyond the crest.[49] Malone has been much criticized for this action and it has been claimed that had his men been in place on the summit they could have repulsed the Turkish attacks which developed on the 10th. This seems doubtful for Malone had only a few hundred men and the Turkish attacks were made in great strength. In any case Malone had no choice. It will be remembered that the summit of Chunuk Bair was enfiladed by positions to the north,[50] and was quite untenable in daylight as long as those positions remained in Turkish hands. Malone chose the only positions possible. Only substantial reinforcements would have saved the British on the 10th and they were not available.

It has often been said that the August attacks from Anzac almost succeeded and it is true that for short intervals troops did hold two of the key summits of the Sari Bair Range. However, these troops were few in number. Also after the machine guns of the New Zealanders on Chunuk Bair had been knocked out,[51] they had nothing more than rifles with which to defend themselves. There was of course no artillery support. In these circumstances it was only a matter of time before these positions were lost to Turkish counter-attacks. To hold the positions in strength almost the entire force at Anzac would have been needed on the crest of the range and given the nature of the country this would have taken many more days to organize than Birdwood had at his disposal, for Turkish reinforcements could always reach the high ground faster from their side of the range than could the Anzacs from theirs.

The point also needs to be considered that even if the entire range from Hill 971 to Battleship Hill had been captured it might have proved impossible to supply such a force across the rugged and twisted ravines. Even the small number of men above the Apex on Chunuk Bair received "little food, less water, little ammunition and no bombs".[52]

In any case even if the ridge had been captured and it had been found possible to supply the men, that was hardly the end of the battle. Birdwood's original plan only saw this as the first stage. The second stage involved pushing reinforcements across the Peninsula under the cover of the force on Sari Bair. In August no reinforcements were available but it is doubtful if they could have been supplied with water had Hamilton been able to offer Birdwood an extra division.

It has been stated, however, that the capture of the ridge would in itself have been decisive. The argument goes that from this position Turkish communications with the Straits could have been cut by artillery fire.[53] It has also been said that once the main ridge was reached the ground from there to the Narrows became much easier and it would have been a relatively simple matter for the Army to have progressed across the Peninsula to Maidos.[54] Concerning the feasibility of cutting Turkish communications from Sari Bair, the officer commanding the artillery in the Australian and New Zealand Division has testified that it would have been extremely difficult even to place heavy guns on top of the ridge. He also stated that from most positions on the ridge the Straits would have been beyond the range of the guns available at Anzac. A further factor was the limited number of guns in the Anzac area. There were only 18 howitzers and eight 18 pounders[55] – hardly enough to lay down a devastating barrage. Nor is the topographical argument any more convincing. A glance at a map shows that although the ground to the east of the main range is not as difficult as that within the Anzac perimeter, it is still precipitous and hardly ideal for the manoeuvring of troops. Also although the summits of the ranges to the east are generally lower than those of Sari Bair, the Anzacs had shown that it was quite possible to hold positions dominated from above. Viewed in this way the Anzac attack was a lost cause before it began except as a further stage in what must be a long process.

The landing at Suvla Bay took place on the night of August 6th. Three beaches were to be used, B and C outside the bay, and A inside. The plan was that the 11th Division would land and seize the heights of Lala Baba, Hill 10 and Ghazi Baba. At the same time the division would throw out a defensive flank between the salt lake and the beaches at B and C. A force would then circle the salt lake in a clockwise direction and attack the Turkish positions on the W and Chocolate hills which overlooked the landing places. A more direct route between the landing places and these objectives was rejected because it was believed that the hills were heavily defended from the north.[56] The 10th Division was to land later in the morning and advance on the main ridge overlooking the bay.

Although the troops taking part in the assault were new they were hardly fresh. By the time they had reached Suvla Bay they had spent most of the night and the previous afternoon on board the transports in stifling and crowded conditions. Many were suffering from diarrhoea and from the after-effects of cholera injections.[57]

There were other problems. Because of the secrecy imposed by G.H.Q. (necessary if the plan was to have any chance) even some of the Brigadiers were unsure about the exact location of the landing points.[58] The troops had almost no idea of what was expected of them.[59] Furthermore, Mudros harbour could not hold all the shipping required, so the 10th Division was sent to Mitylene,[60] which meant that the General commanding (Mahon), despite several attempts, never succeeded in communicating the orders to the brigade which was to make the division's first landing.[61] Some of the brigades had also never practised night marching although this skill was central to the plan.[62]

These were inauspicious signs but it was known that the area was lightly defended and it was hoped that the Turks would be overwhelmed by weight of numbers.

In the event there were no more than 2,000 Turks in the Suvla Bay area. However, despite the fact that 10,000 troops were landed on the first day very little progress was made. The hills overlooking the landing places (Green, Chocolate, W), which were supposed to have been taken by first light, were not assaulted until dusk.

There seem to have been four major causes of the delay. Firstly, one of the brigades (32nd) suffered very heavy casualties, especially in officers, when it tried to advance from the beach. This led to great confusion ( augmented by the dark) and no attempt was made to advance from the water line.[63] Secondly, the 34th Brigade, which was to join the 32nd in assaulting the nearby hills, was thrown into disarray when some of the lighters bringing the troops from the ships grounded on an uncharted reef. Six hours were to pass before the final complements struggled ashore.[64] Thirdly, there was the chaos caused in landing the 10th Division. To avoid the reef which had hampered the 34th Brigade, most of the division was landed outside the bay. However, a later contingent, including Mahon the commander, was landed inside the bay near to the original landing place. Instead of being concentrated for an advance, the division was now strung out across the entire front.[65] Fourthly, a factor by no means confined to Suvla Bay compounded an already chaotic situation. This was the breakdown in communication between commanders in advanced positions and the higher command. The divisional commander (Hammersley), in trying to make the best use of the units of the 10th Division which had unexpectedly arrived in his area, added the 31st Brigade to the forces which were preparing to assault the Green, Chocolate and W hills.[66] The commander of the original force refused to move until new instructions had been confirmed by Hammersley in writing. This situation took the best part of the day to resolve and the attack did not go in until dusk. The attacks on Green and Chocolate were successful but the small Turkish garrison made good their escape and entrenched on the W hills. As night was falling operations were suspended until the 8th.

Thus Hamilton's plan had broken down because of the heavy casualties among the leading battalions, the dislocation in the landings of the 34th Brigade and the 10th Division, the breakdown in communications between the assault troops and the divisional commander, and the reluctance of inexperienced officers to move without detailed instructions. To these factors may be added the inherent defects of the plan. This plan called for two battalions of troops, who had never experienced combat, landed at different beaches, without adequate maps, to conduct complicated and coordinated movements in the dark and then assault objectives, the topography of which was unknown. These complexities certainly invited disaster.

On the 7th, as was characteristic of the first day of battles in the First World War, the influence of the high command was negligible. Stopford, off shore in the Jonquil, had as little idea of what was happening on shore as had Hunter-Weston at Hellas on April 25th. At Imbros, Hamilton received no reports from Stopford throughout the morning. When a message finally came through around noon, it merely stated that the force had been unable to advance beyond the edge of the beach. This was an alarming message and conflicted with other information received by Hamilton that

Turkish opposition was weakening. However Hamilton took over $4^{1}/2$ hours to reply to Stopford, probably because his attention was focused on the crucial day's fighting at Anzac, and then merely urged him to "take every advantage before you are forestalled".[67] He did not intervene further and events at Suvla were left to take their course.

The 8th of August has been characterized as the wasted day at Suvla, the day during which men were seen bathing in the bay or lolling around the beaches drinking tea. Indeed few forward movements were made on the 8th, the only substantial one being several battalions in the centre to link the troops on Kiretch Tepe Ridge to those on the Chocolate and Green hills. Yet the only substantial group of Turks in the entire area was on the W hills to the right. The Anafarta Ridge was unoccupied and remained unoccupied throughout the day. Why was no progress made? One reason is said to have been the lack of water. The troops who landed on the 6th and 7th had only water bottles with them. The main supply was in four lighters which were to arrive early on the 7th but due to various mishaps little water arrived until late on the 8th. In addition the mule teams which were to distribute the water were late in disembarking and this made the movement of water in large quantities from the beaches almost impossible.[68] Thus there is little doubt that there was a water shortage on the 8th, although some units apparently received a supply in the early afternoon.[69] Most of the men, however, had used their water allowance by early on the 7th.

A further factor was the poor physical condition of the troops. On the days following the landing the temperature remained in the 90s, the troops were unused to heat, and dysentry had taken its toll. Taken together with the debilitating effect of nervous strain caused by being in action for the first time and lack of sleep, it can be seen that on the 8th the state of the troops was far from perfect.

These factors were compounded by the reluctance of senior commanders to drive forward men in this condition across difficult scrubby country without adequate artillery support. Hammersley considered the men incapable of further action and thought that an advance might so exhaust them as to render them incapable of resisting an attack.[70] Stopford, under pressure from Hamilton, who had received reports that the Anafarta ridge was still unoccupied,[71] eventually ordered an advance, but made it conditional on no strongly held or entrenched positions being attacked until artillery could be brought up.[72] Under these half-hearted instructions only the most tentative forward movements were made. There seems little doubt that more ruthless commanders could have driven the troops forward to some extent. However, it would have been a formidable undertaking to organize an uphill advance on a five mile front over difficult country for a distance of $1^{1}/2$ miles. Such a feat was never managed at Hellas even by Hunter-Weston who was hardly backward in ordering attacks. Furthermore, who is to say that Hammersley would not have been proved correct? Even if sections of the heights had been taken, exhausted troops may have proved incapable of holding them. Another factor that is often overlooked is the difficulty of supplying a large force on the heights. In the absence of pack transport on the 8th, could ammunition, food and water have been manhandled the three or four miles to the Anafarta Ridge? Finally, the disorganized state of the troops on the Suvla plain should not be forgotten. The 10th Division was still split into two unequal parts, with its commander removed from the main area of action. The 11th Division was scattered all over the central plain, into at least four major groups.[73]

G.H.Q., who intervened more actively on this day, remained convinced that "golden opportunities" were thrown away on the 8th.[74] However, Aspinall, who visited Suvla, only saw the men resting in reserve and although he visited Hammersley, made no extensive tour of troops in the forward areas. Much has been made of Hamilton's intervention late on the 8th. After visiting Stopford, Hamilton ordered Hammersley to place at least one battalion on the high ground immediately.[75] But, the troops were so scattered, and their commanding officer so unfamiliar with their disposition, that it took some hours to concentrate the men in fighting order. Some patrols were even withdrawn from the heights themselves in order to fulfill the order.[76] This is an indication of how difficult it would have been to organise two divisions for an overall advance. In the event the British were forestalled by elements of the Turkish 12th Division which had arrived on the ridge some minutes before.[77] Nevertheless, it is hardly accurate to say that the British lost the battle by these few minutes. The British formations were weak and could have only occupied a small section of the ridge. They would soon have been opposed by the entire Turkish 12th Division and their fate could not have been long delayed.

Thus the Suvla plan failed. Great emphasis in accounts of the battle has been laid on the ineptitude of Stopford and Hammersley, who were both eventually relieved of their commands. The real reason for the failure was that the plan was too ambitious.[78] To succeed, the troops had to overcome a night landing in unknown country, advance across a difficult plain in extreme heat and occupy a ridge five miles long capturing intermediate positions along the way, all in forty eight hours. For troops green from England and in poor physical shape such a task was impossible. Furthermore, it is difficult to see how the operation could have affected the main issue at Anzac even if it had been successful. The axes of advance of the two forces were at an angle and the further the Suvla force pushed on the further it got from Birdwood's troops.[79] Moreover, the Anafarta Ridge, at its highest point, was over four miles from Sari Bair and dominated by it. Therefore in no sense was it a commanding position.[80] Birdwood's contention that the Sari Bair position could not have been held without a success at Suvla hardly applies because the guns that he stated could shell the main ridge were dummies and in any case the position was too far distant for artillery, especially in the small numbers available to the Turks, to be a factor.[81] A further advance from the Anafarta Ridge would also have proved futile for it would have taken the troops _away_ from the main objective, the Narrows forts, and _towards_ the widest part of the Peninsula, where there were many more Anafartas to capture. In short a victory at Suvla would only have been useful if the attack from Anzac had succeeded for in that case it would have provided a well situated base for the northern force

* * * * * * * * * * * * * *

Three chapters of The World Crisis are devoted to the June to August phase of the Dardanelles campaign. For the purposes of this discussion Churchill's narrative can be divided into four sections; the question of reinforcements for Hamilton, June and July at Hellas, naval activity and options during the period, and the August attack from Anzac and Suvla Bay.

The first major issue to be discussed by Churchill is the question of reinforcements for Hamilton. Churchill was of course strongly in favour of sending as many divisions as possible and quotes his paper of June 1st in which he suggested that they should be sent with all despatch.[82] He then describes the Dardanelles Committee meeting of June 7th and the Cabinet of June 9th at which it was decided to send these troops and concludes,

"We had now at length got on June 9 the kind of decisions which were necessary to carry the enterprise through to success. There was no _military_ reason of any kind why the decisions which were reached on June 7 and June 9 should not have been taken within 48 hours of Sir Ian Hamilton's telegram of May 17....But from causes in which the enemy had no part, which arose solely from the confusion into which the governing instrument in this country had been thrown, from a fortnight to three weeks had been lost for ever".[83]

Churchill concludes from this argument that the new divisions could have arrived at Gallipoli in time for an attack in the second week of July. In fact they did not arrive until August, by which time the Turks had been greatly reinforced and, Churchill states, the opportunity lost.[84]

There are several dubious assumptions here. Whether it

was the political crisis or Hamilton's reluctance to ask plainly for reinforcements which caused the delay in the new divisions being despatched to the East is open to question. Certainly Churchill's contention that the collapse of the Government was the sole cause is too simplistic.

Churchill's further point that had the troops arrived in July a victory would have been assured now needs to be considered. His argument assumes that the Turks would not have had the troops available in July that they had in August to stop the Allied advance. However, the reinforcements sent to Gallipoli in that month by the Turks came largely in response to the obvious British preparations for a new offensive. There is no reason to believe that Hamilton's preparations in June would have been any less conspicuous. What was to prevent the Turks matching the British and sending their reinforcements two or three weeks earlier? In any case, unlike the British, the Turks always had a large number of divisions near at hand with which they could have reinforced the Peninsula provided they could delay the attackers until the new divisions arrived. The experience of this campaign showed that they were always apt to do this and in these circumstances Churchill's "lost opportunities" are largely theoretical.

Eventually, of course, two more divisions were sent to Hamilton and Churchill next examines the steps taken by the War Council to send these additional reinforcements. His account of his own role in adding the two divisions (53rd and 54th) to the original force (the 10th, 11th and 13th Divisions) is given and agrees with the conclusion reached earlier, that it was largely due to Churchill's influence that the divisions were sent.[85] He also states that there was no reason why these troops could not have been sent earlier[86] and it is certainly strange that Kitchener did not initially think to provide reinforcements in the event of the battle failing to progress. However, it is hard to see that the late arrival of these divisions decisively affected the August battle at Gallipoli. Churchill states that they had to be thrown into battle direct from their voyage,[87] implying that if they had arrived earlier they could have been used to better advantage. But is it the case that an extra two or three weeks in the East would have greatly benefited these formations? The 10th and 11th Divisions were probably weakened by their early arrival because of their exposure to dysentery. In addition the 53rd and 54th Divisions were little more than half strength, a fact not mentioned by Churchill, and because of this would never have been used by Hamilton as more than a reserve. Thus they could only have played a minor role in the battles and Churchill places too much significance on their late despatch from England.

From consideration of reinforcements for Hamilton Churchill turns to a discussion of the battles at Hellas during June and July. Typical of his treatment of these episodes are his comments on the June 4th action.

> "As in all the battles on the Peninsula, the issue hung in a trembling balance. The Turks were thrown into such confusion that on only two kilometres of their front no less than twenty-five battalions (or parts of battalions) were mingled in the line without any higher organization. In these straits the Turkish Divisional Commander reported that no further British attack could be resisted".[88]

The obvious implication is that had reinforcments been available the British could have broken through. It was suggested earlier that a local success might have been possible had the Corps Commander (Hunter-Weston) handled the reserves in a more imaginative way. However, for reasons that are not obvious Churchill continues the line already adopted in The World Crisis and no word of criticism of this commander appears in the narrative. Perhaps Churchill had obtained his opinion of Hunter-Weston from Hamilton, who always seemed to regard him as a perfectly competent, though somewhat brutal, commander. It was also suggested earlier that even a fresh division may not have led to any more than a slight forward move. Churchill implies however, that much larger results could have been expected. During this period he very rarely states what he expected a British victory would mean. Generally he seems to equate victory with the capture of Achi Baba. Certainly in his paper of June 1st, which is included in The World Crisis, he stated that "As soon as our troops can obtain positions from which the Kilid Bahr plateau can be rendered untenable [i.e. Achi Baba] the whole Turkish army concentrated there is lost".[89] But the comment has been made on several occasions that the capture of Achi Baba would not have made the Kilid Bahr plateau untenable or increased the vulnerability of the Narrows forts in any way. So due caution must be exercised when we read in The World Crisis that these battles could have brought victory. A final point that has to be made about this battle is that if the action failed through the lack of one division, then Churchill must share the responsibility, for at the end of April, when the division should have been despatched, he was silent on the need for extra troops. This point is not mentioned in connection with the June 4th battle in The World Crisis.

It has not been thought worthwhile to describe in detail in the first half of this chapter the other actions (June 28th and July 12-13th) discussed by Churchill.[90] In essence the issues were the same as those on June 4th and are treated in the same way in The World Crisis. Churchill never questions the necessity to fight these actions, although they were in fact the eastern equivalent of such battles as Aubers

Ridge and Festubert, against which he has many harsh things to say. Thus, although he laments the fact that Hamilton's divisions were continually dwindling and that their "deficiences were never overtaken by the drafts supplied by the War Office",[91] he never draws the conclusion that part of their deficiency was caused by these futile and bloody encounters, which were planned and sanctioned by Hunter-Weston and Hamilton, the commanders he apparently held in such high regard.

Churchill next discusses the role of the fleet during June and July at Gallipoli. Generally, Churchill is highly critical of the naval inactivity which he says characterized the period. He states that

"The fact that during all this period the British Fleet neither attacked not threatened the forts at the Narrows nor attempted to sweep the minefields enabled the German and Turkish Commanders to draw upon the medium and mobile artillery which defended the Straits for the purpose of succouring the Fifth Turkish Army in its desperate struggle."[92]

He publishes some of the correspondence between the German Commander of the Straits defences, von Usedom, and the Kaiser[93] and includes the list of guns removed as at 20/7/15 which was discussed earlier and claims that the guns removed "were a vital factor in the defences of the Narrows".[94] The implication of all this is that this period provided an opportunity for the fleet to make another attack on the Narrows. However, Churchill's account ignores two facts. The first is that von Usedom was probably exaggerating the plight of the defence in order to obtain as much help as possible from Germany. The second factor is that von Usedom apparently did not inform the Kaiser that while guns were being taken away from the Straits defences, others were being installed, often in different positions. Unlike the Kaiser, however, Churchill must have been aware of this fact because he had seen the report of the Mitchell Committee, the source from which the information on guns installed, used earlier, was obtained. It was shown that by comparing the two lists of figures a reasonably accurate position of the Straits defences at the end of July could be obtained. The conclusion reached was that, although on balance the defence had lost guns, it still constituted a formidable obstacle and it is doubtful if the fleet had any better chance of success during this period than it had in March. Furthermore, the fleet, from mid-July, was fully occupied in preparing for the new landings and Churchill could hardly expect de Robeck to authorize an attack on the Narrows just before operations which were designed to settle the whole campaign were launched. Nor did the fleet have sufficient ammunition to support an offensive by the military and attack the Narrows. These aspects of the problem are not discussed by Churchill.

Churchill also blames de Robeck for the failure to take up the "option" of landing at Bulair. He states definitely that the "plan fell through largely because of naval difficulties".[95] It is true that de Robeck had severe reservations about the operation. These included the inability of the navy to supply three separate landings, lack of small craft, and the danger from submarines, all of which were important factors in the abandonment of the plan. But, as has been shown, de Robeck's objections were not ill-considered. The difficulties detailed by him were real enough and Churchill makes no attempt to refute them. Furthermore, naval objections were not the only reasons for avoiding Bulair. The strongly defended landing places, the fact that any force landed there would be open to attack from both sides and the great distance from the Narrows were military considerations which weighed heavily with Hamilton, as was shown by his correspondence with Kitchener. In fact Churchill had access to this correspondence but it is noticeable that Hamilton is not criticized in The World Crisis for the fact that the plan was abandoned.

After harshly criticizing the high command of the fleet Churchill proceeds to bestow praise on one facet of the work of the fleet where it was hardly due. In discussing the use of ships' guns by the military as a substitute for heavy mobile artillery he claims that "The observation and direction of the ships' fire attained every week a higher efficiency. This process continued steadily until naval co-operation in land fighting on Gallipoli had become a factor of the utmost value".[96] It is certainly true that the fire of the fleet deterred the Turks to a certain extent from attacking in the open and was also a factor in maintaining the morale of the allied troops. However, it was suggested earlier that the ships' guns were not as efficient as Churchill implies. No doubt co-operation between the Navy and the Army on shore improved as the months went by as Churchill states, but he ignores the fact that this would be offset to a certain extent by the inaccuracies caused by the wear to the ships' guns. Furthermore, it was shown that the ships were never able to obtain the pinpoint accuracy necessary to destroy the Turkish artillery and, although Churchill claims that observation of the ships' fire had improved, he neglects to mention that the aerial spotting force was never large enough to ensure continual good observation for the ships.

As in Churchill's account of the April 25th landings, there is no discussion in The World Crisis of the planning of the August offensive. The explanation for this would seem to be that by avoiding a discussion of the merits and feasiblity of the plan Churchill can focus attention away from the planners and on to the commanders who were to put the plan into operation. This, as will be shown, serves a very useful purpose for Churchill.

For clarity, Churchill's accounts of the Anzac and Suvla offensives will be considered separately.

Churchill's narrative of the Anzac battle opens with brief summaries of the diversions at Hellas and Lone Pine.[97] He states that the Hellas action was a success and that the Turks were able to withdraw only one division from that sector to reinforce Anzac.[98] This is possibly true but Churchill does not draw the attention of the reader to the fact that these men played a crucial part in thwarting the northern advances. Nor does Churchill make clear that the diversions at Hellas soon developed into full scale battles in which the commander (deLisle) seemed to ignore the original objective, and attempted to secure a major victory, the only result being heavy casualties.

The description of the opening day of the battle at Anzac in The World Crisis is brief and generally accurate. More controversial are the conclusions drawn by Churchill from the day's fighting. "Had it been possible to have leap-frogged the exhausted troops by a wave of fresh reinforcements, the whole crest of Sari Bair might well have fallen before noon into our possession".[99] This he calls the "cardinal fatality".[100] This process would have been much more difficult than is implied by this passage. On the left, the problem on the 7th was hardly one of leap-frogging fresh troops through Monash's exhausted column for that formation was hopelessly lost and well away from the main route to the summit. The problem facing a new formation would have been to actually find the correct route to 971 and the experience of the columns from the 13th Division on the 8th (they all lost their way) gives no great cause for optimism. The same factors faced an attempt to relieve the troops in the centre and on the right but to a lesser extent in that the distances were shorter. Another difficulty in using reinforcements on the 7th was the problem of fitting more men into the Anzac perimeter and of supplying them once they were there. In fact Churchill admits these difficulties[101] but gives the impression that they could have been overcome. He does not, however, put forward any explanation as to how these problems might have been solved.

Churchill's description of events on the 8th is barely adequate. He makes no mention of the columns of reserves which did attempt to "leap-frog" through the exhausted men near the summits. The performance of these columns certainly throws grave doubts on Churchill's proposed solution for resuming the attack on the 7th. He also states that the original front of attack was restricted on the 8th to Chunuk Bair and Hill Q.[102] In fact, a decision to this effect was not made until the 9th. On the 8th Monash made a further attempt to advance up Hill 971 though with no result. Furthermore, Churchill adds that Monash and the centre column failed to advance partly because they were "unsupported by any help from Suvla Bay".[103] This is a grossly misleading statement. Even if the Suvla landing had proceeded as scheduled, there is no possible way that Stopford's men could have assisted this column on Hill Q which was many miles from the landing points and at an angle of 90 degrees to the main line of advance. On the left the Suvla force could only have affected the issue if their advance had either outflanked the entire Anzac position causing a general Turkish withdrawal all along the line or if they could have provided more direct assistance to Monash by advancing from Buyuk Anarfarta along the main ridge to 971. In fact, the seizure of the Tekke Tepe ridge would not have outflanked the Turks at Anzac though continued further advances might have. Whether these advances would have been possible will be discussed later. It suffices to say here that they could not have been made by the 8th, the period in which Churchill apparently expected their influence to become important. It is also hard to see how an advance along the main ridge would have been possible by the 8th, for this would have involved further increasing the almost impossible objectives given to the Anzac force. Moreover the country between Buyuk Anafarta and 971 is some of the most difficult and tangled on the Peninsula, a continuation of the series of ridges and ravines which prevented Monash's seasoned troops from discovering the correct route to the summit of the ridge. In these circumstances the task set the inexperienced Suvla divisions by Churchill is clearly impossible.

In describing the battles of the 9th, Churchill concentrates on the dramatic events concerning the Ghurka attack on Hill Q. In fact almost his entire account consists of an extract from the diary of Col. Allanson who led the assault.[104] This extract has since been published many times and in slightly different versions, yet in some ways it seems a very unreliable document. James has pointed out that in the description of the shells incident the words "I saw a flash in the bay" were not included in The World Crisis.[105] Certainly Allanson's account is more credible without the phrase for it is obvious that the bay could not be seen from the reverse slopes. It is not certain if this passage was removed by Allanson or Churchill. There are other curious statements in the extract in The World Crisis. Allanson claims he saw "motors and wheeled transport, on the roads leading to Achi Baba".[106] The Turks however had no motor transport. Also he says "I saw the advance at Suvla Bay had failed, though I could not detect more than one or two thousand against them".[107] Yet it was almost impossible for Allanson to have identified the numbers of Turks at Suvla at that distance, many of whom would have been concealed by the scrub. Moreover, Allanson has seen too much. He has just taken part in a ferocious assault, seen his friends killed at his side, suffered the trauma of having

150 men of his brigade wiped out by shells and been wounded in the leg. Yet he claims he was able to witness the scene at the Straits, at Kilid Bahr at Suvla and recall it in some detail. Though Churchill no doubt included Allanson's account for its vivid and compelling prose these very qualities cast doubts on its veracity. Thus although the actual assault on the ridge no doubt took place much as Allanson described it, his account of what he witnessed from the ridge must be treated with more caution than Churchill does in The World Crisis.

Allanson's account serves another purpose for Churchill. Phrases such as "the key to the whole Peninsula was ours", "we commanded Kilid Bahr, and the rear of Achi Baba and the communications to all their army there" and "Below I saw the Straits"[108] which occur throughout Allanson's account are all designed to impress on the mind of the reader the commanding position which had been reached by Allanson and how near the Anzac attack had been to final victory. However, these sections of Allanson's, and therefore Churchill's, account are no more reliable than those already discussed. It was shown earlier that the British never really commanded Sari Bair in sufficient numbers or over a substantial enough front to claim that the ridge was theirs. Even if Allanson had not been shelled off this ridge the fate of the larger force of New Zealanders on Chunuk Bair is an indication that, unless reinforced in considerable strength, their positions were always vulnerable to counter-attack, especially as the defenders had no heavy or automatic weapons available. Furthermore, there are grounds for thinking that the entire ridge had to be captured before any position on it was secure, for areas like Hill Q and Chunuk Bair could always be enfiladed from sections of the ridge to the north. The difficulty of supplying a large force on the ridge, as with most logistical problems, is not discussed in The World Crisis.

It is even doubtful if the ridge was the "key to the whole Peninsula" as claimed by Allanson and Churchill. Certainly, if the testimony of General Johnson is accurate, large reinforcements or long range artillery would have been needed before the Straits could be dominated, providing of course it proved possible to manoeuvre the guns on to the ridge. Also, Allanson's proposition is based on the fact that, although the Anzacs were able to maintain their positions when the Turks held the heights, with the Anzacs in the dominant position the Turks would have been forced back. Here is a further example of that under-estimation of the fighting quality of the Turks which on many other occasions proved to be disastrously wrong. The final claim that the ridge "commanded Kilid Bahr and the rear of Achi Baba", as a glance at a map will show, is so preposterous that it does not require further comment.

We must now turn to Churchill's description of the Suvla

Bay landing. He states that the Suvla plans involved securing "Suvla Bay as a winter base for Anzac and all the troops operating in that neighbourhood".[109] This it will be remembered was the second version of the plan as modified by Stopford and, although it was suggested earlier that too much has been made by historians of this modification, Churchill seems unaware of the fact that it had even taken place.

The World Crisis then moves on to discuss the events of the 6/7th August. It is noticeable that Churchill's account makes no mention of the fact that the troops were in a poor physical state before the landing, although it was shown earlier that this was a major factor in the lack of progress made on the 7th and 8th. His narrative of the battle instead begins with the landing of the 32nd, 33rd, and 34th Brigades which he says disembarked "without much loss in two or three hours".[110] It is true that two of the brigades suffered few casualties and that the 32nd and 33rd Brigades were disembarked in the time mentioned. However, the grounding of the landing craft of the 34th Brigade was a more important factor than Churchill states and it delayed the landing for a further three hours, making the disembarkation time 6 hours, not the two or three stated in The World Crisis. Nor does he mention that the 32nd Brigade suffered heavy casualties especially in officers, though this is an important factor in the relatively poor showing made by this formation over the next two days.

For the proceedings of the 7th of August at Suvla Bay Churchill's account is completely inadequate.[111] His description of the landing of the 10th Division gives the impression that the event proceeded in an orderly manner. He is apparently unaware of the fact that the landing was disrupted by the decision to land the greater part of it on the right flank and the subsequent decision to land the remainder (with the commander) on the left. This movement in fact disrupted the whole plan, caused great delays and is essential for an understanding of why so little progress was made on the 7th. Indeed it was shown earlier that it was the fact that units of the 10th Division were added to the force that was to attack Chocolate Hill that caused such confusion between the brigades involved and the divisional commander and that most of the day was spent in sorting out the various misunderstandings which occurred. Churchill does not mention any of these facts and offers no explanation at all for the failure to advance more on this day.

Churchill places the entire blame for the failure to advance on the 8th on the local commander, Stopford, who, he says, was concerned that the enemy might be more numerous than the intelligence reports stated and that there might be more Turks in the area than was revealed by aeroplane reconnaissance.[112] He then gives an impression of the scene at Suvla on the 8th, a

"placid, prudent, elderly English gentleman [Stopford]
with his 20,000 men spread around the beaches, the front
lines sitting on the tops of shallow trenches, smoking
and cooking, with here and there an occasional rifle
shot, others bathing by hundreds in the bright blue bay
where, disturbed hardly by a single shell, floated the
great ships of war".[113]

For good measure he then gives Aspinall's impression of the
scene, which was couched in similar terms.[114]

It was suggested earlier that these impressions were
hardly representative of the true state of affairs at Suvla.
Churchill's and Aspinall's account ignore the fact that, in
temperatures to which they were hardly accustomed, most of
the men had been 48 hours without adequate supplies of water
and proper food; that their physical condition before this
ordeal had been poor; that the strain of being in action for
the first time had exercised its debilitating effects and
that many of their leaders, the junior officers, were dead or
wounded and that most of the units of the 10th and 11th
Divisions were hopelessly intermixed. The World Crisis is
more accurate in its description of the supine behaviour of
Stopford, and Churchill is correct in stating that there were
no continuous trench lines and only a few thousand Turks in
front of the British. What he does not explain is how men in
the condition described above and scattered all over the
Suvla plain (the fact that the 10th Division was split in two
is still ignored by Churchill) could have been organized to
advance on a four-mile front, across difficult country, up
hill for $1^{1/2}$ miles. Nor does he explain how supplies
could have been got to the men (no mules had been landed at
the time when Churchill expected the advance could begin) had
such an advance been made or whether, after these efforts, in
his opinion the troops would have been in any condition to
withstand a Turkish counter-attack. It is noticeable that,
although nothing even approaching this feat was attempted by
the aggressive Hunter-Weston at Hellas, Churchill does not
censure him as he does Stopford, for thwarting Hamilton's
plan.

Along with many writers since, Churchill makes far too
much of Hamilton's intervention late on the 8th. Churchill
considers that Hamilton's action could have had decisive
results on the battle had the brigade ordered reached the
heights in time.[115] However, it should be noted that the
force ordered on to the ridge was only a brigade and it is
hardly possible that even had it reached the ridge, it would
have been able to withstand an attack by the two Turkish
divisions which were rapidly approaching the area. In fact
the battle was not lost by Hammersley and Stopford; nor by
the inexperienced troops of the 10th and 11th Divisions, but
by the overambitious nature of the plan. But this is not a
factor mentioned in The World Crisis.

It is surprising to find that the futile and bloody attempts to advance at Suvla during the remainder of August are covered in some detail by Churchill.[116] Perhaps he is trying to emphasize the high cost that was paid for the failure to advance on the 7th and 8th. Another lesson could be drawn from these actions and that is that Stopford, who deprecated any attempt to advance after the failure on the 9th, had a truer view of the likelihood of success than Hamilton, under whose orders these attempts were made. But no criticism of Hamilton is to be found in these pages.

In one respect Churchill's account of the August battles contains a fundamental contradiction. At the beginning of the chapter he says, "The British did not possess any of the preponderance necessary for an offensive. Once their attack was fully disclosed and battle was joined along the whole front, there was no reasonable expectation of their being able to defeat the Turkish Army".[117] Yet this statement is contradicted by the whole thrust of the remainder of the chapter. We have already seen how he considered the Anzac attack came close to decisive results on the 9th. He also says that the decision to place the Turkish reserves marching on Suvla under Mustapha Kemal confided in that officer "the vital fortunes of the whole of the Ottoman Empire",[118] certainly an indication that he considered important issues were at stake. What appears to have happened is that Churchill's first assessment, based on the numbers involved on either side, has been overtaken by the excitement generated by his descriptions of the battles until he has been convinced by his own rhetoric and love of drama that this assessment was wrong.

At the end of this Suvla chapter Churchill includes a table of the numbers of Turkish troops occupying the Peninsula and British troops available for an attack, at various dates from February to August.[119] This replaced a long summary of the naval operation and its prospects with which Churchill originally concluded the chapter.[120] Small sections of the latter were included in a later chapter called "The Consequences of 1915". The rest was omitted. However most of this material made points already covered – no doubt this is the explanation of why it was excluded. Indeed even the table of troop strengths makes the same case that Churchill has been developing from the beginning of the Dardanelles chapters. However, a summary of the case against Churchill's argument may be useful. In the table, Churchill identifies three "favourable occasions" on which success should have been assured. The first is on February 18th when he states that only 5,000 Turkish troops were on the Peninsula and 36,000 Allied troops available for the attack.[121] It will be remembered however that at this time Churchill was assuring his colleagues that troops would not be needed for the purpose of fighting on the Peninsula and it seems hardly appropriate for him in retrospect to identify this as an ideal time for an assault. Furthermore, the 36,000 troops available were the partly-trained Anzacs, a force Churchill said at the time was not capable of even "mopping up" operations without a stiffening of regulars. The second occasion is on March 20th when Churchill says the relative numbers were 14,000 Turks and 60,000 Allied troops. Although Churchill mentions that uncertain weather was a factor at this time, he obviously underrates it because it is clear that he thinks a landing was possible. In fact, the weather was so bad during the next few weeks that this assumption of Churchill is extremely doubtful. Also, although the odds in favour of the Allies were 4 to 1, the landings in April showed that even major landings could be held up by relatively small numbers of troops. Moreover, and this a crucial point that Churchill's table ignores, the Turkish troops listed only had to delay the landings long enough to enable reserves to be brought up. In other words, the Turkish figures are minimums, the Allied maximums. Finally Churchill's third set of figures for July 7th, 70-75,000 Turks to 150,000 Allied troops, presumes that the Allied preparations for battle would not have provoked an equivalent Turkish response and also over-estimates the Allied total by counting all the Divisions at full strength, when some of them were barely 50% effective.

Chapter 10

## THE DARDANELLES V - EVACUATION AND CHURCHILL'S BALKAN POLICY

It has already been related how, after the failure of the
Suvla attack, Hamilton's request for substantial
reinforcements was turned down by the Dardanelles Committee
on the grounds that all troops were needed for the battle in
France. Shortly after this however the fortunes of the
campaign seemed to improve when the French Government
announced that they were preparing an army of four divisions
for the East. It was to be commanded by General Sarrail and
operate on the Asiatic side of the Straits. The French plan
was welcomed by the British but it soon transpired that
Joffre was opposed to the move and this opposition eventually
proved decisive. Later in October the disturbing news of
Bulgarian mobilization reached London. On the 6th Bulgaria
had signed a pact with Austria-Hungary and Germany and plans
for a combined attack on Serbia had been canvassed. When the
intentions of the Central Powers became known, Serbia
appealed to Greece for aid under the terms of a pre-war
treaty and Greece appealed to Britain and France for troops
to enable her to fulfill her obligations to Serbia. Two
divisions (one British, one French) were eventually
despatched from the Dardanelles to Salonica. However, before
more than the advanced guard of these formations had arrived
the pro-allied Venizelos Government fell and was replaced by
a more neutralist administration which immediately repudiated
its treaty obligation to Serbia. The British now argued that
the raison detre of the Salonica plan no longer existed but
suggested that six divisions be sent to the East to be used
in accordance with the developing situation. The French,
however, insisted that the British adhere to the original
plan and under the threat of resignation of Joffre they
reluctantly agreed.

Meanwhile the War Council had decided to recall Hamilton,
who, it was felt, had lost the confidence of the troops.
General Monro was sent from the Western Front to report on
the future of the campaign. Monro favoured evacuation,
especially as Bulgaria had now entered the war on the German

side thus opening a direct route from Germany to Turkey. Kitchener refused to accept this decision before seeing the situation at Gallipoli at first hand. He arrived at the Dardanelles on November 9th and soon came to the same conclusion as Monro. An alternative plan for landing the Gallipoli force at Ayas Bay near Alexandretta was rejected by the reconstituted Dardanelles Committee, now called the War Committee. They also turned down a proposal to retain the bridgehead at Hellas for naval reasons and opted for complete evacuation. At this point Admiral de Robeck returned to England on leave. The naval command passed to Wemyss who immediately offered to renew the naval attack. Perhaps as a result of this new resolve the Cabinet overthrew the decision of the War Committee and decided that the whole question of evacuation should be examined at a conference with the French. At that conference the French, with Russian and Italian support, insisted that Gallipoli should be evacuated and resources concentrated on the defence of Salonica. Despite further attempts by Wemyss to convince the War Committee that a renewed naval attack was feasible the British adhered to the agreed policy. Anzac and Suvla were evacuated on December 19th and 20th and Hellas on January 8th. Surprisingly, in view of the forecasts of up to fifty percent losses, there was hardly a casualty. The Dardanelles Campaign was at an end.

\* \* \* \* \* \* \* \* \* \* \* \* \*

In The World Crisis only the barest outline of the events summarized above is given. Five main topics have therefore been identified as being worthy of further discussion. These are, Churchill's role in the origin of the Salonica expedition, his attitude towards a new naval attack at the Dardanelles, his comments on the missions of Monro and Kitchener to the East, and his account of the final decision to evacuate the Peninsula. It will also be necessary to comment briefly on the summary of the naval war with which Churchill concludes his Dardanelles chapters.

The first area of controversy is Churchill's handling of the origin of the Salonica expedition. He states that

"As a military measure to aid Serbia directly, the landing... at Salonika was absurd. The hostile armies concentrating on the eastern and northern frontiers of Serbia were certain to overwhelm and overrun that country before any effective aid, other than Greek aid, could possibly arrive. As a political move to encourage and determine the action of Greece, the despatch of allied troops to Salonika was justified. But the question arose: Where were the troops to come from? Obviously from the Dardanelles and only from the Dardanelles. A French and a British division, all that could be spared and all that could get to Salonika in time, were accordingly taken from Sir Ian Hamilton's hard-pressed army in the closing days of September."[1]

Churchill goes on to say that "The reader who has a true sense of the values in the problem will not be surprised to learn that this despatch of troops from the Dardanelles produced the opposite effect to that intended or desired."[2] He claims that the Greeks became concerned that the Dardanelles were about to be abandoned and that this made them more determined than ever not to intervene.[3] He concludes that after the change of government in Greece "the object of the expedition to Salonika had entirely disappeared" and that from then on "I continued to point to the Dardanelles as the master key to the problem."[4]

It is difficult, from the passages quoted, to discern what Churchill's own role in the Salonica decision was, or whether he was in agreement with the policy adopted. On the one hand he says that the original decision was justified on political grounds and the only troops that could reach Salonica in time were those from the Dardanelles. On the other hand he says that it was obvious that the move had the opposite effect on Greece to that intended. He is careful however, to frame this point in such a way as to avoid saying that he thought it obvious at the time. What then was Churchill's Salonica policy?

The question of definite aid to Greece and Serbia first came before the War Council on September 23rd. After a discussion of what aid could be sent, Churchill said that

"there would be no great opportunity to clear up the situation in the Dardanelles until about the 15th December ... It would then be the wet weather and Suvla Bay would be difficult to hold ... [if the French Asiatic plan did not develop] it seemed sounder to him to abandon the Suvla "extension" and to hold Anzac and Hellas ... This would enable us to extract four divisions from a bad position in marshy country and use these divisions to strengthen and occupy the uncontested zone [in Serbia] in order to prevent the whole of the Balkans going by the run."[5]

Later he said that "by sending four divisions now rotting at Suvla we might be able to prevent the Austro-German incursion".[6] Thus Churchill was strongly in favour of sending troops to Salonica and it was he who first suggested that a portion of Hamilton's force be used for this purpose. There is no mention of this facet of Churchill's Salonica policy in The World Crisis and to this extent his account is incomplete. As for his argument that the weakening of Gallipoli affected the Greek resolve, it is extremely doubtful if events at Gallipoli weighed greatly with them.

All their actions seemed to be governed by events on the major war fronts and not by what was taking place at the Dardanelles.

Eventually Churchill's plan to occupy part of Serbian Macedonia as a guarantee to Bulgaria was rejected by the War Council. Presumably it was thought that an expedition to save Serbia which forcibly occupied a section of her territory and promised it to her sworn enemy was not likely to further the British cause in the Balkans. There is no mention of this plan in The World Crisis and it is clear that Churchill's account of this incident has been carefully constructed to avoid revealing exactly what his policy was. The reason for this is obvious. Churchill would not want to be identified with the inception of such a fruitless campaign as Salonica. In addition he would not want it known that he once considered emasculating Hamilton's force in favour of the Balkan plan because he considered the force at Suvla to be rotting. Finally he may not have wished the anti-Serb aspects of his policy known.

Churchill's account is much more reliable in dealing with the development of his Salonica policy after the Greek change of government. He claims in The World Crisis that from this point on he opposed strenuously sending troops to Salonica and this claim is borne out by the documents. For example, on October 6th he told the Dardanelles Committee that "it appeared to him that there was no chance of saving the general situation in the Balkans. The only question was whether there was still time to save the situation in Gallipoli".[7] However on October 15th he stated "I believe that the gaining of Greece and Roumania to our side now is a more urgent and a more important objective than forcing the Dardanelles"[8]. But this switch seems to have been an aberration from Churchill's general line which was, as stated in The World Crisis, to focus attention back to the Dardanelles. (It is interesting to note that from this memorandum dealing with the Salonica question sections of which are quoted in The World Crisis, Churchill has omitted the words underlined from the following passage, "Anzac is the greatest word in the history of Australasia. Is it for ever to carry to future generations of Australians and New Zealanders memories of forlorn heroism and of sacrifices made in vain at the incapable bidding of the British Government?"[9] Perhaps he considered it inadvisable for the Dominions to become aware of these sentiments or he may have considered that there was a danger that he would be numbered among the incapable.)

The second area of controversy to be dealt with by Churchill is the matter of a renewed naval attack on the Narrows. He quotes his letter to Balfour of October 6th in which he advocated renewing the naval attack and suggested that "even a few ships in the Marmora would absolutely cut off the Turkish Army and relieve us of all our difficulties".[10] He then chronicles the return of Keyes to London in late October and quotes with approval the Keyes plan. Essentially Churchill says, this plan was for a squadron of the oldest battleships, fitted with mine bumpers and preceded by the best sweepers, to rush the Narrows and attack the forts in reverse. Meanwhile, of the remaining two squadrons, one would attack from below the Narrows and the other bombard from across the Peninsula. This triple assault was to be continued until the forts had been silenced and the Turkish Army cut off from its base.[11] Finally he lists, again with approval, the various attempts by Wemyss to have the naval attack renewed.[12] The questions that now have to be asked are, did the naval attack stand any more chance of success in the later months of 1915 than it did in February and March and, if it succeeded would it have done what its supporters claimed, namely cut off the Turkish Army from its supplies?

Whether the Keyes variation on the Carden plan would have achieved success is as much a matter for speculation as whether a renewed attack would have succeeded after March 18th. Two features of the Keyes plan should however be noted. The first is that it is doubtful if the mine bumpers fitted to the ships would have proved effective, for an efficient anti-mine device, the paravane, was not developed until 1918. Also it seems doubtful whether the squadron firing across the Peninsula could have achieved much, considering that each gun in the forts had to be hit and given the limited quantities of ammunition available. In fact the whole plan really depended on the mine sweepers ahead of the fleet remaining in position through the entire rush, for the chances of a ship hitting a mine in an unswept field were 99 in 100.[13] However, as has been shown in a previous chapter, the minefield defences were, even in October, a formidable obstacle and the odds were surely against the sweepers getting through unscathed. Furthermore, Wemyss' confidence stemmed partly from his view that the efficiency of the minefields had been much reduced during the occupation period.[14] According to the Mitchell Committee this view was incorrect, the mines remaining in place to the end of the campaign. A further aspect of the plan has been questioned by another authority. Admiral Dewar has stated that the forts in the Narrows could not be taken in reverse and were not open to direct fire from the northward.[15] This, it will be remembered, was a crucial aspect of the Keyes plan.

What if the Fleet had got into the Marmora? Could it have starved out the Turkish Army on Gallipoli? Keyes and his supporters considered that all Turkish communications with the Peninsula could have been cut.[16] Others held a different view. De Robeck pointed out that only one of the roads along the Bulair isthmus could be controlled by the navy and then only by day. A second road was out of sight from the sea and could only be bombarded with continual aerial reconnaissance, which was an impossibility due to the distance of Bulair from the nearest island airfield.[17] Another problem was the difficulty of preventing supplies reaching the Turks across the Narrows at night. In addition, it is doubtful if the Fleet could have maintained itself in the Marmora for a long enough period to starve out the Turks. To remain in the Marmora the Fleet would have to have been accompanied by unarmoured colliers and supply ships, which faced a much more hazardous journey than that facing the armoured ships.[18] Once more, the naval prospects seem hardly commensurate with the risks.

We now come to one of the most controversial incidents described in this section of The World Crisis. This is the visit of General Monro to Gallipoli to report on the future of the campaign. Churchill introduces Monro by saying "He belonged to that school whose supreme conception of Great War strategy was 'killing Germans'. Anything that killed Germans was right. Anything that did not kill Germans was useless".[19] He then goes on to describe Monro's visit to Gallipoli in a classic passage which must be quoted at length.

"General Monro's report was awaited with the utmost anxiety. There was however no need for suspense. General Monro was an officer of swift decision. He came, he saw, he capitulated. He reached the Dardanelles on October 28; and already on the 29th he and his staff were discussing nothing but evacuation. On the 30th he landed on the Peninsula. Without going beyond the Beaches, he familiarized himself in the space of six hours with the conditions prevailing on the 15-mile front of Anzac, Suvla and Hellas, and spoke a few discouraging words to the principal officers at each point. To the Divisional Commanders summoned to meet him at their respective Corps Headquarters, he put separately and in turn a question in the following sense: 'On the supposition that you are going to get no more drafts can you maintain your position in spite of the arrival of strong reinforcements with heavy guns and limitless German ammunition? He thus collected a number of dubious answers, armed with which he returned to Imbros. He never again set foot on the Peninsula during the tenure of his command. His Chief-of-the-Staff, also an enthusiast for evacuation, never visited it at all. On October 31 General Monro despatched his telegram recommending the total evacuation of the Gallipoli Peninsula and the final abandonment of the campaign. According to his own statements he contemplated, in addition to the ruin of the whole enterprise, a loss of from thirty to forty per cent of the Army, i.e., about forty thousand officers and men. This he was prepared to accept. Two days later he left for Egypt, leaving the command of the Dardanelles Army temporarily in the hands of General Birdwood."[20]

Before the content of this passage is examined, several points should be made about the way it was written. The final version owed much to an unknown proofreader (perhaps Aspinall or Hamilton) who suggested after reading an early draft that Churchill had not made enough of Monro's visit.[21] Churchill then expanded the material concerned with Monro's tour of the Peninsula and included a sentence suggested by the proofreader to the effect that Monro's Chief of Staff, Lynden Bell, had never visited the Peninsula at all.[22]

When Sir John Edmonds saw this chapter in proof he commented,

"Monro was by no means a man of 'fixed ideas and rapid decision' [this had been Churchill's original phrase]. He was (in 1914-18) a man of considerable [ability?] a 'character' who thought things out carefully & then acted. As commander of the 2nd. Division no one enjoyed more the confidence of [those?] under him. He was looked on by many as the most suitable successor to French in Command of the B.E.F. ... Six hours ashore was ample. What good could he do by wandering around more trenches when he could see all he wanted to see from the water.[23]

Churchill ignored most of the advice contained in this letter. The only concession made was that the words "fixed ideas" were removed from one of the opening sentences. He was by no means ready to forgive so easily the man who had "ruined" the whole enterprise.

This section also contains an interesting illustration of how Churchill laboured to create one of his famous phrases. In summing up Monro's decision to evacuate he first wrote "He came, he saw, he scuttled." He then crossed through "scuttled" and substituted "surrendered", "He came, he saw, he surrendered". Finally he deleted "surrendered" for "capitulated" and produced the infinitely better - because of its alliterative coincidence with the original - "He came, he saw, he capitulated".[24]

We must now turn to the substance of Churchill's charges against Monro. He makes three main points; that Monro had already made up his mind on evacuation before he had objectively assessed the situation; that his visit to the Peninsula was too short to obtain a proper perspective; and that his decision to evacuate was wrong.

In fact Monro's first action when he reached the Dardanelles, indicated that he had not yet decided on evacuation. He telegraphed to Kitchener asking for experienced company commanders, material for shell-proof shelters, and reinforcements for the Territorial divisions; he stated that he was much impressed by the physique and military bearing of the Anzacs.[25] This telegram contradicts Aspinall's recollection that Lynden Bell had said "There is no question about the evacuation; that is entirely determined; what we require, and must have, is local backing".[26] Of course Monro's telegram to Kitchener could have been sent to make it appear that Monro was still undecided as it would have been exceedingly impolitic for him to have mentioned evacuation in his first communication with Kitchener, written only a few hours after his arrival. In these circumstances no final decision is possible but it should be noted that Churchill does not mention Monro's initial telegram. Furthermore, the vital facts needed to decide on the future of the campaign (the Government's commitment to the operation, the number of troops likely to be sent in future) were available in London and did not need an on-the-spot assessment and to this extent Churchill's criticism misses the point.

In criticizing Monro for the precipitate nature of his decision, Churchill has neglected to mention that it was Kitchener who "forced the pace".[27] After receiving Monro's first telegram he replied "Please send me as soon as possible your report on the main issue at the Dardanelles, namely, leaving or staying".[28] This forced Monro to set out for the Peninsula at once and to produce his report just 36 hours later. It is clear that he would have preferred more time and he complained to his military secretary that he did not consider Kitchener's demand for a decision either "fair or reasonable".[29] Concerning the small amount of time spent on the Peninsula, Edmonds' point that the positions were so small they could virtually be seen at a glance seems a reasonable one. Also Monro must have had a good idea of the beachheads from studying maps and charts on the way out.

Was then Monro's decision correct? One of the first documents studied by Monro on his arrival at Gallipoli was an appreciation drawn up by Aspinall. The conclusion reached in this document was that a fresh offensive could not be carried out before the spring of 1916 because of the weather. Aspinall then stated that for good progress to be made an advance on either side of the Straits was necessary and for this 400,000 men plus 20% for drafts would be needed.[30] This was hardly an encouraging document, for Monro must have been aware that there was no chance of troops in this number being made available for the east in 1916. There were other discouraging opinions. Dawnay had drawn up an appreciation decidedly gloomy in tone[31] and two of the Corps Commanders, Byng and Davies, had told Monro that they considered evacuation advisable.[32] Only Birdwood was in favour of holding on although even he admitted that he could not see how good progress could be made.[33] Thus there was a substantial body of local opinion which favoured evacuation. However, evacuation was not likely to be free of cost. Aspinall had mentioned that such an operation would probably cost 40,000-50,000 men, two-thirds of the guns and all the stores[34] and these figures seemed to have been generally accepted. Monro has therefore been blamed by Churchill for coolly contemplating a loss on this scale. But Churchill does not provide evidence to suggest that Monro was the type of officer who would have viewed losses of this size with equanimity. Also the likely loss during evacuation had to be balanced against the loss involved in holding on. From October 23rd until the beginning of the Suvla and Anzac evacuation the casualty rate was approximately 860 per week.[35] At this rate holding on through the winter would have cost about 15,000 casualties, some of whom would have been able to fight again. However to this figure must be added losses from sickness. During October this total was averaging 750 per day, some of whom would never fight again.[36] Sickness from dysentery could be expected to drop with the onset of winter but other complaints such as frostbite, which could permanently incapacitate a man, would rise. Thus the balance sheet was by no means as one-sided as Churchill suggests.

There were, in addition, other good reasons for evacuation. All along the line the Turks held the advantage of position and the winter would have been an unpleasant prospect for the British holding the lower slopes. All chance of surprise, short of another landing, had gone and another landing could not have been sustained by the fleet. The local commanders then were faced with the prospect of making a series of frontal attacks in order to break through and it had been demonstrated time and again that this form of operation was futile. Furthermore, without the numbers mentioned by Aspinall there was no hope of building up the superiority necessary to defeat the 200,000 Turkish troops in the near vicinity of the Peninsula. But even if reinforcements in the numbers suggested by Aspinall were provided it is not clear how the navy could have supplied them. If the force remained on the defensive the question of the value of the exercise has to be asked. No doubt the force was tying down a considerable proportion of the Turkish Army but this could have been accomplished with much less loss if the British had adopted a defensive stance along the line of the Suez Canal. All these points were made in a memorandum written by Monro in November.[37] In retrospect his arguments seem unanswerable but Churchill ignores these points in The World Crisis and concentrates only on the ruin of the campaign. In one respect only is he probably correct. He states in The World Crisis that the Turks could have expected little help from the Germans in the provision of heavy artillery or ammunition.[38] The evacuationists disagreed with this view and dwelt at length on the horrific effects the German guns would have on the British positions.[39]  However, it seems unlikely that the Germans would have withdrawn significant quantities of heavy artillery from their main fronts, where it was desperately needed.  In any case transporting the guns to Gallipoli must have taken a considerable time and it is probable that few additional guns could have arrived before the end of the winter.

It will be remembered that following Monro's decision in favour of evacuation Kitchener visited Gallipoli to see the situation for himself.  Churchill's description of this mission is misleading on one important point.  He gives the impression that Kitchener was in favour of holding on by saying that "His personal inspection of the troops and the defences convinced him that the troops could hold their positions unless confronted with very heavy German reinforcements".[40]  This was true but it did not mean that Kitchener thought the troops should hold on.  In fact he soon endorsed Monro's view, with the exception that he bowed to de Robeck's opinion that Hellas should be retained.[41]

Eventually the Government opted for complete evacuation. In The World Crisis Churchill strongly condemns this decision.  He states that although the Government were able to contemplate the loss of 40,000 to 50,000 men they would not sanction a renewal of the naval attack which might cost only a handful of men and a few old battleships,[42] and he sums up his opinion of their attitude in a memorable phrase, "The determination of the British Government to give in at all costs was now inflexible".[43]  This is hardly a fair summary of the difficulties which faced the Cabinet.  All their naval advisers (except the relatively junior Keyes) had assured them that evacuation was their only option.  This advice was reinforced by the overwhelming majority of military opinion.  The Government were also aware of the cost of maintaining a force on Gallipoli, though Churchill apparently was not.  It would have been a brave or perhaps foolhardy Government which ignored the advice of its military experts.  In short although the decision to evacuate was a difficult one to make it is hard to see how anything else could have been done.

This section of The World Crisis is concluded by Churchill with a short survey of the naval war.  He identifies two schools of naval thought;  the "passive school", which saw the navy's role as subsidiary to the army and advocated the husbanding of naval resources for the Great Battle.  "The opposite view was that the Navy was a gigantic instrument of offensive war, capable of intervening with decisive effect in the general strategy".[44]  This fundamental misconception appears repeatedly in The World Crisis.  Churchill fails to see that Germany, without a vulnerable sea coast and with an army running into millions, was practically immune to offensive operations by the Fleet. In fact Turkey was the only one of the Central Powers with an open sea coast and a small navy and given Churchill's views it seems almost inevitable that he should have attempted to use the navy against her. The theory of "knocking away the props" was then developed to justify this policy. Churchill believes that by the destruction of just one prop, Turkey, the War could have been won in 1915 or early 1916 and he goes on to blame the dominance of the passive school for allowing the Germans 30 months of war to develop their submarine offensive without interruption.[45] However it is yet to be explained how Turkey was propping up Germany or how her defeat would have ensured the collapse of the German Army in the West. This is the major weakness of the "Eastern strategy" and Churchill never convincingly explains how his policies would have seriously weakened the main enemy. Furthermore, the Germans had not planned a submarine offensive on the 1917 scale from the beginning of the war. They only turned to it at the last moment as a desperate measure to save them from defeat. Finally, Churchill is moved to compare two Admirals, one from the forward and one from the passive school. The officers chosen are Beatty and de Robeck.

> "Contrast his [Beatty's] attitude of mind at Jutland, when two of his six ships with 2,500 men had been blown out of existence in a few moments, with that of Admiral de Robeck – an officer of the highest physical courage – but saddened and smitten to the heart by the loss of three obsolete vessels with small loss of life in the numerous fleet which he commanded."[46]

The myth of de Robeck yearning after his lost ships has been dealt with in an earlier chapter. It should only be noted here that the two situations chosen by Churchill to illustrate his theme are hardly comparable. Beatty's decision at Jutland to maintain close contact with the enemy was taken in the knowledge that even with two ships sunk he had (with the 5th Battle Squadron) a good superiority and excellent chances of success. De Robeck's decision was taken in the knowledge that a continuation of the attack would lead nowhere. Churchill never forgave de Robeck for that decision and in The World Crisis he loses no opportunity to denigrate the Admiral, while his extravagant praise of Beatty, which has already been noted as a feature of the book, continues.

## Churchill's Balkan Policy

We now have to consider Churchill's Balkan policy as set down in The World Crisis. Considering his decided views on the subject, surprisingly little material on the Balkans has been included by Churchill and what there is, is scattered throughout two volumes. However the main discussion of his policy takes place in a chapter entitled "The Ruin of the Balkans" and as this is the penultimate of Churchill's "Dardanelles" chapters it seems appropriate to consider it here.

The main features of Churchill's Balkan policy are quite clear. From the beginning of the war he favoured the creation of a Balkan Confederation of Bulgaria, Serbia, Roumania, Montenegro and Greece.[47] He considered that this could have been achieved by the British, French and Russian governments forming a common policy and sending "plenipotentiaries of the highest order to the Balkan Peninsula to negotiate on a clear, firm basis with each and all of these States".[48] He suggests that territory from the Austro-Hungarian and Turkish empires would have provided the inducement for the Balkan states to join the Entente, "For every one there was a definite prize. For Roumania, Transylvania; for Serbia, Bosnia and Herzegovina, Croatia, Dalmatia and the Banat of Temesvar; for Bulgaria, Adrianople and the Enos-Midia line; for Greece, Smyrna and its hinterland."[49] However

"to realize these advantages, certain concessions had to be made by the Balkan states among themselves. Roumania could restore the Dobrudja to Bulgaria; Serbia could liberate the Bulgarian districts of Macedonia; Greece could give Kavalla as a make-weight; and as an immediate solatium to Greece, there was Cyprus which could have been thrown into the scale."[50]

In considering this policy one general point should be kept in mind, that British influence in the Balkans, with the possible exception of Greece, was negligible in 1914. Indeed it is hard to think of an area of the world where British influence counted for less. Trade with the area was minimal, defence links, except with the Greek navy, nil and British representation small. The embassy staff at Bucharest consisted of an ambassador and a clerk. It was therefore hardly Britain's place to take the lead in Balkan negotiations at the beginning of the War. In fact Grey did suggest the formation of a Balkan bloc and deprecated entering into negotiations with any one state,[51] but this policy was immediately undermined by Russia, who as the only Entente power with any influence, took the lead and opened bi-lateral negotiations with Roumania.[52] These discussions culminated in an offer of Translyvania and part of the Bukovina to Roumania in return for a declaration of neutrality.[53] This decision by Russia put paid to any immediate attempt to form a Balkan bloc, for Roumania had now been promised as much as she could have expected from a victorious war,[54] and Greece and Bulgaria would not move without Roumania.[55] Churchill does not explain how these

Russian initiatives could have been prevented in an area traditionally considered to be within the Russian sphere of influence. Nor is it certain that a group of allied "plenipotentiaries" could have accomplished more in the Balkans than was achieved by the regular diplomatic representatives.

Churchill's policy also ignores the fact that these small states were, quite naturally, waiting for a sign from the battlefields as to who would emerge victorious. In the early months of the war these signs were uncertain. The German invasion in the west was offset by the Marne, Russian victories in Galicia, by Tannenburg and the Masurian Lakes. But 1915, the year in which Churchill considered Balkan negotiations could have been pursued to a successful conclusion, was dominated for these states by the succession of Russian defeats; again at the Masurian Lakes in February, at Gorlice-Tarnow in May, at Lemburg in June, at Warsaw and Brest-Litovsk in August and Grodno in September. These defeats were quite often the cause of a breakdown in negotiations with the Balkan states.[56]

Nor were territorial ambitions as easy to reconcile as Churchill seemed to think. The concession which he suggested for Roumania was Transylvania. But Bratiano (the Roumanian Prime Minister) extracted more than that from Russia by promising to remain neutral. Furthermore, as the war progressed so Roumania's price increased. In May her demands included Transylvania, the entire Bukovina to the River Prutt, the Banat of Temesvar and several Hungarian counties,[57] about double the amount of territory suggested by Churchill as adequate compensation. A further problem was that the Banat was on the Serbian list of desiderata, and was considered essential by the Serbs to safeguard Belgrade from bombardment across the Danube.[58] Eventually, all the allies reluctantly acceded to all Roumanian territorial demands and in addition promised to send 200,000 British and French troops to the Balkans,[59] whereupon Roumania increased her price to all the demanded territory and 500,000 allied troops.[60] As the British military attache pointed out, the Roumanians were quite aware that it would have been impossible to supply this number of men in the Danube valley.[61] The sincerity of their repeated assurances that they were about to enter the war must therefore be called into question. In all these negotiations there was never any suggestion on Roumania's part that she would be willing to cede the Dobrudja to Bulgaria.

Similar objections could be applied to Churchill's other suggested territorial concessions. For example, Bulgaria wanted not only the Enos-Midia line, Kavalla and "Bulgarian Macedonia" but Serbian Macedonia as well, and this Serbia refused to concede.[62] Concerning the Greeks, when Cyprus was "thrown into the scale" as suggested by Churchill, it was promptly rejected as inadequate. Eventually not even the offer of Thrace was to move them.[63]

Thus the formation of a Balkan bloc was not as simple as Churchill's exposition of the problem in The World Crisis would have us believe. Indeed this was pointed out to Churchill by Headlam-Morley, a Foreign Office expert, before The World Crisis was published. After reading the proofs he wrote,

"It strikes me on reading this chapter that you hardly recognize sufficiently the difficulties of carrying through the policy which all desired, of founding a Balkan Bloc which should be either neutral or join the Entente. One has always to remember that in this part of the world England really counted very little; the Balkan States were much more influenced by Russia. And we have to remember that, for instance Bulgaria knew that a Russian victory would mean the establishment of Russia in the Straits and at Constantinpole. This they did not wish."[64]

In a later comment he made a similar point about Roumania.[65] Now, Headlam-Morley had been an important influence on Churchill concerning the opening diplomatic chapters of The World Crisis and indeed Churchill had incorporated whole sections of Headlam-Morley's memoranda on pre-war diplomacy in his book.[66] In this instance Headlam-Morley was ignored. The creation of a Balkan bloc is so central to Churchill's thinking on the Dardanelles, it being one of the events to be brought about by the successful forcing of the Straits, that he can hardly concede that it was not possible.

We must now take this investigation one stage further and ask what purpose Churchill hoped to achieve through the formation of a Balkan Confederation. Churchill states that Serbia, Greece, Bulgaria and Roumania disposed of armies which totalled 1,200,000 men (Serbia 250,000, Greece 300,000, Bulgaria 300,000, Roumania 350,000).[67] He considered that "The whole of the forces of the Balkan confederation could then have been directed against the underside of Austria in the following year"[68] and that this "must have involved the downfall of Austria and Turkey and the speedy, victorious termination of the war".[69] Let us now examine this proposition. One fundamental question that has to be asked is how efficient were the Balkan armies Churchill proposed putting into the field against the Austrians and (almost certainly) the Germans. The Roumanian army may be taken as an example. In 1914 the Roumanian army was woefully deficient in modern weapons of war. It had very little heavy artillery and what there was consisted largely of obsolescent pieces.[70] Even the batteries of modern pattern guns were barely mobile, relying on draft oxen to pull them because of a shortage of tractors and horses.[71] Machine guns were in particularly short supply. Eight divisions did not possess any machine guns at all.[72] Those divisions with machine guns had only 12.[73] (A German division in 1916 had up to 324 machine guns.)[74] In 1914 only one machine gun company was added to the army[75] and after the war began all attempts to purchase these weapons from Britain failed because of the shortages in Britain's own army.[76] Then there was the ammunition problem. In 1914 there were only enough shells for two months serious fighting.[77] There was only one armament factory in the country[78] which could only manufacture about one round per rifle daily[79] and two shells per day for each cannon for the artillery.[80] Ironically, the only other source of supply was Germany since many of the guns were made by Krupp.[81] The infantry was also in a sorry plight. Although its nominal strength was about 600,000-700,000 there were only enough rifles for 360,000.[82] Almost all the men were illiterate,[83] which meant company orders and the maintenance manuals for equipment could not be read. Not surprisingly, there was a complete absence of gas equipment and trench mortars.[84] There were virtually no aircraft available for reconnaissance purposes.[85]

The Bulgarian Army was in a somewhat better state with modern guns and a greater number of machine guns.[86] However the standards of equipment were still below those of the Western European nations. Moreover, most of their soldiers were illiterate[87] and had only received minimal periods of training.[88]

Little information has been discovered about the Greek Army. The comment has already been made that in 1914 it was changing much of its armament and was not in a fit state to take the field. It was certainly deficient in all kinds of material and as Greece had no armament industry, replacement of equipment would have been impossible.[89]

These, then, were the armies which Churchill expected to advance several hundred miles over some of the most difficult country in Europe and defeat the Austrians and, even more fantastically, the Germans, who although Churchill does not discuss this possibility in The World Crisis almost certainly would have come to the aid of their ally. It is clear that the primitive Balkan armies would have stood little chance against the more modern forces of the Central Powers. The fate of the Roumanian army in 1916, when the Germans overran most of the country in a campaign lasting only a few months, may be taken as an example of what might have happened earlier had Churchill's strategy been realized. There were other difficulties. The problem of combining the armies of four different nations, with different languages and with very little equipment in common, is not discussed by Churchill. Yet clearly this would have been one of the major difficulties facing a joint operation in the Balkans. The fact that Bulgarian troops would, in all probability, have found it necessary to traverse Serbia in the course of the operations would not have made co-operation any easier.

The poor communications, which were a feature of the area, is another complication not mentioned by Churchill. There was virtually only one major railway, the Sofia-Nish-Budapest line, although Roumania had lines linking Bucharest with the Hungarian capital. The Salonica-Nish line was narrow gauge and had limited carrying capacity. As armies were supplied largely by rail in 1914, these limitations were obviously of crucial importance and it is certain that the Balkan systems would have been unable to support the 1,200,000 troops suggested by Churchill. Indeed we have already seen that the British Military attache considered that not even 500,000 troops could be supported in the Danube valley. Furthermore, it is obvious from the state of their armies that the Balkan countries would have relied on the allies to supply them with ammunition, replacement artillery and probably medical equipment and stores of all kinds. Apart from the fact that Britain and France did not possess surplus material of this kind, the only major ports available for transshipment, Salonica, Constantinople (had the Turks been defeated) and Venice were many hundreds of miles from the main front and of limited capacity. Finally, in the unlikely event of the German and Austrian defenders being pushed back by the Balkan armies, the latter would have been constantly moving away from their main supply bases and their lines of communication would have become greatly extended. When it is remembered that the relatively sophisticated German army was not able to sustain an advance over comparable distances, with the excellent German and Belgium rail systems at its back, this is a factor of no small importance. The Germans and Austrians on the other hand would have been falling back on a much more developed rail network and their lines of communication would have become shorter. In these circumstances an advance by the Balkan armies might have been short lived.

Of course it might be thought that the performance of the Turkish army would disprove the arguments above. It could be argued that this army proved superior to the modern industrial powers against which it was matched. However the circumstances involved at Gallipoli and those envisaged by Churchill's Balkan strategy were entirely different. It was one thing for a peasant army to fight off an invader from behind strongly entrenched positions, quite another to advance against German and Austro-Hungarian armies, themselves sheltering behind fortifications.

Thus on any objective assessment, it seems likely that the accession of the Balkan states to the allied side, would have had very little effect on the outcome of the war. No doubt it would have proved embarrassing to the Central Powers and forced them to open another front. But then by 1915 they already had a front of sorts in the Balkans and were able to overrun Serbia without any substantial diminution of forces from the West. It is hard to avoid Norman Stone's conclusion that belief in the efficacy of the intervention of small states was "The diplomatic equivalent of cavalry"[90] and it is ironic that such a belief should be put forward by Churchill.

## Chapter 11

JUTLAND

On May 31st 1916, the British and German battlefleets met
north-west of Jutland. The meeting was not accidental.
British naval intelligence was aware that the High Sea Fleet
was putting to sea and had ordered Jellicoe and Beatty to
intercept it. Jellicoe was unsure of the purpose of the
German Fleet movement so he placed Beatty with the
battlecruisers and Rear-Admiral Evan-Thomas with the powerful
dreadnoughts of the 5th Battle Squadron well to the south to
prevent a raid on the British coast. Jellicoe remained 70
miles to the north with the Grand Fleet, ready to intercept
any attempt to attack the cruisers maintaining the blockade
line. If the enemy had not been located by early afternoon
it was arranged that Beatty turn north and join the main
fleet.

Beatty's sweep to the south-east proved uneventful.
Then, as he was about to turn north, an unidentified ship was
seen. Further investigation established that the German
battlecruiser force was at sea. Beatty responded by turning
his battlecruisers to the south on a parallel course to the
Germans. Hipper, commanding the German scouting force, also
turned to the south, his aim now being to lure Beatty onto
the High Sea Fleet, still well to the south-east.
Unfortunately for the British the 5th B.S., which Beatty had
placed to his north-west, did not turn and follow the
battlecruisers. The signal to turn made from the Lion had
not been seen by Evan-Thomas, smoke from the ship having
obscured the view. A signal from Beatty ordering his light
forces to the SSE was taken in by the Barham, Evan-Thomas's
flagship, but either it was not passed on to the
Rear-Admiral, or he ignored it as not being applicable to his
squadron.[1] Nor did the 5th B.S. receive the signal from
the usual source, the Tiger, whose duty it was to pass on
Beatty's signals.[2] Eventually the Tiger rectified this
mistake and Evan-Thomas turned and followed the
battlecruisers.[3] By this time the gap between the two
British forces had widened from 4-1/2 miles to 10 and this

prevented the 5th B.S. from playing a full part in the action to follow. Critics of Evan-Thomas have argued that he should have turned toward Beatty on his own initiative. In reply Evan-Thomas has stated that as far as he knew only German light forces were present and therefore there was no reason to concentrate. He also considered that Beatty may have wanted him to the north in the event of the German's attempting to escape in that direction.[4] Of course, as Jellicoe has pointed out, if the original signal had been made by W/T the incident need not have occurred.[5]

The opposing battlecruisers rapidly closed and by 3.48 p.m. they were on parallel courses to the south. Despite a superiority of six to five the action began badly for the British. Their initial salvos were inaccurate and because of an error in the fire distribution signal, for a crucial ten minutes the British did not fire on one of the German battlecruisers (Derfflinger).[6] In addition the Germans had the light advantage. Within half an hour 44 hits had been inflicted on the British, compared with only 17 on the Germans.[7] The climax of this phase of the battle came between 4.00 p.m. and 4.30 when the Indefatigable and the Queen Mary blew up and sank.

Beatty had now lost one-third of his battlecruiser force. He was soon to realize that he was in grave danger of losing the remainder. At 4.38 one of his cruiser screen reported: "Urgent. Priority. Have sighted Enemy battle-fleet".[8] This report came as a shock to the British who had been assured by an earlier Admiralty signal that the High Sea Fleet was still in harbour.

Beatty immediately turned north and with the Germans following headed towards the Grand Fleet. Disaster now almost struck the British. Evan-Thomas had not seen Beatty's signal to turn, which had once more been made by flags. The two squadrons passed, Evan-Thomas heading directly towards the entire German fleet. Beatty once more signalled him to turn but by an incredible lapse, the signal officer on the Lion, the unfortunate Seymour, neglected to haul down the signal (that is make it executive) for a period of seven minutes.[9] This placed the turning point of the 5th B.S. within range of Scheer but by the greatest good luck the squadron emerged from the hail of shells virtually unscathed and was able to join Beatty in the "run to the north". Of course Evan-Thomas could have avoided the situation by disobeying the signal and turning his squadron independently, but as Marder has remarked independent action was not the habit of flag officers in those days.[10]

It was of paramount importance during the run north that Beatty keep Jellicoe informed about the state and position of the German fleet. At this point Jellicoe's knowledge of the encounter was hazy. He knew Beatty had been in action and that the enemy battlefleet was at sea. No one had advised him of the loss of the two battlecruisers. Nor was he to find Beatty's subsequent signals particularly informative. Eighty minutes elapsed from the time of Beatty's northward turn at about 4.40 until the moment the Lion was sighted by Jellicoe. Yet during this period Jellicoe did not receive one accurate report on the course or composition of the High Sea Fleet.[11] Partly this can be explained by the fact that the firing of the guns had upset the ships' compasses which led to inaccuracies in the positional reports. However, the fact remains that most ships which were in a position to send vital information concerning the High Sea Fleet neglected to do so and some of the light cruiser squadrons failed even to keep in touch with the German formations.

Despite these lapses the northward run favoured the British. Over 20 hits were scored on the German battlecruisers, several of which became little better than wrecks.[12]

On learning that Beatty was engaged with the enemy Jellicoe increased the speed of the dreadnought fleet, which was in six parallel columns of four ships, to 20 knots, its maximum speed. At the same time he endeavoured to obtain additional information by pushing forward the cruisers of the 1st and 2nd C.S., and by sending Hood with the 3rd B.C.S. to assist Beatty.[13] In the event Hood, without an accurate idea of Beatty's position, moved too far to the east to aid either the battlecruiser force or provide information and the old cruisers of the 1st and 2nd C.S. were scarcely faster than the dreadnoughts. Jellicoe could have used the much faster 4th L.C.S. as scouts but chose not to do so. Perhaps he was reluctant to send lightly armoured ships into the unknown. In any case they too would probably have gone too far east to provide accurate information.

As the two forces closed, W/T contact was established with Beatty's force. Reports continued to be conflicting but at 6.00 the Lion appeared about six miles away to the starboard of the Grand Fleet. From previous reports Jellicoe had expected Beatty's flagship to be dead ahead and 12 miles distant. Thus Jellicoe realized that he had considerably less time in which to deploy the battlefleet than he had initially thought. In addition Beatty had still not informed him of the position of Scheer and a further ten minutes was to go by before this vital information reached the British flagship.[14]

At 6.10 Beatty informed Jellicoe that the enemy battlefleet was to the S.S.W. Ahead were Hipper's battlecruisers which were being forced eastwards by a large turning movement by Beatty. This manoeuvre had the disadvantage of taking Beatty across the front of the Grand Fleet but it also hid Jellicoe's force from Scheer. The Germans were at a considerable disadvantage. Scheer had 16 dreadnoughts and 6 ageing pre-dreadnoughts against Jellicoe's 28 dreadnoughts (including the 5th B.S. which was about to join the Grand Fleet.) However Jellicoe remained unaware of his great superiority until after the battle for he never saw more than three or four German ships at a time and no one in the battlecruiser force informed him of the size or composition of Scheer's fleet.

Jellicoe had now to deploy the Grand Fleet in a single fighting line. How was this to be accomplished? Jellicoe decided to deploy on the port column. He reasoned that this movement would cross the enemy's T, gain the light advantage and cut Scheer off from his base. These arguments have been rejected by Jellicoe's critics. They claim that a starboard deployment would have brought the Grand Fleet into action earlier, at a point in the late afternoon when every minute of daylight was valuable. It would also have brought the British battle line much closer to the German, thus making full use of British superiority in gunfire and would have made it more difficult for Scheer to escape by turning away. These are important points but there were dangers in such a movement. For example, it is certain that the starboard column would have masked the fire of other British ships at the crucial moment of deployment. Also because of the proximity of the turning point to the German Fleet Scheer would have been in a position to straddle the British line as it turned. As it was, even with the port deployment, several ships at the end of the line were straddled as they turned. Furthermore, Jellicoe considered a starboard deployment could expose the head of the British line to mass torpedo attacks from the flotillas which he expected to be ahead of the main German line. In fact these flotillas were well to the east and not in a position to attack but Jellicoe was unaware of this for at the moment of deployment he had not sighted a single German ship.[15]

Theoretically there was a third alternative open to Jellicoe. He could have deployed on the centre column and led the van himself. This would have placed him closer to the German line than the port deployment but still in a position to bar Scheer's line of retreat. It would also have left the British with the light advantage. In fact the movement was never a possibility. A centre deployment involved a considerable amount of intricate manoeuvring. The danger was that this would lead to confusion just as the British line was coming into battle. Also at the head of a line of ships 5 miles long, Jellicoe could have lost control of the rear squadrons and perhaps of the whole battle.

As it was there was confusion enough. At deployment Beatty was still crossing in front of Jellicoe; the 1st C.S. almost collided with Beatty as it came charging towards Scheer (two ships of the squadron were blown up seconds later); Hood's flagship, the <u>Invincible</u>, blew up and sank, making the third British battlecruiser to suffer this fate; and at the rear of the line, as the 5th B.S. wheeled into position, the <u>Warspite</u>'s helm jammed and it took no further part in the battle.

It has often been suggested that Jellicoe should have made better use of the 5th B.S., which consisted of the world's most powerful dreadnoughts but was destined to remain impotent at the rear of the British line. One suggestion is that Evan-Thomas should have been ordered to the disengaged side of the German fleet where he could have fallen on the weak pre-dreadnought squadron. This theory ignores the fact that Jellicoe did not know at this point the exact position of Scheer's line, the position of the pre-dreadnoughts in it, or even if the pre-dreadnoughts were at sea.[16] Neither is it clear how the 5th B.S. could have got to the disengaged side of the enemy from its position at deployment. A glance at a chart shows how difficult this would have been.[17] Also the Barham's W/T had been destroyed which would have caused communication problems.[18] Finally, if the manoeuvre had been attempted, it is possible that the 5th B.S. would have been caught by Scheer when the Germans executed their first battle turn.

Just after 6.30 some order developed in the British line and Jellicoe opened fire. Twelve hits were scored without reply. Scheer, realizing for the first time that the entire Grand Fleet was at sea, executed a 16 point turn and disappeared in the mist.[19] Several British ships saw this manoeuvre[20] but none reported it to Jellicoe, who merely assumed that the German line had been obscured by low cloud and smoke.[21] With the exact position of the Germans now in doubt, Jellicoe ordered a wide turning movement designed to ensure that Scheer's retreat was blocked. This was not a turn away, as some have held, but an interim manoeuvre designed to maintain a favourable position.

The Grand Fleet was now heading south, not in a continuous line but in echelons by division. At this point Scheer reappeared out of the mist, heading directly for the centre of the British line. Jellicoe opened fire to great effect, 34 hits being scored.[22] Scheer immediately executed a second battle turn and ordered a torpedo attack. In all 31 torpedos were fired.[23] Jellicoe at once altered course away from the enemy. For this he has been much criticized. It has been stated that he should have turned towards the attack bringing his fleet much closer to Scheer who was retiring in some disorder. However, this manoeuvre involved much more risk than turning away[24] and had not been practised by the Grand Fleet. Moreover, it is doubtful if Jellicoe could have overtaken Scheer before nightfall, even had he turned towards the torpedo attack. One historian has estimated that even the slower German squadrons would have been 16,000 yards from the nearest British ship at nightfall, that is out of effective range.[25]

In any case even if Jellicoe had turned towards Scheer it would have been difficult for him to order a general pursuit, for once again Jellicoe had not seen the battle turn. Yet again some of his battlefleet captains had witnessed the manoeuvre but none had transmitted this information to the flagship.[26]

Even though night was falling Jellicoe made a last attempt to engage the High Sea Fleet. He knew that Scheer was somewhere to the west and at 7.35 he altered course towards him. It is in this context that Beatty's signal made at about 7.50, "Submit van of Battleships follow Battlecruisers. We can then cut off whole of enemy's battle-fleet"[27] should be read. Some have seen this signal as evidence of Beatty urging a reluctant Jellicoe to renew the attack before it was too late. But Jellicoe had been steering directly for Scheer for some time before receiving this signal and in any case the battlecruisers had long been out of sight of the van of the Grand Fleet, so "following" would have been difficult.

Jellicoe had rejected an attempt to fight a night action as involving far too many risks and likely to nullify the great British superiority in fire power. At 9.15 he therefore disposed the Grand Fleet in night cruising formation. Beatty was placed at the head of the dreadnought fleet, which was in five columns in echelon. The light forces were ordered to prolong the line astern. Jellicoe had every hope that with this formidable line of ships between Scheer and his base the battle would be renewed in the morning. Yet Scheer crashed through the British light forces and escaped. What went wrong on the British side? The answer partly lies in a miscalculation as to Scheer's route home. Jellicoe knew of three channels through the Heligoland minefields available to Scheer. The British commander calculated on the basis of the last visual sighting of the High Sea Fleet that Scheer would choose the southern route.[28] However, this involved Scheer in travelling the greatest distance to safety and would have left him short of his base by daylight. Two northern routes provided a much more direct course but Jellicoe ignored them. Because previous Admiralty intelligence had proved faulty he also ignored an Admiralty signal that Scheer might use a northern passage.[29] The Admiralty was partly to blame for Jellicoe's attitude towards this message. Their advice was in fact based on accurate intelligence of Scheer's route but they neglected to pass on this vital information to Jellicoe in the proper form. Had they done so there is little doubt that Jellicoe would have revised his opinion as to Scheer's route.[30]

As it was, at 11.00 p.m. the High Sea Fleet broke through the British light forces and escaped. Only one of the captains of the British flotillas which were engaged reported Scheer's presence to Jellicoe and that message was jammed.[31] Consequently the Grand Fleet did not intervene. No doubt other destroyer captains should have attempted to contact the flagship. However, Jellicoe too showed little initiative during this period. Even when he saw starshells and searchlights to the north he made no enquiries, assuming that only a minor encounter between opposing light forces was involved.[32]    This    partly    reflected    the    strength    of Jellicoe's conviction that Scheer would choose the southern route home.   Nevertheless, given that this route was only one out of several possibilities, Jellicoe can be criticized for not investigating the activity to the north.   As he did not do so, the morning of June 1st brought, instead of the prospect of a renewed battle, an empty sea.

Nevertheless,   as   with   so   many   aspects   of   Jutland, probably far too much has been made of the opportunity lost by the failure to anticipate correctly Scheer's route.    In yearning for a decisive battle on June 1st historians have neglected the state of the weather on that day.   At daybreak, visibility near Horns Reef was no more than three or four miles.   In these conditions there would have been difficulty in even locating the German squadrons.   The possibility of a prolonged encounter, necessary if the British were to score a conclusive victory, was nil.[33]

Thus Jutland ended in an inconclusive stand-off.   The British suffered the heavier losses - 14 ships (including three battlecruisers) and over 6,000 officers and men.   The Germans lost 11 ships (including one battlecruiser and one pre-dreadnought battleship) and over 2,500 officers and men.[34]   Do the disparate losses indicate the superiority of German materiel?

Three British battlecruisers were blown up at Jutland and it has been argued that this demonstrated the inferiority of British    design.    It    is    certainly    true    that    German battlecruisers had thicker belt armour, greater internal subdivision, better damage control and wider beams, all of which made them very hard to sink.   Yet it was not these factors which saved the German ships at Jutland.   The destruction of the three British ships was caused by flash penetration to the magazine.   German battlecruisers also had this design flaw, but due to a lucky discovery during the Dogger Bank encounter had rectified it in time for Jutland.[35]    Thus    the    sinking    of    the    three    British battlecruisers at Jutland is hardly relevant to the controversy over British and German ship design.

Jutland has also been widely held to have demonstrated the inferiority of British shells, which it is claimed were not powerful enough to sink the German ships.   Yet if the punishment received by the respective battlecruisers can be taken as a guide this assertion seems very dubious.   The table below gives the number of hits scored on British and German battlecruisers at approximately 6.15 p.m.[36]

Table 11.1

Hits suffered by British and German Battlecruisers
at Jutland - 6.15 p.m.

| Hits on British Battlecruisers 3.48 - 6.15 p.m. | | Hits on German Battlecruisers 3.48 - 6.15 p.m. | |
|---|---|---|---|
| Lion | 13 | Lutzow | 9 |
| Princess Royal | 7 | Seydlitz | 11 |
| Tiger | 15 | Moltke | 5 |
| New Zealand | 1 | Von Der Tann | 4 |
| | | Derfflinger | 5 |

Source:  Based on a list compiled by J. Campbell :
         Beatty Papers.

If the state of the two battlecruiser squadrons at 6.15 p.m. is now compared, it will be found that on the British side the Lion had one turret out of action and the Princess Royal, Tiger and New Zealand were fighting with all guns. On the German side the Lutzow was completely wrecked and had to leave the line, the Derfflinger was in a "sorry condition", the Seydlitz was awash and the Von Der Tann had no turrets in action. Only the Moltke was fully effective.[37] Yet it can be seen from the table that the number of hits received by the two squadrons was approximately equal. How then could British shells be held to be inferior? If British shells were inefficient, as post-Jutland investigations appeared to show, then the German shells must have been just as bad.[38]

What of battle tactics? Jellicoe has been criticized for overcentralizing control in the flag ship and for not allowing squadron commanders any initiative. A survey of the Grand Fleet Battle Orders, at the time of Jutland expanded to the size of a small book, lends weight to this criticism. These orders envisaged a battle fought at long distance in a single line controlled from the flagship. This supposed that the Germans would be willing to participate in such an action though outnumbered. It also supposed that Jellicoe would be able to control a five mile line of ships from the flagship. Both were dubious assumptions. However Jellicoe's battle orders had one supreme advantage. Providing the British line remained intact there was almost no chance that it could be defeated. More adventurous tactics could have led to the destruction of a detached British squadron which would have left the rival fleets dangerously equal. This was a risk that Jellicoe rightly considered was not worth running.

It may be appropriate at this point to discuss the view that Jellicoe fought the battle of Jutland along rigidly preconceived lines as laid down in his Memorandum of October 1914. In that document he drew the attention of the Admiralty to his belief that in any future encounter the Germans would endeavour to lead the Grand Fleet into a mine and submarine trap. His answer would be to refuse to follow the Germans onto such a trap but to move the battlefleet to a flank before deployment.[39] In fact Jutland was not fought along these lines. On May 31st it was Scheer who had been led into a trap, not Jellicoe. There was therefore no chance that the Germans had laid mines or had placed submarines in waters near the scene of the action. Jellicoe of course realized this. His "refusal" to follow the German Fleet sprang not from the hidden dangers of mines and submarines, but from the fact that he was unaware that Scheer had turned away. His movement to a flank was designed to maintain a superior situation not to avoid mines and submarines and in any case was made after deployment not before.

Historians love a decisive battle and Jutland was anything but that. They have therefore tended to concentrate on what might have happened had either side scored a victory. Most agree on the results that would have flowed from a German victory. Britain's communications with France and the outside world would have been cut, and essential supplies would not have reached the army or the civilian population. Peace on German terms would probably have followed.

A British victory presents more imaginative possibilities. In a recent book, Arthur Marder lists four far-reaching effects of a British victory.[40] The first of Marder's points is that the troops kept in England to repel an invasion could have been released to the Western Front. However, it is difficult to see that this relatively small number of men could have decisively tipped the scales in the Allies' favour. The second effect listed is that a British victory would have allowed the Grand Fleet to enter the Baltic. Once there it could have cut off German ore supplies from Sweden, aided a Russian landing in Pomerania, opened a supply route to Russia, and thus have prevented the March 1917 revolution. It is possible, with the High Sea Fleet gone, the British would have been able to dominate the Baltic. However enemy submarines, mines and torpedo craft would have still represented formidable obstacles. Landing a Russian force in Pomerania was a Fisher day-dream which presupposed that the Russians had a well supplied, skilled, mobile force supported by a sophisticated system of logistics to enable the army to be reinforced and supplied. In fact no such force or system existed. In any case the Germans would always have been able to reinforce their armies at a faster rate than the invaders. That victory at Jutland could have prevented the Russian revolution relies on the theory that it was shortage of supply which led to Russian defeats, and it was the defeats which caused the revolution. This theory ignores the complex social discontents which contribute to a revolution. Moreover, it is by no means certain that Russian shortages could have been overcome by the Allies had a supply route been opened. In 1916 Russia received via the White Sea 2.5 million tons of supplies. Because of shipping shortages this amount could only have been increased to 2.7 million tons in 1917 even if the Baltic had been opened.[41] An additional factor is the inability of the Russian communication system to handle more supplies. By 1917 100,000 tons of supplies had built up at Murmansk, of which only 3,000 tons could be shifted daily.[42] In any case the main Russian problem was not shortage of supplies. In January 1917 the Russian supply of shells was comparable to 1916 averages for Britain and France.[43] As Norman Stone has indicated it was the lack of organization and trained personnel to use the materiel produced, rather than materiel shortages, which caused the Russian downfall.

The third effect of a British victory listed by Marder is that German submarines, deprived of the support of the High Sea Fleet, could have been blocked in by mines and destroyer flotillas and the submarine campaign of 1917 prevented. However, with their main fleet gone the Germans could have turned to submarine warfare in 1916. Any attempt to block the Heligoland Bight with mines must have failed at this stage of the war because the British did not produce an effective mine until 1917 and these were not available in any quantity until 1918 when convoy had already thwarted the submarine. Destroyer flotillas, released from the Grand Fleet to hunt submarines, may have been little more successful. To be effective these flotillas relied on hydrophones and depth charges neither of which was perfected until 1918.

The last point raised by Marder concerns morale. Obviously British morale would have been raised by a "new Trafalgar" but it is hard to see how this factor could have contributed to the defeat of the German Army. A German defeat undoubtedly would have been a great blow to the Central Powers but even Marder says "it is very unlikely that [a defeat] would have resulted in an early German surrender. The Fleet had nothing like the prestige of the Army in Germany".[44]

* * * * * * * * * * * * * *

We now turn to Churchill's treatment of Jutland in The World Crisis. Churchill's chapters on the battle deal with events which took place while he was out of office. For the first time he is describing events in which he did not participate. One advantage we might expect from this section is that Churchill will be able to take a more detached view, his distance from the event giving him a truer perspective on the major controversies and issues. On the other hand, it must be realized that these chapters could suffer from a serious drawback. The first two volumes were enlivened and informed by the extensive use of Admiralty documents and sources of information. For this period Churchill is cut off from this inside information. Could we expect then that Churchill's account, though more detached, will in some ways be less valuable to the reader because of a lack of proper documentation? These questions will have to be kept in mind during the course of the following discussion.

When Churchill first contemplated writing a chapter on Jutland he soon realized that he knew little about the detailed course of the battle and he began to cast about for material to read and for some expert naval advice. He contacted Beatty, at that time First Sea Lord, who put Kenneth Dewar from the naval staff at his disposal.[45] Dewar, with his brother Alfred, was responsible for the compilation of the controversial "Naval Staff Appreciation of Jutland", which was very critical of Jellicoe and was called by him (Jellicoe) "a purely B[attle] C[ruiser] F[leet] account looked at with BCF eyes".[46] This was probably the first account of the battle read by Churchill who thought it "admirable"[47] and, although he was to read many other narratives of the battle, including the more pro-Jellicoe Harper Record,[48] it will be seen that it was the Staff Appreciation which made the greatest impression on him.

Others to assist Churchill on this section were Keyes and Beatty who both read the chapters in draft and made detailed criticisms. The effect of these advisers on Churchill's narrative will be revealed in the course of the discussion.

No section of The World Crisis provoked more controversy than Churchill's criticisms of the handling of the 5th B.S. in the opening phase of the battle.[49] A lively correspondence on the subject was opened in the columns of The Times and Churchill was even accused of bringing on the heart attack suffered by the unfortunate Evan-Thomas shortly after the publication of Volume 3 of The World Crisis. Certainly Churchill's account is highly critical of Evan-Thomas. However modern scholarship would probably endorse his view that whatever qualities Evan-Thomas showed as a commander, initiative was not among them. Nevertheless in certain ways Churchill's handling of this phase of the battle lacks balance. Thus while Churchill examines the mistakes made by Evan-Thomas in some detail, no mention is made of Beatty's contribution to the mishandling of the 5th B.S. For example, it is noticeable that Churchill fails to mention that if Beatty's original signal to Evan-Thomas had been made by W/T instead of flags, surely a reasonable course given the notorious difficulty in reading the Lion's signals, there could have been no confusion. Furthermore Churchill does not mention the failure of the Tiger to pass Beatty's signals on to Evan-Thomas and it is doubtful if he was aware that such an arrangement existed. Finally, Churchill does not make clear that although a signal from Beatty ordering a change of course was probably taken in by Evan-Thomas, this message was specifically directed to Beatty's light forces and this was why it was ignored by the 5th B.S.

Churchill's description of the battlecruiser action is in the main accurate but in three important areas his account cannot be accepted. It is not clear from The World Crisis that the shooting of the German ships was much more accurate than the British, particularly in the early phase of the battle. The number of hits scored (44 v. 17) is not recorded and the impression is left that, apart from the unlucky destruction of two British battlecruisers, the gunnery of both scouting forces was approximately equal. Furthermore, he describes the muddle over the fire distribution signal thus; "The chances of the battle on either side led to discrepancies in the selection of targets, and sometimes two British ships were firing at one German, while another was ignored, or vice versa".[50] By using a neutral phrase such as "the chances of the battle" Churchill glosses over the fact that an actual mistake was made and neatly avoids blaming anyone. Moreover, his "vice versa" implies that similar mistakes were made by Hipper's squadron when there is no evidence to suggest that this was so. Thus the reader is left with the erroneous impression that both sides were of equal incompetence. This impression, reinforced by the fatalism of "the chances of the battle", subtly deflects criticism from the British battlecruiser squadron.

The second area of dubious accuracy concerns the 5th B.S. Churchill assigns all the blame for that squadron's delayed turn at 4.53 to Evan-Thomas. He states that "the Rear-Admiral, having been slow in coming into action, was inclined to be slow in coming out".[51] But as has been shown, Evan-Thomas' failure to turn earlier was the result of his not having seen Beatty's 4.40 signal until 4.57. No doubt Evan-Thomas demonstrated his usual lack of initiative but the system of signalling used by the flagship can hardly be excluded from blame.

To sum up, Churchill's description of the opening phase of the battle is very favourable to Beatty. The repeated signalling errors of the battlecruiser fleet are glossed over and the blame largely assigned to Evan-Thomas for not anticipating Beatty's intentions correctly. Also, the fact that Beatty had been out-manoeuvred and out-fought by Hipper is not made clear by Churchill, although he is correct in saying that the British had the better of the later stages of the run north.

For the clash of the battle fleets Churchill invites the reader to "take his mental station on the bridge of the Iron Duke".[52] He correctly stresses that Jellicoe's prime need at that moment was for information about the enemy and that he could get it in two ways; by W/T from the Battle Cruiser Fleet already engaged with Scheer or by sending forward his own scouts to obtain visual contact with the two fleets. We have already seen that the information passed on to Jellicoe by the Battle Cruiser Fleet was sparse and often inaccurate. Churchill excuses Beatty on the grounds that he had no time to pass on signals "while in heavy action" himself.[53] Yet for much of the time during the run to the north Beatty was <u>not</u> in action and, although during this phase he was at times out of contact with the German fleet, he could easily have informed the C-in-C of Scheer's last known position and of the loss of the <u>Queen Mary</u> and the <u>Indefatigable</u>. But Churchill ignores this and blames Jellicoe for not sending forward the fast cruisers of the 4th L.C.S. to obtain information for himself.[54] This is a valid criticism for these ships could have been sent forward any time after Jellicoe learned that the two fleets were in action. Nevertheless Churchill errs in exonerating Beatty from all blame for Jellicoe's lack of information. Of course, Churchill has failed to realize that during this time the information which Jellicoe had on the whereabouts of the German fleet was based on inaccurate reports. In fact, Jellicoe believed it to be much further to the east and there is no guarantee that his scouts would have met Scheer even had they been sent out.

After describing in an uncontroversial manner the minor disasters which on the British side attended the closing of the two battle fleets, Churchill turns to Jellicoe's deployment of the Grand Fleet. He discusses the two alternatives which Jellicoe believed were possible, namely, deployment on the port versus the starboard wing. Although not blaming Jellicoe for choosing the "safer course",[55] Churchill concludes that

> "[in the light of present knowledge] he could have deployed on the starboard wing without misadventure. The 5th Battle Squadron ... was in fact about to take the van ahead of the <u>Marlborough's</u> division of older Dreadnoughts. Beatty's battle cruisers were already steaming upon the exact course. Still farther ahead in front of all Hood in lively comprehension was about to wheel into the line".[56]

In fact, this picture of exactitude and order at the head of the British line is quite misleading and presumably results from a postwar study of the battle charts. From a diagram it can be seen that the 5th B.S. (minus of course the <u>Warspite</u>) would eventually have come into battle at the head of the line, but it is by no means certain that it could have arrived before the fire of the High Sea Fleet became effective. In any case, Evan-Thomas would have masked the fire of the <u>Marlborough</u>'s division while providing a concentrated target for the leading German ships. Beatty was further to the east and too fully engaged with Hipper to relieve some of the pressure on the leading British ships. The same objections apply to Hood who was even further away. Thus the principal objection to the starboard deployment, noted earlier, that the head of the British line could have been smothered with fire by Scheer, still holds. Moreover, the manoeuvre would still have risked a mass torpedo attack from German destroyers. Finally, even if Churchill had been correct, Jellicoe had none of Churchill's "present knowledge".

Churchill then discards <u>both</u> of these alternatives, claiming that "out of a tangle of uncertainties and out of a cruel dilemma ... [there] was a sure, prudent and glorious middle course".[57] This was the controversial deployment on the centre column. The dangers in this manoeuvre have already been set down and even Churchill admits it was a "complicated evolution".[58] Yet he still puts it forward as the ideal solution, ignoring the fact that Jellicoe could hardly risk having the Grand Fleet fall into disarray at this critical moment to gain a mere 4,000 yards. The answer to Churchill's point that the Grand Fleet was not under fire when deployment commenced and was therefore quite safe is that the fleet would come under fire <u>during</u> deployment on the centre column, thus adding to the difficulties of an already delicate manoeuvre. Also, it is hard to see why Jellicoe, by adopting this deployment, "would have retained the greatest measure of control over his Fleet",[59] as Churchill claims. Jellicoe would have been at the very tip of a line of ships 5 to 6 miles long instead of in the centre of the line. In this situation the rear squadrons would have been beyond his control altogether unless a system of signal relays had been improvised, a difficult feat in the midst of battle. Presumably Churchill's answer to this would be that Jellicoe was at fault for not making the fleet familiar with the centre column deployment, but it is doubtful if a manoeuvre involving three groups of ships steaming in different directions at the critical moment before battle was joined would have been practical under any conditions.

The advantages obtained by the British from the starboard deployment are not mentioned by Churchill. His total prejudice against the movement is indicated by the fact that he describes it as a "retirement".[60] He does not explain how a manoeuvre, which cut off Scheer from his base, crossed his T, and brought a concentrated fire to bear on the head of his line in such conditions of light that the enemy could hardly reply, could possibly be regarded as a retirement.

Churchill's next assertion is that Jellicoe missed a good opportunity for destroying at least two or three of the enemy's older battleships, the pre-dreadnought "<u>Deutschlands</u>". He believes that this could have been accomplished by detaching the four (in fact, there were only three - Churchill has forgotten the crippled <u>Warspite</u>) - <u>Queen Elizabeths</u> to the disengaged side of the enemy to attack the old German ships. It was shown earlier that

Jellicoe did not have the information about the composition or position of the German fleet necessary to order such a movement and that in any case it would have been almost impossible to execute. Furthermore, Churchill is apparently not aware that the squadron would have risked being trapped by the High Sea Fleet after their first battle turn. How Jellicoe was to communicate with the squadron with the Admiral's W/T out of action is another problem not discussed. Finally, even supposing the movement had been possible, his contention that Scheer would have been forced to rescue these ships and thus commit himself to battle is not supported by previous experience. For example, the Blucher was left to her fate at the Dogger Bank and Von Pohl abandoned Hipper's entire squadron during the Scarborough raid.

The later editions of The World Crisis have nothing to say about the manoeuvring of the British Fleet at the time of Scheer's first turn away. No mention is made of Jellicoe's "failure" to pursue the German fleet at this stage. However, in the 1st Edition of Volume 3 Churchill had Jellicoe turning away from the torpedo stream "according to his long-resolved policy".[61] This section was later dropped, probably on the advice of Kenneth Dewar, who told Churchill that he doubted very much if this was the correct reason for Jellicoe's turn.[62] Apparently Churchill was not prepared to credit Jellicoe with any tactical reason for making the turn (it will be remembered that Jellicoe was anxious to ensure that Scheer remained cut off from his base) and in the later editions of The World Crisis only the movements of the German fleet are given during this period and no explanation at all is offered for Jellicoe's movements.

Churchill returns to the attack on Jellicoe by criticizing the turn away from the torpedo attack which accompanied Scheer's second battle turn. He states that Scheer's manoeuvre "might well have been fatal to the Germans",[63] and castigates Jellicoe for not turning towards the attack and dividing the Fleet with the object of catching the disarrayed High Sea Fleet between two fires. This criticism is hardly justified. We saw earlier that it would have been impossible for Jellicoe to divide his squadrons, for the exact position of Scheer was not known. Nor of course did Jellicoe know that the High Sea Fleet was retreating in disarray. Also, division of the Fleet would have risked the annihilation of the detached squadron if any miscalculation was made. Moreover, if the calculations outlined in the first part of this chapter are accepted as being even approximately accurate, Jellicoe could not have caught the Germans before dark, even if he had turned towards the torpedo attack. Furthermore, Churchill does not point out that turning towards a torpedo attack involved much more risk than a turn away (according to Frost six times the risk.) Commanders on both sides (including Beatty and

Hipper) invariably turned away from torpedo attacks during the course of the war.

Churchill's account of the daylight action at Jutland ends with a discussion of Beatty's "follow me" signal. This section was only added after the proof stage had been reached[64] and was included on the advice of Kenneth Dewar.[65] Not surprisingly it follows closely Dewar's own account in the Naval Staff Appreciation. Churchill implies that only Beatty sought to renew the action during these hours.[66] This was not the case. As stated earlier, the van of the Grand Fleet was at this time actually steering more directly for the High Sea Fleet than was Beatty. Furthermore the van, led by Jerram's squadron, was out of sight of the battlecruisers when the signal was sent and would have found any order to "follow" difficult to obey. Finally, even if Jerram had known Beatty's position, he was too far astern to join an action before nightfall. Thus this incident was hardly the missed opportunity for a general engagement that Churchill suggests.

How does Churchill deal with the problems which faced Jellicoe at the beginning of the night action? We saw earlier that there were three main escape routes open to Scheer. To these Churchill adds a fourth, the Kattegat route. Churchill admits that it was an unlikely choice because he claims Scheer could have been brought to battle during the next day.[67] Still he thinks that Jellicoe should have guarded against this possibility by sending a few light cruisers "to watch the area".[68] But even if Jellicoe had done this and the cruisers had seen the High Sea Fleet and informed Jellicoe at once, there was no chance that the British could have caught the Germans that day. The distance between the two fleets would have been about 150 miles and the British fleet was certainly not more than 4 knots faster than the German. It would therefore have taken 38 hours to overhaul Scheer. Thus contrary to Churchill's opinion, Jellicoe's exclusion of this route as a possibility seems quite reasonable.

In discussing the remaining three escape routes available to Scheer, Churchill is critical of Jellicoe for concluding that the southerly (Ems) route was the most likely. Churchill's opinion that this decision was "contrary to the main weight of evidence"[69] is reasonable considering that by using this route Scheer would run the risk of being brought to battle in daylight. However, in this section Churchill does not make clear the contribution to Scheer's escape made by the Admiralty. It was noted earlier that had Naval Intelligence passed their information to Jellicoe in the correct form, there could have been little doubt as to Scheer's intention. Churchill omits this point altogether, although he must have been aware of the Admiralty blunder because it was discussed in the Jutland volume of the Official History, published four years before Volume 3 of The

Churchill is on stronger ground in criticizing Jellicoe for remaining passive in the face of evidence that an action of some form was taking place to the north of the main British line. Churchill's implication that Jellicoe should have taken steps to investigate this disturbance is surely reasonable.

Of course Churchill, in common with other naval historians, assumes that Jellicoe's failure to predict correctly Scheer's route cost the British the chance of a decisive victory on June 1st. Given the uncertain state of the weather in the likely area of the battle, this is a very dubious assumption indeed.

Churchill now proceeds with an examination of the materiel used by the British and German fleets. He concludes that because of their better distribution of armour, German battlecruisers were superior to the British types. Yet, in the next paragraph Churchill accepts that flash penetration to the magazine almost certainly destroyed the British battlecruisers that were sunk. It will be remembered that this defect was not a matter of superior design for at the Dogger Bank the turret of the Seydlitz was penetrated in a similar manner to the Queen Mary, Indefatigible and Invincible.[71] Churchill thus contradicts his own argument but still leaves the impression that Jutland proved the inferiority of British ship design.

Churchill also accepts the orthodox opinion that British shells were inferior to those used by the Germans, although in a post-war letter he stated that the difference between the two was "much exaggerated".[72] Evidence was brought forward previously which would indicate that this latter belief might have been more accurate. Privately Churchill was prepared to accept responsibility for the poor standard of British shells. After the war he wrote, "I suppose I am to blame for our shells not being as good as the German. I assumed our constructors and ordnance experts were the last word in their science".[73] In fact it was during Churchill's administration that 13.5" shells were found to be defective and there were, therefore, good reasons why he should not have gone on trusting the experts. However in The World Crisis Churchill is silent on his own responsibility for the poor state of British shells and he is merely content to warn Naval Ordnance Boards against the complacency which allowed that situation to develop.

We have seen that Churchill has been very critical of Jellicoe's conduct of the battle. On the other hand, he is very conscious of the "unique" responsibilities of the British C-in-C and tries to give them full weight in his account.

"His responsibilities were on a different scale from all others. It might fall to him as to no other man - Sovereign, Statesman, Admiral or General - to issue orders which in the space of <u>two or three hours</u> might nakedly decide who won the war....Jellicoe was the only man on either side who could lose the war in an afternoon".[74]

How does Churchill think this responsibility affected Jellicoe's tactics?

"All he knew was that a complete victory would not improve decisively an already favourable naval situation, and that a total defeat would lose the war. He was prepared to accept battle on his own terms; he was not prepared to force one at a serious hazard. The battle was to be fought as he wished it or left unfought."[75]

Churchill apparently agrees with this strategy. He continues,

"A British Admiralissimo cannot be blamed for making these grave and solid reasons the basis of his thought and the foundation from which all his decisions should spring."[76]

It was, therefore, not Jellicoe's general strategic conception with which Churchill disagreed, but the way in which that conception was translated into action. It was his opinion that "a perception that a decisive battle is not a necessity in a particular situation, and ought not to be purchased at a heavy risk, should not engender a defensive habit of mind or scheme of tactics."[77] Thus the nub of Churchill's criticism is that while not risking the Grand Fleet, Jellicoe should have developed offensive tactics which sought to make the most of all opportunities to annihilate the enemy. Yet it was shown earlier that Jellicoe did not fight the battle of Jutland with a "defensive habit of mind" or use a "defensive scheme of tactics". The whole sweep into the southern section of the North Sea was offensive. His deployment, far from being defensive, was designed to gain solid advantages of light and position for the opening phases of the action. His circling movement after deployment was not a "retirement" but designed to maintain those advantages. If he failed to follow Scheer's second battle turn, it was not because he wished to avoid action but because he was unaware that the German fleet had turned away. From that moment until dark he continually sought to renew the action and, had Jellicoe been correct about Scheer's escape route, he would have undoubtedly sought a decision on the morning of June 1st. Why then did Churchill think that Jellicoe had fought a purely defensive battle?

The most obvious reason is that Churchill was convinced that
Jellicoe had fought the battle along the lines laid down in
his letter to the Admiralty in October 1914. It is true that
in the situation there outlined Jellicoe proposed to adopt
defensive tactics, but it was shown earlier that at Jutland
Jellicoe soon realised that this situation did not apply.
The letter therefore played no part in the C-in-C's
thinking. However, it was Churchill who sanctioned the
tactics laid down in the 1914 letter and he is obviously
concerned to dissociate himself from them.

A second reason is that Churchill has consistently looked
at the battle from a theoretical point of view. He has
studied the naval charts without making himself familiar with
the information available to Jellicoe at the time. By this
method it is possible to see several "opportunities" lost
through the use of defensive tactics. Only one example need
be given. The 7.20 battle chart shows the High Sea Fleet
retreating in disarray. The Grand Fleet, instead of
immediately turning and pursuing it, "defensively" continues
to steam in a southerly direction. To Churchill this looked
like a missed opportunity to inflict a crushing blow on the
enemy. In reality, with the limited amount of knowledge
available to Jellicoe at the time, it was nothing of the
kind. However, this theoretical approach is a constant
element in Churchill's account.

There is a more general reason for Churchill's harsh
treatment of Jellicoe. Not only was a "defensively-minded"
commander against Churchill's natural inclination for the
attack but also against "the best traditions of the Navy".
To whom were future generations to look to maintain the
"golden links" with such heroes as Rooke and Nelson? Not to
Jellicoe, says Churchill, but to "Beatty and the
battle-cruisers, to Keyes at Zeebrugge, to Tyrwhitt and his
Harwich striking force".[78] This is grossly unfair to
Jellicoe while vastly overrating the contribution of such
minor figues as Keyes and Tyrwhitt. In fact the main raison
d'etre of British seapower has always been to keep Britain's
sea lanes open and to prevent the invasion of the homeland.
This was Jellicoe's purpose as it was Nelson's. Nelson was
able to achieve this purpose by a series of battles,
culminating in Trafalgar. Jellicoe achieved the same results
without a battle.

Churchill's criticism of Jellicoe for over-centralising
command has some substance. It was shown earlier how this
hampered Jellicoe's conduct of the battle and robbed his
subordinate commanders of what little initiative they had.

Churchill's discussion of the results which might have
flowed from a British victory is full of interest. He was
first inclined to believe that a "new Trafalgar" would have
left the two antagonists approximately where they had been
before. This was certainly the line he had taken in his

<u>London Magazine</u> article of 1916. However, after reading the
Naval Staff Appreciation he wrote to Keyes, "I am shaken in
my view as to the small consequences which would have
resulted from a complete victory at Jutland."[79] But when
the time came to write the Jutland chapters of <u>The World
Crisis</u> he reverted to his original view. In the first proof
he wrote,

> "If the German Fleet had been decisively defeated on May
> 31, 1916, in battle off Jutland, that superb and glorious
> episode would not have decided the general course of the
> war. It would not have improved the control of the sea
> communications of the Allies by the British Navy. It
> would not have directly increased the stringency of the
> blockade. It would not have prevented the U-boat attack
> of 1917 which the Germans were actively preparing. On
> the contrary, it might well have led to a greater
> concentration of skilled men and resources upon the
> development of the U-boat campaign. It would not have
> supplied the Admiralty with the driving power and daring
> to attack the German naval bases in the Elbe and other
> river mouths in the North Sea....It would have brought
> the entry into the Baltic into immediate practical
> possibility. But that entry was a great new operation of
> war which in the absence of a German battle fleet,
> certainly in the presence of a reduced German fleet,
> would have presented features of extreme complexity and
> required long preparation. Moreover, the Russians at
> this date were no longer in a condition to profit from
> the British entry and control of the Baltic by descending
> with their armies upon the northern coasts and striking
> at Berlin....the disappearance of the German battle fleet
> would probably not have influenced the course of the war
> as a primary factor on land".[80]

This paragraph brought a chorus of protests from
Churchill's naval advisers. Beatty and Dewar wrote to
Churchill, urging him to change his mind.[81] Keyes also
strongly dissented and pencilled suggested amendments in the
margin of the proof.[82] The impact of this criticism can be
seen in the published version of this paragraph on page 983.
On five of the seven points mentioned above Churchill
completely reversed his stand and the other two were
omitted. Most of Keyes' suggestions were accepted.
Churchill now held that if the High Sea Fleet had been
defeated, the Admiralty might well have moved against the
German bases and this could have frustrated the U-boat
attack. The difficulties accompanying a British entry into
the Baltic are now forgotten and we find that this movement
might have prevented the Russian revolution although
Churchill admits that this is a "speculative question". (He
had originally written "highly speculative".)[83] The aid

which the Navy could have given the Army is now emphasized rather than played down. It is not known why Churchill changed his mind on this issue. No reasons for their points of view were advanced by Dewar, Beatty and Keyes in their correspondence with him. No doubt Churchill was more than willing to believe that decisive results should flow from a decisive battle. In the discussion on this point earlier in this chapter considerable doubt was cast on this view. The conclusions reached were more in line with Churchill's first thoughts than with his published version. On this occasion Churchill, seemingly, was not well served by his advisers.

It can now be seen that neither expectation raised in the opening paragraph of this section came to pass. On the first issue, that of the availability of information, it is clear that Churchill's account has not suffered from a lack of documentary material. In fact through his naval advisers Churchill had access to expertise and unpublished sources available to few historians at the time. In minor ways his account has profited from these privileges. His maps and diagrams were all either taken from unpublished accounts or drawn especially for him. He was able to use papers prepared for him on such technical subjects as flash penetration and shell design. In such aspects therefore Churchill's account has not been noticeably impaired by the fact that he was out of office.

However it is also clear that the second expectation, that Churchill's account would prove less partisan, has also not been fulfilled. The lavish praise of Beatty, which has been noted in the pre-Jutland chapters of The World Crisis, is continued in this section where Beatty's dubious tactics during the battle are completely overlooked. Conversely, the antipathy displayed towards Jellicoe in earlier chapters is again evident in Churchill's allocation to him of the whole blame for the indecisive daylight action and for Scheer's escape at night. It would therefore appear that Churchill has not been able to detach himself from the strong convictions which he formed during his period in office. This is especially true in relation to Beatty and Jellicoe where Churchill's attitudes to both men were formed in the pre-war years. This pro-Beatty anti-Jellicoe stand has also affected Churchill's choice of advisers, for it is noticeable that they are all representative of only one facet of naval thinking on Jutland, the anti-Jellicoe school. The similarity of approach between Churchill and his advisers is often very obvious. It was noted earlier that Churchill's criticisms of Jellicoe were frequently based on a combination of hindsight and neglect of practical problems. Compare this with Dewar's approach which has also been described as savouring "too much of theoretical tactics combined with being wise after the event".[84] Certainly Churchill made no attempt to balance his account by consulting experts more kindly disposed to the Commander-in-Chief. Beatty was able

to comment on the draft chapters of <u>The World Crisis</u> but not
Jellicoe, Keyes but not Bacon, Dewar but not Harper. Rather
than providing a counterweight these men reinforced
Churchill's prejudices and a partisan account was the result.

## Chapter 12

## THE SOMME AND THE CASUALTY STATISTICS CONTROVERSY

### Churchill and Strategic Options 1916

Churchill begins his discussion of strategy in 1916 with a survey of the choices facing the German Commander-in-Chief, Falkenhayn, in that year. Essentially, Churchill states, Falkenhayn's choices were to attack in the East or in the West.[1] Churchill considered that it was in Germany's true interest to attack in the East. He states, "The vital need for Germany was to break the blockade", and adds that this could only have been done by acquiring the rich food-growing areas of the Ukraine.[2] An attack on Russia by Germany would have had the added advantage for the Central Powers of isolating Roumania, which could have been induced to join the German side, but Falkenhayn turned his back on the East and attacked the French at Verdun.[3]

Readers of the earlier chapters will not be surprised to find Churchill advocating an eastern policy for Germany. It is in fact his Dardanelles strategy transferred to Berlin. Is there any reason to suggest that the strategy would have proved more successful for the Germans in 1916 than it had for the British and French in 1915? In a qualified sense the answer is yes. The Germans had a much more important and coherent objective in the East than did the Entente. The overthrow of Russia would have enabled Falkenhayn to move vast numbers of troops to the main theatre. If this could have been accomplished in 1917 instead of 1918 the immediate superiority of the Germans might have proved decisive or at least enabled them to negotiate an armistice on favourable terms. However, as Falkenhayn realized, Germany did not have the resources to embark on such an undertaking and even if large numbers had been taken from the West to attack the East, the opening of the Anglo-French attack on the Somme must have meant their return. Furthermore, the Russians in mid-1916 were far from beaten. Their supplies of munitions had improved greatly in the first six months of the year and Brusilov was to show that they still retained an offensive capacity. Finally Churchill's strategy assumes that the adhesion of Roumania to the Central Powers mattered. Our earlier discussion of the state of the Roumanian army would indicate that it was very unlikely that these peasant levees would have tipped the scale either way. Even the Russians might have attacked the Roumanians with some prospect of success.

It can of course be argued that the strategy eventually adopted by Falkenhayn proved a dismal failure and that Churchill is justified in pointing out an alternative. However, it is likely that in 1916 Germany simply did not have the power to force a decision on either front. Standing, as the German army did in 1916, on enemy territory a prudent strategy would have been to conserve life and remain on the defensive in the hope that war weariness would cause the allies to negotiate. But these Fabian tactics had no appeal for Falkenhayn in 1916, nor to Churchill ten years later in his commentary on "Falkenhayn's choice".

If Churchill's discussion of the dilemma facing the German High Command is open to a certain amount of criticism, it is a model of sober reflection compared to his section on the alternatives facing the allies in 1916. Churchill writes, "the plan of British and Allied war which according to this account would best have served our interests in the year 1916 would have been a surprise attack upon the Dardanelles".[4] He considers that this move would have parried a German thrust to the East, brought in Roumania and brought aid to Russia, and so might well have been decisive. The force that Churchill would have used to execute his plan was the large number of allied troops in Egypt and Salonica, which he claims could have been rapidly concentrated for a landing on the Gallipoli Peninsula.[5]

It is noticeable that in this discussion Churchill says nothing about the strategy to be adopted on the Western Front. However, it is hard to see that a call for a British offensive there could or would have been resisted once the French had been attacked at Verdun. Thus, as in 1915, the British would have found themselves supporting two offensives with only the munitions and reinforcements for one. As for Churchill's proposal that the Dardanelles be attacked again, it is not necessary to restate the arguments already produced to show why even a success at Gallipoli would not have greatly affected the course of the war. However, it should be mentioned that surprise in mounting an attack would not have been as easy to achieve as Churchill seems to believe. The marshalling of shipping for twenty divisions could hardly have gone unnoticed in the East. Furthermore, nothing like twenty divisions could have been accommodated on the Gallipoli Peninsula and, if a landing in the Gulf of Enos or on the Asiatic shore was proposed, it must be remembered that the long period of time necessary to land such a large force would have enabled the Turks to have brought in reinforcements to thwart the British plan. In addition, the Straits defences and minefields remained intact during 1916 and no easy passage would have been open to the Fleet. Finally, after the experiences of 1915 it is hard to believe that any responsible commander would have been prepared to undertake such an operation and it is noticeable that Churchill did not put it forward at the time. Even in The World Crisis he apparently only added this section as an afterthought.[6]

Writing About The Somme

Before Churchill's account of the Somme is discussed, it is necessary to correct a common misapprehension about the sections of The World Crisis which deal with events post 1915. It has been claimed that for the 1916-18 period Churchill lacked those primary sources which leant weight to the first two volumes of The World Crisis and that "for much of his account he had to rely on external, published sources".[7] The Churchill Papers reveal that this was not the case. In the course of writing Volume 1 of The World Crisis Churchill sent his chapter on Antwerp to Sir John Edmonds, the compiler of the Official British History of the war, for comment. While Churchill was writing Volume 3, their co-operation developed to a much greater extent. The full extent of the remarkable collaboration between the two men is best illustrated by Churchill's chapter on the Somme. Edmonds, whose own volumes on the subject did not appear until the 1930's, seemed to be more than willing to supply Churchill with any documents that he requested. To a certain extent, as will be shown, he also seems to have used Churchill as a means of putting forward ideas considered too frank for the Official History. In any case Edmonds supplied to Churchill all the General Staff appreciations relating to the Somme and Haig's reports and correspondence with Robertson. In addition he sent translations of various German accounts of the battle, including "Die Schwaben an der Ancre" quoted by Churchill on pp. 1045-6, "Die 27 Infanterie Division im Weltkrieg" quoted on p. 1051, as well as his own account of "The Assault on the Orvillers Spur by the 8th Division" which forms the basis of Churchill's narrative on pp. 1046-7.[8]

Edmonds helped Churchill in more direct ways. The description of the opening hours of the battle of the Somme, which appears on p. 1044 of The World Crisis, was entirely written by Edmonds and incorporated into the text without change by Churchill.[9] However, when Edmonds saw the first draft of Churchill's Somme chapter (this unfortunately does not seem to have survived) he was unhappy with the tone of some of Churchill's criticisms of the British High Command. He suggested to Churchill that "in view of your high & esteemed position in the hearts of your countrymen I think you might cut out some of the sarcasm about the military leaders".[10] Churchill responded positively to this suggestion.

"Of course the sarcasms and asperities can all be pruned out or softened. I often put things down for the purpose of seeing what they look like in print. Haig comes out all right in the end because of the advance in 1918. Without this the picture would be incomplete. As you know, this Somme chapter was written a very long time ago. I am anxious to vindicate my own appreciation of the position at the time, and of course my General argument against these [offensives?]. But this Somme chapter certainly requires a strong addition showing the undoubtedly deep impression made upon the Germans by the wonderful tenacity of our attack. If you have anything that bears on this, perhaps you could bring it along with you".[11]

Unfortunately without the first draft there is no way of knowing exactly how Churchill went about toning down the chapter. The "balancing" German material was, as we have seen, supplied by Edmonds and appears on p. 1051 of The World Crisis. It is possible that he also suggested the quotation from Ludendorff's memoirs which discusses the terrible effect of the battle on the German Army and which Churchill also uses.

Churchill seems to have suggested some additions to his chapter which met with no response from Edmonds. Concerning the artillery aspect of the battle Churchill wrote "I think I ought to introduce into the Somme chapter some account of the creeping barrage and who has the credit for its inception. It surely was the one great new tactical feature at this stage to aid the offensive".[12] This was an important point, for Western Front battles are often referred to as being totally lacking in innovation and as being essentially the same in 1918 as they were in 1915. This was of course not the case and the creeping barrage marked a major step forward in battle tactics.[13] Unfortunately Edmonds does not seem to have responded to Churchill's suggestion and possibly for this reason no mention of the creeping barrage is to be found in the Somme chapter of The World Crisis.

Eventually Edmonds was well satisfied with Churchill's efforts. He told Churchill "I can find nothing against your general line of argument" and "The Somme chapter is a work of art, it takes up every important factor and shows extraordinary insight and is perfectly fair".[14] This was astounding praise from a historian whose published line of argument (that the Somme in terms of casualties and morale was a British victory) was so different from that adopted by Churchill in The World Crisis. Perhaps Edmonds underwent a comprehensive change of mind before he published, or perhaps he felt obliged in an official history to produce a document more sympathetic to Britain's military leaders. However, his unqualified praise of a chapter which contained an analysis of casualty statistics directly opposed to his own argument on this subject defies explanation.

No hint of the Edmonds-Churchill partnership leaked out over the years. Nor did Churchill ever acknowledge the help given him by Edmonds in the writing of The World Crisis. This secrecy was not Churchill's wish, but Edmonds'. None of the British documents which he supplied to Churchill was generally available to other historians and there no doubt would have been an outcry if it had become known that Churchill was receiving special treatment. Edmonds' reaction to a possible public acknowledgement of his assistance is summed up in a letter he wrote to one of Churchill's research assistants in connection with a later book by Churchill, "The Eastern Front".

> "On no account should my name or mention of the Branch [Historical Branch, C.I.D.] appear. We should have all sorts of people clamouring for help, apart from possible trouble in Parliament. Please thank W.S.C. for his kindly thought, but say it is wisest to omit reference to the Section and that I was glad to help in any way".[15]

## The Somme

In his discussion of the Somme battle Churchill's first point is that a major mistake was made by the British and French Commanders in selecting "as the point for their offensive what was undoubtedly the strongest and most perfectly defended position in the world".[16] Is he correct in stating that the Somme location was chosen by the British as well as the French commanders and thus including Haig as well as Joffre in his strictures? The evidence is contradictory. Joffre claims that it was he who first suggested the area to Haig[17] and in early January Haig did report that he was working out plans for an attack to the north of the Somme while Foch considered an attack to the south.[18] However, Joffre intended that the British contribution to this battle should be in the nature of a wearing out attack undertaken some months before the main French offensive.[19] Haig was opposed to these tactics. He had been preparing plans for an offensive in Flanders to be part of a co-ordinated spring campaign and to be undertaken at the same time as the French attack south of the Somme.[20] But he now suggested, perhaps to avoid what he regarded as the premature and unco-ordinated British attack on the Somme planned by Joffre, that the British contribution to this plan be extended and undertaken simultaneously with the French.[21] To this Joffre agreed. Then the Germans attacked at Verdun and the French component of the offensive was thrown into doubt. Haig did not favour a lone British attack on the Somme and immediately informed Kitchener of his intention to revert to his northern plan. He was assured that although the French contribution to the battle would be scaled down it would still be considerable and the joint

Somme attack was therefore adhered to.[22]

Is it possible from this contradictory evidence to decide exactly what the attitude of the British High Command to the Somme location was? The following points can perhaps be isolated.

(1) Joffre first chose the Somme location probably because it was the point at which the British and French armies joined and therefore he would be able to a certain extent to control the scope and duration of British participation.

(2) Haig rightly regarded the British contribution to this attack as subsidiary to the main effort which would be made by the French on the Somme and by the British in Flanders – hence his preparations for an offensive in that area.

(3) In February Haig came to see the virtues of an attack on a broad front and suggested that the British portion of the Somme attack be increased to form part of a major Franco-British offensive.

(4) When French divisions were diverted to Verdun Haig, considering that the British alone were not strong enough to obtain any worthwhile strategic objectives (which on the Somme front were quite distant), reverted to his northern schemes where important objectives such as strategic railways and the Belgian Coast were considered to be within striking distance of the front line.

(5) When the French announced that they were prepared to participate in the Somme offensive though on a reduced scale, Haig considered that the combined armies were strong enough to break the German line and allowed the joint attack to take place.

Thus Haig neither proposed the Somme battlefield as implied by Churchill nor strongly resisted it as stated by Haig's apologists. He apparently saw it as the area in which an attack on the broadest possible front could be made and he considered that this type of attack had the best chance of success. In either case the question is a great deal more complicated than is implied by Churchill in The World Crisis.

Churchill's second point is that he considered the Somme area to be unsuitable as a prospective battlefield because it was so strongly defended. But the question has to be asked, given the fact that it would have been necessary for the British to have attacked somewhere in 1916, what easier alternative theatres of action did they have? To the north of Ypres there were impassible inundations: the area around the Lys and Loos was an industrial wilderness. Much of the French sector was even less promising. South of Verdun there are rivers, forests and mountains. Champagne and Artois had been the locations of the disastrous French attacks in 1915. This left the Somme and the Ypres salient; and the Third Battle of Ypres in 1917 amply demonstrated the difficulties of attacking in Flanders. Thus the Somme as a location seems no worse than any other area and it is noticeable that no alternative to that site is offered by Churchill in The World Crisis.[23]

Churchill next turns to a discussion of Haig's objectives in fighting the battle. He claims that it is clear from the unprecedented artillery bombardment and the positioning of the cavalry near the front line that a major rupture of the German line was sought.[24] This has been denied by others who have seen the main purpose of the battle as the relief of the French at Verdun and a battle of attrition with the object of killing as many Germans as possible.[25] Once again the evidence is contradictory. When it was obvious that the British were to play a major role in the battle Haig spoke of the object of the attack as being not only "to defeat the enemy on the front of attack [but].... such a victory over the enemy's forces as will compel him to retreat and thereby open up possibilities of further tactical and strategical success".[26] In contrast Rawlinson, the army commander who was to carry out the attack, was in favour of only attempting the seizure of the German front line before regrouping for a second attack.[27] Eventually Haig realized that because of the diminution of the French contribution the objectives would probably have to be scaled down and he then spoke of the Montauban Ridge just beyond the German second line as being the objective, further action to be dependent on "developments".[28] However, it is clear that Haig continued to hanker after larger results and he told Rawlinson that he should consider reaching Combles on the German third line on the first day.[29] (Combles fell in October.) Later Haig urged Rawlinson to keep the cavalry close up in case the resistance of the enemy broke and it proved possible to get through into open country;[30] and in a note to Joffre just before the battle Haig identified as the fourth stage of the action a move forward to a line Cambrai-Douai, many miles beyond the German positions and not reached until the end of the war.[31]

At the same time, however, Haig began to speak of the operation as having the sole object "of relieving the pressure on Verdun"[32] and Robertson could tell the War Committee that "there was no idea of any attempt to break through the German lines, it would be only a move to 'digeuger' the French."[33] Thus once more Haig seems to have followed a complicated course. Originally he had hoped for a decisive breakthrough, and although he modified his objectives later, he still hoped to capture the entire German defensive positions. However, as the weeks went by and the French contribution to the battle dwindled, Haig shifted the emphasis in his appreciations from breaking through to relieving pressure on the French. At the same time he never gave up his hope that a decision could be reached. To this extent Churchill is justified in his claim that the Somme was meant to produce a victory and did not form a part of an

216

overall campaign to wear down the German army. Also if attrition had been Haig's sole aim then surely the battle could have been planned differently. For example, an attack on a narrower front would have increased the weight of artillery per yard to the advantage of the British. Then, when sections of the enemy's front line were captured, they could merely have been held in expectation of the counter-attacks which inevitably would have developed. But far from adopting this policy the British attacked in a manner most likely to cause heavy casualties to their own side and kept on attacking until some of their formations cracked.34 To a certain extent they were saved by the equally inept German policy, especially noticeable later in the battle, of counter-attacking with no worthwhile objectives in mind. One must conclude therefore that if Churchill is wrong and Haig did only plan to fight a battle of attrition, then he did so in the most inappropriate way.

Turning to the opening of the battle, Churchill laments the lack of surprise caused by the "vast uncamouflaged preparations" and the week-long preliminary bombardment.35 Yet it is hard to see how an attack by over 14 divisions could have been "camouflaged". Throughout the course of the war it was not found possible to disguise the preparations36 for any major battle as distinct from pin-pricks such as Cambrai and Messines. Also, although Churchill does not seem to be aware of it the length of the preliminary bombardment was a matter of great controversy between Haig and Rawlinson. From the first Rawlinson favoured a long bombardment. He thought only by prolonged shelling could he be sure that the German wire was cut. This plan would also prevent the Germans from bringing up food and ammunition and make sleep impossible.37 He told his Corps commanders "nothing could exist at the conclusion of the bombardment in the area covered by it".38 Haig proposed a hurricane bombardment of short duration in order to achieve surprise39 but Rawlinson argued that there was little chance of surprise anyway40 and after a long struggle he persuaded Haig to change his point of view.41 Thus Rawlinson must bear the main responsibility for the long opening bombardment but this fact is not mentioned in The World Crisis.

Of the effect of the bombardment Churchill says,

"The seven-days' bombardment had by no means accomplished what had been expected. Safely hidden in the deep dugouts, the defenders and their machine guns were practically intact. From these they emerged with deadly effect at the moment of assault or even after the waves of attack had actually passed over and beyond them".42

It is thus clear that in Churchill's estimation over-confidence in the effect of the bombardment caused the collapse of the initial attack and the high number of casualties suffered on the first day. This view certainly seems to be correct. Indeed it is surprising that he is not more criticial of Haig and Rawlinson on this point, for there is evidence to suggest that it was already known before the attack commenced that the dugouts had not been destroyed nor the wire cut. For example, the depth and method of construction of the German dugouts was well known to the British commanders[43] and it should have been possible to calculate that by far the larger number of British shells did not have the power to penetrate to those depths. Furthermore, interrogation of prisoners revealed that "The trenches are very good and the dug-outs are very deep and [the] prisoner has never known a shell to get through into a dug-out".[44] As late as the 29th of June the Intelligence Summary stated "The dug-outs are still good. The men appear to remain in these dug-outs all the time and are completely sheltered".[45] As for wire cutting, on the 26th the 8th Corps reported that their trench raids had been unsuccessful due to uncut wire,[46] the 10th Corps reported some uncut wire on the 29th[47] and the 3rd Corps stated the night before the attack that the wire on their front had been damaged but not cut sufficiently.[48] All these signs were ignored by Haig who was able to write on the 30th, "The wire has never been so well cut, nor the Artillery preparation so thorough".[49] Rawlinson also thought that the "wire cutting has been well done",[50] although he did comment that he was not satisfied with the work done on the 8th Corps front and on the 30th wrote, "I am not quite satisfied that all the wire has been cut and in places the front trench is not as much knocked about as I should like".[51] Yet although the whole plan hinged on the conditions that nothing could live in the area covered by the bombardment and that the wire would be totally destroyed, neither Rawlinson nor Haig made any attempt to investigate further the disturbing Intelligence reports or to modify their attack to avoid areas such as the 8th Corps front where there were obvious difficulties. They would therefore seem to be even more culpable for the disaster on the first day than is implied by Churchill in The World Crisis.

Of course it is possible that Churchill was not aware of all the facts set down above at the time he wrote his Somme chapter. However he seems particularly anxious to avoid an investigation of the part played by Rawlinson in the battle. In fact a remarkable feature of Churchill's Somme chapter is that Rawlinson's name does not appear at all. A portrait of Rawlinson does appear in The World Crisis but it comes much later in Churchill's account in connection with the Battle of Amiens in 1918.[52] That action was one of Rawlinson's notable successes and he is described by Churchill as "keen, practical, resolute" with a "strongly-marked capacity".[53] Rawlinson undoubtedly deserved some praise for he was one of

the few army commanders who showed any flexibility and he had
a certain ability to learn from mistakes. Yet the mistakes
which he did make on the Somme were not of a minor nature.
Nor were they the kind of error that normally escaped the
attention of Churchill. But no criticism of Rawlinson
appears in The World Crisis. Perhaps this can be put down to
the fact that Rawlinson and Churchill became good friends
after Churchill became Secretary of State for War in 1919
when they often shared the pursuits of painting and boar
hunting.[54]

Churchill's account of the first day's fighting on the
Somme, though brief, is generally accurate and is enlivened
by eyewitness accounts from troops on both sides.[55] He
sums up the day's fighting thus, "Nearly 60,000 British
soldiers had fallen, killed or wounded, or were prisoners in
the hands of the enemy. This was the greatest loss and
slaughter sustained in a single day in the whole history of
the British Army. Of the infantry who advanced to the
attack, nearly half had been overtaken by death, wounds or
capture."[56] It is accounts such as this that have given
wide currency to the view that the British Commanders were
totally insensitive to the losses being suffered by the
troops and sent wave after wave of men to their doom when the
prospects of success were negligible. Enough has already
been said in this chapter to indicate that Rawlinson and Haig
had many failings. An attempt was also made to show exactly
where their responsibilities lay for the heavy casualties
suffered on the first day. However, writers such as
Churchill often ignore the real difficulties faced by
commanders in the First World War in trying to control a
battle on the scale of the Somme. For example, on the first
day when the men left their trenches it was almost impossible
for the High Command to establish the course of events on the
other side of the front line. In discussing why formations
were repeatedly ordered to attack when their predecessors had
suffered heavy casualties, Keegan has written, "most
important of all was the simple ignorance of what was
happening which prevailed almost everywhere on the British
side of no-man's-land throughout most of the day."[57]
Keegan goes on to give an example of a Colonel who received
no news from the front in the first two hours although it was
only 1,000 yards away.[58] Montgomery, the C.O.S. to
Rawlinson, later wrote, "Failure of 3 out of the 5 Corps on
the 1st July was not fully realised for quite a long time.
Hopeful reports kept coming in from Corps and it was very
difficult to know which reports were accurate and which were
not .... The severity of the losses was not realized for
several days."[59] Rawlinson himself noted in his diary,
"9.20 a.m. The battle has begun well .... We captured all
the front line trenches easily."[60] In fact at this time in
excess of 30,000 casualties had been suffered and long
sections of the enemy line were untouched.[61] It is hard to

see how the difficulty in communicating across trench lines could have been overcome. Runners were often killed before they could return to their own lines. In any case the information they carried was often out of date. Deep telegraph and telephone lines stopped at the front trench and hastily laid cables were vulnerable to shell fire.[62] Radio technology was not sufficiently developed to be used.

The responsibility for continuing the battle of the Somme until November was of course Haig's. The necessity to prolong the battle for five months has been a matter of some controversy, commentators such as Terraine holding that this aided Haig's overall strategy of wearing down the German forces, others stating that it was wearing down the British army to a greater degree and obtaining no worthwhile objectives. Churchill is of the latter school but while holding to the view that there were no good strategic reasons for continuing the battle, he is prepared to be lenient towards the Commander-in-Chief over this question. Churchill states that the need to keep pressure away from the French and the fact that Haig was continually fed with false intelligence by his own Intelligence Department concerning relative German-British casualties and the state of enemy morale may have contributed to the Commander-in-Chief's decision.[63]

But did the misleading evidence from the Intelligence Department play a part in Haig's decision to continue the campaign? It is understandable that in the early phase of the battle Haig accepted without question the reports of his Intelligence Department and was able to state that "signs of serious demoralization in the ranks of many of the enemy's units have been evident."[64] It is harder to explain Haig's continuing belief in these reports two or three months later which led him to make such statements as "evidence of a growing deterioration in his morale accumulates daily"[65] and "It is not possible to say how near to breaking point the enemy may be but he has undoubtedly gone a long way towards it."[66] By this time (October) it would not have been unreasonable for Haig to have viewed with some scepticism the reports of deteriorating German morale from his Intelligence Department. Furthermore there is evidence that Haig meant to continue the attack even if German morale held. On September 19th Rawlinson reported "Kig[gell] says D.H. means to go on until we cannot possibly continue further either from the weather or want of troops. I'm not so sure that he is right."[67] Three weeks later he wrote "[Haig] is bent on continuing the battle until we are forced to stop by the weather indeed he would like to go on all through the winter."[68] There is no mention of impending victory or imminent collapse of German morale here, and indeed for Haig the battle seemed to have developed a momentum of its own and he appeared determined to continue with it whatever the circumstances. Clearly then not all the blame for the long months of attrition on the Somme can be borne by the Intelligence Department.

What of Churchill's contention that it was necessary to continue the battle for the purpose of keeping pressure off the French at Verdun? This could certainly have been a factor in the British decision to attack on July 1st (although it provided a convenient excuse if the attack failed) and no doubt Verdun played some part in the decision to keep on attacking. However, the French position soon improved and by July 14th they felt strong enough to begin preparations for a small counter-attack at Verdun. Moreover, all through September and October they began to build up supplies for a larger movement and on October 19th their opening barrage commenced.[69] Thus October 19th was the last date on which relief of the French at Verdun should have been a consideration for Haig. Yet the Somme battle continued for another month at a cost of 70,000 men. On this basis it is hard to accept that Verdun was of overriding importance to Haig during the latter months of the battle. Furthermore it must not be forgotten that the French participated in the Somme at a final cost of almost 200,000 men. If the sole object of the British attack was to relieve the French because of their desperate position, the killing or wounding of an additional 200,000 Frenchmen seems a strange way of going about it. Surely if the French had been in such dire straits their part in the battle would have been closed down and the British left to attack alone. The fact that this was not done throws doubt on the whole argument.

## Churchill and the Casualty Statistics Controversy

Churchill had been interested in the question of relative German and British casualty statistics since 1916 when he had written a memorandum to the Cabinet claiming that contrary to published reports the British were suffering many more casualties than the Germans. When he began writing The World Crisis Churchill was anxious to vindicate his wartime memorandum and in 1921 he obtained through Lord Curzon, the Foreign Secretary, a set of German casualty statistics from the British Embassy in Berlin.[70]

However, he then dropped the subject until late 1923 when he had definitely decided to add a third volume to The World Crisis. He apparently requested more detailed information from Berlin and when the figures arrived he informed Edmonds, "They absolutely confirm the argument [that the British and the French had suffered higher casualties than the Germans] but with the most surprising features. I have in consequence recast the first three chapters [of volume three] with a new chapter full of [graphics?] called "The Blood Test."[71] As Churchill's volume neared publication Edmonds warned Churchill that the German figures were misleading as they did not include the lightly wounded.[72] Apparently he supplied

Churchill with figures from the German VII Army Corps to prove his point.[73] Churchill immediately recognized the fundamental weakness in Edmonds' argument. He pointed out to Edmonds that if the figures for the VII Army Corps were representative, then 40% would have to be added to the total German wounded while the total German dead remained the same. If this were done it would destroy the ratio of one killed to two wounded which Churchill, on the basis of his present statistics, considered common for all three major armies in the West.[74]

Churchill had hit on a very important point here, for logic would dictate that over four years of war between armies similarly equipped the ratio of killed to wounded should be similar. Unfortunately, the only comparative British and German figures for killed and wounded that now exist contain such a large number of undistributed "missing" that no accurate comparisons can be made.[75] In the figures supplied to Churchill this category had been distributed between wounded and killed although the result of this allocation no longer exists. However, in the absence of any indications that the distribution of the German casualties should differ from the French and British it seems likely that these final figures would confirm Churchill's assertion. Churchill did not receive any answer on this point from Edmonds who could apparently offer no explanation.

Nevertheless Churchill thought Edmonds' criticisms worthy of further investigation and he wrote to Hume, who had worked on the subject while attached to the British Embassy in Berlin, to have the point re-examined.[76] Hume promised to obtain an authoritative answer from the Germans but proffered his own opinion that the lightly wounded had been included.[77] While this investigation was under way Edmonds returned to the attack, telling Churchill, "It was ... notorious that the Germans did not include 'lightly wounded' ... in the casualties.'[78] He added, however, that as this fact was so well known, "I have never troubled to collect any statements on the subject."[79] Despite Edmonds' lack of evidence these criticisms clearly worried Churchill. His whole chapter depended on the reliability of the figures. He therefore wrote again to Hume emphasizing the importance of the German researches, and asking him to check that the lightly wounded were included in the German figures. "I am founding a considerable argument on these figures which in their present form bear out all I thought and wrote at the time in Official memoranda about what was taking place at the front. I am extremely anxious to be on the right side in all these calculations and to make assurance doubly sure."[80]

Hume replied a few days later enclosing a letter from Herr Stinger from the Reichsarchiv.[81] In that letter Stinger emphatically denied that the lightly wounded had been excluded from the figures and he also claimed that the sick and wounded who died later were also reallocated to killed.[82] This reply satisfied Churchill that his basic figures were correct. He now asked Hume to have his final calculations verified by Stinger. In reply Hume informed Churchill that Stinger regarded the figures as being as good as any likely to be obtained.[83] These figures, with minor changes, are used in The World Crisis.[84]

Clearly Churchill went to a great deal of trouble to establish the reliability of his figures. How does he use them to "prove" his case? Churchill draws two main conclusions from his tables of casualty statistics. (1) "During the whole war the Germans never lost in any phase of the fighting more than the French whom they fought, and frequently inflicted double casualties upon them."[85] (2) "In all the British offensives the British casualties were never less than 3 to 2, and often nearly double the corresponding German losses."[86] He therefore concludes that the great battles of attrition on the Western Front left the British and French weaker in relation to the Germans than before they commenced. He also claims that the Germans did not lose in these battles enough men to balance their annual intake and under the prevailing conditions they would have had sufficient men to last indefinitely.[87]

It is not surprising that many historians have rejected these arguments, for Churchill is claiming that the great allied offensives from 1916, although prodigious in their slaughter, were totally futile in their results. The case against Churchill made by his major critics will now be examined.

It has already been noticed that Sir John Edmonds did not accept Churchill's German figures as accurate. He continued this scepticism into his volumes of the Official History, concluding that 30% had to be added to all German totals to include the lightly wounded.[88] It was also noted however that in correspondence with Churchill Edmonds did not produce any evidence with which to back up this assumption, merely stating that the fact that the lightly wounded were not included was "notorious". Eventually as justification for this thesis Edmonds pointed to a quotation in the German Official History (Vol. XII) which said that "the great losses of the summer of 1916, since the beginning of the year without the wounded whose recovery was to be expected within a reasonable time amounted to a round figure of 1,400,000, of whom 800,000 were between July and October."[89] This would seem to indicate that the Germans indeed did not include their lightly wounded. However it has been demonstrated by M.J. Williams that this passage actually read, "The great losses of the summer of 1916 had made considerably more difficult the reinforcement supply of the Field Army. They amounted, since the beginning of the year, without the wounded whose recovery was to be expected within a reasonable time...etc."[90] As Williams comments the passage used by Edmonds "occurs in the context of a general discussion of the

German reinforcement position in 1916 ... Here it would be natural to ignore lightly wounded who would soon rejoin their units and would not need to be replaced...Clearly this passage does not constitute a general admission that lightly wounded were omitted from the returns of specific battle losses in Der Weltkreig."[91] In an earlier article Williams attacked the very basis of Edmonds' 30% addition.[92] He noted that Edmonds' case contained a major flaw which arose from the incorrect labelling of certain figures as "net" or "gross" of the lightly wounded. Edmonds claimed that two different sets of figures were available, those from the Reichsarchiv compiled from unit returns being "net" and those from the Nachweiseampt being "gross". For any particular battle therefore a comparison between the two figures would yield the percentage of lightly wounded. For Verdun, Edmonds selects Churchill's total German casualty figure of 426,519 and compares it with a figure of 336,831 calculated by a German military historian, Wendt. Defining these figures as "gross" and "net" respectively Edmonds calculated that the understatement in the German figures was 33%. However, as Williams has pointed out, Churchill's figure, as stated clearly in The World Crisis, [93] is based on the Reichsarchiv statistics and therefore, according to Edmonds' own claim, should be "net". Wendt's figures were based mainly on the actual unit returns and would therefore have the same base as Churchill's. In fact, the difference between the two sets of figures is attributable to differences in time periods and to the fact that Wendt's relate to Verdun only and Churchill's to the Western Front as a whole. Therefore the basis of Edmonds' calculations is entirely fallacious.[94]

It should be noted that Edmonds uses similar sleight of hand on the British figures. Thus, for the Somme he lists the British losses as 419,654.[95] This is of course a Somme only figure and should not be compared (as Edmonds does) with a German figure which represents losses on the Western Front as a whole.

Another critic is Sir Charles Oman, who in a contribution to a volume "The World Crisis: A Criticism", questioned the reliability of Churchill's figures for the Somme.[96] Oman was employed on casualty statistic calculations during the war and he claims that by adding up the German losses as published in their official Verlustliste he arrives at a figure of 420,000 for the period July-late October.[97] He then adds 60,000 for the period late-October-November not covered by the Verlustliste and another 50,000 for the ancillary units (artillery, engineers etc.) to arrive at a total of 530,000. This total is then compared with Oman's British and French figures for the Somme only of 489,334[98] to obtain a result that brings the allies out on the right side. However, Oman has not compared like with like. As Williams points out, "Sir Charles assumed that all the published losses for units that had been engaged on the Somme had been suffered there."[99] This was clearly not the case as the lists were often four or five weeks old and in the meantime the German units had often been engaged elsewhere on the Western Front. Thus Sir Charles is comparing a <u>Western Front</u> figure for Germany with a <u>Somme only</u> figure for Britain and France.

Churchill's German figures have also come under attack from John Terraine who accepts Edmonds' contention regarding the lightly wounded.[100]  After the work of Williams this position is clearly untenable but Terraine, while stating that the addition of a flat 30% is too crude, goes on to claim that a <u>variable</u> percentage should be added - sometimes 30%, sometimes 25% or 20%, but probably never as low as 15%.[101]  Terraine then proceeds to select the example of Passchendaele and adds 20% to a figure quoted in the Official German account (260,000) to arrive at 312,000 which he claims is approximately equal to the combined British and French losses.[102]  Several points should be noted here. The first is that Williams did not query the actual percentage figure derived by Edmonds but destroyed the entire basis for adding anything at all. Furthermore, although Terraine claims that the German figures are not exact, he does not put forward any evidence to explain why they should be any less exact than the British. As he then suggests that 20-25% should be added on to the German figure, it can only be assumed that despite Williams' work Terraine still accepts Edmonds' basic contention. Moreover, it seems very convenient that Terraine's chosen figure of 20% enables the casualty figures of the two sides for Passchendaele to balance. In conclusion it must be said that Terraine has produced no new evidence for questioning the reliability of the German figures as used by Churchill.

Terraine has also called into question the validity of Churchill's British casualty statistics. In his book on Passchendaele already quoted he has pointed out that the source used by Churchill, <u>Statistics of the Military Effort of the British Empire</u>, contains not one set of casualty figures for Passchendaele but three.[103]  This is also true of other battles and the various lists in the <u>Military Effort</u> will now be compared to see if any discrepancies arise. Churchill's figures are taken from "Approximate Casualties by Months in the Expeditionary Force, France", on pp. 263-5 and appear in the first column below. The other figures come from a table of comparative British and German casualties on the British Sector of the Western Front, also taken from the <u>Military Effort</u>. It is noticeable that the two columns vary throughout the whole period with the exception of the first and the last three pairs of figures - a coincidence which would suggest a common source. It is also noticeable that Churchill has chosen the higher set of figures. However this makes little difference to his case.

Table 12.1    British Casualties on the Western Front
1914-18

| Period | Military Effort Figures as used By Churchill | | Military Effort Section 7 Figures |
|---|---|---|---|
| Aug '14–Jan '15 | 102,196 | | 102,196 (a) |
| Feb–Mar '15 | 33,678 | | 30,937 |
| Apr–May '15 | 96,994 | | 92,157 |
| June–July '15 | 38,878 | | 36,801 |
| Aug–Oct '15 | 100,111 | | 94,820 |
| Nov–Dec '15 | 20,380 | | 17,882 |
| Jan–Feb '16 | 23,989 | | 21,343 |
| Mar–June '16 | 105,978 | | 97,332 |
| July–Aug '16 | 271,330 | | 257,642 |
| Sept–Oct '16 | 181,908 | | 170,147 |
| Nov–Dec '16 | 60,041 | | 54,053 |
| Jan–Apr '17 | 187,287 | | 170,477 |
| May–June '17 | 151,163 | | 140,524 |
| July–Sept '17 | 247,024 | | 230,964 |
| Oct–Dec '17 | 232,316 | | 217,650 |
| Jan–Mar 20 '18 | 22,851 | (b) | 19,252 |
| 21 Mar–30 Apr '18 | 316,889 | (c) | 302,869 |
| May–July '18 | 134,047 | | 125,573 |
| Aug '18 | 122,272 | | 122,272 |
| Sept '18 | 114,831 | | 114,831 |
| Oct '18 | 121,046 | | 121,046 |
| Total | 2,685,209 | | 2,540,768 |

(a)   No separate figure available

(b)   Jan–Feb Figure

(c)   March–Apr Figure

Source:   Churchill's Military Effort figures, The World Crisis, Appendix J p.1423;   other figures Military Effort p.359–62.


The overall difference between the columns is 6.5%, for the periods of the Somme 5.9%, and neither percentage is high enough to make the allied casualties lower than the German.

There is another set of figures in the Military Effort. These cover selected periods only and begin on July 1st 1916.

Table 12.2    British Casualties on the Western Front –
              Selected Periods 1916-1918

| Period | Churchill's Figures | Military Effort Table XIII-XV |
|--------|---------------------|-------------------------------|
| July-Nov '16 | 499,476 | 474,974 |
| 9 Apr-6 June '17 | 196,110(a) | 178,416 |
| 7 June-30 July '17 | 159,818 | 103,505 |
| 31 July-30 Dec '17 | 394,645 | 380,002 |
| 21 Mar-14 Nov '18 | 830,010(b) | 755,665 |
| | 2,080,059 | 1,892,562 |

(a)   April-May figures

(b)   March-November figures

Source:   Churchill's figures, The World Crisis, Appendix
J;   other figures, Military Effort, p. 325-28.

As noted in the table, time periods dealt with in the two
columns are not quite identical and some of the variation in
the statistics was undoubtedly caused by this factor.   For
example, the wide discrepancy between Churchill's figure for
June and July 1917 and the figure given in the Military
Effort for 7th June – 30th July 1917 can largely be explained
by the fact that the casualties for the first day of the
Third Battle of Ypres, which commenced on the 31st July, are
not included in the lower total.   Because of the differing
time periods it is therefore difficult to compare the two
sets of figures.   But the fact that the total given in the
Military Effort is 10% lower than the figures used by
Churchill does nothing to invalidate his overall case that
the allies suffered more casualties than the Germans on the
Western Front for, even if the lower total is used, the
balance is still in Germany's favour.

Thus, although Terraine deserves credit for pointing out
the variations in the Military Effort and has provided a
useful warning that no set of figures can be regarded as
absolute, the variations do not prove on inspection to be
wide enough to alter Churchill's contention that overall
German casualties were less than those of the allies.

In fact British casualty figures can be checked against
two other sources, medical statistics and the casualty
returns in the Annual Reports of the British Army.   For the
medical statistics yearly totals only are available and,
although these sometimes show significant variations from
Churchill's figures (9% lower for 1917), overall they are
virtually identical.[104]   The lists in the Annual Reports of
the British Army have been called by one authority as "the

most reliable treatment of British War Casualties".[105] Unfortunately the figures exclude Colonial casualties while Churchill's tables include them but if the Colonial casualties (which in any case form only a small proportion of the total) are added to the Annual Report figures for Britain and compared with Churchill's total, then they are found once more to be almost identical.[106] Thus an exhaustive check on British and German casualty statistics reveals that Churchill has used figures that are as reliable as any available.

Of course Churchill's overall argument that the Germans suffered less than the British and French could still be invalidated if Churchill's French statistics proved to be substantially inaccurate. Unfortunately I have been able to discover little about Churchill's French figures. They derive from the official returns presented to the Chamber of Deputies in 1922.[107] The apparent lack of controversy over them could indicate that they are accepted as accurate or that no other figures are available or that the source of the figures has been destroyed. However, even if Churchill's French statistics were unreliable for any particular battle for the war as a whole they would need to be inaccurate by a factor of about 100% for the overall balance to be altered in favour of the allies. For the war as a whole the Germans suffered 5,383,000 casualties on the Western Front. As reported by Churchill the British suffered 2,758,000 and the French 4,974,000.[108] Considering that the British and German figures are as accurate as any likely to be obtained, Churchill's French figure would have to be reduced from 4.97 million to 2.6 million to bring the balance out on the side of Edmonds, Terraine and Oman. It is extremely unlikely that Churchill's French figures are as inaccurate as that.

Can Churchill's figures be criticized in any other way? It should be noted that his statistics do not relate to particular battles but include the Western Front as a whole. Churchill suggests that to obtain casualty figures specific to any one battle 1/8th should be deducted from these figures to account for losses on the quiet sectors of the front. However, the discussion of the French and German figures for the Somme for July-October revealed that approximately 2/5ths and 1/4 respectively of the casualties were suffered on "quiet fronts". For the British the figure would be about 1/10th.[109] Clearly the ratio varies greatly for each army. In the case of the Somme, to arrive at the casualties suffered in that battle only 140,000 has to be deducted from Churchill's German figures (the casualties suffered on quiet fronts) and 175,000 from his figure for the French and British. These deductions hardly invalidate his case, however, for they still leave 600,000 allied casualties against 400,000 German. Churchill's figures are obviously less reliable for any particular battle than for the war as a whole but it should be remembered that if the Germans did suffer more losses than the allies in a specific battle, this would tilt the statistics for the remaining actions even more heavily in the Germans' favour.

Thus, when all factors are taken into account Churchill's figures seem to prove his contention that the allies always lost more men in their offensives than the German defenders. (The 1918 British offensive is conveniently ignored by Churchill and does not fit his argument. The casualty ratios during the British advance (Aug-Nov) were practically equal. Nevertheless this does not invalidate his larger argument for the war as a whole.)

However, in conclusion it must be said that a "blood test" is a very crude way of comparing the ability of modern states to wage war. Troops in the line are only one facet of a state's war-making capacity. Thus, although Churchill could well be correct in claiming that the allies suffered for the war as a whole more casualties than the Germans, it is still possible that Germany was being worn down at a faster rate. For example, "attrition" seems to have been at work on the transportation system of Germany. Because so much German production was devoted to munitions other machinery, such as railway equipment, suffered. The production of railway machinery declined by approximately 100% between 1914 and 1918.[110] This meant, for example, that by the end of the war coal could not be transported to where it was needed and many blast-furnaces were idle as a result.[111] In general, industrial production declined by 1/4 during the course of the war.[112] Food production was also affected by military requirements. There was a shortfall of labourers, horses, fodder, agricultural machinery and the fuel to run it.[113] Due to conscription for the army the civilian labour force declined by 4,000,000 during the war.[114] Taken together with the shortages of raw materials, the result was that "consumer goods" production did not exceed 50-60% of the pre-war levels.[115] Germany's financial capacity to carry on the war was also undergoing a process of attrition. By 1918 three quarters of her gold reserves and almost all holdings of foreign securities had gone.[116] Almost all of these factors can be related to the impingement of the army on the economy. In other words the crucial factor may have been that the German economy could not bear the strain placed upon it by the maintenance of an army of 8 million men and their accompanying equipment for four years. Britain and France, with greater financial resources and a wider economic base, may have been in a better position to endure longer. In Germany's case economic collapse and military collapse could be inter-related. The question of why the war was won (or lost) is then a good deal more complicated than the tables of figures produced by Churchill would indicate.

Nevertheless, of the four authorities mentioned, Churchill has handled his material with the greatest perspicacity and was scrupulous in his attempts to check its validity. The need to prove a case eventually led Edmonds, Oman and Terraine into error. Churchill too may have been seeking to prove a case, but in this instance it is the amateur historian who has demonstrated the superior analytical ability.

Chapter 13

CHURCHILL AND THE TANK 1914-1918

Invention

It was the difficulty of rapid movement brought about by
trench warfare on the Western Front that lay behind the
evolution of the first tanks. Early attempts to adopt
mechanical traction to the prevailing war conditions have
very little in common with the tank as it was finally
developed, but as they are well established in the mythology
with which the invention of the tank is surrounded, several
of the most important experiments should be briefly examined.

One of the earliest developments arose out of the
activities of the Royal Naval Air Service around Dunkirk. To
protect the aerodromes from incursion by German cavalry
formations, patrols of motor vehicles fitted with armour
plate were developed.[1] This experiment was countered by
the Germans who adopted the simple expedient of digging
ditches across the major roads.[2] In November 1914 Admiral
Bacon of the Coventry Ordinance Works suggested to Churchill
that this problem could be overcome by the use of an armoured
tractor which would lay a series of girders across the gaps
in the road.[3]

However, a machine that was prepared by Bacon was a
wheeled[4] armoured tractor and its only purpose was to
bridge gaps in the road. Obviously this device bore only a
remote resemblance to the tank and little was lost when it
was eventually cancelled.

Meanwhile a more promising idea had been put forward by
Lt.-Col. Swinton, the official war correspondent
(Eye-witness) attached to GHQ in France. In October 1914
Swinton arranged a meeting with Hankey, and told him that he
had seen Holt Caterpillar tractors at work in France hauling
artillery and it had occured to him that some of these could
be modified into fighting machines.[5] On the 2nd of January
1915 Swinton passed on his idea for a "machine gun destroyer"
to the War Office.[6] His basic idea was for a modified Holt
Caterpillar with a top speed of 4 miles per hour, designed to
carry 10 men, 2 machine guns and one light quick firing
gun.[7] The machines were to be specifically adapted to

enfilade enemy trenches with machine gun fire while the crew was protected by the armour. It was thought that the caterpillar tracks would be able to crush the enemy wire.[8] Under the stimulus of Swinton's concept Hankey had also taken up the idea of a "trench-crossing" device. His plan was for a caterpillar to be fitted with heavy-rollers in order to crush the barbed-wire by sheer weight. Such machines would give some protection to the advancing infantry and could be fitted with machine guns to support the advance.[9] This paper was read by Churchill who, in a letter to Asquith, strongly supported Hankey's ideas. He thought

> "It would be quite easy in a short time to fit up a number of steam tractors with small armoured shelters, in which men and machine guns could be placed, which would be bullet-proof. Used at night they would not be affected by artillery fire to any extent. The caterpillar system would enable trenches to be crossed quite easily, and the weight of the machine would destroy all wire entanglements. 40 or 50 of these engines prepared secretly and brought into positions at nightfall could advance quite certainly into the enemy's trenches, smashing away all the obstructions and sweeping the trenches with their machine-gun fire and with grenades thrown out of the top. They would then make so many points d'appui for the British supporting infantry to rush forward and rally on them."[10]

It should be noted that both Hankey's and Churchill's proposals differed significantly from Swinton's. Hankey had merely proposed a form of armoured steam roller; Churchill's machine was meant to carry substantial numbers of infantry, intended for use at night, and was clearly not designed to capture more than one line of enemy trenches at a time.

With Swinton's, Hankey's and Churchill's proposals before them the War Office acted. Scott-Moncrieff (Director of Fortifications and Works) thought Swinton's suggestion well worth trying and asked permission to form a committee to investigate his "machine gun destroyer".[11] A trial took place on February 17th. The Holt Caterpillar climbed the wire entanglements but fell into a trench and the slippery ground prevented it from getting out.[12] The idea was then allowed to drop. The War Office has often been described as obscurantist for allowing this promising development to lapse so easily and it is certainly true that the officials involved showed little persistence or imagination. However the trials had demonstrated one of the fundamental drawbacks of the early tank, the difficulty which the machines had in operating over wet and boggy ground. This virtually precluded their use in winter on the Western Front and made their utilization on the low-lying ground of Flanders doubtful at any time of the year. Thus the immediate utility of the weapon must have been placed in doubt and it is possibly this reason rather than a resistance to new ideas which led to the demise of the project.

Meanwhile, interest in a trench crossing machine had revived at the Admiralty. In January Churchill wrote to Sueter (Director, Air Division RNAS) asking him to investigate the possibility of crushing trenches with two steam-rollers tied together.[13] Experiments showed, however, that the rollers bogged too easily and investigations were halted.[14] In February a proposal for a "land battleship" was put to Churchill by Major Hetherington of the R.N.A.S.[15] Hetherington envisaged a huge platform mounted on 40 foot wheels carrying two four inch guns and powered by an 800 h.p. engine.[16] Churchill passed this proposal on to Fisher who in turn consulted Tennyson d'Eyncourt, the Director of Naval Construction.[17] D'Eyncourt considered the proposition unworkable. The machine would weigh over 1,000 tons and be a conspicuous target for enemy artillery. He thought, however, that the idea was interesting and suggested investigations be made into smaller alternatives.[18] Churchill therefore appointed d'Eyncourt to head a small Committee, consisting of Hetherington, Col. Dumble from the War Office and Col. Crompton, a well known engineer.[19] Thus was born the Admiralty Landships Committee.

The Committee held their first meeting on February 22nd and decided to proceed with the building of two prototypes, one employing wheels and the other caterpillar tracks.[20] In view of the confusion which has arisen concerning these designs it is important to realize exactly what was proposed. The wheeled type was based on a design by Crompton and consisted basically of a platform, armoured and closed, fitted to an existing wheeled tractor to carry 50 men and machine guns.[21] The caterpillar type was virtually identical, merely substituting tracks for the wheels.[22] Thus both proposals were in line with Churchill's original idea for an armoured infantry carrier mounting machine guns. These weapons were clearly designed to transport the infantry across no-mans land with as few casualties as possible. Once the enemy trenches had been reached the infantry would have presumably decamped from the landships, taken the trench line and then re-loaded for an assault on the second line. Obviously this was a different concept from the tank as eventually developed.

Soon after the meeting, the two designs were submitted to Churchill who authorized d'Eyncourt to proceed "As proposed and with all despatch".[23] The committee decided to engage Fosters of Lincoln to build 6 of the "big wheel" type and use Pedrail tracks to construct 12 of the caterpillar type.[24] The cost of these machines was estimated at £70,000 and authorization to spend this money was given by Churchill. It was expected to produce the first "big wheel" type in 12

weeks and the first caterpillar two weeks later.[25] In the
event technical difficulties were to delay the production of
the two landships for a much longer period. With the
caterpillar type it was found that to accommodate 50 men the
vehicle had to be 40 feet long. This produced intolerable
strains on the chassis and it was thought that the vehicle
would be unable to negotiate the narrow roads in France,[26]
so it was cut in two and the two halves articulated
together.[27] It was then discovered that the Pedrail system
was not strong enough for the articulated machine so a new
type, the "Bullock creeping grip" was ordered from
America.[28] Meanwhile the "big wheel" type had been
abandoned. The design was found to be practicable but it
formed a very large target and would have been a menace to
other wheeled traffic in the event of a break down.[29]
Fosters then turned to other alternatives.[30] At this point
the Admiralty was contacted by the War Office and a decision
taken to form a joint Committee on landships.[31]

The revived interest in the "tank" by the War Office may
be put down to Swinton. In early June he had placed his
paper on machine gun destroyers before the
Commander-in-Chief, Sir John French. French passed the paper
on to the War Office with the remark that the machines
appeared to be of "considerable tactical value".[32] Another
trial was held using a Foster-Daimler 105 h.p. tractor,[33]
but at this point the War Office learned of the seemingly
more promising Admiralty experiments and the joint Committee
was formed.

The intervention of the War Office had one immediate
effect. They informed the Landships Committee that the
machines "should be designed to carry a minimum of men and a
maximum of gun fire" and suggested that 2 x 2 pounder pom
poms and two machine guns be carried in each portion of the
articulated machines.[34] Obviously although the War Office
reduced the number of infantry to be carried and increased
the emphasis on fire power the Landship was still largely
considered to be an infantry platform for they also specified
that loopholes be cut out for musketry fire.[35] Soon
however, the War Office requirements underwent another change
to bring them more in line with Swinton's original
conception. They asked for a vehicle with a top speed of
four miles per hour able to climb an earth parapet 5' thick
and 5' high and to bridge a gap of 5'. It should carry 10
men, 2 machine guns and one light quick firing gun.[36] Thus
due to the intervention of Swinton and the War Office the
type of machine being investigated by the Landships Committee
changed from an armoured transport for troops to a form of
light mobile artillery. The course was now clear for the
invention of the tank proper.

The War Office specifications caused a split within the
Landships Committee. Crompton was convinced that only an
articulated machine would meet the new weight

requirements.[37]    D'Eyncourt    thought    a    single
non-articulated machine should be built and he instructed a
Mr Tritton of Fosters to proceed with one half only of the
articulated model "to have the Bullock tracks, a superimposed
gun carriage on top with two-pounders fitted in it".[38]
Immediate difficulties were encountered in the construction
of this machine which afterwards became known as "Little
Willie". Placing the gun turret on top of the body raised
the centre of gravity which meant that the machine tended to
tip over when mounting a parapet.[39]   Also it was found that
the Bullock track was not strong enough and had a tendency to
fly off the chassis.[40]   The work of the Committee appeared
to have come to nothing, for "Little Willie" as well as
having these defects did not meet the War Office
specification concerning the climbing of a 5' parapet.
Considering conditions in France this was an essential
attribute. At this stage Lt Wilson of the R.N.A.S., who had
been working with Tritton, suggested that the problem of the
high centre of gravity could be solved if the tracks were
raised to encircle the entire sides of the tank.[41]   By
elongating those sides to form a rhomboid greater length of
track and therefore greater traction could be provided. The
problem of the position of the guns was solved by placing
them in detachable "sponsons" on the sides. According to
Tritton this suggestion also came from Wilson.[42]   There
was, however, one major technical problem to be solved before
a prototype of the Tritton-Wilson tank (later called
"Mother") could be built. None of the existing tracks were
of sufficient strength for the new design. In the relatively
short time of a month Tritton and Wilson had solved this
problem,[43] and in October work began on the new
design.[44] By December work on "Mother" had been completed
and successful trials were conducted in front of a large
gathering of military and civilian officials at Hatfield Park
on February 2nd, 1916.[45]

* * * * * * * * * * * * * *

We must now examine Churchill's account of the invention
of the tank to which a separate chapter in Volume 2 of The
World Crisis has been devoted.[46]   One general point should
initially be made. With minor emendations the account given
by Churchill from page 510 to page 516 has been taken from
his Statement to the Royal Commission on Awards to Inventors
which sat in 1919.[47]   The duty of this body as far as the
tank was concerned was to ascertain the persons responsible
for its invention and to allocate monetary rewards to them.
Churchill from the first waived his claim to any cash
payment,[48] but in the document submitted set out to make
the best case for himself that he could. Obviously this part
of his account in The World Crisis is not a cool and detached
history, but rather a narrative originally written to

convince a court of its validity.

The opening two pages of Churchill's narrative, however, are not taken from his Royal Commission statement although they follow the same line. In these pages Churchill describes the experiments conducted by Admiral Bacon to find a bridging device to cross ditches. Bacon's work is described by Churchill as one of the first steps in the "chain of causation" leading to the invention of the tank.[49] It is hard to avoid the conclusion that Churchill has made too much of these experiments and that they occupy an inordinate amount of space in his brief account. It has been shown that all Bacon was attempting to do was to equip a tractor with a form of portable bridge which it laid across a trench and then pulled up after passing over. This machine was surely a far cry from the idea of the tank. Neither did Bacon's experiments lead on to future developments and this is admitted by Churchill.[50] Yet prominence is still given to Bacon's ideas, the possible reason being that Churchill is anxious to establish the antecedents of the tank as far back as possible and to establish them firmly among developments initiated by the Admiralty. Finally Churchill is incorrect in stating that Caterpillar traction was used on Bacon's tractor.[51] Descriptions of the machine given by others make it quite clear that the machine was a conventional wheeled tractor.

Following the detailed narrative of Bacon's work Churchill has a brief paragraph on the early contributions of Hankey and Swinton.[52] However, no description of the weapons devised by the two men is included. With Hankey's idea this is of little importance as his device was merely a form of steam roller. The omission of Swinton's conception is more important. It is quite clear from the description given earlier that Swinton envisaged a machine which was recognizably like the original tanks but by not giving the necessary details Churchill is able to make the statement that all concerned were working on the same type of machine.

Churchill is also rather severe on the War Office authorities, who stopped work on the project after seeing a caterpillar perform under adverse conditions.[53] The facts were that no competent design existed that would work and the War Office authorities were quite correct in seeing that any such machine would have great difficulty in operating on the Western Front. Therefore to put down the demise of this experiment to "official obstruction"[54] would seem to be going too far. Where Churchill is correct is in attacking the lack of persistence and imagination which led these authorities to abandon the attempt after one trial.

The formation of the Admiralty Landships Committee is next discussed by Churchill,[55] but his account of the working of this Committee is unreliable. He states that the placing of orders for 12 of the caterpillar type and 6 of the big wheel type developed by the Committee was the "moment when the actual manufacture of the first tanks was definitely ordered".[56] He further states that "an effective machine was designed as the direct outcome of this authorization".[57] He also considers that the efforts of Swinton "were brought to nothing by the obstruction of some of ... [his] superiors" and that Swinton was "unfortunate in not being able to command the resources necessary for action, or to convince those who had the power to act".[58] Not one of these claims is correct. Regarding the first claim, Churchill never gives a description in The World Crisis of the two types of machine which were being built by the Admiralty Committee. However it has been shown that they were not actually tanks in the true sense of the word but merely armoured infantry carriers, designed to transport 50 men across no-mans land. This was a completely different weapon and concept from the first tanks. Therefore it is hardly correct to say that the orders placed for these machines amounted to the moment when the manufacture of the first tanks was authorized. Nor is Churchill correct in claiming that an effective machine was built as the direct outcome of this order. It was shown in some detail earlier that eventually the work of the Landships Committee finished in a series of blind alleys and impractical designs. What saved their work from oblivion was the introduction of the War Office specifications. These were of crucial importance for they changed the concept under consideration from an infantry carrier into the tank proper. Thus it was this order that led to the building of "Mother" and not the order for the original 18 machines signed by Churchill. Obviously then, Churchill is again in error in claiming that Swinton's ideas came to nothing through War Office obstruction, for it has been seen that the final War Office specifications were based fairly closely on Swinton's original idea and although the War Office had been very slow to respond to Swinton's proddings there is no evidence to suggest that they deliberately tried to stifle his invention. Indeed as has been shown it was the War Office that took the initiative in establishing the joint Committee under whose auspices "Mother" was developed.

Finally, Churchill details the honourable part he played in ensuring that the Landships Committee was retained by the Admiralty. He then goes on to say

"[the Admiralty] decided that the construction of one experimental machine should be proceeded with. One alone survived. But this proved to be the 'Mother Tank' which, displayed in Hatfield Park in January, 1916, became the exact model of the tanks which fought on the Somme in August, 1916."[59]

This statement is largely at variance with the facts. There never seems to have been a decision to concentrate on one

"tank" only, although, as we saw earlier, D'Eyncourt
instructed Tritton to push ahead with one half of the
articulated caterpillar because of lack of progress on the
original design. (The "big wheel" type had already been
cancelled due to technical difficulties.) This machine was
therefore developed ahead of the articulated design but it
was not "Mother" as implied by Churchill but "Little
Willie". "Mother", as has been shown, was developed
independently by Tritton and Wilson while work was still
progressing on "Little Willie". Furthermore it should be
clear that even "Little Willie" did not arise out of the
initial Landships Committee's design but as a result of the
War Office specifications.

What has Churchill attempted to do in this chapter of The
World Crisis? Largely he has attempted to establish a direct
link between Admiralty experiments on landships and the
"Mother" tank and he postulates a chain of causation thus:[60]

In fact the chain should run

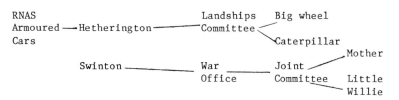

It can be seen at a glance from the second chart that
Churchill has omitted from his account the vital role played
by Swinton and the War Office and has completely confused the
process whereby "Mother" evolved out of the work of the joint
Committee which incidently is not even mentioned in The World
Crisis. Thus when Churchill claims that he is entitled to
the credit "for initiating and sustaining the action which
led to the tanks being produced",[61] this is at best a half
truth. He is entitled to credit for establishing and
sustaining the Landships Committee which provided the
expertise that enabled the Swinton-War Office specifications
to be quickly translated into a practical machine. Thus
although Churchill played an honourable role in the inception
of the first tank it was rather more indirect than has been
indicated in The World Crisis.

Utilization

Somme

Churchill concludes his section on Tanks in Volume 2 of The World Crisis by giving a brief description of the use to which tanks were put in the battle of the Somme.62 This material is expanded and augmented in Volume 3 where two pages of a chapter on the Somme are devoted to tanks.63 In his analysis of this phase of the battle Churchill's main point is that the tanks were used prematurely and "the immense advantage of novelty and surprise was thus squandered".64 How valid is this criticism? During the battle of the Somme it was clearly suggested to Haig that he withhold the tanks until larger numbers were available. However Haig was convinced that his September plan was the last opportunity to shift the enemy from the entrenched position before autumn. The examination of prisoners and captured documents had convinced him that German morale was cracking and he considered the coming battle could be decisive. He therefore felt bound to use any available weapon including the tanks.65 This explanation has been accepted by Terraine who strongly disagrees with Churchill's line and says that it was "absurd" to suppose that Haig would hold back a new weapon in a decisive battle.66 This statement begs the important question of whether there was any reasonable expectation that the September battle would be decisive. Even with the contemporary evidence available to Haig the prospects did not seem hopeful. Fewer divisions would be engaged than on the first day of the battle. The only reserves available were the remains of divisions that had fought in the opening phases of the Somme.67 There was also no sign of German morale on the battlefield cracking on a large scale as against the possibly low morale of small groups of prisoners. Furthermore the ground over which the tanks were to be used was particularly unsuitable, being torn up and cratered. The assumption of success then would appear to be wildly optimistic and to this extent Churchill's criticism of Haig for using the tanks in what could only be a minor success would appear to be justified.

However, there is another side to the story. There is always a case to be made for using a new weapon in small numbers at first and not making the offensive dependent absolutely on its performance. Thus of the tanks which fought on the Somme Swinton recorded "progress ... was hampered in every direction by the frequent failure of the machines, owing to minor defects. There were, in addition, the inevitable difficulties with guns, mountings and various small fitments."68 In other words the Mark I tank was not a particularly efficient fighting machine and one tank Commander regarded "as too appalling to contemplate the prospect of attacking with 300 or 400 Mark I tanks absolutely untested in battle."[69] There was the further point that a small scale trial enabled a group of battle-experienced crew to be built up and used to train the men for the larger number of tanks that were being produced. Thus Fuller, hardly an apologist for the General Staff, thought that the lessons learned on the Somme fully justified the employment of tanks.[70] In The World Crisis Churchill has ignored the benefits that accrued to the Tank Corps in battle-trained men and more efficient machines from the experience on the Somme. On balance it seems that these advantages, although they played no part in Haig's decision to use the tanks, outweighed the disadvantages of exposing them to the enemy, especially, as Churchill himself admits, as the Germans made no use of the disclosure to build their own tanks.[71]

## Cambrai

On November 20th, 1917 the British Third Army broke into the Hindenburg defences on a six mile front to a depth of six miles. There had been no preliminary bombardment and for the first time tanks had led the attack en masse. The plan had been to break through the three lines of the defences with a view to allowing the cavalry through to Valenciennes-Douai to cut the communications of the German forces further to the north.[72] In fact the third line of the Hindenburg system was not pierced except in a few isolated sections. The attack slowly developed into a slogging match for the heights of Bourlon Wood and eventually it petered out. On November 30th the Germans, attacking without tanks, recaptured almost all the ground gained by the British, and the battles ended in an inconclusive draw.

Churchill makes a series of important statements about this battle in The World Crisis. He ascribes most of the success in the early part of the battle to the tanks.[73] He claims that "there was no reason why a battle like Cambrai could not have been fought a year before, [or on a larger scale] or better still, why three or four concerted battles like Cambrai could not have been fought simultaneously in the spring of 1917".[74] He is clearly aware of the audacity of these statements and of the arguments that can be brought against them:

> "it will be said, such assertions take insufficient account of the practical difficulties, of the slowly gathered experience, of the immense refinements of study, discipline and organization required. Could, for instance, 3000 Tanks have been manufactured by the spring of 1917? Could the men to handle them have been spared from the front? Could their tactical training have been perfected behind the line and out of contact with the enemy? Could the secret have been kept? Would not preparation on so large a scale, even behind the line,

have become apparent to the enemy? To all these questions we will answer that one-tenth of the mental effort expended by the Headquarters Staff on preparing the old-fashioned offensives of which the war had consisted, one-twentieth of the influence they used to compel reluctant Governments to sanction these offensives, one-hundredth of the men lost in them, would have solved all the problems easily and overwhelmingly before the spring of 1917".[75]

This harsh indictment of the General Staff is obviously central to Churchill's entire argument against the Western Front battles and it will be necessary to consider each of the points raised in some detail.

Were the tanks the decisive factor at Cambrai as claimed by Churchill? Clearly they were important especially in keeping British casualties low. The commander of the 6th Division states "I attribute the very light casualties and success to the Division on 20th November firstly of course to the moral effect of the tanks."[76] By 6 p.m. the six British divisions had suffered only 4,000 casualties[77] whereas on the Somme often one division had recorded more than this total on the first day. However it is clear from the detailed divisional reports that there were other factors contributing to the easy success. For example the 187th Brigade (62nd Division) got ahead of its supporting tanks but still managed to advance to timetable.[78] The right wing of the 20th Division arrived at the second objective at 11.30 a.m. in spite of the fact that all 11 tanks accompanying it had been knocked out.[79] On the 6th Division front the troops pushed through gaps left by the enemy in the wire largely without the help of tanks.[80] Finally we find later in the day the 187th Brigade reporting "The tanks did good work at the start, but the battalion soon outstripped them, advancing steadily for some 1,400 yards up the Hindenburg front system behind a barrage which moved with remarkable precision."[81] Obviously then, tanks were not the only factor in the rapid advance. The important contribution made by the artillery barrage was identified in the last quotation. This is mentioned by Churchill[82] but it is hardly given the prominence it deserves. The new methods of ranging meant that the German batteries were immediately blanketed with fire and their response was quite ineffectual.[83] It should be made clear however that the development of the tank enabled the artillery to concentrate on the enemy's artillery and rear positions rather than on the destruction of the wire and to this extent the tank and the effectiveness of the artillery barrage were interrelated.[84]

A second factor however was the state of the German defenders occupying the Hindenburg line at Cambrai. Ludendorff has testified that because of Passchendaele the

line was weakly held by tired or landwehr divisions.[85]
Thus without the battle in the north, so condemned by
Churchill, the initial breakthrough at Cambrai could have
been much more difficult. In addition, the British had a
superiority of three to one over the battle front.

Thirdly, fog, a factor that often came to the aid of the
attacker in 1917 and 1918, played its part at Cambrai. It
was found to be especially effective in deadening the noise
of the assembling tanks.[86]

Clearly tanks were but one factor in the new methods of
warfare introduced in late November 1917.

What of Churchill's claims that Cambrai could have been
fought on a larger scale? Certainly more tanks were
available than the 400 used. By October 27th 824 Mark IV
tanks had been handed over to the Army by the Ministry of
Munitions.[87] However the problems of assembling a great
number of tanks at the front would have been formidable. In
the first place there were only two cranes in France at this
time capable of unloading tanks and this severely limited the
speed of delivery from England.[88] Furthermore wagons to
transport tanks remained in short supply throughout 1917. To
transport the 400 tanks to Cambrai improvised wagons had to
be used and many of these were found to be too damaged after
one journey to be used again.[89] In addition the supplies
needed by the tank corps were enormous. To keep the 400
tanks used at Cambrai in action for 10 hours were needed
28,000 gallons of petrol, 2,000 gallons of oil, 16,000
gallons of water, 6,000 gallons of gear oil and 2,800 lbs of
grease.[90] Also 500,000 rounds of 6 lb shell and 5,000,000
rounds of machine gun ammunition were stockpiled.[91] It is
extremely doubtful if double the number of wagons and double
the amount of stores, tank supplies and ammunition could have
been concentrated with the facilities available in 1917 and
it would seem that these logistic factors have been ignored
by Churchill in his claim that Cambrai could have been fought
on a larger scale.

It seems even more unlikely that Cambrai could have been
fought a year earlier. It was shown in our earlier
discussion that the first tanks were built in a remarkably
short time and that the delay in reaching a satisfactory
design was due to neither War Office nor Admiralty
obstruction but was caused by the technical difficulties
involved. The date of the authorization for the first tanks
(Feb. 12th 1916)[92] does not seem unreasonable. The number
originally sanctioned (100) might appear modest but it has to
be remembered that the weapon was untried and that the figure
had been suggested as the maximum desirable at this stage by
Swinton.[93] Now for "Cambrai" to have taken place in
November 1916 it would have been necessary to build 400
machines by October at the latest, that is in a period of 8
months. For this to have been achieved a rate of about 50
tanks per month was needed, an extremely difficult task with

the limited facilities available.[94]  Also, had these tanks been built they would have been Mark I's, the Mark IV being developed out of the lessons learned on the Somme.  To have entered a battle with 400 Mark I tanks would have been very risky indeed.  On the Somme 25% of the numbers engaged broke down before they reached the start line and 25% of the remainder broke down on the start line.[95]  Of those remaining, 50% did not catch up with the infantry.[96]  Thus the projected attack would have been supported not by 400 tanks but by a little over 100.  In fact the confusion of large scale breakdowns could have turned the battle into a shambles.

Could three or four battles like Cambrai have been fought in the spring of 1917 as suggested by Churchill?  It is clear from The World Crisis that Churchill envisaged these battles taking place simultaneously, so approximately 1200 to 1600 tanks would have been required.  It would have been essential for these tanks to have been the new Mark IV type for after the Somme the Germans developed an armour piercing bullet that could penetrate Mark I armour.[97]  The new design which incorporated many other refinements was not ready until February 1917[98] and production commenced in the first week of April.[99]  Even allowing "spring" to extend to June 1st it was clearly not possible to build 1200 Mark IV tanks in two months.  Moreover, the logistic factors which, as was shown, would have ruled out a Cambrai fought with double the number of tanks would have applied in greater force six months earlier and with double the number of tanks again to contend with.  Finally, it has to be remembered that Cambrai was chosen carefully because of the good going it offered to the tanks.  Could two or three similar battlefields have been selected?  Flanders would always have presented difficulties because of the low lying ground and the devastation caused by previous battles.  Also Cambrai had special features such as large woods close by in which it was possible to conceal the tanks and it is doubtful if these conditions could have been duplicated in the northern section of the British front.

By now it should be obvious that Churchill's statements to the effect that the problems facing extended tank battles could have been solved by G.H.Q., had they applied their minds to them, are specious.  The major difficulty to be overcome related to tank design and production and it was hardly within the province of G.H.Q. to solve these technical and industrial problems.  Nor could they conjure heavy cranes, railway wagons, road transport, and light railways out of nowhere.  The problems to be faced were hard ones of logistics and communications and they cannot simply be dismissed with the vague generalities which Churchill uses in The World Crisis.

In the later volumes of The World Crisis are included many papers on strategy written by Churchill when out of office and as Minister of Munitions, in which tank policy occupies a prominent position. The message of these papers is always the same, that not enough is being made of this new weapon by G.H.Q. and that many more should be built. For example Churchill prints his paper of November 9th 1916 which advocated the immediate construction of 600 tanks and sketched out the plan for a battle in which they could be used to the best effect.[100] In a later chapter is published a paper written soon after he became Minister of Munitions in which he forecast tanks in greatly increased numbers for 1918 and lamented the fact that the number of men assigned to the Tank Corps was so severely limited.[101] In the "Munitions Budget" for 1918, reproduced in full in The World Crisis, he commented,

"Tanks have never yet been used in numbers under conditions favourable to their action. Nor have we ever yet had a sufficiently reliable kind of tank, nor nearly enough of them .... In consequence the army consider that they cannot allocate more than 18,500 men to the tank corps. This limits the number of fighting tanks required to an establishment of 1,080 .... There will be no difficulty in supplying this requirement, but the new designs will not be available in full numbers until July, 1918. Thereafter considerable expansions would be possible."[102]

Further papers reprinted throughout Volume 3 take up the theme of the restriction on the number of men allotted to the Tank Corps and its projected expansion.[103] In the later document Churchill stated "the resources are available, the knowledge is available, the time is available, the result is certain: nothing is lacking except the will."[104] He then reprints his letter to the Deputy C.I.G.S. informing him that in spring 1919 3,629 heavy tanks would be available plus nearly 1000 from the Anglo-American tank factory at Chateauroux. By June another 1180 and 900 tanks respectively could be added to those totals which with existing models would give over 7,000 tanks. He suggested that numbers greatly in excess of these could be supplied if the direction was given.[105] He states that his vision of the future was "10,000 fighting tanks, large and small, specially adapted to the ground they had to traverse, moving forward simultaneously behind the artillery barrage on fronts of assault aggregating 300 or 400 kilometres."[106] In a final paper, dated September 9th, 1918 he claims that although the Tanks Corps personnel had been increased to 35,000 this number would still be inadequate for the tanks being produced and that "you [Lloyd George] will have large numbers of these invaluable weapons without the men to man them".[107]  He continued,

"What has made it so difficult to develop a good policy about tanks has been the repeated shifts of opinion for and against them. Every time a new success is gained by their aid, there is an immediate clamour for large numbers. The moment the impression of that success passes away, the necessary men and material are grudged and stinted".[108]

Thus Churchill's message is clear. Before he became Minister of Munitions the authorities neither at home nor in the field appreciated the value of the tank as a weapon. After he became Munitions Minister he continually pressed for the use of more and more tanks on the Western Front and although considerable quantities were supplied they were never used in the numbers he would have liked, due to the repeated shifts in position by the military authorities. How accurate is this view of tank development in 1917 and 1918?

An examination of the attitude of the military authorities to tanks does not bear out the impression conveyed by <u>The World Crisis</u> that they were reluctant to employ this new weapon. Only a few days after the tanks first went into action on the Somme a conference between senior staff officers and Swinton recommended to Haig that 1000 tanks be ordered in addition to the number in hand.[109]  Haig immediately agreed to this figure and informed the War Office accordingly.[110]  This policy was confirmed at a meeting between Haig, War Office authorities and Col. Stern of the Mechanical Warfare Supply Department[111] (formerly Tank Supply Department).  Haig stated that tanks were required in as large numbers as possible and while improvements in design were desirable he considered almost any design better than no tank.[112] Supply figures for the new Mark IV tank for 1917 were set at March 120, April 120, May 140, June 200, July 240, August 260, September 280.[113]  In April, Stern, who was hardly enamoured with the military authorities, recorded an interview with Haig in which Haig

"said he would do anything to help me; that a division of Tanks was worth 10 divisions of infantry and he probably underestimated it - told me to hurry up as many as I could - not to wait to perfect them but to keep sending out imperfect ones as long as they came out in large quantities".[114]

Later in the year the number of tanks required by the army was increased to 1600 heavy, 1200 medium and 800 supply tanks.[115]

However the Mechanical Warfare Supply Department failed to produce anything like the quantities requested by the army. Their performance for the programme for the Mark IV was March nil, April 88, May 122, June 142, July 169, August 128, September 176, a total of 825 tanks against a projection of 1,360.[116] This shortfall can be attributed to a combination of factors. There was some delay in developing the new Mark IV design but there were also problems with steel castings, a bottleneck in the production of tank tracks and inefficiences within the Mechanical Warfare Supply Department.[117] Thus it can be seen in this early period that the tardy development of the tank did not arise out of a reluctance on the part of the army to use the weapon, because G.H.Q. consistently ordered more tanks than the Mechanical Warfare Supply Department could supply. The delays arose out of difficulties in establishing quickly an efficient organization to launch the new weapon and because of technical problems that were probably inevitable in the design of such a relatively complex machine as the tank.

What of the period when Churchill became Minister of Munitions? When Churchill took up his post the position in regard to tanks was: of the 1000 Mark IV tanks requested by the War Office about 500 had been delivered.[118] In addition the War Office had asked for 700 Mark V, 600 of a lighter tank yet to be designed and 450 supply tanks by the 1st March 1918.[119] Churchill was forced to admit that although every effort would be made he feared that no more than 200 of the new heavy Mark V and 250 of the medium tanks could be supplied by that date.[120] The War Office responded to the news by slightly reducing the number of heavy tanks required (to 600) and by extending the March 1st deadline to June 1st.[121] In the event not even these revised totals were supplied by the Ministry of Munitions and by June 1st only about 400 Mark V and 130 of the new light tanks, the medium A, had been delivered.[122]

It should be noted, however, that Churchill often brushed aside the reality of what the Ministry could deliver and set about proposing grandiose schemes of his own. The Tank Co-ordinating Committee of the Ministry recorded that on December 29th Churchill had proposed a maximum programme of 10,000 tanks per annum, 4,500 to be built in Britain and 5,500 by the Joint Anglo-American factory in France.[123] What the Co-ordinating Committee thought of this proposal was not stated but it should be noted that it would have involved a 400% increase in the manufacture of 6 pounder guns and a 10 fold increase in personnel for the tank corps.[124] Churchill's paper of October 21st which he quotes in The World Crisis should be read in the light of these facts. It is now clear that his lamentations about the fixed ceilings for the Tank Corps were made in relation to the future expansion which he foresaw for tanks rather than to what was actually being produced. For the War Office quota of 18,500 was adequate for their suggested programme[125] and the

Ministry of Munitions in the early months of 1918 was not capable of meeting even that requirement.

So far was the Ministry falling behind War Office demands that as early as January 20th 1918 Churchill had to issue revised figures of output for the Mark V tank.[126] He was bitterly disappointed with this result and asked the newly appointed head of the yet again reorganised Mechanical Warfare Department, Admiral Moore, when production could be expected to meet the required number of 400 tanks per month.[127] Moore optimistically estimated that this figure would be reached by June and maintained after August.[128] Consequently Churchill informed the War Office that 4,459 tanks could be built by the Ministry between February 1st 1918 and the 31st March 1919[129] and the next day this was approved by Lloyd George even though it went beyond the numbers requested by the War Office.[130] This state of affairs however did not last. In May the Supreme War Council called for a greatly increased tank programme[131] and as a result the War Office expanded their demands to 5,440 tanks from England and 1,500 from the Anglo-American factory at Chateauroux.[132] The Ministry of Munitions however proved incapable of meeting even the original War Office programme. When Admiral Moore who had "not been a success"[133] was removed from office it was found that, although 900 Mark V**tanks had been ordered in September 1917, almost a year later not one had been delivered. The supply of medium D and C tanks was in a similar position.[134] In fact from April to July tank production as a whole had fallen 50% below the estimates.[135] As a result of these disclosures a new Tank Board to supervise production was formed.[136] The Board was confronted almost immediately by a War Office demand for almost 6000 tanks of all types[137] but before it could be considered the Armistice intervened.

It is now worth considering what tanks were actually produced by the Ministry of Munitions. In 1918 1136 heavy fighting tanks and 148 medium tanks were assembled.[138] Of the 700 Mark V ordered in 1917 400 were made, of 1000 Mark V* 632, of 900 Mark V** one, of 900 Mark VII one, of 1750 medium C and D nil.[139] Only one tank was ever produced at Chateauroux. Thus not even the 1917 War Office Programmes were met by the Ministry and in some weeks production of heavy tanks had fallen below 20.[140] Why were so few produced? There were many factors involved, some of which indicated that Britain had virtually reached the limit of the resources that could be devoted to war production. For example, there were component shortages of all kinds including ball-bearings for the medium A and B tanks, gearboxes for all types, as well as engines and driving chains.[141] In addition there were inefficiencies within the Mechanical Warfare Department. McClean found on taking over that 1755 alterations to the working drawings supplied to contractors had taken place in the six months from

February to July 1918.[142] Each one involved delays in production. He also found that although the supply of armour plate had been adequate no proper steps had been taken to have the "raw" plate machined to fit it for tank production, with the result that shortages had been caused by the Mechanical Warfare Department itself. This in turn had caused problems when men left tank factories on the Clyde to take up other work as a result of the lack of finished plate.[143] Of course a recurring problem throughout Churchill's administration was the shortage of skilled labour. This undoubtedly caused some reduction in output but it is hard to say exactly to what extent. For instance the difficulty with ball-bearing production did not stem from a shortage of skilled labour but the absence of any firms in the country capable of manufacturing to the required standard.[144] The same could be said for gear boxes, many of which had to be rejected by the main suppliers.[145] Furthermore, labour difficulties on the Clyde seem to have been artificially caused by the Ministry itself.

Thus it should now be clear that Churchill has given a quite misleading picture regarding tank production in 1917 and 1918. By reprinting many of his memoranda from the period he has given the impression that he was one of the few people urging tank production forward, and that there was a vacillating and generally negative attitude by the military to its use. This impression has been achieved not so much by what he has said but by the unspoken assumptions behind the memoranda and the periodical repetition throughout the third volume of the "tank message". The facts, as has been shown, were very different and the military programmes exceeded, except for a brief period, even the estimates produced by the Ministry of Munitions. Thus it was not the will that was lacking as claimed by Churchill but the means of production. Nor could Churchill claim that lack of military enthusiasm for the tank meant that he was deprived of essential materials for its construction. As has been shown material stocks seem to have been adequate. The country just did not have a reservoir of skill large enough to enable large scale production to be improvised quickly. Inefficiencies under Admiral Moore, a Churchill appointee, were also a factor. It would not be right, however, for Churchill to be blamed for these inadequacies. The situation was largely not of his making and was beyond the power of any Minister to rectify. On the other hand it is clear that the picture of the tank "prophet in the wilderness" presented in The World Crisis also cannot be accepted.

Chapter 14

CHURCHILL AND THE SUBMARINE WAR

Churchill devotes only 45 of the 1,500 pages of The World Crisis to submarines. In these circumstances a detailed examination of the submarine war would be unjustified. However several interesting issues arise out of Churchill's narrative of this aspect of the war at sea and these will be briefly discussed.

The First U-Boat Campaign - 1915

By giving his chapter on this period the title of the "First Defeat of the U-Boats" Churchill leaves the reader in no doubt of his view of the eventual outcome of the U-Boat campaign. In a discussion of Admiralty counter-measures which were taken after the German announcement of the campaign, Churchill reprints a long memorandum which he wrote on February 11th. The steps taken by the Admiralty are listed as; netting the Straits of Dover, the north channel between Scotland and Ireland and the Southern Irish Sea; providing trawler and destroyer patrols for these defences; patrolling the Southampton-Havre troop convoy route; institution of a coast watch in areas likely to be used by U-Boats; arming as far as possible the patrolling trawlers, drifters and yachts, and development of the decoy or Q ship strategem.[1] In addition, scientific investigation was ordered into such devices as hydrophones, bomb lances and explosive sweeps. Churchill is convinced that these measures achieved success. He points out that in March 6,000 vessels entered or left British ports and only 21 were sunk; that the Dover barrage proved a great success and forced U-boats to make the long north about journey around Scotland to reach the Western approaches; that the merchant seamen became increasingly confident in their approach to the U-boat; and that the patrolling flotillas of small craft and the Q ships became increasingly effective.[2] He concludes that the Germans suffered substantial U-boat losses and "by May their premature and feeble campaign had been completely broken, and for nearly eighteen months, in spite of tragic incidents, we suffered no appreciable inconvenience".[3]

Has Churchill given a fair picture of the first U-boat campaign?

The immediate Admiralty response to the U-boat menace was a good deal more lethargic than the impression given by Churchill's account. On the outbreak of war for reasons not altogether obvious, the Admiralty Submarine Committee was dissolved.[4] Despite such obvious German successes as the torpedoing of the three cruisers in September no more thought seems to have been given to anti-submarine warfare until the return of Fisher to the Admiralty in November. Then on the Fourth Sea Lord's prompting[5] an anti-submarine Committee under Commander Donaldson was set up.[6] It was this committee that recommended most of the measures mentioned by Churchill in The World Crisis.[7] Thus these early anti-submarine measures owe less to Churchill's initiative than the contents and context of his memorandum of February 1915 would lead us to believe.

Churchill is also misleading on the effectiveness of several of the measures adopted during this period. For example, although he claims the Dover barrage forced U-boats to travel around the north of Scotland, this was true of the larger boats only. The small German B and C boats based in Flanders repeatedly passed the Straits during 1915,[8] and it has been estimated that in the last six months of the year over 100 vessels were sunk by mines laid by these craft.[9] As for bomb lances and hydrophones, the former device was eventually found to be totally ineffectual and no submarines were ever sunk by it. Hydrophones were introduced in 1915[10] but efficient sets were not ready until 1917[11] and eventually proved of limited use. Q ships had no success during Churchill's period in office though they did sink three submarines between July and September 1915.[12] In an early draft of this chapter Churchill was preparing to make large claims for Q ships. "Ultimately during the great submarine campaign in 1917 as many as – were constructed and commissioned, and during the whole course of the war – submarines were entrapped and destroyed by this device alone, a number exceeding those destroyed by any other single agency".[13] The blanks in Churchill's deleted paragraph can now be filled in. About 215 Q ships were commissioned and 10 U-boats were sunk by them in the course of the war but none after August 1917.[14] Nor was Churchill correct in his assumption that Q ships sunk more submarines than any other agency. Mines, depth-charges and ramming all caused more U-boat sinkings than Q ships, and gunfire caused just as many.[15] Perhaps it was a realization of this fact that led Churchill to omit the paragraph. There is no doubt however, that the Q ship appealed to Churchill as a weapon of war.

Nor were the hundreds of armed yachts, trawlers and drifters which were pressed into service particularly effective during this period.[16] By the end of December

250

1915 the patrols had accounted for only one or two enemy submarines.[17]

What of Churchill's claim that by May 1915 British counter-measures had defeated the U-boats and that the campaign had been an abject failure? In fact under Churchill's administration only four U-boats were sunk[18] and if German U-boat strength is taken at the beginning of the campaign (February) and at the end (October) it will be found that during the period the number of U-boats had increased by 26.[19] Statistics of shipping losses are hardly more favourable to the British. From February to December 1915, 30 German submarines had torpedoed 220 British ships, a total gross tonnage loss of 731,788. Approximately 140 ships (gross tonnage 680,000) had been damaged in the same period. So far from May seeing the demise of the campaign as claimed by Churchill, the highest losses for the year were reached in August (135,153) and September (89,693).[20] In the autumn 92 ships were sunk in the Mediterranean by only 6 U-boats.[21] Equally alarming was the fact that although since the beginning of the war Britain had built 1,326,529 tons of merchant shipping, for the period of the U-boat campaign only 650,919 tons had been built.[22] That is, the losses had not been made up. Furthermore, as the table shows, output was decreasing.[23]

Table 14.1
Merchant Ship Production, 1915

| Period | UK Merchant Shipping Output (Gross Tonnage) |
|---|---|
| 1915, 1st quarter | 266,267 |
| 2nd " | 146,870 |
| 3rd " | 145,070 |
| 4th " | 92,712 |
| Total | 650,919 |

Thus by whatever criteria that are used, the first German U-boat campaign cannot be called a failure and in giving his chapter the title of "The First Defeat of the U-boats", Churchill misleads the reader. Furthermore, it is quite obvious from the literature that British counter-measures were not the reason that the campaign was reconsidered by the German government in October. The Government of the United States had protested to Germany immediately a war zone had been declared around Britain on February 18th and stated that they would hold Germany responsible for the loss of any American lives.[24] American protests over the sinking of the Lusitania in May 1915, in which many Americans were lost, led to restrictions being placed on U-boat captains.[25] Finally, after a stiff American note had followed the sinking of the Arabic in August 1915, U-boats were withdrawn from all northern waters except the North Sea.[26] Thus it was American pressure and not British counter-measures which brought the campaign to an end. However, it should be noted that even then Germany did not forgo the use of U-boats altogether. Rather they concentrated their attention on the Mediterranean, where there were far fewer American targets. The tables of losses show that 150,000 tons of British shipping was lost in November and December,[27] that is after the official end of the campaign.

## The Final Phase 1916-18

Unlike any of the other wartime chapters of The World Crisis, Churchill's final chapter on the U-boat war is substantially based on the work of one of his naval advisors, as the following letter makes clear. Churchill to Kenneth Dewar:

"I send you a very rought draft of the U-boat chapter. You will see that I have re-written your excellent account in the more highly coloured and less technical style suited to the lay reader, to whom the rudiments have to be explained. I should be so much obliged if you would make any corrections or improvements which occur to you".[28]

In fact Churchill's account of the last phase of the U-boat campaign is even briefer, for the time span covered, than his sections on the earlier campaign. The main interest in the chapter therefore lies in a comparison between Dewar's paper and the material published by Churchill in The World Crisis. In making such a comparison it can be seen how Churchill changed Dewar's draft into his own more "highly coloured" prose, and what sections of it he chose for inclusion in The World Crisis and what material he chose to omit.[29] However because of their importance his handling of the introduction of the convoy system and the failure of British defensive measures of 1916-7 will also be discussed.

The first area of comparison between Dewar's and Churchill's account of the submarine war is that of language. Dewar's autobiography (The Navy From Within) and the many articles published by him reveal him as an interesting and forceful writer well able to express vividly his often highly unorthodox (for the Navy at least) ideas. No doubt it was these qualities that first recommended him to Churchill. One would not expect his account of the submarine war to be a bland narrative filled with statistics and tables. Nor is it many phrases which appear in The World

Crisis and would seem to have a Churchillian origin are in fact Dewar's. Thus it was Dewar who originally wrote of the "dark doom" awaiting the Flanders U-boats, described the operations division of the Admiralty as "troubled like Martha over many things" and suggested that hunting a U-boat was like blind man's buff in an unlimited space of three dimensions".[30] Yet as stated in his letter to Dewar, Churchill still felt the need to "improve" on Dewar's prose. He usually did this by adding even more adjectives or by making events revolve more around personalities. Several examples may be given. In writing of the effect of the increasingly efficient anti-submarine methods on the U-boats crews, Dewar said,

> There is no doubt that in these circumstances the original high morale of the submarine crews was put to a terrible strain and declined rapidly during 1918. The presentiment of a sudden and awful death, the continual attacks by escort vessels, and the fear of mines, produced a state of nervous tension which was reflected in the surrender of more than one undamaged submarine and in numerous cases of boats putting back for small repairs a few days after leaving harbour".[31]

In The World Crisis this becomes:

> "The unceasing presentiment of a sudden and frightful death beyond human sight or succour, the shuddering concussions of the depth charges, the continual attacks of escort vessels, the fear of annihilation at any moment from mines, the repeated hair-breadth escapes, produced a state of nervous tension in the U-boat crews. Their original high morale declined rapidly during 1918 under an intolerable strain. The surrender of more than one undamaged submarine and numerous cases of boats putting back for small repairs a few days after leaving harbour showed that even in this valiant age the limits of human endurance had been reached".[32]

Thus when Churchill's amendments are placed together, (unceasing, frightful, beyond human sight or succour, shuddering concussions of the depth charges, annihilation at any moment, repeated hair-breadth escapes, intolerable, valiant, limits of human endurance) we can see that his version of events is indeed more highly coloured than Dewar's.

A further example of this type of treatment may be found in the "rival" descriptions of the Zeebrugge operation. Of that action Dewar wrote:

> "The full story of that heroic action is well known. The harbour was completely blocked for about three weeks and it was dangerous for submarines for a period of two months. By dint of strenuous efforts the entrance was

partially cleared, but the obstacles formed by the sunken ships prevented the full use of the port. After 23rd April no operations of any importance were carried out by the Flanders destroyers, which were seriously impeded in entering and leaving the harbour. In consequence of these measures the losses in the English Channel were reduced from about 20 to 6 a month, and the minefields laid by Flanders boats fell from 404, or 33 a month, in 1917 to 64, or 6 a month, in 1918".[33]

In The World Crisis we find,

"The famous story of the blocking of Zeebrugge on St. George's Day by Admiral Keyes and the Dover Force cannot be repeated here. It may well rank as the finest feat of arms in the Great War, and certainly as an episode usurpassed in the history of the Royal Navy. The harbour was completely blocked for about three weeks and was dangerous to U-boats for a period of two months. Although the Germans by strenuous efforts partially cleared the entrance after some weeks for U-boats, no operations of any importance were ever again carried out by the Flanders destroyers. The results of Admiral Keyes' command at Dover reduced the Allied losses in the English Channel from about twenty to six a month, and the minefields laid by the Flanders boats fell from thirty-three a month in 1917 to six a month in 1918. These results, which constitute a recognizable part of the general victory, were achieved notwithstanding the fact that the numbers of U-boats in commission were maintained by new building at about two hundred".[34]

In Churchill's account we are told, in addition to Dewar's facts, that the famous story of Keyes and Zeebrugge, which took place on St. George's day, was probably the finest feat of arms in the Great War and unsurpassed in British Naval history. Later we are reminded that the good results which flowed from the action were achieved under Admiral Keyes' command at Dover and constitute a recognizable part in general victory. Thus does Churchill emphasize the romantic, historic, adventurous and important nature of Zeebrugge. At the same time he leaves the reader in no doubt that it was Keyes who supplied the inspiration behind the operation.

As well as examining the differences in the language used by Dewar and Churchill it is instructive to look at the different way the same aspect of the submarine war has been treated in their respective accounts. A good example is the activities and effectiveness of Q ships. Dewar devotes just under a page to a discussion of this strategem. He states that "Four submarines were destroyed by this method in 1915, two in 1916, and five in 1917". He adds "The system had its limitations, however, for the Q ship was frequently disabled

or sunk before the submarine could be enticed into a
favourable position. A vivid example of this stands out in
the action between the Dunraven and U61".[35] A brief
description of this action follows, and Dewar concludes

> "The last submarine destroyed by a Q ship was U88, in
> September 1917, and after that the strategem had lost its
> power. Submarines were taking no more risks. From first
> to last it had accomplished the destruction of 11
> submarines with the loss of 20 decoy ships, some of them
> with all hands".[36]

Although Churchill's section on Q ships is clearly based
on Dewar's account it differs from it in several important
ways. It has already been noticed that Churchill, in an
earlier chapter, greatly over-emphasized the importance of
this anti-submarine device and he now continues this
process. Firstly he states that 11 U-boats were destroyed by
Q ships during 1915 and 1916[37] when Dewar's account made it
clear that these successes were spread over three years. He
also omits the point made by Dewar that the Q-ship was often
sunk before the submarine, and the figures which show that
almost twice as many Q-ships were sunk as submarines.[38] He
then makes the assertion, certainly not supported by Dewar's
paper, that it was the activities of Q-ships that forced
submarines to rely "more and more upon their torpedoes".[39]
(In fact more important factors in instituting these changed
tactics were the different nature of the unrestricted
campaign of 1917-18 and the vastly increased numbers of armed
merchantmen.) Furthermore where Dewar devotes only a few
sentences to the Dunraven incident Churchill spends 2 1/2
pages or 1/8 of the total space on the 1917-18 submarine war
in describing this action.[40] Finally, where Dewar used the
action to illustrate the limitations of the Q ship method,
Churchill omits this point and merely publishes the story as
a stirring tale. Certainly he never draws attention to the
fact that it was the submarine which won the encounter and
the Q ship which was sunk.

A further example of the difference in approach between
Dewar and Churchill is illustrated by their sections on
convoy. Because of the importance of convoy in combatting
the German submarine campaign it is not surprising to find
Dewar devoting a great deal of attention to it. In fact it
takes up about one third of his paper. This emphasis was not
adopted by Churchill. Although Churchill calls the
introduction of convoy "the decisive step" in the submarine
war,[41] little more space is devoted to convoy in The World
Crisis than was used to describe the Dunraven incident. Thus
much of the material on convoy supplied by Dewar was omitted
from Churchill's account. In this category fall tables of
convoy losses, the escort problem, troop convoys, convoy in
the Mediterranean and Scandinavian convoys.[42] Yet these
were all important subjects and certainly more worthy of

inclusion in a general survey than Churchill's relatively trivial Q ship material. However, Churchill obviously felt that his readers required occasional stirring tales to hold their interest rather than an undramatic narration of convoy facts and figures. After reading both Churchill and Dewar the impression remains that Dewar has struck the more correct balance.

The way in which Churchill decided to adapt Dewar's section on convoy has one curious feature. The controversy surrounding the introduction of convoy and the question of whether the Admirals or the politicians took the initiative is well known. Here it seems would be an ideal opportunity for Churchill to mount another attack on Admiralty inactivity, especially as Jellicoe was the main figure concerned. Furthermore as the imposition of convoy upon the reluctant Admirals was widely held to be one of Lloyd George's major contributions to victory, it might have been expected that Churchill would emphasize his leader's decisive role. In fact neither of these expectations wholly comes to pass. While making it quite clear that he considers the Admirals responsible for the tardy introduction of convoy, Churchill also lists the difficulties which led to their hesitations. Moreover his narrative does not revolve around the criticism of personalities and Jellicoe's name is not mentioned at all. Finally Lloyd George's contribution is dismissed in one sentence, Churchill merely saying "The trial of the convoy system was urged upon the naval authorities by the Cabinet, and in this the Prime Minister took a decisive part".[43]

Yet some years later Churchill wrote an article on convoy in which he described at length and in sarcastic tones the victory of the "amateur politicians" over "the competent, trained, experienced experts at the Admiralty", clearly identified Jellicoe as the main villain and set down in detail the famous visit of Lloyd George to the Admiralty.[44] What caused this difference in approach? One possible explanation is that the two pieces on convoy were written by Churchill under different guises, the first by Churchill the historian, the second by Churchill the journalist. Thus in The World Crisis Churchill adopts a more sober approach, eschews personalities, and while coming down on the side of the politicians, is careful to consider the difficulties facing the Admiralty. In the article (originally published in the Daily Telegraph) he feels able to adopt a more partisan approach, no doubt more in keeping with the readership of a popular journal. However, there is another explanation less flattering to Churchill. It is possible that Churchill avoided criticizing (or praising) individuals in his section on convoy because of his own noticeable absence from the ranks of those advocating this solution. Alternatively, perhaps Churchill's lack of involvement at the time with the convoy issue led to his showing a certain lack of interest in the subject when writing The World Crisis and under these conditions he was quite willing to follow Dewar's account without embellishment.

Thus Churchill's need to tell a more "colourful" story than Dewar has led him to produce a slightly less balanced account. However most of the elements which made up the final submarine campaign are present in The World Crisis and the factual material provided by Dewar and included by Churchill can hardly be faulted. Churchill of course never reveals that the chapter was largely ghost-written by Dewar but no doubt Dewar, like Edmonds concerning the Somme material, would not have wanted this fact to be made public.

Chapter 15

THE WRITING OF THE WORLD CRISIS 1916-1918

We must now turn our attention to the later chapters of The World Crisis which deal with the 1917 and 1918 campaigns. At first glance, considering the amount of space devoted to this period of the war, the chapters may seem to require detailed criticism along similar lines to those on Jutland and the Somme. However when Churchill's material is examined in detail it is found that much of it consists of quotations from memoranda and letters written by Churchill and the reproduction of maps and diagrams. Further, Churchill was not at the centre of power in this period and many of the memoranda on policy reprinted in The World Crisis had no discernible impact. When these documents are deducted from the total amount of space devoted to the 1918 battles we find only 69 pages remain. Obviously then Churchill's discussion of any one battle is very brief and in fact many of his battle pieces are merely chronicles with little attempt made critically to appraise the events discussed. Therefore a detailed investigation of these chapters would appear unwarranted.

However the Churchill Papers contain much interesting material on how these chapters were written and it is proposed to deal with the historiographical aspect of Churchill's later chapters.

The method adopted is to examine the major contributions made to the book by the more important of Churchill's advisers.

One of the first to read the draft chapters of Volume 3 of The World Crisis was Lord Beaverbrook. After reading the proofs he commented to Churchill, "My principal general criticism is that there is no home politics whatever in this volume".[1] He also considered that Churchill had not adequately recognized the contribution made by Lloyd George to the final victory.[2] Churchill's initial reason for omitting domestic politics from his book is not hard to find. During this period he was out of office, and then as Minister of Munitions he was not in the Cabinet. He also took no part in the manoeuvrings which preceded the main political event of the period, the replacement of Asquith as Prime Minister by Lloyd George. However, perhaps as a result of Beaverbrook's criticism, a chapter entitled "A Political Interlude" was eventually included.[3] It deals in rather summary fashion with the defects of the coalition government from May 1915, the conscription issue, the power of the press in wartime and the formation of the Lloyd George coalition. As usual Churchill adds a personal note by including a discussion of his secret session speech of May 10th 1917 which, he claims, was instrumental in Lloyd George's decision to include him in the government in July.

Churchill also tried to meet Beaverbrook's argument about Lloyd George. "L.G. I have added a short passage of appreciation at the end of "A Political Interlude" which I trust will repair the deficiency you notice".[4] This appreciation of Lloyd George can be read on p. 1115-6 of The World Crisis. However a section of it owes more to Hankey, who was also assisting Churchill at this point, than to Churchill. In a letter to Churchill Hankey detailed some of the qualities of Lloyd George.

> "For example, his habit of snatching advantage out of disaster always strikes me as one of his outstanding merits. Thus, out of the terrible losses from submarines in the Spring of 1917 he obtained the adoption of the convoy system (for which however I think you have given him credit). From the disaster of Caporetto he secured the establishment of the Supreme War Council. From the disaster of March 21st he secured the unified command".[5]

This should be compared with the following passage from The World Crisis:

> "Mr. Lloyd George in this period seemed to have a peculiar power of drawing from misfortune itself the means of future success. From the U-boat depredations he obtained the convoy system: out of the disaster of Caporetto he extracted the Supreme War Council: from the catastrophe of the 21st of March he drew the Unified Command and the immense American reinforcement".[6]

Beaverbrook, however, was still not satisfied that Churchill had treated Lloyd George generously enough. Indeed, the chapters of The World Crisis on the Nivelle offensive, Passchendaele and the build-up to the German Spring offensive of 1918 contain many references unflattering to the Prime Minister. Churchill speaks of Lloyd George's "facile acceptance of the Nivelle schemes", laments his weakness in agreeing to the prolongation of Passchendaele and clearly disagrees with the policy which left the British Army under strength through the winter of 1917-18.[7] He was not prepared to alter these judgments. He wrote to Beaverbrook,

> "I am grieved that the story should produce the impression on your mind of hostility to L.G. I think now, as I said then, that he was utterly wrong about Nivelle, about not stopping Passchendaele and about not reinforcing the army in the winter of 1918. He would have had far more authority over G.H.Q if he had not chopped and changed so much about offensives in the west. Every three or four months he was in a new mood. They at any rate were consistent in always wanting to attack. I was consistent in always trying to stop them. L.G. figures on both sides of the account with a contradiction which history is bound to note, because all the documents exist. In the upshot he was always wrong. He encouraged the Nivelle offensive which ended in disaster. He discouraged the final advance in 1918 which ended in success. He gave way about the prolongation of Passchendaele against a true conviction. Still there is no doubt that he was much better as No. 1 than anybody else. The same may be said of Haig. The truth is that armageddon was quite beyond the compass of anybody, even including you and me".[8]

Thus, although Churchill was prepared to include sections in The World Crisis praising Lloyd George, he was not prepared to remove the criticisms. Lloyd George is therefore handled in a much more direct way than was noticed in Volume 1 where several unflattering references to the then Chancellor of the Exchequer were carefully removed. But in 1921 and 1922 when Volume 1 was written Churchill and Lloyd George were colleagues in government, Churchill being the junior partner. By 1926 they were no longer colleagues. Nor were they likely to be aligned politically in the future and this fact may have led Churchill to reject further attempts by Beaverbrook to alter The World Crisis in Lloyd George's favour.

On a separate occasion Beaverbrook complained of Churchill's treatment of Bonar Law. Churchill amended his account and Beaverbrook replied, "I do not see any objection whatever to the text as amended. I am sure it gives a fair impression of Bonar Law".[9] Unfortunately the material omitted by Churchill cannot be identified. It could not have been concerned with events described in "A Political Interlude" for that chapter was only included later. Yet there are no other references to Bonar Law in Volume 3. Perhaps Churchill transferred the omitted material to a later chapter in which Bonar Law appears in a not unfriendly light.[10]

Despite the criticisms of Beaverbrook about the political aspects of The World Crisis it was the final military chapters which gave Churchill the most trouble in the construction of Volume 3. Although Edmonds continued to supply him with material and documents, Churchill felt the lack of advice from a serving officer, a military equivalent of Keyes, who had read all the naval chapters. The problem was that Churchill was hardly persona grata with a considerable section of the army who were well aware of his opinion of their capabilities. Also Sir Henry Wilson, who would have been a possible candidate, was dead. Churchill then hit upon the startling idea of approaching Sir Douglas Haig for help on his military chapters. Churchill had established good relations between himself and the Commander-in-Chief during Churchill's period as Minister of Munitions. Haig had been particularly impressed at the way in which losses in materiel caused by the German spring offensive had been promptly replaced by Churchill's Ministry.[11] After the war the friendly relations had been maintained and Haig had been sent a presentation copy of Volume 1 of The World Crisis. Nevertheless the possibility of literary collaboration between the two men must have seemed fairly unlikely. Even a cursory reading of The World Crisis reveals Churchill's hostility to the policy adopted by G.H.Q. in France from 1915 onwards. Such statements as "if only the Generals had not been content to fight machine-gun bullets with the breasts of gallant men, and think that that was waging war"[12] can hardly have endeared Churchill to Haig. However, the need to ask Haig's permission to quote from conversations between Churchill and the Commander-in-Chief led Churchill to include the chapters in which they were contained for Haig's comments. Churchill's letter continued,

> "The four chapters in which they [the conversations] occur may perhaps interest you, and I dare say you will not be discontented with them....On the other hand, as you may perhaps remember, I was a convinced and outspoken opponent of our offensive policy at Loos, on the Somme and at Passchendaele, and the argument of the book turns strongly against it. Therefore, in considering whether you care to allow these personal quotations to appear in the latter part you ought to bear in mind the criticisms of the earlier years which are also included in the work. I need scarcely say that these criticisms are expressed in terms appropriate to the pleasant personal relations which have for so many years and in such varied circumstances existed between us".[13]

Haig responded positively to Churchill. He was apparently willing to balance the criticisms of Part 1 of Volume 3 with the praise bestowed in Part II. He not only gave Churchill permission to quote from the conversations but sent him some extracts from his diary to show what he thought to be the facts at the time. He also added, "It has been a very great pleasure to read your very brilliant account of those anxious weeks".[14] Churchill was delighted with Haig's reply. "You take, if you will permit me to say so, a broad-minded view about criticisms, as is right in regard to matters which belong to history and will for generations be argued about".[15] He thanked Haig for his criticisms of the four chapters and included more for Haig's perusal and he also asked permission to reproduce Haig's famous "backs to the wall" message in facsimile.[16] This was duly given and the reproduction appears on p 1273.[17] From this point on, the unlikely partnership between Churchill and Haig developed. Haig read most of the chapters of Volume 3 of The World Crisis from the Nivelle Offensive on, and as will be shown made a considerable contribution to the book. At the end of their collaboration Haig wrote,

"The book will have an honoured position in my library here, and I feel sure that I shall read all you have written with the greatest pleasure, as I have already greatly enjoyed reading the extracts from the Book which have appeared in the 'Times'. In order to enjoy reading your writings it is not, I find, necessary to agree with all the opinions which you express. And as for criticisms of what I did or did not do, no one knows as well as I do how far short of the ideal my own conduct both of the 1st Corps & 1st Army was, as well as of the B.E.F. when C in C. But I do take credit for this, that it was due to the decisions which I took in August and Septr 1918 that the war ended in Nov....I hope that if you ever happen to be in this neighbourhood, or passing through that you will arrange to spend a day or two with us".[18]

As will be shown the line suggested by Haig, that he was largely responsible for the decision to press for decisive action in 1918, was the line adopted by Churchill in The World Crisis. It is then indeed ironic that Churchill, usually regarded as the bête noir of G.H.Q. and the scourge of the "westerners", should enlist the willing cooperation of the arch westerner in writing The World Crisis. Surely this is one of the strangest secrets that the Churchill Papers have to reveal.

Of course the adoption of a more pro-Haig line by Churchill produced trouble for him with some of his other advisers who were usually to be found in the other camp. Beaverbrook considered that "On both Jellicoe and Haig you give the impression of hedging, [it is hard to see how Churchill could be accused of hedging on Jellicoe!] though no doubt the historian of the future, reading between the lines will see clearly enough what you really thought of them".[19] Churchill was quick to correct Beaverbrook's assumptions, though his reply is much more appropriate to the

view of Haig given in The World Crisis than to that of
Jellicoe.

> "There is no doubt that both Jellicoe and Haig were
> absolutely at the top of their professions from every
> point of view; and apart from the erroneous doctrines
> which led one to fight as little, and the other as much,
> as possible, they played worthy parts and rendered great
> services and bore a noteworthy share in the eventual
> success. Therefore it would not be just, apart from
> other considerations, to frame a hard partisan indictment
> and omit all recognition of the other side. I do not
> seek to condemn individuals, but to establish certain
> impersonal views upon the war by sea and land. If I can
> do this satisfactorily while avoiding recriminations, I
> am quite content. As a matter of fact my subsequent
> study of the war has led me to think a good deal better
> of Haig than I did at the time. It is absolutely certain
> there was no one who could have taken his place".[20]

It is interesting to note that Churchill thought he had
avoided giving a "hard indictment" of Jellicoe in The World
Crisis. Concerning Haig, it is hard to judge if Churchill's
modified view of the Commander-in-Chief came about as a
result of their collaboration or was the initial cause of
it. Whatever the reason Churchill's portrait of Haig
contains elements of balance lacking in his treatment of
Jellicoe.

The results of the Haig-Churchill partnership must now be
examined in more detail. Only the more important of the
changes suggested by Haig will be included here.

In his criticisms of the later chapters of The World
Crisis Haig consistently showed concern over the picture
given by Churchill of the relationship between himself and
the leading French Generals and the relative contributions
made by the British and French Armies to the final battles.
Haig seemed concerned to show that while his personal
relations with Nivelle, Foch and Petain were always good, and
while he was always willing to accede to any reasonable
French request, he firmly rejected unreasonable interferences
and at all times maintained the independence of the British
Army.

The first of Haig's suggested amendments to The World
Crisis in this area can be seen in relation to the Nivelle
Offensive in the spring of 1917. Nivelle had requested that
the British launch a preparatory attack near Arras and
Churchill had originally written of this, "Haig met the
request of General Nivelle by a statement of his difficulties
and burdens. He had hoped to be allowed to mass his reserves
for an offensive on the Belgian coast - an earlier and more
propitious Passchendaele".[21] On Haig's suggestion this was
changed to read:

"Haig was not unwilling to meet the wishes of the French Command. He was in favour of renewing the offensive in France and was ready to fall in with Nivelle's views as to its direction and scope. Moreover, when the French wished to assume the brunt of the new attack and asked for assistance for this purpose, it was hardly for the British to refuse. On December 25 therefore Haig wrote to Nivelle. 'I agree in principle with your proposals and am desirous of doing all I can to help you on the lines you suggest'".[22]

Of the two versions, Haig's as used by Churchill in The World Crisis seems to be more accurate. There is no evidence to suggest that Haig put forward his northern plan as an alternative to Nivelle's offensive. However, Haig was preparing for an earlier Passchendaele[23] and as a result of his emendations this fact was not included in The World Crisis.
Thus Haig was anxious to show that he was willing to cooperate with Nivelle. On the other hand he was also anxious to show that the plan, which placed the British Army under Nivelle for the duration of the offensive, had not originated with him. He therefore supplied Churchill with a narrative of the Calais Conference at which this decision was made. Whether Churchill had an earlier version of this event is not known but the influence of Haig's account becomes apparent when it is compared with that which appears in The World Crisis. Haig wrote,

"During Jan... Traffic difficulties had become so acute that a break down of the Nord system appeared probable. I referred the matter home and another conference was ordered - This time at Calais on 26th and 27th February 1917. Transportation was not discussed, but Nivelle's operations were! Then the French produced a detailed scheme of organisation for an Allied G.H.Q. in France - This provided for a French Generalissimo, and H.Q. Staff of French & Brit. officers with a British C of S. The British C in C was to be retained but only in name to do A.G.'s work but to have nothing to do with operations. This proposal was pronounced to be unworkable, but an agreement was drawn up placing the control of the forthcoming operations solely in Nivelle's hands, and the British Army under his orders".[24]

Churchill's version in The World Crisis reads,

"During January the inadequacy of the rolling stock on the Nord railway became so marked that after strenuous British protests another conference was convened at Calais on February 26. The French then produced a detailed scheme of organization for an allied G.H.Q. in

France. This provided for a French Generalissimo with a Headquarters Staff of French and British Officers under a British Chief of Staff. A British Commander-in-Chief was to be retained in name for Adjutant-General's work, but without influence upon operations. The immediate resistance of the British Generals led to this proposal being put aside, and instead an agreement was drawn up placing the control of the forthcoming operations solely in Nivelle's hands and the British Army under his orders for that period".[25]

The next of Haig's important comments on the subject of Anglo-French relations came in a chapter of Churchill's entitled "The Turn of the Tide". This chapter is concerned in part with the accumulation of reserves by Foch for the French Counter-attack of July 1918. To free French divisions for the battle, Foch wanted Haig to move British divisions into the French Zone. Of this request Churchill originally wrote, "[Foch] also on the 12th and 13th demanded four British divisions from Haig to be followed when necessary by four more".[26] Haig apparently objected to the word "demanded" which implied that he had been reluctant to part with his divisions. To remove this impression he wrote an expanded version of this incident for Churchill which stressed that the initial four divisions were sent by G.H.Q the moment Foch's request arrived.[27] This version of events was incorporated almost entirely into The World Crisis.[28] Of the sequel to this event Churchill's account originally had Haig moving two of the additional divisions requested but refusing to despatch the remaining two and finally, after a conference with Foch, "submitting" to their removal.[29] However, Haig suggested that Churchill make it clear there was no point blank refusal on the British side but a request that a decision be deferred until Haig could meet Foch to discuss this point.[30] A sentence to this effect was added to The World Crisis.[31] Haig also objected to the word "submitted"[32] and Churchill changed this in the text to "agreed".[33]

In relation to this incident Churchill had written of Foch before the battle,

"He is fighting two battles already behind the front: one to claw his counter-stroke troops from Petain's reserves; the other to coax four - and it must be eight - divisions from Field-Marshal Haig. He has yet a third battle to fight behind the line".[34]

In the light of Haig's comments Churchill could hardly maintain this line and eventually he merely said of Foch, "He has battles to fight behind the line as well as in front of it".[35]

Thus far Haig was mainly concerned to show that he was always anxious to help the French where possible. From the battle of Amiens on, however, he clearly saw it as his major task to ensure that Churchill did not underrate the contribution made by the British Army (and of course Haig) to final victory. In fact there had been a slight tendency on Churchill's part to emphasize the French contribution but, after Haig's comments, the "balance" was restored. For example, in continuing the narrative of the battle of Amiens Churchill wrote, "The victory of August 8 was no sooner ended and the German front stabilized than Foch wished to renew the attack".36 After Haig's comments this read, "The victory of August 8 was no sooner ended, than both <u>Foch and Haig</u> sought to renew the attack".37

Haig continued to be concerned that the role of the British Army (and himself) in the last months of the war would not be appreciated by Churchill and he wrote a general note on the subject for Churchill's guidance.

> "The attacks by the British Army were regulated by me. Foch's order was to drive back Germans so as to clear Longaux Railway Centre and main line from Amiens to Paris. It was I who decided to bring in the 3rd Army [Byng] on the left of Rawlinson <u>contrary to Foch's orders</u> [for the August 21st Battle]. It was also I who planned to bring Horne (1st Army) in to the Battle (with the Canadian attack on Monchy le Preux and Drocaut-Queant lines) on the left of Byng. Foch had nothing to do with that strategy – His strategy consisted in saying & making the French Army act on his saying 'Tout le monde a la bataille'... He got the best out of the French Troops & without Foch they would have given in".38

After receiving this note Churchill completely re-wrote his paragraph on the rival strategies after Amiens. The result can be seen on p. 1340-1. It follows closely the lines suggested by Haig. The tribute paid to Haig and the British Army later in the chapter may also have been added as a result of Haig's comments.39

A further major concern of Haig's was the relationship between G.H.Q. and the British Government and he was careful to scrutinize closely Churchill's handling of this topic. Haig's first comments in this area concerned Churchill's discussion on the failure of Lloyd George to supply Haig with reinforcements during the winter of 1917-18.

Originally Churchill had been fairly sympathetic to Lloyd George. He initially wrote, "To meet the German onslaught when it came – if it came – everything must be thrown in: but the Prime Minister feared lest our last resources should be expended in another Passchendaele",40 and then continued, "That this was no idle fear is shown by the following remarkable passage in Colonel Boraston's account".41 He had then inserted a quotation from Boraston's book to the effect that a defensive policy had

266

only been adopted by G.H.Q because their divisions were under strength.[42]    Churchill had then concluded: "All this written long after the event, and with full knowledge of the Commander-in-Chief's mind, justifies the fears of the War Cabinet that the sending of large additional reinforcements would only have led to their improvident consumption before the German offensive fell upon us".[43]    Haig was unhappy with this section.  He protested to Churchill that "I am not responsible either for facts or opinions expressed in this Book!....Boraston wrote the communiques at G.H.Q. and did that work extremely well.  He occasionally came to dinner – It was not until I became C in C in London that he joined my Staff as Priv Sec in 1919".[44]    Churchill then removed the whole passage, including the quotation from Boraston.  The line eventually taken in The World Crisis was that the responsibility for the weakness of the British front lay with the Government for withholding troops but that Haig had contributed to this situation by the prolongation of Passchendaele.[45]    However, Boraston was closer to the mark than is implied by Haig's comments.  On January 7th 1918 Haig noted in his diary that he considered that the Germans would attack in the west in the Spring and that "In my opinion, the best defence would be to continue our offensive in Flanders, because we would then retain the initiative and attract the German Reserves against us".[46]    Whether Haig would have carried out this policy had he been reinforced is another matter but, given his past performance, Lloyd George's fears do seem to have been justified.

Haig's second intervention in a section of The World Crisis concerning the British Government came in Churchill's description of the Battle of Arras.  On two occasions Churchill has originally inserted that the British High Command had unnecessarily prolonged this battle, causing heavy casualties as a result.[47]    Haig protested that Lloyd George had urged that "Arras" be continued and he produced operational telegrams showing that in any case he had ordered the attacks to be of a strictly limited nature.[48]    He also supplied some notes on the battle which Churchill seems to have substituted[49] (though with changed wording) for his first paragraph critical of G.H.Q.  The following statement almost certainly originated with Haig.

"Haig had originally intended to close these operations [to the east of Arras] after the capture of Monchy-le-Preux and to begin as soon as possible the attempt to clear the coastal sector by the capture of the Messines and Passchendaele ridges.  But the conditions prevailing in the French Army and in Paris were such that it was thought dangerous to relax even for a few weeks the pressure upon the enemy".[50]

Thus, in the changed version Churchill exonerates Haig

only been adopted by G.H.Q because their divisions were under strength.[42]    Churchill    had    then    concluded:    "All    this written long after the event, and with full knowledge of the Commander-in-Chief's mind, justifies the fears of the War Cabinet that the sending of large additional reinforcements would only have led to their improvident consumption before the German offensive fell upon us".[43]    Haig was unhappy with this section.  He protested to Churchill that "I am not responsible either for facts or opinions expressed in this Book!....Boraston wrote the communiques at G.H.Q. and did that work extremely well.  He occasionally came to dinner – It was not until I became C in C in London that he joined my Staff as Priv Sec in 1919".[44]    Churchill then removed the whole passage, including the quotation from Boraston.  The line eventually taken in The World Crisis was that the responsibility for the weakness of the British front lay with the Government for withholding troops but that Haig had contributed    to    this    situation    by    the    prolongation    of Passchendaele.[45]    However, Boraston was closer to the mark than is implied by Haig's comments.  On January 7th 1918 Haig noted in his diary that he considered that the Germans would attack in the west in the Spring and that "In my opinion, the best defence would be to continue our offensive in Flanders, because we would then retain the initiative and attract the German Reserves against us".[46]    Whether Haig would have carried out this policy had he been reinforced is another matter but, given his past performance, Lloyd George's fears do seem to have been justified.

Haig's second intervention in a section of The World Crisis concerning the British Government came in Churchill's description of the Battle of Arras.  On two occasions Churchill has originally inserted that the British High Command had unnecessarily prolonged this battle, causing heavy casualties as a result.[47]    Haig protested that Lloyd George had urged that "Arras" be continued and he produced operational telegrams showing that in any case he had ordered the attacks to be of a strictly limited nature.[48]    He also supplied some notes on the battle which Churchill seems to have substituted[49] (though with changed wording) for his first paragraph critical of G.H.Q.  The following statement almost certainly originated with Haig.

> "Haig had originally intended to close these operations [to the east of Arras] after the capture of Monchy-le-Preux and to begin as soon as possible the attempt to clear the coastal sector by the capture of the Messines and Passchendaele ridges.  But the conditions prevailing in the French Army and in Paris were such that it was thought dangerous to relax even for a few weeks the pressure upon the enemy".[50]

Thus, in the changed version Churchill exonerates Haig

divisions be created behind the Western Front to meet the coming (Spring 1918) German offensive. This plan was espoused by Lloyd George and opposed by Haig. In The World Crisis Churchill had initially been inclined to side with the politicians against G.H.Q., again using Boraston's account as a basis for his criticism.

"His [Haig's] Staff Officer [Boraston] in his account is scornful of the idea of an "Executive Committee" doling out reserves on to a moving battlefield such as existed during the retreat of March 21st. Now that the commanding genius of Marshal Foch belongs to history, we can say with certainty that thirty divisions in his hands would have brought a far more timely, abundant and skilful succour to the last heroic struggles of the Fifth Army than was ever derived from the arrangements of mutual assistance made between Haig and Petain. Sir Douglas Haig however preferred to trust to these arrangements, though they appeared both exiguous and complicated, and though they proved, when required, almost entirely illusory".[60]

However, following Haig's comments a more pro-Haig, and it must be said more accurate statement, was substituted.

"There is no doubt that had this plan [for a general reserve] been put immediately into execution, and had Foch been armed with thirty divisions specifically assigned to the support of whatever part of the front was attacked, larger resources would have been secured to Haig in his approaching hour of supreme need. Haig did not however welcome the proposal. He declared that he had no divisions to spare for the general reserve, and that there were not even enough for the various army fronts. In such circumstances the earmarking of particular British divisions for service elsewhere could have been little more than a formality. None could have been taken from him unless the attack fell elsewhere".[61]

With Haig as Churchill's chief adviser it was inevitable that Edmonds should play a lesser role in these final chapters. However, he continued to be an important source of information for Churchill, supplying him with the records of the Doullens Conference, German operation orders for March 1918,[62] an account of the Lys Offensive and of the French advance (August to November).[63] He also wrote a small section which Churchill used virtually unchanged, on British Intelligence reports of the impending German withdrawal in March 1917.[64] Edmonds' comments were usually confined to general remarks such as stating that "The Climax chapter is magnificent"[65] or that "The Teutonic Collapse is a very fine chapter".[66]

Probably Edmonds' major contribution to these chapters was to supply on request examples of "good fights" on March 21st 1918, for Churchill incorporated the encounters chosen by Edmonds virtually unaltered.[67]

Two more features of the writing of these later chapters should be noted. It is interesting to note that after completing a lengthy chapter on the preparation, cause and consequences of the French Spring Offensive in 1917, The World Crisis contains only the most sketchy account of the battle of Passchendaele. This is especially surprising as Passchendaele is used as one of the supreme examples of military folly in "The Blood Test". The reason for this omission is not clear. No clue is provided by the Churchill Papers. Lack of material could not have been a factor for Edmonds supplied Churchill with at least one document on Passchendaele[68] and would presumably have been prepared to supply others. Perhaps Churchill considered that any points he could make in relation to the battle would merely repeat those made in the Somme chapter. Perhaps he considered a detailed analysis of the battle could not be made without requiring a protracted criticism of Lloyd George's vacillating policy towards the attack and its continuation. Clearly he preferred to concentrate his attention on Cambrai, which occupies a good proportion of this chapter, and to use that battle to drive home his point about the futility of attrition.

The section of The World Crisis which deals with the events of 1917 provides the only instance where Churchill omitted a draft chapter altogether. The chapter was originally to be titled "The Offensive Problem by Land and Sea" and was to consist largely of two memoranda written by Churchill - "Mechanical Power in the Offensive 7/11/16" and "Naval War Policy 1917 (7/2/17)".[69] Churchill moved the former memorandum to his first "munitions" chapter[70] and retitled the now purely naval chapter "Thoughts on a Naval Offensive".[71] The main thrust of this chapter, which now almost entirely consisted of the naval paper, was that the policy being followed at sea was too passive and that what was needed was an offensive scheme that would force the German navy to fight. Churchill thought that this could be achieved by the old plan of the capture of a German island, either Borkum or Sylt. The details of how such an operation would be carried out were then given in some depth.[72] However, in retrospect Churchill was not entirely confident of the soundness of the scheme and, before making a final decision on whether to include the chapter, he sent it to Keyes, asking if he thought it would be ridiculed by service opinion.[73] After considering the chapter Keyes pointed out to Churchill that a similar scheme had been studied by the Plans Division of the Admiralty in 1917 and had been found to be totally impractical.[74] This decided Churchill. He replied to Keyes, "So many thanks for your searching criticisms of my Borkum plan. It has proved fatal to the inclusion of the chapter in any form, which is probably a good thing".75

## CONCLUSION

For convenience and clarity this assessment of The World Crisis will take the following form: first, the three main constituent parts of the book - the naval war, the Dardanelles, and the war in 1916-18 - will be considered as entities; then themes which have emerged as common to the whole book will be discussed; and then a final summing-up will be attempted.

### The Naval War

Two questions must first be asked of Churchill's account of the naval war. How adequate is his coverage of the main events? And has he managed to strike the right balance between the episodes chosen for inclusion? A glance at a list of the main subjects dealt with by Churchill in The World Crisis (Heligoland, Scarborough Raid, Dogger Bank, Goeben, Coronel, Falklands and Jutland) reveals that it has been the description of battles with which Churchill has been most concerned. There is little on the organizational aspects of the submarine war, and nothing on commerce protection, the relationship between British sea-power and trade, or the work of the Grand Fleet in maintaining the blockade. These are important omissions, especially when it is realized that some of the actions described in their stead were of minor importance. Nevertheless Churchill has some justification for his choice of events. In the first place he no doubt included those incidents which he considered would have the most appeal to a wide readership. Secondly he was writing a personal tale and there seems little doubt that at the Admiralty he took an interest in battles, even to the extent of writing operational orders, which did not extend to, say, seaborne trade. The type of account he has chosen to write can therefore be defended on the grounds of personal involvement as well as a desire to tell an exciting story.

This justification can also be extended to the amount of space devoted to each incident. It is doubtful if in any general history of the war an historian could give good grounds for including a whole chapter on the Scarborough Raid, the escape of the Goeben, the Dogger Bank or even Coronel. Churchill, however, witnessed these events from the Admiralty and a proportion of each account is spent on valuable descriptions of how naval battles were viewed from Whitehall. We must be grateful to Churchill for recording these rarely-chronicled scenes, and on these grounds partly excuse him for concentrating so much on relatively unimportant incidents.

As far as reliability is concerned, Churchill's narrative can be criticized on three counts. Firstly, he has a tendency to exaggerate the successes of the naval war and overstate the benefits which flowed from them. Heligoland and the Dogger Bank, as has been shown, were in reality hardly more than minor skirmishes that did little to alter the naval balance in Britain's favour. Yet for Churchill Heligoland allegedly affected German naval policy for the rest of the war, and Dogger Bank is described as a smashing victory. In dealing with the Scarborough Raid, certain aspects of the Dogger Bank encounter, and Jutland, Churchill agonizes over a series of "lost opportunities". In fact even if the British had destroyed entirely the opposing German force the naval war would have been little affected. Lost opportunities also play a large part in Churchill's account of Jutland. About these two things must be said. First, it is highly problematical whether the opportunities ever existed. Secondly Churchill fails to recognise, at least in the published version of The World Crisis, the highly speculative nature of the results which he claims would have followed a British victory at Jutland. The second point to be made about reliability is that Churchill is always prone to ignore the difficulties faced by local commanders, and to deny that those difficulties were sometimes compounded by the actions of the Admiralty. This is particularly noticeable in Churchill's description of the Goeben incident where most of the responsibility for the escape of the German ship is placed upon Milne and Troubridge. The ambiguity and often the incompetence of Admiralty instructions is glossed over. Churchill's treatment of Cradock falls into the same category. And even the difficulties of Admiral Christian, forced to patrol a narrow stretch of water close to enemy bases, are not taken into account. Nevertheless it should be noted that Churchill's treatment of these men stops a long way short of vilification and that his version of their actions is lent plausibility by the fact that in various ways Milne, Troubridge, Cradock and Christian all fell considerably short of what might have been expected of a British Admiral in wartime.

Thirdly, Churchill's account of the naval war can also be criticized as being unduly theoretical. Mundane factors such as the state of visibility and knowledge available to Admirals at the time of battle are often ignored. These factors are particularly relevant to a discussion of Churchill's Jutland chapters where his suggested tactics for Jellicoe, while always elegant and seemingly well-thought-out, are completely impractical.

Another criticism that can be made of the naval chapters of The World Crisis concerns Churchill's handling of the leading naval personalities and particularly his treatment of Beatty and Jellicoe. As has been shown Churchill hardly loses an opportunity to praise Beatty. The Admiral's errors at Scarborough, Dogger Bank and Jutland are entirely overlooked. In contrast Jellicoe's contributions to the Heligoland battle and the Scarborough Raid are ignored by Churchill, and his hypercritical attitude towards the British Commander-in-Chief at Jutland resulted in a narrative which lacks balance and comprehension. Contrary to Churchill's accounts in their overall strategic and tactical outlook little separated the two Admirals, as Beatty's tenure in charge of the Grand Fleet revealed. In The World Crisis Churchill completely loses sight of this point and continually contrasts the dashing Beatty with the cautious and dour Jellicoe. Clearly Churchill was attracted by Beatty's style of command, of which informality and panache were key features, and repelled by the unassuming Jellicoe. Of course there is something to be said for Churchill's point of view. Despite his faults Beatty made an excellent Commander-in-Chief and it is hard to identify a contemporary who could have taken his place. Despite his virtues Jellicoe's pessimism later distorted his judgement and eventually led to his dismissal. However, in The World Crisis Churchill exaggerates the faults of Jellicoe and the virtues of Beatty to the point of caricature and his portraits of the two Admirals must be treated with extreme caution.

In contrast to his attitude to Jellicoe, there are many occasions in The World Crisis where Churchill moderates or conceals the patent failings of some of his colleagues. Thus there is no mention of Prince Louis' glaring errors before Coronel. Criticisms of Milne, Troubridge and Sturdee are tempered. In some ways this policy is self-serving. Churchill's desire that the reputation of Prince Louis remain intact had an ulterior motive; harsh criticisms of Milne, a Churchill appointee, might have raised awkward questions; Troubridge had been a close colleague; denigration of Sturdee might have detracted from the victory at the Falklands. Thus Churchill's treatment of these men could be put down to self-interest. On the other hand the position could be more complicated than this. It seems possible that in dealing with these incidents Churchill is consciously trying to distance himself from the events and take a more objective view. Thus tempering criticism of Milne, Troubridge and Sturdee not only serves Churchill's own purpose but is demanded in a work whose opening chapters proclaim it to have a wide historical sweep. In this way Churchill the historian protects Churchill the politician.

Finally, it remains to assess what Churchill's account of the naval war has to offer the reader. Firstly, there is the prose style in which the book is written. Although this wears a somewhat archaic air and is too florid for many tastes, Churchill is nevertheless rarely dull and is always able to marshall his arguments and describe complicated actions with admirable clarity. Secondly, because of Churchill's deep involvement with his subject his narrative has an immediacy that other more detached historians have not been able to match. A good example of this is his description of the Antwerp expedition in which the atmosphere of the war-torn city is vividly recaptured. More importantly, The World Crisis gives a powerful impression of the naval war as seen by one of the most important participants on the allied side. Especially important is its portrayal of how naval actions appeared to those giving the directions at the Admiralty. For these reasons this section of the book will retain its value despite Churchill's often questionable interpretation of events.

## The Dardanelles

Because of Churchill's close and continual involvement with the Dardanelles campaign his section on the operation occupies almost one-third of The World Crisis and is of extraordinary interest. Nevertheless it should be apparent that Churchill's Dardanelles chapters are liable to heavier and more consistent criticism than any other section of the book. These criticisms should now be summed up. Turning first to the earlier Dardanelles chapters it will be remembered that they were misleading in three ways. First, the rationale put forward by Churchill in the The World Crisis for investigating alternative theatres of war was that action elsewhere was necessary to break the deadlock in the west. This was shown to be fallacious as the planning of four out of five of them (Holland is the exception) began long before that deadlock set in. This particularly applies to the Dardanelles which was first investigated by Churchill in October 1914. A related point is that in The World Crisis Churchill exaggerates the importance he placed on the Dardanelles scheme at the time. Thus in his discussion of events of January 1915 virtually all mention of other operations (Zeebrugge, Borkum, Holland) is excluded, when, as has been shown, active discussions on all of these plans continued throughout the period. Apparently Churchill is anxious in The World Crisis to establish the view that action at the Dardanelles was his one consistent strategic idea since the beginning of the war. In fact it was merely one (and not always the most important) of a bewildering number of alternatives.

A second facet of Churchill's early Dardanelles chapters that can be criticized is his assertion that a decision was made in favour of an attack at the Dardanelles because there was an overwhelming consensus of political and naval opinion in agreement with it. It has been suggested that this was certainly not the case as far as Churchill's naval advisers were concerned, not one of whom seems to have supported the naval operation without reservations. Nevertheless it was also shown that Churchill was able to construct a plausible case because of the vacillating and contradictory nature of the naval advice which he was given. Jackson always hedged on the vital issues, Wilson did not regard the decision as his particular problem, Bartoleme's equivocations made his advice worthless, Oliver was mainly in favour because the Dardanelles distracted Churchill from the more dangerous Borkum plan, Fisher refused to make his position clear and continually shifted his ground when confronted by Churchill. The World Crisis is more reliable on the attitude to the operation of Churchill's political colleagues, many of whom expressed great enthusiasm for the plan. However, Churchill does not make the point that their enthusiasm partly resulted from his own rather dubious assurances that the naval attack would not need supporting troops. Indeed it was suggested that Churchill may have deliberately refrained from raising the question of troops at this early stage of the debate.

This point brings us to a third area where The World Crisis misleads. Churchill's discussion of the use of troops to support the fleet contains a number of contradictions and inconsistencies. His own two changes in attitude on this subject (one in early February when he become convinced that military operations would have to be undertaken; a second in early March when his confidence in the navy's ability to succeed alone reasserted itself) are concealed. He also does not admit in The World Crisis that Kitchener withheld troops partly because whenever he pressed Churchill on the chances of the purely naval plan, he was reassured that the fleet could do the job alone. Eventually this contradiction forces Churchill in The World Crisis into the untenable position of berating both Kitchener for failing to supply troops and de Robeck for suggesting that they were essential. Such is the skill with which the book is written, however, that this contradiction has received little attention from historians.

Churchill's later sections on the naval and military aspects of the campaigns are extremely variable in quality. The most satisfactory section is perhaps his description of the naval attack up to the 18th of March. The naval operations are set down in some detail and most of the facts are correctly summarized. However, Churchill's basic assumption that the naval plan as developed by Carden and the Admiralty Staff was sound, leads him to put forward specious reasons for its failure such as the timidity of Carden and de Robeck and the "misuse" of the Queen Elizabeth. With de

Robeck's accession to the command Churchill changes this approach somewhat and claims that the plan was abandoned at the very moment when success was assured. All these assertions were shown to be very far from the truth. The reason for failure, which is never admitted in The World Crisis, is that the task facing the fleet was too great.

Churchill's military chapters on Gallipoli are some of the most disappointing in the whole book. There is no discussion of the planning of the April 25th landings and Churchill's account of the Hellas landings does not analyse the controversial decision to evacuate Y beach. The same can be said for his descriptions of Suvla Bay. Again there is little on the planning of the operation and such key events as the causes of the delayed landing at A beach and the dislocation of the 10th Division's landing are not mentioned at all. Whether Churchill adopted this sketchy approach to avoid criticizing the actions of his friend Hamilton, is not known, but the result is most inadequate.

The theoretical nature of Churchill's writing on strategy which was noted in the naval chapters is again very much in evidence in his Gallipoli account. His repeated assertions that one (or two) extra divisions would have, at various points, turned the scale in the allies' favour ignore the difficult logistical problems that the deployment of additional divisions on the Gallipoli Peninsula would have caused. In similar fashion he moves divisions over battlefields like chess pieces, in the case of the August attack at Anzac, completely disregarding the nature of the ground over which the troops would have had to manoeuvre. The tendency to ignore logistic factors and the state of the troops involved in an attack also allows Churchill to disregard the real difficulties facing Stopford on August 7th and 8th.

Churchill also confuses the attainment of immediate objectives with the successful conclusion of the campaign. Thus we are successively told that the seizure of Achi Baba, Sari Bair, the Anafarta Ridge or the Narrows forts would have meant victory. In the case of the first three objectives this was very far from the truth, and in the last case highly speculative. It has been shown that the appearance of the fleet before Constantinople might not have produced a Turkish surrender. And even if it had done, this might not have meant a speedy termination of the war. Thus, as with the naval battles, so with Gallipoli, Churchill overstates the results of successful action.

There are other parallels between the Gallipoli sections and those on the naval war. Churchill's treatment of Keyes and de Robeck is very similar to his handling of Beatty and Jellicoe. For Churchill, Keyes can do no wrong and his often wildly unrealistic schemes for renewing the naval attack are greeted with enthusiasm in The World Crisis. Keyes' dashing and flamboyant personality and often heroic actions appealed to Churchill in a way that the more sober and cautious approach of de Robeck did not. Thus de Robeck is treated with little understanding and no sympathy, his rational arguments often being dismissed as emotional reactions to the loss of ships.

It cannot be said that Churchill's discussion of the diplomatic aspects of Gallipoli is any more reliable than his military sections. The effect on the Balkans, first of the opening bombardment of February 19th and then of the military landings, is greatly exaggerated. Nowhere in The World Crisis is it admitted that the events on the Eastern Front were the major considerations influencing the actions of the Balkan states. Churchill's solution to the allies' Balkan dilemma would almost certainly have failed had it been put into effect, and his formulation ignores the practical difficulties for Grey caused by pre-war Russian pretensions in the area. Finally, Churchill's view that the antiquated Balkan peasant armies could have proved the decisive factor in the war was shown to be based on a complete disregard of the immense problems both in combining the armies of five different countries and the state of the armies themselves.

Churchill's later Gallipoli chapters occupy much less space than his account of the genesis of the operation. Political events in particular are downplayed, Churchill confining himself to a discussion of the May political crisis and of various meetings of the War Council/Dardanelles Committee. His narrative of the May crisis gives a full account of Fisher's resignation and is quite accurate up until May 17th. From then on Churchill conceals his own attempts to cling to office and the bitterness which he felt towards Asquith and Bonar Law for their part in his downfall. In dealing with the War Council meetings, The World Crisis is characterized by continued criticisms of Kitchener for failing to choose between east and west. As has been shown this was not the case. The British war plan ensured that their major effort would be made on the Western Front but Churchill never accepts this fact, even though The World Crisis makes it clear that he had been sent to the Admiralty to ensure that this policy would be adopted.

A further comment is appropriate at this point. Throughout The World Crisis Churchill points to the "fates" as a major factor in the thwarting of the Dardanelles operation. As was shown this process commenced well before the Dardanelles section of the book was reached. It was in the chapters on the escape of the Goeben that readers were first reminded that even then the fates were working against British policy in the East. In fact the arrival of the German battlecruiser at Constantinople was not related even in the remotest way to the failure of the Dardanelles plan but Churchill is clearly anxious to introduce to the reader as early as possible the idea of fatalistic causation as an explanation for that failure. As The World Crisis progresses we find that the fates are invoked to explain the Russian veto on Greek participation at Gallipoli, the delay in the dispatch of the 29th Division from England, and the decision to break off the naval attack when the Turks were out of ammunition. In reality these supposed interventions by the fates can usually be explained in terms of political calculation or human error, and the several occasions where Churchill characterizes their intervention as "decisive" were shown to be not decisive at all. Yet by adopting this approach Churchill is able to divert attention from the more prosaic explanations for the collapse of the operation such as the lack of adequate resources, the absence of a well-thought-out plan and the piecemeal nature of British involvement. In short Churchill uses the fates not to explain events but to explain them away.

The Dardanelles chapters of The World Crisis certainly prove, if proof was needed, that it is quite possible to base a narrative on an enormous number of documents and still produce a misleading account. It was noted that at times over 40% of Churchill's Dardanelles section was taken up with the publication of memoranda and letters. In his introduction Churchill puts forward the view that these documents would prove his case. All they prove, however, is that Churchill has adopted an adept process of selection. Also, many of the documents are his own memoranda and the case presented in them is merely stated rather than argued or critically examined. Finally, it was noted, Churchill is not averse from deleting key sections of documents.

Considering this extensive list of criticisms is there anything positive than can be said about this section of The World Crisis? Churchill's Dardanelles chapters do contain examples of powerfully written descriptive passages. In this category fall his account of the great naval attack on March 18th, and his graphic description of the carnage on V beach on April 25th. However, what holds the attention of the reader through nearly 400 pages is the enthusiasm of the writer for his subject and the skill with which his case is unfolded. At the time that The World Crisis was written the Dardanelles campaign had provided both the high and the low point in Churchill's political life. His overwhelming desire from 1915 onwards was to vindicate his own part in events and it was this need that makes Volume 2 of The World Crisis the best example of Churchill's skill as an apologist. In none of his other historical works does Churchill's prose achieve the same force, and in reading The World Crisis it is quite possible to admire Churchill's achievement while disagreeing almost entirely with the argument he propounds.

1916-1918.

The third volume of The World Crisis was found to be a curious mixture. Some sections of it, such as Churchill's discussions of the High Command of the opposing armies, the

Roumanian Campaign, and British strategy in the autumn of 1917, were not worthy of detailed consideration. Also an inordinate amount of space was found to consist of Churchill's own relatively unimportant (in terms of any influence they may have had) papers and memoranda.

It is also hard to avoid the conclusion that when Churchill wrote this volume the failure at Gallipoli was still very much on his mind. Thus throughout the first half of the volume Churchill is anxious to demonstrate the immense cost of the war on the Western Front and to point to easier alternatives in the east. For 1916 he actually recommends a second invasion of Gallipoli. In 1917 his major plan consists of a landing in Palestine. The "Blood Test" and Somme chapters are designed to show what the failure at Gallipoli meant in terms of manpower. The section on tanks demonstrates to his own satisfaction the incorrigibility of the military, whom it is claimed were incapable of adapting to this new and cheaper way of waging war.

Nevertheless Volume 3 does contain two of Churchill's best efforts as a 'detached historian'. "The Blood Test" represents the most exhaustive and balanced effort yet made to construct a general critique of the war around casualty statistics, and Churchill must be given great credit for the care with which he assembled his material. It was suggested that an interpretation based on casualty statistics ignores the many social and economic factors which might have played a part in the German defeat. But taken on its own terms this chapter is a considerable scholarly achievement.

Similarly, Churchill's account of the battle of the Somme contains a balance which was lacking in other chapters written by Churchill about events in which he did not take part. Whether this aspect of Churchill's account of the Somme was due to the influence of Edmonds or whether Churchill had already determined to consult Haig on the later chapters and tempered his narrative of 1916 in anticipation is not known. What is clear is that Churchill has taken some trouble to understand the difficulties, instead of merely listing the deficiencies, of the British High Command.

Other areas of this volume are also quite reliable in the facts presented. Although in his last chapter on the submarine war Churchill fudges his discussion of convoys, and spends rather too much time discussing trivial issues such as Q ships, he has, with the considerable aid of Kenneth Dewar, constructed a perfectly adequate basic account of the struggle. Also with the help of Haig, Beaverbrook and Hankey, Churchill's chronicle of the 1918 battles generally strikes the correct balance and is judicious in allotting responsibility and praise between the various allied commanders.

It must be admitted, however, that Churchill's third volume does contain serious defects. The absence of any detailed discussion of the Third Battle of Ypres seems an error of judgement, despite the duplication in argument with the Somme chapter that its inclusion might have caused. In addition, Churchill's tank material is quite misleading in its intent and the reader emerges with a totally erroneous view of tank possibilities in 1917 and 1918. Notwithstanding its merits, the Somme chapter never really conveys the problems faced by lower order commanders during the battle, Rawlinson is exonerated from all responsibility and even Haig's role in the disaster of the first day is not made clear.

Nevertheless this volume is probably more reliable in its interpretation of events than the others. On the whole, though, this volume of The World Crisis lacks the interest which carried the reader through the earlier sections. Except for a few chapters Churchill merely provides a chronicle of events. The spirited if partial arguments which enlivened the earlier volumes are missing. It is then almost possible to establish a direct relationship between interest, involvement and reliability. The last volume of The World Crisis, which is probably the most reliable, holds our interest least. The Dardanelles account is at the same time the least reliable and the most interesting. The first volume lies somewhere in between.

It now should be possible to make some general comments about The World Crisis as a whole.

In his original preface Churchill claimed that he was not writing history but presenting his book as a contribution to history. And to a certain extent it is true that Churchill is largely telling his own story. But, as has been shown, there are many indications all through The World Crisis that Churchill is trying to take a more detached view of events than is usual in a work of pure memoir. Thus even when Churchill is describing events with which he was intimately involved the book is often characterized by a breadth of outlook more commonly found in scholarly histories. Of course Churchill's approach is often self-serving and the supporters of Jellicoe, de Robeck and Monro may question the entire concept of Churchill's detachment. However it is not argued that this is Churchill's constant approach or even that it is particularly widespread. What is suggested is that in a work of this type it is unusual to find the memoirist attempting historical detachment at all. It is perhaps this quality which raises The World Crisis above the intellectual level of most war memoirs.

Having said this it must also be said that Churchill's technique as a historian has several notable defects. The first of these concerns the documents quoted in The World Crisis. The reader is never sure that the version given by Churchill is complete, or if material damaging to the case Churchill is building up has been omitted, or if any deletions made have been indicated in the text. Enough examples of this type of practice have been found to show that it was reasonably common throughout The World Crisis.

A second more complicated point arises out of this. The Churchill Papers reveal that many of what seem to have been Churchill's true thoughts about men and events never found their way into The World Crisis but were deleted by the author before publication for reasons of expediency or occasionally charity. It might be said that the decision to exclude material is the prerogative of any author but The World Crisis would have been more revealing about Churchill's views had the deleted material been retained, and from the standpoint of a scholar of the period the omissions represent a great loss.

Many of the amendments made to The World Crisis were the result of advice given to Churchill from a wide range of colleagues and friends who read the book before publication. What overall effect these men had on the book and whether on balance they improved Churchill's narrative is difficult to assess. Certainly Edmonds, Dewar and Aspinall provided Churchill with a number of useful documents that would not otherwise have been at his disposal. Also Beaverbrook, Hankey, Keyes and Haig all contributed to making Churchill's last volume better balanced both in content and approach. Nevertheless it seems that Churchill's advisers were not generally able to push him in a direction in which he was not already going. His fundamental redrafting of the passage on the possible results of a British victory at Jutland perhaps represents the only occasion on which this does not hold true. In most other cases he rejected unpalatable advice and listened to those who reinforced the general line of approach that he had already adopted. Thus he ignored Edmond's ideas on Monro and incorporated Aspinall's; refused to bring his later chapters into line with Beaverbrook's opinion of Lloyd George; and consulted Haig on the 1918 battles but not on the British offensives of 1916 and 1917. In adopting this approach Churchill substantially remained his own man and the impact of his advisers on the book, though it was sometimes important and often, as in the case of Haig, fascinating, should not be exaggerated.

One issue that should be raised at this point is what The World Crisis tells us about Churchill's attitude to war. Two passages have already been quoted which indicate that Churchill was acutely conscious of the horrors of the new style of warfare that was being fought in France and Flanders. There are many other such passages throughout the book. Clearly this type of warfare did not accord with Churchill's more romantic notions of the military art and to some extent his endeavours to find alternative theatres of operations should be viewed in this context. What is never recognized in The World Crisis is that the defeat of the German army, which was necessary for victory, was bound to be an extremely bloody and protracted affair.

Churchill's passages on the horrors of modern warfare also indicate that although he confessed to finding war exciting he never lost his humanity or forgot what the cost of the war was. Critics of Churchill have usually fastened on to the first of these characteristics and forgotten the second. But the evidence of <u>The World Crisis</u> indicates that Churchill was not the militarist of popular legend.

This thread of humanity which runs through <u>The World Crisis</u> and which is so noticeably absent from the works of some of Churchill's colleagues, such as Grey and Asquith, will be one of the reasons why Churchill's book will continue to be read. Despite its errors and mis-statements it does possess breadth of vision to a degree quite unusual in a work of this type. Other reasons too should ensure the book's continued popularity. These include, apart from Churchill's later reputation, the power and stately nature of the writing, and the lucidity with which Churchill is able to discuss often quite complicated events. More important, however, than all these factors in compelling interest, is the commitment with which the book has been written. Churchill clearly set out to vindicate his actions and point of view and performed these tasks with verve for most of the book. Commitment is often a characteristic decried in historical writing; and in Churchill's case the price paid for the heightened interest, in distortions and lack of balance, would undoubtedly be regarded by some readers as too high. But the fact remains that it is this quality which will ensure that <u>The World Crisis</u> continues to be read when many less committed though more accurate works have been long forgotten.

## Introduction

1. For the publication details of The World Crisis see Woods F. A Bibliography of the Works of Sir Winston Churchill (2nd ed), London, Kay and Ward, 1969, p. 50 and Churchill Papers 8/38 and 8/50.

2. Guinn P British Strategy and Politics 1914 to 1918, Oxford U.P., 1965, Chapter 11 p.48-80.

3. James R R, Gallipoli, London, Batsford, 1965, p.352.

4. Ashley M, Churchill as Historian, London, Secker and Warburg, 1968.

5. See his essay in Churchill: Four Faces and the Man, London, Allen Lane, 1969.

6. Lord Sydenham et al, The World Crisis: A Criticism, Port Washington, Kennikat Press, 1970 (Reprint of the 1928 edition).

7. See Churchill Papers 8/180, 8/111, 8/41.

8. Churchill to Curtis Brown (his literary agent) 16/1/28, Churchill Papers 8/207.

## Chapter 1

### The Escape of the Goeben

1. The above account is based on the operational telegrams in Adm 137/19, Adm 137/879 and Adm 116/3109.

2. The World Crisis, p.180. Because the volumes of the 1950 Odhams reprint used here do not correspond to the original volumes only the page numbers will be quoted.

3. Admiralty to Milne 3/8/14, Adm 137/19; Admiralty to Milne 4/8/14, Adm 137/879.

4. The World Crisis, p.180.

5. Ibid., p.202-3.

6. Churchill Papers 8/64.

7. Ibid.

8. The World Crisis, p.203-4.

9. Ibid., p.204.

10. Ibid., p.202.

11. Milne Sir Berkeley, The Flight of the Goeben and Breslau, London, Eveleigh Nash, 1921, p.111.

12. The World Crisis, p.209.

13. Ibid.

14. The telegrams are contained in Adm 137/19.

15. _The World Crisis_, p.208-9.


Chapter 2

Coronel and the Falklands

1. Admiralty to Cradock 14/9/14, Adm 116/3486.
2. Admiralty to Cradock 16/9/14, Adm 116/3486.
3. Sturdee and L.B. to S.N.O. Malta 18/9/14, Adm 137/20.
4. Cradock to the Admiralty 18/9/14, Adm 137/1022.
5. Cradock to the Admiralty (Received 11/10/14 and 12/10/14), Adm 116/3486.
6. Minute by Churchill 12/10/14, Adm 116/3486; Churchill to Prince Louis 14/10/14, Adm 137/26.
7. Admiralty to Cradock 14/10/14, Adm 137/26.
8. Cradock to the Admiralty 27/10/14, Adm 116/3486.
9. Admiralty to Cradock 28/10/14, in Ibid.
10. Oliver to Churchill 29/10/14, Adm 116/3486.
11. The above account is based on the operational telegrams in Adm 137/43, Adm 137/304 and Sturdee's report in Adm 137/1027.
12. _The World Crisis_, p. 370.
13. Preston A, _Battleships of World War I_, N.Y., Galahad, 1972, p. 101.
14. Marder A J, _From the Dreadnought to Scapa Flow : The Royal Navy in the Fisher Era_ V2, London, Oxford U.P. 1965, p. 106 (Hereafter Scapa Flow)
15. Pitt B, _Coronel and the Falklands_, London,

Cassell, 1960, p. 28.
16. Grant H, H.M.S. Canopus, _Naval Review_, V 11, 1923, p. 527.
17. Bennett H T, Twenty One Years Ago : The Tragedy of Coronel, _The Argus_ (Melbourne) 2/11/35. (Bennett was navigating officer on the _Canopus_ at the time of Coronel)
18. Marder A J, _Scapa Flow_ V2, p. 106.
19. _Canopus_ Log for 1914, Adm 53/69505.
20. Note in _Naval Review_, V 51, January 1963, p. 125-6.
21. Richmond Diary 6/10/14, Richmond Papers, RIC 1/10.
22. Von Spee to his wife 2/11/14, Adm 137/1022.
23. See Churchill Papers 8/64. The paragraph removed criticized Prince Louis for exonerating Sir Berkeley Milne from blame over the escape of the _Goeben_.
24. Fisher to Pamela McKenna 3/10/14, McKenna Papers, MCK 6/7.
25. _The World Crisis_, p. 378.
26. Ibid., p. 390.


Chapter 3

The North Sea 1914-15

1. See Admiralty operations orders for Heligoland in Adm 137/1943 and reports on the operation in Adm 137/551.
2. Churchill Papers 8/66.
3. _The World Crisis_, p. 261.
4. Ibid.
5. _Arethusa_ Report

30/8/14, Adm 137/551.

6. Ibid.

7. Ibid.

8. The World Crisis, p. 261.

9. Quoted in Ibid, p. 262.

10. Marder A J, Scapa Flow, V2, p. 42.

11. Corbett Sir J, Naval Operations V 1, London, Longmans, 1920, p. 171.

12. Ibid.

13. Churchill to Prince Louis 18/9/14, Adm 137/47.

14. Admiralty to Admiral Christian 19/9/14, Adm 137/47. In the margin of one of the proofs of this chapter was written, probably by Churchill's naval adviser Thomas Jackson, "I think Adml. Sturdee ackd. his responsibility for the orders of the 19th." Churchill Papers 8/123.

15. Admiral Christian's Report 22/9/14, Adm 137/47.

16. Corbett Sir J, Naval Operations V1, p. 175-6.

17. Gilbert M, Winston S Churchill V 3, London, Heinemann, 1971, p. 86. The pamphlet was written by the London journalist Gibson Bowles.

18. The World Crisis p. 276-7.

19. Keyes to Leveson 21/8/14, Keyes Papers, 4/30.

20. Richmond Diary 26/8/14, Richmond Papers, RIC 1/9.

21. Lady Richmond Diary 16-22/9/14, Richmond Papers, RIC 1/16.

22. Keyes Sir Roger, The Naval Memoirs of Admiral of the Fleet Sir Roger Keyes: The Narrow Seas to the Dardanelles 1910-1915, London, Thornton Butterworth, 1934, p. 105-6.

23. The World Crisis, p. 279.

24. Court of Enquiry Into Loss of Aboukir, Cressy and Hogue on September 22, 1914 - Minutes 30/9/14, Adm 137/47.

25. Admiral Christian to Jellicoe 29/9/14, Jellicoe Papers, Add/Mss 49035.

26. Admiral Christian - Report 22/9/14, Adm 137/47.

27. For the signals and ships' reports on the operation see Adm 137/295.

28. The World Crisis, p. 422N2.

29. Ibid., p. 427-8.

30. Lion Report 19/12/14, Adm 137/295.

31. Marder A J, Scapa Flow V 2, p. 140N.

32. Lion Report 19/12/14, Adm 137/295.

33. Southampton Report 18/12/14, Adm 137/295.

34. Minute by Churchill N.D., Adm 137/295; Asquith to Venetia Stanley 6/1/15, quoted in Gilbert M., Winston S. Churchill V3 Companion Documents, London, Heinemann, 1972, p. 381. (Hereafter C.V.3.)

35. The World Crisis, p. 419.

36. These exaggerated expectations were mirrored on the German side, the Germans concentrating on the narrow margin by which the British ships avoided the High Sea Fleet. However, as Churchill rightly points out (The World Crisis p. 426) there was no need for the faster British squadrons to engage in an action against their will.

37. Crutwell C.R.M.F,

The Great War, London,
Oxford U.P., 1934, p. 312.

38. Churchill to the
Mayor of Scarborough
20/12/14, The Times,
21/12/14.

39. Churchill Papers
8/129.

40. The World Crisis, p.
418. He also removed "good"
from the following sentence
"The Admiralty spread the
good tidings" (about the
bombardment).

41. See the signals and
ships' reports in Adm
137/305 and Adm 1/8413/54.

42. The World Crisis, p.
561.

43. Ibid., p. 567.

44. Ibid., p. 568.

45. Chalmers W, The Life
and Letters of David, Earl
Beatty, London, Hodder and
Stoughton, 1951, p. 196.

46. The World Crisis, p.
568.

47. Churchill Papers
8/138.

48. Minute by Churchill
11/2/15, Adm 137/305.

Chapter 4

Antwerp

1. See Edmonds Sir J,
Military Operations: France
and Belgium 1914, 2 vols.,
London, Macmillan, 1933 &
1935.

2. The World Crisis, p.
298.

3. Ibid., p. 299.

4. Churchill to Grey,
Kitchener and Asquith
7/9/14, quoted in Ibid., p.
299.

5. Ibid.

6. Ibid., p. 299 and p.
302.

7. Ibid., p. 302.

8. Ibid., p. 299.

9. Villiers to Grey
2/10/14, quoted in Ibid., p.
305-6.

10. Ibid., p. 307.

11. Ibid., p. 310-12.

12. Ibid., p. 312,
319-21.

13. Ibid., p. 323.

14. Ibid., p. 324.

15. Ibid., p. 326-7.

16. Morning Post
13/10/14, quoted in Gilbert
M, Winston S. Churchill V3,
p. 126.

17. Daily Mail 14/10/14,
quoted in Ibid., p. 126.

18. Hopwood to
Stamfordham 6/10/14, C.V.3,
p. 173-4.

19. Asquith to Venetia
Stanley 10/10/14 & 13/10/14.
C.V.3, p. 184 & 188.

20. Sunday Pictorial
19/11/16, p. 5, 26/11/16, p.
5-6.

21. The material used
from the Sunday Pictorial
appears on p. 322, 325-27 &
p. 333.

22. Churchill to Grey,
Asquith and Kitchener
7/9/14, C.V.3, p. 97-9.

23. Churchill to Grey
20/8/14, C.V.3, p. 46-7.

24. He told Grey "I
expect [the Belgians] will
hang on to Antwerp",
Kitchener to Grey 7/9/14,
C.V.3, p. 97.

25. Grey of Fallodon
Viscount, Twenty Five Years
1892-1916, V.2, London,
Hodder and Stoughton, 1925,
p. 79.

26. Ibid., p. 80.

27. Edmonds to Villiers
24/6/23, Cab 45/158.

28. Villiers to Edmonds
26/9/23, in Ibid.

29. Asquith to Venetia

Stanley 5/10/14, C.V.3, p. 165-6.

30. The World Crisis, p. 319.

31. Asquith to Venetia Stanley 13/10/14, C.V.3, p. 188-9.

32. Gilbert M, Winston S. Churchill, V3, p. 125.

33. Churchill to Kitchener 3/10/14, Adm 1/8397/362.

34. Churchill to Kitchener 5/10/14, in Ibid.

35. French Sir John, 1914, London, Constable, 1919, p. 191-2.

36. The World Crisis, p. 964.

37. Ibid., p. 963.

38. Ibid., p. 298.

39. Edmonds Sir J, 1914, V2, p. 121N & p. 122N.

40. Ibid., p. 465.

41. See Map Annex in Ibid, Map 6.

42. The World Crisis, p. 324.

43. Churchill Papers 8/68, emphasis added.

44. Ibid., emphasis added.

45. The World Crisis, p. 322.

46. Liddell Hart B.H, A History of the World War 1914-1918, London, Faber, 1930, p. 91; Crutwell C.R.M.F., The Great War, p. 96; Edmonds Sir J, 1914, V2, p. 62-3.

47. Edmonds to Churchill 12/1/20, Churchill Papers, 8/38.

Chapter 5

Strategic Options 1914

1. The World Crisis, p. 461.

2. Ibid., p. 466.

3. Ibid., p. 473.

4. Ibid., p. 467-72

5. Ibid., p. 467.

6. Ibid., p. 472.

7. Ibid., p. 473.

8. Stone Norman, The Eastern Front 1914-1917, London, Hodder and Stoughton, 1975, p. 48.

9. The World Crisis, p. 437.

10. Ibid., p. 436.

11. Ibid., p. 441.

12. Ibid., p. 443.

13. Ibid., p. 450.

14. Ibid.

15. Ibid., p. 488.

16. Ibid., p. 479-83.

17. Ibid., p. 478.

18. Ibid.

19. Ibid., p. 490.

20. Ibid., p. 507.

21. Trumpener U, Germany and the Ottoman Empire 1914-1918, Princeton, N.J., Princeton U.P., 1968, p. 14-15.

22. Ibid., p. 54.

23. Ibid., p. 24.

24. Admiral Kerr (C-in-C of the Greek Fleet) to Churchill 9/9/14, Grey Papers, F.O. 800/63.

25. Cunninghame T.M, (British Military Attache in Athens in 1914), "The Greek Army and the Dardanelles", National Review, V92, September 1928, p. 124.

26. This was the opinion of Col. Metaxas, the Vice-Chief of the Greek General Staff. See the evidence of Cunninghame at the Dardanelles Commission 13/3/17, Q 22, 444, Cab 19/33.

27. Minute by Col. Talbot (a W.O. representative who attended both meetings) 5/9/14. W.O.

106/1463.

28. Cilbert M, Winston S. Churchill V3, p. 204-5. Gilbert is quoting from the Pease Diary.

29. The World Crisis, p. 446.

30. Memorandum by Slade 31/10/14; Limpus to Admiralty 2/11/14, Adm 137/96.

31. F.R. Maunsell (former Military Attache, Constantinople) to Aspinall-Oglanger 1/11/23, Cab 45/243.

32. Trumpener U, "German Military Aid to Turkey in 1914: An Historical Re-appraisal", Journal of Modern History, V32, 1960, p. 147-8.

33. G.H.Q. Constantinople: Answers to Mitchell Committee Questions, Adm 116/1714.

34. Von Usedom to the Kaiser 14/11/14, Cab 45/215.

35. The file is in the Churchill Papers 8/45.

36. Admiral Carden to the Admiralty 3/2/15, Adm 137/96.

37. It is interesting to note that the section of The World Crisis which deals with the November discussions is a slightly reworded version of Churchill's evidence to the Dardanelles Commission. See Churchill Papers 8/75.

38. Note by Admiral Jackson, Adm 137/456; Jellicoe to the Admiralty 27/7/14, Adm 137/995; Memorandum by Wilson 10/9/14, Adm 116/1350; Memorandum by Churchill 2/12/14, Adm 137/452; Memorandum by Oliver 15/12/14, Adm 116/1350.

39. Churchill Papers 8/134.

40. Ibid 8/182.

41. Keyes to Churchill 1/12/26, in Ibid 8/174.

42. Churchill to French 9/12/14, C.V.3, p. 300.

43. Churchill to French 11/1/15, C.V.3, p. 401-2.

44. See Churchill Papers 8/135.

45. Churchill to French 15/11/14; Churchill to Fisher, Wilson and Oliver 19/11/14, C.V.3, p. 265 and p. 269.

46. French to Churchill 29/11/14, C.V.3, p. 282.

47. Rhodes James R, Gallipoli, London, Batsford, 1965, p. 31.


Chapter 6

The Dardanelles I — The Decision

1. Lloyd George — "Suggestions As To The Military Position", Lloyd George Papers, C/16/1/7,

2. Churchill to Asquith 29/12/14, Asquith Papers, 13/242-3.

3. Churchill to Asquith 31/12/14, Asquith Papers, 13/244.

4. Fisher to Hankey 2/1/15, Hankey Papers, Cab 63/4.

5. Ibid.

6. Buchanan to Grey 1/1/15, C.V.3, p. 359-60.

7. Kitchener to Churchill 2/1/15, C.V.3, p. 360.

8. Kitchener to Churchill 2/1/15, C.V.3, p. 360-1.

9. Fisher to Churchill 3/1/15, C.V.3, p. 367-8.

10. Dardanelles Commission-Fisher's Evidence 11/10/16, Q3115, 3117; Oliver's Evidence 5/10/16, Q1772-5, Cab 19/33.

11. Churchill to Carden 3/1/15, Adm 137/96.

12. Dardanelles Commission-Churchill's Evidence 4/10/16, Q1261, Cab 19/33.

13. For example see James, Gallipoli, p. 31.

14. Churchill to Fisher, Wilson & Oliver 3/1/15, Adm 137/452; Churchill to Jellicoe 4/1/15, Jellicoe Papers, Add/Mss 48890.

15. Richmond Diary 4/1/15, Richmond Papers, RIC 1/11; Fisher to Churchill 4/1/15, C.V.3, p. 372.

16. Churchill to Fisher 4/1/15, C.V.3, p. 71.

17. Lady Richmond Diary 5/1/15, Richmond Papers, RIC 1/17,

18. Carden to Churchill 5/1/15, Adm 137/96.

19. Churchill to Carden 6/1/15, in Ibid.

20. Dardanelles Commission-Churchill's Evidence 28/9/16, Q1131, Cab 19/33.

21. Ibid., Carden's Evidence 6/10/16, Q2838.

22. Fisher to Churchill 5/1/15, C.V.3, p. 380.

23. Dardanelles Commission-Churchill's Evidence 28/9/16, Q1260-5, Cab 19/33.

24. "Note on Forcing the Passage of The Dardanelles and Bosphorus By the Allied Fleets, In Order to Destroy The Turco-German Squadron and Threaten Constantinople, Without Military Co-operation", Adm 116/3491. Were the last

three words added by Jackson as a warning?

25. Hanbury-Williams to Kitchener 3/1/15, Kitchener Papers, Pro 30/57/67.

26. Hardinge to Nicolson 6/1/15, Nicolson Papers, F.O. 800/377.

27. War Council Minutes 7/1/15, Cab 42/1/11.

28. Ibid, 8/1/15, Cab 42/1/12.

29. Fisher to Churchill 9/1/15, C.V.3, p. 399.

30. Churchill to French 11/1/15, C.V.3, p. 401-2.

31. Carden to Churchill 11/1/15, Adm 137/96.

32. Dardanelles Commission-Churchill's Evidence 28/9/16, Q1140, Cab 19/33.

33. Ibid, Oliver's Evidence 5/10/16, Q1814-5; Jackson's Evidence Q2110-1.

34. Appendix 1 to "Coast Defences of the United Kingdom and the Question of a Coast Watch" - Joint War Office-Admiralty Report 25/2/14, Cab 39/27/19.

35. Dardanelles Commission-Oliver's Evidence 5/10/16, Q1868, Cab 19/33.

36. See Godfrey Papers, Imperial War Museum, 69/33/1.

37. "Report of the Committee Appointed to Investigate the Attacks delivered on and the Enemy Defences of the Dardanelles Straits 1919", p. 74. Hereafter Mitchell Committee Report.

38. Churchill to Limpus 9/9/14, Adm 116/1336.

39. See Mallet to Grey 10/9/14, in Ibid; Mallet to Grey 11/9/14, Grey Papers, F.O. 800/80.

40. Churchill to Grey 11/9/14, Grey Papers, F.O.

800/88,

41. Churchill to Fisher 23/12/14, C.V.3, p. 327.

42. Jellicoe to Churchill 8/1/15, C.V.3, p. 397-8.

43. War Council Minutes 13/1/15, Cab 42/1/16.

44. Ibid.

45. Ibid.

46. Fisher to Oliver 12/1/15, Oliver Papers, OLV/5.

47. Churchill to Fisher and Oliver 13/1/15, C.V.3, p. 412-3.

48. Ibid.

49. Jackson - "Remarks On Vice-Admiral Carden's Proposals As to Operations In Dardanelles 15/1/15, Adm 116/3491.

50. Ibid.

51. Dardanelles Commission-Bartoleme's Evidence 5/10/16, Q1584-5, 25/10/16, Q5341, Cab 19/33.

52. Oliver-Draft Autobiography p. 147, Oliver Papers, OLV/12.

53. Lady Richmond Diary 20/1/15, Richmond Papers, RIC 1/17.

54. Ibid., 3/1/15.

55. Dardanelles Commission-Oliver's Evidence 5/10/16, Q1814, Cab 19/33.

56. Note by Wilson on Jackson's Paper 7/1/15, Adm 137/1089.

57. Dardanelles Commission-Wilson's Evidence 5/10/16, Q1998 and 1926, Cab 19/33.

58. See, for example, Churchill to Fisher 30/8/16, telling him that he has completed his statement and suggesting that they meet and "discuss particular points and documents", C.V.3, p. 550.

59. Dardanelles Commission-Fisher's Evidence 11/10/16, Q3201-3, Cab 19/33.

60. Quoted in Dardanelles Commission, First Report, London, H.M.S.O., 1917, p. 21.

61. Dardanelles Commission-Fisher's Evidence 11/10/16, Q3148 and Q3124, Cab 19/33.

62. Churchill to Carden 14/1/15, Adm 137/96.

63. Churchill to the Comte de Sainte-Seine 16/1/15, C.V.3, p. 458.

64. Fisher to Jellicoe 19/1/15, C.V.3, p. 429-30.

65. Fisher to Jellicoe 21/1/15, C.V.3, p. 436.

66. Fisher to Churchill 20/1/15, C.V.3, p. 435n2.

67. Fisher to Churchill 20/1/15, C.V.3, p. 435.

68. Churchill to Fisher 20/1/15, C.V.3, p. 433-5.

69. Fisher to Churchill 25/1/15, C.V.3, p. 451.

70. "Memorandum By the First Sea Lord On The Position Of The British Fleet and Its Policy Of Steady Pressure" 25/1/15, Cab 42/1/24.

71. Churchill to Fisher 27/1/15, Cab 42/1/24.

72. Churchill to Fisher 26/1/15, C.V.3, p. 458.

73. Churchill to Fisher 28/1/15, C.V.3, p. 462.

74. Jellicoe to Churchill 15/1/15, C.V.3, p. 417-8; Richmond Diary 19/1/15, Richmond Papers, RIC 1/12.

75. Memorandum by Lord Esher 22/1/15, Kitchener Papers, Pro 30/57/57.

76. French to Churchill 23/1/15, C.V.3, p. 444-6.

77. Dardanelles Commission - Churchill's

Evidence 28/9/16, Q1184, Cab 19/33.

78. Asquith to Venetia Stanley 28/1/15, C.V.3, p. 462-3.

79. War Council Minutes 28/1/15, Cab 42/1/26.

80. Lord Fisher, Memories, London, Hodder & Stoughton, n.d., p. 80.

81. Dardanelles Commission - Fisher's Evidence Q3196; Balfour's Evidence Q4179; Haldane's Evidence Q4493; Asquith's Evidence Q5481, Cab 19/33.

82. War Council Minutes 28/1/15, Cab 42/1/26.

83. Lord Hankey, The Supreme Command V 1, London, Allen & Unwin, 1961, p. 269.

84. Dardanelles Commission - Crewe's Evidence 30/10/16, Q5676; Balfour's Evidence 13/10/16, Q4144, Cab 19/33.

85. Grey, Twenty Five Years V2, p. 154.

86. Grey to Churchill 2/2/15, C.V.3, p. 480-1.

87. Dardanelles Commission - Lloyd George's Evidence 30/10/16, Q5676, Cab 19/33.

88. Balfour - "Notes on Lord Fisher's Memorandum" 1/2/15, Balfour Papers, Add/Mss 49712.

89. Dardanelles Commission - Churchill's Evidence 28/9/16, Q1190, Cab 19/33.

90. Fisher to Churchill 29/1/15, C.V.3, p. 471.

91. Lloyd George to Kitchener 29/1/15, Kitchener Papers, Pro 30/57/80; Churchill to Asquith 7/2/15, C.V.3, p. 495-6; Callwell to Robertson 30/1/15, Robertson Papers, 1/8/1.

92. "The War: Attack on the Dardanelles" : Note by the Secretary 2/2/15, Cab 42/1/33.

93. War Council Minutes 9/2/15, Cab 42/1/33.

94. Jackson - "Attack on Constantinople" 13/2/15, Adm 116/3491.

95. Ibid.

96. Richmond - "Remarks on Present Strategy", Richmond Papers, RIC 14/3.

97. War Council Conclusions 16/2/15, Cab 42/1/35.

98. War Council Minutes 19/2/15, Cab 42/1/36.

99. Ibid.

100. Ibid.

101. Minutes of the C.I.D. 28/2/07, Cab 38/13/12.

102. Churchill to Kitchener 18/2/15, Kitchener Papers, Pro 30/57/72.

103. War Council Minutes 19/2/15, Cab 42/1/36.

104. The World Crisis, p. vii.

105. Ibid., p. 527.

106. Ibid., p. 578.

107. Ibid., p. 531-2.

108. Ibid., p. 532.

109. Ibid.

110. Ibid.

111. See C.V.3, p. 371.

112. The World Crisis, p. 532.

113. Ibid., p. 446.

114. Ibid., p. 533.

115. Ibid.

116. Ibid., p. 547.

117. Ibid., p. 602.

118. Ibid., 533 & 536.

119. Ibid., p. 533.

120. Ibid., p. 530.

121. Churchill Papers 8/78.

122. The World Crisis, p. 536.

123. Ibid.

124. Ibid., p. 576.

125. Ibid., p. 577.

126. Ibid.
127. Ibid., p. 578-88.
128. Ibid., p. 589.
129. Ibid., p. 591.
130. Ibid., p. 591-2.
131. Churchill Papers 8/80. Churchill has got the quotation wrong. Butler actually wrote, "He that complies against his will is of his own opinion still" Butler, "Hudibras", Part III, Canto III, line 547-8.
132. Churchill Papers 8/80.
133. The World Crisis, p. 538.
134. Churchill Papers 8/137.
135. The World Crisis, p. 536.
136. Churchill Papers 8/78, emphasis added.
137. The World Crisis, p. 553.
138. Ibid., p. 576.
139. Ibid., p. 552-3.
140. Churchill to Fisher & Oliver 13/1/15, C.V.3, p. 412-3.
141. The World Crisis, p. 545.
142. Ibid., p. 537.
143. Ibid., p. 541.
144. Ibid., p. 538-40.
145. Ibid., p. 604.
146. Ibid., p. 602.
147. Ibid., p. 604.
148. Ibid., p. 602-3.
149. Ibid., p. 597.
150. Ibid., p. 598.
151. Ibid., p. 599.
152. For January 13th see The World Crisis, p. 542-3, January 28th, p. 589-90. February 9th, p. 601, February 16th, p. 603-4, February 19th, p. 604-5.
153. The World Crisis, p. 591.
154. Ibid., p. 593.
155. Ibid., p. 594.
156. Churchill Papers 8/139. See The World Crisis, p. 594.

Chapter 7

## The Dardanelles II - The Naval Debacle

1. Dardanelles Operations Orders 5/2/15, Adm 137/1089.
2. Admiral Carden-Narrative of Events 19th February to 16th March, Adm 137/38.
3. Corbett Sir J, Naval Operations V 2, London, Longmans, 1920, p. 144-5.
4. Ibid., p. 145.
5. Jones H.R, The War In The Air V 2, London, Hamish Hamilton, 1969, p. 13. (Reprint of 1928 ed.)
6. Carden-Narrative, Adm 137/38.
7. Keyes to his wife 20/2/15, Keyes Papers, 2/8.
8. Admiral Carden, "Orders for the forcing of the Dardanelles by the Allied Squadron" 14/2/15, Adm 137/38.
9. Mitchell Committee Report, p. 35.
10. Corbett Sir J, Naval Operations V 2, p. 148.
11. Carden-Narrative, Adm 137/38.
12. War Council Minutes 24/2/15, Cab 42/1/42.
13. Ibid.
14. Ibid.
15. Ibid.
16. Jones, The War In The Air V2, p. 15.
17. Carden-Narrative, Adm 137/38.
18. Diary of Lt. Macleish 25-26/2/15, Macleish Papers (Macleish

was aboard the Agamemnon.)

19. Stewart A.T. & C.J.E. Peshall, The Immortal Gamble, London, Black, 1917, p. 17.

20. Carden to Churchill 25/2/15, C.V.3, p. 565.

21. Carden to the Admiralty 27/2/15, Adm 137/109.

22. War Council Minutes 26/2/15, Cab 42/1/47.

23. These points were made in a memorandum by Balfour on 24/2/15 (W.O.159/3). It seems to have been ignored.

24. War Council Minutes 26/2/15, Cab 42/1/47.

25. Ibid.

26. Bax-Ironside to Grey 23/2/15, F.O. 371/2243; Bax-Ironside to Grey 10/3/15, Adm 116/1336.

27. Eliot to Grey 1/3/15, C.V.3, p. 603.

28. Lady Richmond Diary 1/3/15, Richmond Papers, RIC 1/17.

29. Ibid., 4/3/15.

30. Fisher to Beatty 20/2/15, Beatty Papers. (It will be remembered that it was Fisher who proposed sending the Queen Elizabeth).

31. Fisher to Jellicoe 28/2/15, in Marder A.J, Fear God and Dreadnought : The Correspondence of Admiral of the Fleet Lord Fisher of Kilverstone V 3, London, Cape, 1959, p. 161-2, (Hereafter Fear God).

32. Churchill to Grey 28/2/15, Grey Papers, F.O. 800/88.

33. Churchill to Oliver, Jackson, Fisher, 28/2/15, Adm 137/1089.

34. Churchill to Carden 28/2/15, Adm 137/109.

35. "After the

Dardanelles : The Next Steps" 1/3/15, Cab 42/2/1.

36. War Council Minutes 3/3/15, Cab 42/2/3.

37. Carden to Churchill 4/3/15, C.V.3, p. 625.

38. Churchill to Kitchener 4/3/15, Kitchener Papers, Pro 30/57/61.

39. Churchill to Grey (not sent) 4/3/15, C.V.3, p. 634.

40. Buchanan to Grey 3/3/15, F.O. 371/2243.

41. Buchanan to Grey 8/3/15, in Ibid.

42. Elliot to Grey 6/3/15, in Ibid.

43. Churchill to Grey (not sent) 6/3/15, C.V.3, p. 645.

44. Elliot to Grey 3/3/15, F.O. 371/2243.

45. Cunninghame, The Greek Army and The Dardanelles, p. 130-1.

46. Bax-Ironside to Grey 4/3/15, Adm 137/109.

47. Bax-Ironside to Grey 10/3/15, Adm 137/1336.

48. Napier Lt.-Col., H.D, The Experiences of a Military Attache in the Balkans, London, Dranes, 1924, p. 126. Napier saw the King on 7/3/15.

49. Elliot to Grey 4/3/15, F.O. 371/2243.

50. Carden-Narrative, Adm 137/38.

51. Triumph Report 3/3/15, Adm 137/38.

52. Corbett Sir J, Naval Operations V2, p. 181-2.

53. Carden to the Admiralty 10/3/15, Adm 137/38.

54. War Office to Maxwell 27/2/15, W.O. 158/574.

55. Corbett Sir J, Naval Operations V2, p. 186-7.

56. See Map "The Dardanelles" in Ibid.

57. "Defences of the Dardanelles" by General Percival, Adm 116/1713.

58. Birdwood to Kitchener 5/3/15, Birdwood Papers, AWM File 419/10/17.

59. Rear-Admiral Second in Command, Eastern Mediterranean Squadron, "Appreciation of present position in Dardanelles and proposals for future operations" 9/3/15, Godfrey Papers, Imperial War Musuem, 69/33/1.

60. Carden to the Admiralty 10/3/15, Adm 137/1089.

61. Dewar K.G.B, The Dardanelles Campaign, Naval Review, V 45, April 1957, p. 153. (Dewar is quoting from Wemyss' Diary).

62. Asquith to Bonar Law 8/3/15, Bonar Law Papers, 36/6/23.

63. War Council Minutes 10/3/15, Cab 42/2/5.

64. Ibid.

65. Ibid.

66. Instructions For The General Officer Commander-in-Chief, The Mediterranean Expeditionary Force 13/3/15, C.V.3, p. 684-6.

67. Ibid.

68. Churchill to Jellicoe 9/3/15, Jellicoe Papers, Add/Mss 48890.

69. Churchill to Carden 5/3/15, Adm 137/109.

70. Churchill to Carden 11/3/15, C.V.3, p. 677-8.

71. Carden to Churchill 14/3/15, C.V.3, p. 693.

72. Fisher to Churchill 4/3/15, C.V.3, p. 636.

73. Fisher to Churchill 12/3/15, C.V.3, p. 680.

74. Fisher to Jellicoe 15/3/15, C.V.3, p. 701.

75. Fisher to Jellicoe 16/3/15, Jellicoe Papers, Add/Mss 49006.

76. Jackson to Oliver 11/3/15, C.V.3, p. 676-7.

77. Memorandum by deRobeck 12/4/15, Adm 116/1434.

78. Carden to Churchill 16/3/15, C.V.3, p. 703.

79. Fisher to Churchill 24/3/15, C.V.3, p. 730.

80. Birdwood to Kitchener 23/3/15, Kitchener Papers, Pro 30/57/61.

81. Churchill to deRobeck 17/3/15, C.V.3, p. 706.

82. Dardanelles Commission- deRobeck's Evidence 10/10/16, Q2707-9, Cab 19/33; deRobeck to Churchill 18/3/15, Adm 137/110.

83. Corbett Sir J, Naval Operations V 2, p. 218-224.

84. DeRobeck-Report 24/3/15, Robeck Papers, 4/4.

85. Keyes to his wife 21/3/15, Keyes Papers, 2/9.

86. DeRobeck to Wemyss 18/3/15, Hamilton Papers, 17/7/25/4.

87. Wester-Wemyss Admiral of the Fleet Lord, The Navy in the Dardanelles Campaign, London, Hodder & Stoughton, 1924, p. 43.

88. Meeting of Captains 19/3/15, Robeck Papers, 4/5.

89. DeRobeck to Hamilton 19/3/15, Hamilton Papers, 5/4.

90. War Council Minutes 19/3/15, Cab 42/2/14.

91. Admiralty to deRobeck 20/3/15, C.V.3, p. 718-9.

92. Weather Reports in Adm 116/1713.

93. DeRobeck to the Admiralty 21/3/15, Adm 137/110.

94. Keyes - Naval Memoirs V 2, p. 186.

95. "A.W.C." The Immortal Gamble, Naval Review, V 53, April 1965, p. 146.

96. Hamilton to Churchill 21/6/23, Hamilton Papers, 1/15.

97. Kitchener to Hamilton 19/3/15, in Ibid 15/17.

98. Dardanelles Commission - Hamilton's Evidence 13/10/16, Q4385-6, Cab 19/33.

99. DeRobeck to Churchill 23/3/15, Adm 137/110.

100. Gilbert M, Winston S. Churchill V 3, p. 365-6.

101. Churchill to deRobeck 24/3/15, Adm 116/1348.

102. DeRobeck to Limpus 26/3/15, Limpus Papers.

103. DeRobeck to Churchill 27/3/15, Adm 116/1348.

104. Ibid.

105. Churchill to deRobeck 27/3/15, C.V.3, p. 753-4.

106. Mitchell Committee Report, p. 436.

107. G.H.Q., Constantinople - Answers given to the Mitchell Committee, Adm 116/1714.

108. James, Gallipoli, p. 64; Aspinall-Oglander C, Military Operations : Gallipoli V 1, London, Heinemann, 1928, p. 105N.

109. Mitchell Committee Report, p. 437-8.

110. Quoted in Germains V, The Tragedy of Winston Churchill, London, Hurst and Blackett, 1931, p. 195N.

111. Mitchell Committee Report, p. 71.

112. Ibid., p. 436.

113. G.H.Q. Constantinople-Answers given to Mitchell Committee, Adm 116/1714.

114. Mitchell Committee Report, p. 71.

115. Moorehead A, Gallipoli, London, Hamish Hamilton, 1956, p. 75.

116. Mitchell Committee Report, p. 50.

117. Ibid.

118. Marder A.J, From The Dardanelles to Oran, London, O.U.P., 1975, p. 24-5.

119. Ibid.

120. Ibid, p. 23.

121. Preston, Battleships of World War I, p. 121.

122. The reinforcements ordered by the Admiralty did not include a dreadnought.

123. Enver Bey (C.O.S. to Souchon) to the Mitchell Committee. See Mitchell Committee Report, p. 382.

124. Von Sandars, Five Years In Turkey, London, Baulliere, Tindall & Cox, 1927, p. 47.

125. G.H.Q. Constantinople-Answers given to Mitchell Committee, Adm 116/1714.

126. Morganthau H, Ambassador Morganthau's Story, N.Y., Doubelday, 1919, p. 195.

127. Ibid.

128. Dardanelles Commission-Hall's Evidence 24/10/16, Q4906, Cab 19/33.

129. G.H.Q. Constantinople-Answers given

to Mitchell Committee, Adm
116/1714.
130. Mitchell Committee
Report, p. 211.
132. The World Crisis, p.
6061
132. Ibid., p. 605-6.
133. Ibid., p. 609-10.
134. Ibid., p. 605.
135. Ibid., p. 612.
136. Ibid.
137. Ibid., p. 613.
138. Ibid.
139. Ibid., p. 623.
140. Ibid., p. 625.
141. Ibid.
142. Ibid., p. 633-4.
143. Ibid., p. 636.
144. Ibid., p. 639-43.
145. Ibid., p. 613-4.
146. Ibid., p. 614.
147. Ibid., p. 616.
148. Ibid., p. 632.
149. Ibid., p. 629.
150. Ibid., p. 618.
151. Ibid., p. 617.
152. Ibid., p. 620.
153. Ibid., p. 619.
154. Venizelos to
Churchill 6/11/23, Churchill
Papers, 8/45.
155. The World Crisis, p.
661.
156. Ibid., p. 664.
157. Ibid., p. 647.
158. War Council Minutes
6/4/15, Cab 42/2/17.
159. Churchill to Balfour
8/4/15, C.V.3, p. 780.
160. Churchill Papers
8/143.
161. Hamilton to
Churchill 21/6/23, Churchill
Papers 8/44.
162. The World Crisis, p.
648.
163. Churchill Papers
8/183.
164. The World Crisis, p.
660.
165. Ibid., p. 672.
166. Ibid.

167. Ibid.
168. Ibid.
169. Ibid., p. 673.
170. Note by the Mitchell
Committee, Adm 116/1713.
171. The German figures
are on p. 674 of The World
Crisis.
172. Ibid., p. 673.
173. Ibid.
174. Ibid., p. 673.
175. Ibid., p. 675.
176. Ibid., p. 676.
177. Ibid.
178. See Chapter XXI
179. Churchill Papers
8/91.
180. The World Crisis, p.
679-81.
181. Mitchell Committee
Report, p. 85-7.
182. Ibid., p. 86.
183. Ibid., p. 87.
184. Ibid.
185. The World Crisis, p.
680.
186. Mitchell Committee
Report, p. 86.
187. Ibid.
188. Ibid.
189. The World Crisis, p.
681-3.
190. Edmonds to Churchill
2/7/23, Churchill Papers
8/44.

Chapter 8

The Dardanelles III –
Military Failure

1. Dardanelles
Commission-Braithwaite's
Evidence 25/1/17, Q13250,
Cab 19/33.
2. Dardanelles
Commission-Statement by
Captain H.P. Douglas R.N.
(Hydrographic Department),
Cab 19/32.
3. See General Staff
War Diary 18/3/15, W.O.

95/4263.

4. Hamilton to Kitchener 23/3/15, G.H.Q. War Diary, W.O. 95/4264.

5. Appreciations by Generals Paris and Hunter-Weston, Hamilton Papers, 17/7/30-1.

6. Hamilton to Kitchener 18/4/15, G.H.Q. War Diary, W.O. 95/4264.

7. Hamilton to Clive Wigram 16/4/15, Hamilton Papers, 5/9.

8. Fisher to Churchill 27/3/15, Churchill Papers 8/177; Fisher to Churchill 28/3/15, C.V.3, p. 757-8; Memorandum by Fisher 27/3/15, C.V.3, p. 754-5; Memorandum by Fisher 31/3/15, in Marder A.J, Fear God V 3, p. 179-81.

9. Hamilton, Tudor and Lambert to Fisher 7/4/15, Adm 1/8440/341.

10. Fisher to Hamilton, Tudor and Lambert 8/4/15, C.V.3, p. 783-5.

11. Memorandum by Fisher 8/4/15, C.V.3, p. 781.

12. Lady Richmond Diary 11/4/15, Richmond Papers, RIC 1/17.

13. Fisher to Jellicoe 22/4/15, Jellicoe Papers, Add/Mss 49007.

14. Swiftsure Report 5/5/15, Adm 116/1434.

15. Ibid.

16. DeRobeck - "Orders For Combined Operations" 12/4/15, Adm 116/1434.

17. Hamilton to Clive Wigram 16/4/15, Hamilton Papers, 5/9.

18. Wemyss to Cornwallis 24/4/15, Robeck Papers, 4/23.

19. Albion Report 4/5/15, Adm 137/40.

20. Note by Brig-Gen Percival on Information given by C.O.S. 9th Turkish division 6/5/19, Adm 116/1713.

21. For S see 2nd Battalion South Wales Borderers War Diary 25/4/15, W.O. 95/4311. For Y, Lt-Col Matthews Report 27/4/15, G.H.Q. War Diary, W.O. 95/4264.

22. G.H.Q. War Diary 25/4/15, entry for 9.21 a.m., W.O. 95/4263.

23. Ibid., entry for 10.00 a.m.

24. 1st Battalion, Royal Inniskilling Fusiliers War Diary 25/4/15, W.O. 95/4311.

25. Aspinall-Oglander, Gallipoli V 1, p. 245.

26. "Report of the Landing of the 29th Division on April 25th", W.O. 95/4263.

27. 87th Infantry Brigade War Diary, W.O. 95/4311. The troops of the 87th Brigade covering X beach remained in the same position on the 26th as on the previous night. They had to await the capture of the high ground above V before advancing. As this was not taken until 4 p.m. on the 26th their advance was postponed.

28. Aspinall-Oglander, Gallipoli V 1, p. 280-1.

29. Ibid., p. 283.

30. Miles Major S, "Notes on the Dardanelles Campaign of 1915", The Coast Artillery Journal, V 62, 1925, p. 127.

31. Mitchell Committee Report, Map. 13.

32. Ibid., Map 15.

33. Aspinall-Oglander, Gallipoli V 1, p. 294.

34. Ibid., p. 292.

35. Ibid., p. 291.

36. 29th Division War

Diary 28/4/15, W.O. 95/4304.

37. Dardanelles
Commission-Statement by
Lt-Col Patterson, Cab 19/30.

38. "Note on The Landing
Near Cape Hellas" by
Brig-Gen A.W. Roper 10/5/15,
W.O. 95/4264.

39. Williams O.C, "The
Gallipoli Tragedy",
Nineteenth Century, V 106,
July 1929, p. 87.

40. "Notes on Landing at
W beach" by Major
Striedenger, W.O. 95/4304.

41. Bean's Diary, quoted
in Bean C.E.W, Gallipoli
Mission, Canberra,
Australian War Memorial,
1948, p. 306.

42. Miles, "Notes on the
Dardanelles Campaign, 1925,
p. 34; See also General
Egerton's Diary (1934) in
Cab 45/249; Harrison W.R.G,
Gallipoli Revisited, Journal
of the Royal Artillery, V49,
October 1932, p. 293; Head
Lt-Col C.O., A Glance at
Gallipoli, London, Eyre and
Spottiswoode, 1931, p. 78.

43. James, Gallipoli, p.
107.

44. Mitchell Committee
Report, Map 16.

45. Bean, Gallipoli
Mission, p. 277-8.

46. Miles, "Notes on the
Dardanelles Campaign", 1925,
p. 130.

47. Aspinall-Oglander,
Gallipoli V 1, p. 347.

48. Brereton C.B, Tales
of Three Campaigns, London,
Selwyn and Blount, 1926, p.
116-7. Brereton was with
the New Zealand contingent.

49. Bean, Gallipoli
Mission, p. 301-2.

50. For Roumania see
Smith C.J, The Russian
Struggle For Power

1914-1917, N.Y.,
Philosophical Library, 1956,
p. 290-1; for Bulgaria,
Bax-Ironside to Grey 8/5/15,
F.O. 371/2245.

51. Bax-Ironside to Grey
9/5/15, F.O. 371-2245.

52. Churchill to
Kitchener 26/4/15 (not
sent), C.V.3, p. 816-7.

53. Quoted in Hamilton
Ian, The Happy Warrior : A
Life of General Sir Ian
Hamilton, London, Cassell,
1966, p. 427.

54. Churchill to
deRobeck 27/3/15, C.V.3, p.
755-6.

55. DeRobeck to
Churchill 29/3/15, C.V.3, p.
759.

56. Cassar G, The French
and the Dardanelles : A
Study of Failure in the
Conduct of War, London,
Allen & Unwin, 1971, p. 124;
Keyes to his wife 10/5/15,
Keyes Papers, 2/11.

57. DeRobeck to the
Admiralty 10/5/15, Adm
137/154.

58. Keyes to Braithwaite
1/5/15, Keyes Papers, 5/2.

59. War Council Minutes
14/5/15, Cab 42/2/19.

60. Ibid.

61. Ibid.

62. Memorandum by
Churchill 14/5/15, C.V.3, p.
885-7.

63. Crease to Churchill
29/10/23, Churchill Papers
8/48.

64. Fisher to Churchill
15/5/15, C.V.3, p. 887.

65. Asquith to Fisher
15/5/15, C.V.3, p. 888.

66. Churchill to Fisher
15/5/15, Fisher to Churchill
16/5/15, Churchill to Fisher
16/5/15, Fisher to Churchill
16/5/15, C.V.3, p. 888-92.

67. 2nd, 3rd, 4th, Sea Lords to Churchill and Fisher 16/5/15, Adm 1/8440/341.

68. Hamilton (2nd Sea Lord) to Jellicoe 16/5/15, quoted in "A Reply to Criticism", Jellicoe Papers, Add/Mss 49041.

69. Gilbert M, Winston S. Churchill V 3, p. 457.

70. Hankey Diary 20/5/15, Hankey Papers, 1/1.

71. Asquith to Lord Stamfordham 17/5/15, Asquith Papers, 27/162.

72. Wilson to Bonar Law 16/5/15, C.V.3, p. 894.

73. Fisher to Bonar Law 17/5/15, Bonar Law Papers, 37/2/35.

74. Lloyd George D, War Memoirs V 1, London, Ivor Nicolson, 1933, p. 228-9.

75. Churchill to Asquith 17/5/15, C.V.3, p. 898.

76. The Times 18/5/15 and 16/5/15

77. Churchill to Asquith 18/5/15, C.V.3, p. 902-3.

78. Ibid.

79. Asquith to Fisher 17/5/15, quoted in Marder A.J, Fear God V 3, p. 239.

80. Bonar Law to Fisher 17/5/15, Bonar Law Papers, 37/5/25.

81. Esher to Fisher 16/5/15, quoted in Mackay R, Fisher of Kilverstone, London, O.U.P., 1973, p. 499.

82. Fisher to Asquith 19/5/15, C.V.3, p. 906-7.

83. Balfour to Selborne 20/5/15, Selborne Papers, 1/151-2.

84. According to Donald, Fisher's return was still under consideration when this letter arrived "and stopped negotiations". Donald to Fisher 8/6/15, Donald Papers, D/4/12.

85. Wilson to Asquith 19/5/15, C.V.3, p. 916.

86. Churchill to Asquith 20/5/15, C.V.3, p. 920.

87. Jellicoe to Hamilton 19/5/15, Hamilton Papers, HTN/125.

88. Fisher to Bonar Law 19/5/15, Bonar Law Papers, 50/3/1.

89. Emmot to Asquith 20/5/15, C.V.3, p. 919.

90. Pringle to Asquith 20/5/15, C.V.3, p. 919.

91. Hankey Diary 19/5/15, Hankey Papers, 1/1.

92. Fisher to Bonar Law, 19/5/15, C.V.3, p. 915.

93. Churchill to Asquith 21/5/15, C.V.3, p. 925.

94. Churchill to Bonar Law 19/5/15, C.V.3, p. 908.

95. Bonar Law to Churchill 21/5/15, C.V.3, p. 924.

96. Churchill to Asquith 21/5/15, C.V.3, p. 926.

97. Asquith to Churchill 21/5/15, C.V.3, p. 926-7.

98. Gilbert M, Winston S. Churchill V 3, p. 479.

99. The World Crisis, p. 666.

100. Ibid., p. 630.

101. Ibid., p. 636.

102. Ibid., p. 684-6.

103. Ibid., p. 686.

104. Ibid., p. 687.

105. Aspinall-Oglander to Churchill 8/8/23, Churchill Papers 8/45.

106. Hamilton Sir Ian, Listening For the Drums, London, Faber, 1944, p. 254.

107. Hamilton to Churchill 28/6/23, Churchill Papers 8/44.

108. Hamilton Sir Ian, Listening For the Drums, p. 254.

109. The World Crisis, p.

708.

110. Ibid., p. 713-4.
111. Ibid., p. 745.
112. Churchill Papers 8/149.
113. The World Crisis, p. 727.
114. Ibid.
115. Ibid., p. 728.
116. Ibid.
117. Hamilton to Churchill 28/6/23, Churchill Papers 8/44.
118. The World Crisis, p. 730.
119. Ibid., p. 732-3.
120. Ibid., p. 733 (emphasis added).
121. Van Creveld M, Supplying War : Logistics from Wallenstein to Patton, London, Cambridge U.P., 1977, p.2.
122. Churchill Papers 8/148.
123. The World Crisis, p. 736.
124. Ibid., p. 743.
125. Churchill Papers 8/149 (emphasis added).
126. The World Crisis, p. 742.
127. Churchill Papers 8/87.
128. The World Crisis, p. 745.
129. Ibid., p. 754.
130. Ibid., p. 755.
131. Ibid., (1st Edition) p. 358.
132. Ibid., p. 761.
133. Churchill Papers 8/150.
134. The World Crisis, p. 767.
135. Ibid.
136. Ibid., p. 768.
137. Beaverbrook Lord, Politicians and the War 1914-1916, London, Collins, 1960 (reprint of the 1928-32 edition), p. 116.
138. The World Crisis, p. 768.
139. Ibid., p. 771.
140. Churchill Papers 8/150.
141. The World Crisis, p. 769-776.
142. Ibid., p. 772 and 776.
143. Churchill Papers 8/150.
144. Ibid.
145. Ibid.
146. The World Crisis, p. 775.
147. Churchill Papers 8/150. The recent election probably refers to the 1922 General Election after which Bonar Law became Prime Minister. The "three times" refers to the formation of the first and second wartime coalitions and the demise of Lloyd George in 1922, which is also the "palace revolution" referred to. In 1922 Churchill was Colonial Secretary in the Lloyd George coalition. The "palace revolution" lost him his Cabinet post, the ensuing General Election his parliamentary seat.
148. The World Crisis, p. 774.
149. Churchill to his wife 11/12/15, quoted in Gilbert M, Winston S. Churchill V 3, p. 607.
150. The World Crisis, p. 773-4.
151. Ibid., p. 643.
152. Ibid., p. 739.
153. Ibid.

Chapter 9

The Dardanelles IV - The Terrible If's

1. Dardanelles

Commission – M.E.F. Weekly
Returns, Cab 19/31.
  2.  Hamilton to
Kitchener 17/5/15, W.O.
159/13.
  3.  Hamilton to
Kitchener 3/6/15, Hamilton
Papers, 15/17.
  4.  42nd Division, War
Diary 4/6/15, 1/6
Manchester's, W.O. 95/4316.
  5.  8th Corps War Diary
4/6/15, W.O. 95/4273.
  6.  42nd Division War
Diary 4/6/15, W.O. 95/4316.
See entries for 1/5, 1/6,
1/8 Manchesters.
  7.  Aspinall-Oglander,
Gallipoli V 2, p. 53.
  8.  Hamilton to
Kitchener 6/6/15, Dawnay
Papers, Box 17.
  9.  Dardanelles
Committee Minutes 7/6/15,
Cab 42/3/1.
  10.  Churchill to
Kitchener 15/6/15, C.V.3, p.
1017-8.
  11.  Churchill to
Asquith, Bonar Law, Balfour
and Curzon 11/6/15, C.V.3,
p. 1003-4.
  12.  Memorandum by
Ashmead-Bartlett 11/6/15,
C.V.3, p. 1004-8.
  13.  W.O. to Hamilton
11/6/15, Dawnay Papers, Box
17.
  14.  Hamilton to W.O.
12/6/15, Hamilton Papers,
15/17.
  15.  DeRobeck to the
Admiralty 12/6/15, Adm
137/155.
  16.  Keyes to his wife
13/6/15, Keyes Papers, 2/12.
  17.  H.M.S, London,
Gunnery Report 10/10/15;
H.M.S. Implacable, Gunnery
Report 29/9/15, Adm
1/8440/335.
  18.  Admiral Stuart

Nicholson Report 21/6/15,
Adm 137/774.
  19.  H.M.S. Implacable,
Gunnery Report 29/9/15, Adm
1/8440/355.
  20.  B.H.S.", Dardanelles
Details, Naval Review, V 24,
1936, p. 89.
  21.  von Usedom to the
Kaiser 20/7/15, Cab 45/215.
  22.  Mitchell Committee
Report, p. 446-7.
  23.  Ibid., p. 457.
  24.  Aspinall-Oglander,
Gallipoli V 2, p. 74.
  25.  Braithwaite to
Stopford 22/7/15, W.O.
158/576.
  26.  Braithwaite to
Stopford 29/7/15, in Ibid.
  27.  Memorandum by
Stopford 31/7/15, in Ibid.
  28.  Quoted in Stopford's
Report on Suvla Operations
26/10/15, W.O. 106/708.
  29.  Aspinall-Oglander,
Gallipoli V 2, p. 185.
  30.  Miles, Notes on the
Dardanelles Campaign, 1925,
p. 214.
  31.  Powles Col C.G.
(Ed.), History of the
Canterbury Mounted Rifles,
Auckland, Whitcombe and
Tombs, 1928, p. 46-9.
  32.  Dardanelles
Commission – Lt-Col. C.
Allanson's Evidence 19/1/17,
Q11746, Cab 19/33.
  33.  4th Australian
Brigade War Diary, W.O.
95/4353.  (150 wounded, 50
killed).
  34.  Bean C.E.W, The
Story of Anzac V 2, Sydney,
Angus & Robertson, 1938, p.
635.
  35.  North John,
Gallipoli : The Fading
Vision, London, Faber, 1966
(reprint of 1936 ed.), p.
111.

36. Aspinall-Oglander, Gallipoli V 2, p. 105-7.

37. Malthus C, Anzac : A Retrospect, Auckland, Whitcombe and Tombs, 1965, p. 111.

38. Ibid., p. 115-7. Bean states that the ground over which the New Zealanders advanced was hidden from Battleship Hill. See The Story of Anzac V, p. 638.

39. Aspinall-Oglander, Gallipoli V 2, p. 209.

40. Bean C.E.W, The Story of Anzac V 2, p. 658-662.

41. 38th Infantry Brigade War Diary 8/8/15, W.O. 95/4302.

42. "Report of Fighting on 8/8/15 on Chunuk Bair", N.Z. and Australian Division, New Zealand Infantry Brigade, Wellington Battalion, W.O. 95/4352.

43. Aspinall-Oglander, Gallipoli V 2, p. 216.

44. Dardanelles Commission - Lt-Col. Allanson's Evidence 19/1/17, Q11792, Cab 19/33.

45. Allanson's Diary, Copy in Bush Papers, 75/65/3.

46. Dardanelles Commission - Lt-Col. Allanson's Evidence 19/1/17, Q11854, Cab 19/33.

47. See Log Of Bacchante 9/8/15, Adm 53/34649; Bean C.E.W, The Story of Anzac V 2, p. 694.

48. Hamilton to Birdwood 11/9/15, Hamilton Papers, 5/10.

49. Bean C.E.W, Gallipoli Mission, p. 212.

50. Statement by Major Harston of the Wellington Regiment (Malone's Adjutant) Cab 45/234.

51. "Report of Fighting on Chunuk Bair", W.O. 95/4352.

52. Malthus, Anzac, p. 119.

53. See the introduction by Sir Ian Hamilton to Pemberton T.J, Gallipoli Today, London, Benn, 1926.

54. Miles, Notes on the Dardanelles Campaign, 1925, p. 137.

55. Dardanelles Commission-Brig-Gen G.N, Johnston's Evidence 2/5/17, Q26644-47, Q26658, Cab 19/33.

56. 11th Division's orders, Cab 45/227.

57. General Hammersley's Report 20/7/16, W.O. 32/5123.

58. Col H.T. Goodland (30th Brig, 10th Division) to Aspinall-Oglander 26/3/31, Cab 45/242.

59. Capt. A.E. Bancroft (signals) to Aspinall-Oglander 9/2/31, Cab 45/241.

60. Account of the Suvla Bay landing in the Miller Papers, PP/MCR/16.

61. Dardanelles Commission-Statement by General Mahon, Cab 19/30.

62. 32nd Brigade (11th Division) War Diary 30/7/15, W.O. 95/4299.

63. "The 32nd Infantry Brigade at Suvla Bay", Hamilton Papers, 6/6.

64. 34th Brigade War Diary 6/7/15, W.O. 95/4299.

65. "Suvla Bay", Notes by Admiral Christian (the local naval commander) 7/8/15, Robeck Papers, 4/34.

66. Report by Brig-Gen. F.F. Hill, Cab 45/242; 31st Brigade War Diary 7/8/15, W.O. 95/4296.

67. G.H.Q. War Diary 7/8/15, W.O. 95/4264.

68. Dardanelles Commission-Statement by Aspinall, Cab 19/28.

69. "The 32nd Infantry Brigade at Suvla Bay", Hamilton Papers, 6/6.

70. General Hammersley's Report, W.O. 32/5123.

71. G.H.Q. War Diary 8/8/15, W.O. 95/4264.

72. Stopford to the 10th and 11th Divisions 8/8/15, 9th Corps War Diary, W.O. 95/4276.

73. See the map facing p. 281 in Aspinall-Oglander, Gallipoli V 2.

74. Aspinall to Hamilton 8/8/15, G.H.Q. War Diary, W.O. 95/4264.

75. 32nd Brigade War Diary 8/8/15, W.O. 95/4299.

76. Ibid.

77. Mitchell Committee Report, Map 35.

78. This was the conclusion of a War Office Committee set up to examine the reasons for the Suvla failure. See the report in W.O. 32/5119.

79. Miles, Notes on the Dardanelles Campaign, 1925, p. 143.

80. Ibid.

81. Dardanelles Commission-Birdwood's Evidence 6/3/17, Q21308, Cab 19/33.

82. The World Crisis, p. 791.

83. Ibid., p. 795.

84. Ibid., p. 795-6.

85. Ibid., p. 799-801.

86. Ibid., p. 796.

87. Ibid., p. 826.

88. Ibid., p. 811.

89. Ibid., p. 792.

90. Ibid., p. 812.

91. Ibid.

92. Ibid., p. 813-4.

93. Ibid., p. 814-5.

94. Ibid., p. 814n.

95. Ibid., p. 799.

96. Ibid., p. 816.

97. Ibid., p. 830.

98. Ibid.

99. Ibid., p. 832.

100. Ibid.

101. Ibid.

102. Ibid., p. 836.

103. Ibid.

104. Ibid., p. 837-8.

105. James, Gallipoli, p. 290n.

106. The World Crisis, p. 837.

107. Ibid., p. 837-8.

108. Ibid., p. 837.

109. Ibid., p. 828.

110. Ibid., p. 833.

111. Ibid., p. 833-4.

112. Ibid., p. 839.

113. Ibid.

114. Ibid., p. 840-1.

115. Ibid., p. 842-3.

116. Ibid., p. 844-5.

117. Ibid., p. 829.

118. Ibid., p. 836.

119. Ibid., p. 847.

120. Churchill Papers 8/91.

121. All references are to The World Crisis, p. 847.

Chapter 10

The Dardanelles V – Evacuation and Churchill's Balkan Policy

1. The World Crisis, p. 864.

2. Ibid.

3. Ibid., p. 865.

4. Ibid.

5. Dardanelles Committee Minutes 23/9/15, Cab 42/3/28.

6. Ibid.

7. Ibid., 6/10/15, Cab 42/4/3.

8. Memorandum by

Churchill 15/10/15, C.V.3, p. 1220-4.

9. See Churchill Papers 8/155 and The World Crisis, p. 874.

10. Churchill to Balfour 6/10/15, quoted in The World Crisis, p. 866.

11. The World Crisis, p. 880-2.

12. Ibid., p. 888-891.

13. Mitchell Committee Report, p. 72.

14. Wemyss to Jackson 15/12/15, Jackson Papers.

15. Dewar K.G.B, "The Dardanelles Campaign", Naval Review, V45, October 1957, p. 396.

16. Keyes to deRobeck 18/10/15, Keyes Papers, 5/17.

17. DeRobeck to C-in-C Med Force 30/10/15, Adm 137/2168.

18. Limpus to deRobeck 12/11/15, Limpus Papers.

19. The World Crisis, p. 877.

20. Ibid., p. 878.

21. Churchill Papers 8/155.

22. Ibid.

23. Edmonds to Churchill 20/7/23, Churchill Papers 8/183.

24. Churchill Papers 8/93.

25. Monro to Kitchener 28/10/15, G.H.Q. War Diary, W.O. 95/4265.

26. Report of a Conversation between Aspinall, Roch, Wedgewood and Hamilton 8/1/19, Hamilton Papers, 17/5/13.

27. James, Gallipoli, p. 323.

28. Aspinall-Oglander, Gallipoli V 2, p. 401.

29. Quoted in Barrow, General Sir George, The Life of General Sir Charles

Carmichael Monro, London, Hutchinson, 1931, p. 69.

30. Untitled Appreciation by Aspinall 22/10/15, W.O. 158/575.

31. Appreciation by Dawnay 30/10/15, Dawnay Papers, Box 17.

32. Davies to Monro 1/11/15; Byng to Monro 2/11/15, W.O. 158/578.

33. Birdwood to Kitchener 2/11/15, Birdwood Papers, AWM File 419/10/7, Box 213.

34. Appreciation by Aspinall 22/10/15, W.O. 158/575.

35. Dardanelles Commission-Dardanelles Casualties, Weekly Reports, Cab 19/31.

36. Aspinall-Oglander, Gallipoli V 2, p. 389.

37. Memorandum by Monro 12/11/15, W.O. 158/578.

38. The World Crisis, p. 870-2.

39. See Monro's Appreciation quoted above.

40. The World Crisis, p. 883.

41. Kitchener to Asquith 15/11/15, Cab 42/5/20.

42. The World Crisis, p. 891-2.

43. Ibid., p. 892.

44. Ibid., p. 897.

45. Ibid., p. 898.

46. Ibid., p. 897.

47. Ibid., p. 442.

48. Ibid., p. 850.

49. Ibid., p. 849.

50. Ibid., p. 849-50.

51. Grey to Bax-Ironside 21/8/14 and Grey to Elliot 27/8/14, quoted in "The Balkans 1914-15 from the Outbreak of War to the Offer to Bulgara" by E.C. Percy 9/7/15, F.O. 371/2264. (Hereafter, "The Balkans

1914-15").

52. Barclay to Grey
12/8/14, quoted in Ibid.

53. Foreign Office
Memorandum, N.D., F.O.
371/2241.

54. Barclay to Nicolson
14/11/14, Nicolson Papers,
F.O. 800/376.

55. Dallin A. (Ed.),
Russian Diplomacy and
Eastern Europe 1914-1917,
N.Y., King Crown Press,
1963, p. 214; "The Balkans
1914-15", p. 7.

56. e.g. Buchanan to
Grey 18/2/15, giving the
Russian defeat at the
Masaurian Lakes as the
reason for the lapse in the
Roumanian negotiations, F.O.
371/2243; Chirol to Grey
10/8/15, saying that the
fall of Warsaw had prevented
any chance of Roumanian
intervention, FO 371/2259.

57. Dallin A.(Ed.),
Russian Diplomacy and
Eastern Europe, p. 255.

58. Crewe to des Graz
10/7/15, F.O. 371/2261.

59. Grey to Barclay
12/10/15, F.O. 371/2273.

60. Barclay to Grey
16/10/15, in Ibid.

61. Grey to Barclay
16/10/15, in Ibid.

62. "Precis of Documents
and Proceedings Connected
with the Political and
Military Developments in the
Balkan Peninsula from
September 1 to 28 inclusive,
1915", Cab 42/4/21.
(Hereafter, Precis).

63. Precis October
14-21, Cab 42/4/21.

64. Headlam-Morley to
Churchill 10/1/23, Churchill
Papers 8/44.

65. Headlam-Morley to
Churchill 22/2/24, in Ibid
8/185.

66. See Churchill Papers
8/180 and 8/41.

67. The World Crisis, p.
473.

68. Ibid., p. 474.

69. Ibid., p. 849.

70. Barclay to Grey
1/4/15, Adm 137/1089;
Kiritescu C, La Roumanie
dans la Guerre Mondiale
1916-1919, Paris, Payot,
1934, p. 265.

71. Kiritescu C, Guerre
Mondiale, p. 265.

72. Petrie Charles, The
Roumanian Campaign 1916,
Army Quarterly, V14, 1927,
p. 341.

73. Seicaru P, La
Roumanie dans la Grande
Guerre, Paris, Minard, 1968,
p. 346.

74. Kiritescu C, Guerre
Mondiale, p. 265.

75. Barclay to Grey
30/6/14, F.O. 371/2089.

76. General Brade to
Foreign Office 15/11/15,
F.O. 371/2274.

77. Barclay to Grey
1/4/15, Adm 137/1089.

78. Seicaru P, La
Roumanie, p. 289.

79. Napier to Grey
6/12/15, F.O. 371/2274.

80. Seicaru P, La
Roumanie, p. 289.

81. Kiritescu C, Guerre
Mondiale, p. 54.

82. Napier Lt-Col. H.D,
Experiences of a Military
Attache, p. 105.

83. Stone N, The Eastern
Front, p. 264.

84. Petrie C, The
Roumanian Campaign, p. 341.

85. Kiritescu C, Guerre
Mondiale, p. 265.

86. Biranek Jan,
Bulgaria's Forces, Purnell
History of the First World
War, p. 1079.

87. Ibid.

88. Bax-Ironside to Grey 23/3/14; "Bulgaria, Annual Report 1913", F.O. 371/1918.

89. Cunninghame, The Greek Army and the Dardanelles, p. 122.

90. Stone N, The Eastern Front, p. 109.

Chapter 11

Jutland

1. The former was Evan-Thomas' contention-Note in Evan-Thomas Papers, Add/Mss 52506.

2. Chalmers, Beatty, p. 227.

3. Waller A.C, 5th Battle Squadron at Jutland, R.U.S.I. Journal, November 1935, p. 791-9. (Waller was the Captain of the Barham).

4. Note by Evan-Thomas, Evan-Thomas Papers, Add/Mss 52504.

5. Jellicoe to Evan-Thomas 3/6/23, in Ibid.

6. Corbett Sir J, Naval Operations V 3, London, Longmans, 1923, p. 334.

7. Roskill S, Admiral of the Fleet Earl Beatty : The Last Naval Hero : An Intimate Biography, London, Collins, 1980, p. 161.

8. Quoted in, Official Despatches Relating to The Battle Of Jutland 30th May to 1st June 1916 with Appendices and Charts, London, H.M.S.O., 1920, (CMD 1068) (Hereafter, Official Despatches).

9. Ibid., p. 453.

10. Marder A.J, Scapa Flow V 3, p. 64.

11. Official Despatches, p. 450-3.

12. List of hits compiled by A. Campbell, Beatty Papers; see also Bennett G, The Battle of Jutland, London, Batsford, 1964, p. 93.

13. Official Despatches, p. 451.

14. Ibid., p. 457.

15. Jellicoe to Beatty 4/6/16, Beatty Papers.

16. Ibid.

17. Jellicoe makes this point - See "The Grand Fleet and Jutland", Jellicoe Papers, Add/Mss 49041.

18. Godfrey Captain J.H, "Seven Lectures on Jutland" (No. 4), Cab 45/269 Pt.II.

19. Scheer Admiral, Germany's High Sea Fleet in the World War, London, Cassell, 1920, p. 152-3.

20. See for example "Extract from Officers Report H.M.S. Benbow" 10/6/16, Adm 137/302.

21. Dreyer A.C, Sea Heritage, London, Museum Press, 1955, p. 150.

22. Campbell List, Beatty Papers.

23. Frost H.H, The Battle of Jutland, Annapolis, Maryland, U.S. Naval Institute, 1964, p. 269-70.

24. Frost calculated that Jellicoe could have expected six hits had he turned towards the enemy attack. See The Battle of Jutland, p. 376.

25. Bacon Admiral Sir Reginald, The Jutland Scandal, London, Heinemann, 1924, p. 82 and The Life of John Rushworth, Earl Jellicoe, London, Cassell, 1926, p. 285.

26. For example see the reports of Marlborough, Revenge, Agincourt, Valiant

in Adm 137/302.

27. Official Despatches, p. 466.

28. Ibid., p. 476.

29. Bacon, Jellicoe, p. 298-90.

30. Marder A.J, Scapa Flow V 3, p. 151-2.

31. Official Despatches, p. 478.

32. Jellicoe - "Proposed Appendix to 'The Grand Fleet'", Jellicoe Papers, Add/Mss 49040.

33. Marder A.J, Scapa Flow V 3, p. 157.

34. Ibid., p. 202-4.

35. Ibid., p. 172.

36. Table based on the Campbell List in the Beatty papers. Note: The British ships which blew up are excluded as their destruction was caused by the one exceptional factor.

37. Marder A.J, Scapa Flow V 3, p. 101.

38. The Post Jutland Committee on Shells drew attention to the fact that as early as 1914 it had been discovered that a 13.5" shell fired against a 6" plate at an angle of 20 degrees failed to penetrate. See "Ammunition for Naval Guns", Technical History Section, Admiralty, May 1920, TH 29.

39. Jellicoe to the Admiralty 30/10/14, Adm 137/995.

40. For Marder's discussion see Scapa Flow V 3, p. 210-11.

41. Fayle C. Ernest, Seaborne Trade V 3, London, Murray 1924, p. 33.

42. Stone N, The Eastern Front, p. 158.

43. Ibid.

44. Marder A.J, Scapa Flow V 3, p. 209.

45. Churchill to Keyes 19/6/26, Keyes Papers, 15/5.

46. Jellicoe to Frewen 6/11/22, Frewen Papers, Add/Mss 53738.

47. Churchill to Keyes 25/8/24, Churchill Papers, 8/196.

48. Ibid.

49. See The World Crisis, p. 994-5.

50. Ibid., p. 997.

51. Ibid., p. 1002.

52. Ibid., p. 1006.

53. Ibid., p. 1008.

54. Ibid., p. 1010.

55. Ibid., p. 1016.

56. Ibid.

57. Ibid.

58. Ibid. It is certain that Churchill got this idea from reading the Naval Staff Appreciation which also advocates the centre deployment. The deployment diagrams used by Churchill on p. 1009 were sent to him by Kenneth Dewar, one of the authors of the study. Dewar to Churchill 10/11/26, Churchill Papers 8/204.

59. The World Crisis, p. 1016.

60. Ibid.

61. The World Crisis, First Edition, p. 152.

62. Dewar to Churchill 9/3/27, Churchill Papers 8/186.

63. The World Crisis, p. 1022.

64. Churchill Papers 8/99.

65. Dewar to Churchill 10/11/26, in Ibid 8/204.

66. The World Crisis, p. 1022.

67. Ibid., p. 1027.

68. Ibid.

69. Ibid., p. 1029.

70. Corbett Sir J, Naval

Operations V 3, p. 402.

71. The World Crisis, p. 1036.

72. Churchill to Bridgeman (1st Lord) 15/11/26, Churchill Papers 8/204.

73. Ibid.

74. The World Crisis, p. 985.

75. Ibid., p. 1004.

76. Ibid., p. 984.

77. Ibid., p. 990.

78. Ibid., p. 1039.

79. Churchill to Keyes 25/8/24, Churchill Papers 8/196.

80. Churchill Papers 8/158.

81. Beatty to Churchill 11/11/26, Churchill Papers 8/204; Dewar to Churchill 1/11/26, Churchill Papers 8/187.

82. Churchill Papers 8/158.

83. Ibid.

84. Marder A.J, Scapa Flow V 3, p. 109.

Chapter 12

The Somme And The Casualty Statistics Controversy

1. The World Crisis, p. 945.

2. Ibid., p. 957 & p. 960.

3. Ibid., p. 961.

4. Ibid., p. 953.

5. Ibid.

6. Churchill Papers 8/96.

7. Plumb J.H, "The Historian" in Churchill : Four Faces and the Man, London, Allen Lane, 1969, p. 143.

8. See the Churchill Papers 8/203 for the Churchill-Edmonds correspondence.

9. Churchill papers 8/189.

10. Edmonds to Churchill 6/7/26, Churchill Papers 8/203.

11. Churchill writes "defences" in the original, but this is clearly an error for offensives".

12. Churchill to Edmonds 7/7/26, Churchill Papers 8/203.

13. See Becke Major A.F, The Coming of the Creeping Barrage, Journal of the Royal Artillery, V58, 1931-2, p. 19-42.

14. Edmonds to Churchill 8/7/26 and 6/8/26, Churchill Papers 8/203.

15. Edmonds to Col. Horden 21/8/31, Churchill Papers 8/287.

16. The World Crisis, p. 1040.

17. Joffre to Haig 26/12/15, quoted in The Memoirs of Marshal Joffre V 2, London, Bles, 1932, p. 417.

18. Haig to Robertson 3/1/16, Robertson Papers, 1/27/6.

19. Edmonds Sir John, Military Operations : France and Belgium, 1916 V 1, London, Macmillan, 1932, p. 27.

20. Haig-Diary 14/1/16, quoted in Blake R. (Ed.), The Private Papers of Douglas Haig 1914-1919, London, Eyre & Spottiswoode, 1952, p. 125.

21. Haig to Joffre 1/2/16, W.O. 158/14.

22. Haig-Diary 25/2/16, Blake p. 133.

23. For a longer discussion of the

prospective battlefields see Keegan J, The Face of Battle, London, Cape, 1976, p. 210-11.

24. The World Crisis, p. 1042-3.

25. Blake, Editorial Notes, p. 152.

26. Haig to Joffre 10/2/16, W.O. 158/14.

27. Somme Draft Plan 3/4/16, 4th Army War Diary, W.O. 158/321.

28. Haig to Joffre 10/4/16, W.O. 158/14.

29. Rawlinson Diary 23/5/16, Rawlinson Papers, 1/5.

30. Memorandum by Kiggell 16/6/16, W.O. 158/234.

31. Haig to Joffre 26/6/16, W.O. 158/14.

32. Haig to Robertson 1/6/16, W.O. 158/21 and Haig to Robertson 10/6/16, W.O. 158/14.

33. War Committee Minutes 30/5/16, Cab 42/14/12.

34. The 115th Brigade of the 38th division "failed to attack" on July 7th and another Brigade on the night of the 7/8th. The division was withdrawn. Horne to Haig 13/7/16 and notes by Haig 15/7/16 and Rawlinson 14/7/16, W.O. 158/234.

35. The World Crisis, p. 1042.

36. As against the scope and main thrust of an attack. Both these features were disguised by the Germans in their attack of March 21st, 1918.

37. Rawlinson to Haig 19/4/16, 4th Army War Diary, W.O. 158/321.

38. Edmonds Sir J, 1916 VII, p. 288.

39. Haig to Rawlinson 13/4/16, 4th Army War Diary, W.O. 158/321.

40. Rawlinson to Haig 19/4/16, in Ibid.

41. Rawlinson Diary 13/5/16, Rawlinson Papers, 1/5.

42. The World Crisis, p. 1044. Actually this section was written by Edmonds.

43. e.g. "Information Gained From The Raiding Party On The Night Of The 5th", 4th Army Intelligence Summary 8/6/16, W.O. 157/171.

44. 4th Army Intelligence Summary 7/6/16, in Ibid.

45. 4th Army Intelligence Summary 29/6/16, in Ibid.,

46. 4th Army War Diary 26/6/16, W.O. 158/327.

47. 4th Army War Diary 29-30/6/16, in Ibid.

48. 4th Army War Diary 30/6/16, in Ibid.

49. Haig-Diary 30/6/16, Blake, p. 151.

50. Rawlinson Diary 30/6/16, Rawlinson Papers, 1/5.

51. Ibid.

52. The World Crisis, p. 1337.

53. Ibid.

54. Gilbert M, Winston S. Churchill V 4, London, Heinemann, 1975, p. 384-7.

55. The World Crisis, p. 1044-7.

56. Ibid., p. 1047.

57. Keegan, Face of Battle, p. 256-7.

58. Ibid., p. 259.

59. Montgomery to Edmonds 5/11/30, Cab 45/190.

60. Rawlinson Diary 1/7/16, Rawlinson Papers, 1/5.

61. Middlebrook M, The

First Day On The Somme,
London, Allen Lane, 1971, p.
148.
    62. Keegan, Face of
Battle, p. 260.
    63. The World Crisis, p.
1059-60.
    64. Haig to Robertson
8/7/16, W.O. 158/21.
    65. Haig to Joffre
11/9/16, W.O. 158/15.
    66. Haig to Robertson
7/10/16, W.O. 158/21.
    67. Rawlinson Diary
19/9/16, Rawlinson Papers,
1/5.
    68. 6/10/16, Rawlinson
Papers, 1/7.
    69. Horne A, The Price
of Glory : Verdun 1916,
London, Penguin, 1964, p.
298 and p. 309-11.
    70. Lord D'Abernon to
Curzon 26/7/21, Churchill
Papers 8/188.
    71. Churchill to Edmonds
29/8/23, in Ibid 8/203.
    72. Edmonds to Churchill
14/10/26, in Ibid 8/188.
    73. Churchill to Edmonds
15/10/26, in Ibid 8/203.
    74. Ibid.
    75. British and German
ratios are 1 killed to 4.5.
wounded and 1: 3.9.  If
8/10ths of the missing are
assigned to the killed the
ratios are 1: 2.8 and 1:
1.75. However the German
"missing" constitute 25% of
their total casualties while
the British figure is only
11% and this makes any
similar distribution to both
sides unlikely.  Clearly a
higher proportion of the
German missing has to be
added to their killed
category than British
missing to their killed and
this would tend to even up
the killed to wounded ratios.

    76. Churchill to Hume
21/10/26, Churchill Papers
8/203.
    77. Hume to Churchill
9/11/26, in Ibid 8/204.
    78. Edmonds to Churchill
18/11/24, in Ibid.
    79. Ibid.
    80. Churchill to Hume
12/11/26, in Ibid.
    81. Hume to Churchill
19/11/26, in Ibid.
    82. Stinger to Hume
18/11/26, in Ibid.
    83. Hume to Churchill
27/11/26, in Ibid.
    84. See Tables A and B
on p. 933-4.
    85. The World Crisis, p.
935.
    86. Ibid., p. 936.  That
is the offensives of 1915,
1916 and 1917.  Churchill
continually ignores the 1918
British offensive in which
the losses of the two sides
were approximately equal.
    87. Ibid., p. 936.
    88. Edmonds Sir J, 1916
V 1, p. 496-7.
    89. Edmonds Sir J,
Military Operations : France
and Belgium 1917 V 1,
London, Macmillan, 1940, p.
88 note 1.
    90. Williams M.J,
"Treatment of the German
Losses on the Somme in the
British Official History :
Military Operations France
and Belgium, 1916, V II",
R.U.S.I. Journal, V 111,
February 1966, p. 70.
    91. Ibid.
    92. Williams M.J,
"Thirty Per Cent : A Study
In Casualty Statistics",
R.U.S.I. Journal, V 109,
February 1964, p. 51-55.
    93. The World Crisis, p.
932-4.
    94. Edmonds goes through

similar arithmetical and mental gymnastics to arrive at a figure of 27% to be added to the Somme figures. See Williams, "Treatment of German Losses".

95. Edmonds Sir J, 1916 V 1, p. 497.

96. Oman Sir Charles, "The German Losses On The Somme", in The World Crisis : A Criticism, Port Washington, N.Y., Kennikat, 1970, (Reprint of 1928 Ed), p. 40-65.

97. Ibid., p. 51.

98. Ibid., p. 52-3.

99. Williams, Treatment of German Losses, p. 70.

100. Williams, Thirty Per Cent, p. 51; See also Terraine John, Douglas Haig : The Educated Soldier, London, Hutchinson, 1963, p. 321.

101. Terraine John, The Road to Passchendaele : The Flanders Offensive of 1917 : A Study in Inevitability, London, Leo Cooper, 1977, p. 347.

102. Ibid.

103. Ibid., p. 344.

104. Mitchell Major T.J. and G.M. Smith, Casualties and Medical Statistics of the Great War : Official Medical History of the War, London, H.M.S.O., 1931. See pages 122, 136, 149, 158, 168.

105. Winter J.M, Some Aspects of the Demographic Consequences of The First World War in Britain, Population Studies, V30, p. 541.

106. General Annual Reports of the British Army For the Period From 1st October 1913 to 30th September 1919, London, H.M.S.O., Cmd. 1193, 1921.

107. The World Crisis, Table A, p. 933.

108. The approximate difference between Churchill's Western Front figure for July-October 1916 and Edmonds' Somme only figure for the same period.

109. Military Effort, p. 362.

110. Grebler Leo and Wilhelm Winkler, The Cost of the World War to Germany and to Austria-Hungary, New Haven, Conn., Yale U.P., 1940, p. 57 and 87. (Published for the Carnegie Endowment For International Peace).

111. Ibid., p. 57-8.

112. Ibid., p. 27.

113. Hardach Gerd, The First World War 1914-1918, London, Allen Lane, 1977, p. 112.

114. Grebler and Winkler, The Cost of the World War, p. 30.

115. Ibid., p. 27.

116. Ibid.

Chapter 13

Churchill and the Tank 1914-18

1. History of the Ministry of Munitions, London, Ministry of Munitions, 1921, V 10, Supply of Munitions-Part 3-Tanks, p. 5-6. (Hereafter Ministry of Munitions, Tanks).

2. Ibid., p. 6.

3. Ibid.

4. Swinton Sir Ernest P, Eyewitness : being personal reminiscences of certain phases of the great war, including the genesis

of the tank, London, Hodder, 1932, p. 102.

5. Ibid., p. 81.
6. Ibid., p. 94.
7. Memorandum by Swinton, "Caterpillar Machine Gun Destroyer", N.D., W.O. 158/831.
8. Ibid.
9. Memorandum by Hankey 28/12/14, C.V.3, p. 339.
10. Churchill to Asquith 5/1/15, C.V.3, p. 377-8.
11. Scott-Moncrieff to Von Donop 5/1/15, Mun 5/211/1940/13.
12. Col. Holden to the Director of Armaments 18/2/15, in Ibid.
13. Sueter Rear-Admiral Sir Murray, The Evolution of the Tank : A Record of Royal Naval Air Service Caterpillar Experiments, London, Hutchinson, 1937, p. 53-4.
14. Ibid., p. 55-6.
15. Ministry of Munitions, Tanks, p.7.
16. Memorandum by Hetherington, N.D., Stern Papers, 1/C/1.
17. Ministry of Munitions, Tanks, p. 8.
18. Minutes by D'Eyncourt 18/9/16, Adm 116/1339.
19. Ibid.
20. Ibid.
21. Col. R.E. Crompton, "A Self Moving Armoured Fort for the Attack and Destruction of Enemy's Trenches" 22/2/15, Mun 5/210/1940/22.
22. Landship Committee Minutes 22/2/15, Adm 116/1339.
23. D'Eyncourt to Churchill 24/2/15 and Minutes by Churchill 24/2/15, Mun 5/210/1940/22.

24. Landship Committee-Progress Report 19/3/15, and D'Eyncourt to Churchill 20/3/15, Adm 116/1339.
25. Minutes of a meeting between Crompton, Director of Air Division's Representatives and Director of Contracts 24/3/15, Stern Papers, 1/C/1.
26. Ministry of Munitions, Tanks, p. 12.
27. Progress Report on the "Pedrail", Unsigned memorandum 11/6/15, in Ibid.
28. Ibid.
29. Landships Committee Minutes 14/6/15, in Ibid.
30. Fosters to Crompton 5/6/15, in Ibid, 01/7.
31. W.O. to Admiralty 21/6/15; Admiralty to W.O. 30/6/15, Adm 116/1339.
32. Undated note by French, W.O. 158/831.
33. Mun, 5/211/1940/13.
34. Landships: Preliminary Work-Memorandum by D'Eyncourt 16/6/15, Stern Papers, 1/C/1.
35. Landships Committee-Progress Report 23/6/15, in Ibid.
36. Minute by W.O. 1/7/15, Mun 5/210/1940/22.
37. Ministry of Munitions, Tanks, p. 20.
38. Minutes of Proceedings before the Royal Commission on Awards to Inventors-Tritton's Evidence 21/10/19, Q2818, Mun 5/210/1940/33.
39. Ibid., Q2579.
40. Memorandum by D'Eyncourt, N.D., D'Eyncourt Papers.
41. Royal Commission on Awards to Inventors-Tritton's Evidence 21/10/19, Q2580, Mun

5/210/1940/33.

42. Ibid., Q2597-2602.
D'Eyncourt claimed he
invented the sponson. See
Memorandum by D'Eyncourt in
D'Eyncourt Papers.

43. Ibid-Wilson's
Evidence, Q3084-9.

44. Minute by D'Eyncourt
16/10/15, Stern Papers,
1/C/1.

45. Ministry of
Munitions, Tanks, p. 28.

46. The World Crisis, p.
508-26.

47. Copy N.D, D'Eyncourt
Papers.

48. Ibid.

49. The World Crisis, p.
508.

50. Ibid., p. 509.

51. Ibid.

52. Ibid., p. 510.

53. Ibid., p. 512. The
names missing from the
minutes quoted by Churchill
are, in the first letter
written by Scott-Moncrieff,
Col. Jackson and Holden, and
Col. Holder later in the
same letter. The second
minute was from
Scott-Moncrieff to Holden
and the third was written by
Holden.

54. Ibid., p. 513.

55. Ibid., p. 512-4.

56. Ibid., p. 515.

57. Ibid.

58. Ibid.

59. Ibid., p. 516.

60. Ibid., p. 515.

61. Ibid.

62. Ibid., p. 525.

63. Ibid., p. 1052-3.

64. Ibid., p. 525.

65. Haig to Robertson
29/7/16, W.O. 158/843. See
also Edmonds, 1916 V 2, p.
233-5.

66. Terraine John, Haig,
p. 222-3.

67. Rawlinson Diary
30/8/16, Rawlinson Papers,
1/5.

68. Swinton, Eyewitness,
p. 261.

69. Edmonds, 1916 V 2,
p. 365-6.

70. Fuller Col. J, "The
History, Organization, Ideas
and Training of Tanks",
March 1917, Fuller Papers,
TS/8.

71. The World Crisis, p.
525 and p. 1053.

72. Draft Scheme for
Operation GY Third Stage,
W.O. 158/349.

73. The World Crisis, p.
1188-9.

74. Ibid., p. 1189.

75. Ibid., p. 1190.

76. Sixth Division
Report 17/12/17, W.O.
158/357.

77. Miles Captain W,
Military Operations : France
and Belgium 1917 V 3,
London, H.M.S.O., 1948, p.
88-9.

78. Ibid., p. 60.

79. Ibid., p. 53.

80. Sixth Division
Report 17/12/17, Appendix A,
W.O. 158/357.

81. Miles, 1917 V 3, p.
61.

82. The World Crisis, p.
1188.

83. Kirke Col. R.M. St.
G, "Some Aspects of
Artillery Development during
the First World War on the
Western Front", Journal of
the Royal Artillery, V 101,
Sept. 1974, p. 139.

84. Brooke Major A.F,
"The Evolution of Artillery
in the Great War: VII : The
Evolution of Artillery
Tactics" (3), Journal of the
Royal Artillery, 1926-7, p.
321.

85. Ludendorff General, My War Memoirs 1914-1918 V 2, (3rd Ed.), London, Hutchinson, N.D., p. 494.

86. Fuller Col. J, "Results and Deductions [from Cambrai], Fuller Papers, 1/165.

87. Tank Supply 1917-18, Mun 4/775.

88. Henneker Col. A.M, Transportation On The Western Front, London, H.M.S.O., 1937, p. 306.

89. Ibid., p. 306. See also the narrative "Cambrai" in Cab 45/200.

90. Training Note No. 16-Tank Tactics Feb. 1917, Fuller Papers, TS/6.

91. Cooper Bryan, The Ironclads of Cambrai, London, Pan, 1970, p. 71.

92. Minute by Lloyd George 12/2/16, Mun 5/210/1940/10.

93. Swinton, Eyewitness, p. 214.

94. For Tank production figures see Mun 4/744-775 and Mun 2/15-17.

95. Orgill Douglas, The Tank : Studies in the Development and Use of a Weapon, London, Heinemann, 1970, p. 21.

96. Ministry of Munitions, Tanks, p. 36.

97. Elles and Chamberlain, AVF of WWI, p. 36.

98. Ibid.

99. Tank Supply 1917, Mun 4/774.

100. Mechanical Power in the Offensive 9/11/16, The World Crisis, Appendix N, p. 1437-1440.

101. Memorandum by Churchill 21/10/17, in Ibid., p. 1442.

102. Ibid., p. 1167.

103. Man-Power and The Situation 8/12/17, in Ibid, p. 1225.

104. Munitions Programme, 1919, 5/3/18, in Ibid, p. 1241.

105. Churchill to Harington 21/6/18, in Ibid, p. 1315-7.

106. Ibid., p. 1322.

107. Churchill to Lloyd George 9/9/18, in Ibid, p. 1349.

108. Ibid., p. 1350.

109. See W.O. 158/836.

110. Haig to W.O. 2/10/16, in Ibid.

111. Ministry of Munitions, Tanks, p. 39.

112. Montague (Minister of Munitions) to Stephenson Kent 23/11/16, Mun 5/210/1940/10.

113. Stern to Elles? January 1917, Stern Papers, 1/C/3.

114. Stern-Diary 24/4/17, Stern Papers, 1/C/3.

115. W.O. to Ministry of Munitions 24/8/17, Mun 5/211/1940/37.

116. Tank Supply 1917, Mun 4/774. The August figures were reduced because the tank factories apparently shut for a week's holiday.

117. Ministry of Munitions, Tanks, p. 49.

118. Tank Supply 1917, Mun 4/774. Exact figure 521 to end of July.

119. Minutes of a Conference at the Ministry of Munitions with War Office Representatives 29/9/17, Mun 5/211/1940/37.

120. Ibid.

121. W.O. to Ministry of Munitions 15/10/17, Mun 5/12/200/56; Ministry of Munitions, Tanks, p. 56.

122. For production figures see Mun 4/775 and Mun 2/15.

123. Minutes of the Tank Co-ordinating Committee 7/1/18, Mun 4/5160.

124. Ministry of Munitions, Tanks, p. 58.

125. Minutes of a Conference at the Ministry of Munitions with War Office Representatives 29/9/17, Mun 5/211/1940/37.

126. Minutes of a Meeting at the Ministry of Munitions 11/2/18, in Ibid.

127. Churchill to Moore 20/2/18, in Ibid.

128. Munitions Council-Committee 57-Tanks-Minutes 27/2/18, in Ibid.

129. Minutes of a Joint War Office-Admiralty-Munitions Meeting 7/3/18, Mun 5/210/1940/3.

130. Minutes of a Meeting at the Ministry of Munitions 8/3/18, Mun 5/211/1940/37; Diary of Sir Henry Wilson 8/3/18, Wilson Papers, DS/Misc/80/8.

131. Ministry of Munitions Note 1/6/18, Mun 5/211/1940/9.

132. Moore to Churchill 20/6/18, Mun 5/211/1940/37.

133. Churchill to Lloyd George 10/8/18, quoted in Gilbert M, Winston S. Churchill V 4 Companion Documents, London, Heinemann, 1977, p. 370-1.

134. "Report on Condition of Mechanical Warfare Supply Department at August 1918 by J.B. Maclean", Mun 5/211/1940/37.

135. Memorandum by Col. Stern 8/8/18, D'Eyncourt Papers.

136. Tank Board, Minutes of First Meeting 15/8/18, in Ibid.

137. Tank Board Co-ordinating Committee, Minutes 25/10/18, Mun 4/5160.

138. See Mun 4/775 and Mun 2/15-17.

139. History of the Ministry of Munitions V 12, Part II, Appendix VI.

140. See Mun 2/16 weeks ending July 6, August 17, September 21. The tank production figures are again short for a week in August 1918.

141. Ministry of Munitions, Tanks, p. 60-9.

142. Report by Maclean August 1918, Mun 5/211/1940/37.

143. Ibid.

144. Ministry of Munitions, Tanks, p. 66.

145. Minutes of a Meeting at the Ministry of Munitions with the Major Tank Contractors 20/6/18, Mun 5/211/1940/37.

Chapter 14

## Churchill and the Submarine

1. The World Crisis, p. 697-701.

2. Ibid., p. 702-4.

3. Ibid., p. 704.

4. Memorandum by Admiral Tudor (4th Sea Lord) 26/2/16, Adm 137/1159.

5. Memorandum by Tudor 24/11/14, Adm 137/968.

6. Donaldson to Fisher 28/11/14, in Ibid.

7. Memorandum by Donaldson 9/12/14 and Remarks on Submarine Attack by the Naval War Staff Feb. 1915, in Ibid.

8. Gayer Captain A, "Summary of German Submarine Operations in the Various Theatres of War, from 1914

to 1918", U.S. Naval Institute Proceedings, V 51, 1926, p. 627.

9. Chatterton E. Keble, Fighting the U-Boats, London, Hurst & Blackett, 1942, p. 100.

10. Memorandum by Captain Dumas, Adm 137/1047.

11. Marder A.J, Scapa Flow V 2, p. 350.

12. Grant Robert M, U-Boat Intelligence 1914-1918, London, Putnam, 1969, p. 182-3. Contains the most reliable list of U-Boat's sunk.

13. Churchill Papers 8/146.

14. Grant, U-Boat Intelligence, p. 182-190.

15. Ibid.

16. By April 60 yachts had been armed and 500 trawlers and drifters, with another 120 being fitted out. Corbett Sir J, Naval Operations V 2, p. 389-90.

17. Grant, U-Boat Intelligence, p. 182-3.

18. Ibid. Two were probably sunk by their own mines, one by a Russian mine and the cause of one loss is not known.

19. Jameson Rear-Admiral William, The Most Formidable Thing : The Story of the Submarine from its earliest days to the end of World War I, London, Hart-Davis, 1965, p. 174; Hezlet Vice-Admiral Sir Arthur, The Submarine and Sea Power, London, Peter Davies, 1967, p. 46-7 and p. 52.

20. The Admiralty, Merchant Shipping Losses, London, H.M.S.O., 1919, Table A and C.

21. Gibson R.H. and M. Prendergast, The German Submarine War 1914-1918, (2nd Ed.), London, Constable, 1931, p. 80.

22. Great Britain-Parliament, Merchant Shipping and the Submarine, London, H.M.S.O., 1918, (CMD 9221).

23. Ibid.

24. May Ernest R, The World War and American Isolation 1914-1917, Cambridge (Mass.), Harvard U.P., 1966, p. 123. (Harvard Historical Studies V71).

25. Ibid., p. 208-9.

26. Ibid., p. 219-27.

27. Admiralty-Merchant Shipping Losses, Table A.

28. Churchill to K.G.B. Dewar 14/11/26, Churchill Papers 8/204.

29. It would be unnecessarily tedious to list all the sections of The World Crisis which Churchill has taken directly from Dewar's account, or those he has merely paraphrased or rearranged. It is sufficient to indicate that p. 1201 to p. 1218 (including the diagram) very largely comes from Dewar's paper. See Churchill Papers 8/187.

30. Churchill Papers 8/187; The World Crisis, p. 1193, 1203, 1213.

31. Churchill Papers 8/187.

32. The World Crisis, p. 1213 and 1218. Churchill's major additions are underlined.

33. Churchill Papers 8/187.

34. The World Crisis, p. 1212. Churchill's major additions are underlined.

35. Churchill Papers 8/187.

36. Ibid.
37. The World Crisis, p. 1196.
38. Ibid.
39. Ibid.
40. Ibid., p. 1196-8. Dewar supplied Churchill with a book from which Churchill took his account. Dewar to Marsh 11/11/26, Churchill Papers 8/187.
41. The World Crisis, p. 1203.
42. Churchill Papers 8/187.
43. The World Crisis, p. 1207.
44. Churchill W.S, Thoughts and Adventures, London, Odhams, 1947, "The U-boat War", p. 92-9.

Chapter 15

Writing The World Crisis 1916-1918.

1. Beaverbrook to Churchill 23/11/26, Churchill Papers 8/204.
2. Ibid.
3. The World Crisis, p. 1098-1116.
4. Churchill to Beaverbrook 27/11/26, quoted in Gilbert M, Winston S. Churchill V 5 Companion Documents, London, Heinemann, 1979. Hereafter, C.V.5.
5. Hankey to Churchill 8/12/26, Churchill Papers 8/204.
6. See The World Crisis, p. 1115-6.
7. Ibid., p. 1136, 1178, 1181-2, 1220-7.
8. Churchill to Beaverbrook 30/11/26, C.V.5, p. 890.
9. Beaverbrook to Churchill 24/10/26, Churchill Papers 8/203.
10. The World Crisis, p. 1140.
11. Haig-Diary 27/4/18, Blake, p. 306.
12. The World Crisis, p. 1190.
13. Churchill to Haig 20/11/26, C.V.5, p. 884.
14. Haig to Churchill 1/12/26, Churchill Papers 8/204.
15. Churchill to Haig 6/12/26, in Ibid.
16. Ibid.
17. Haig to Churchill 15/12/26, in Ibid. Haig's only condition was that 100 extra copies be duplicated by the printer for him to autograph to raise funds for ex-servicemen.
18. Haig to Churchill 13/3/27, Churchill Papers 8/211.
19. Beaverbrook to Churchill 22/11/26, in Ibid 8/204.
20. Churchill to Beaverbrook 23/11/26, C.V.5, p. 884-5.
21. Churchill Papers 8/161.
22. Ibid. See The World Crisis, p. 1123-4.
23. Haig to Nivelle 6/1/17, Blake, p. 190-1.
24. Churchill Papers 8/161.
25. The World Crisis, p. 1125.
26. Churchill Papers 8/171.
27. Ibid.
28. The World Crisis, p. 1325-6.
29. Churchill Papers 8/171.
30. Ibid.
31. See The World Crisis, p. 1326 (The last

sentence of the first paragraph).

32. Churchill Papers 8/171.

33. The World Crisis, p. 1329.

34. Churchill Papers 8/171.

35. The World Crisis, p. 1327.

36. Churchill Papers 8/172.

37. The World Crisis, p. 1340, emphasis added.

38. Churchill Papers 8/172.

39. The World Crisis, p. 1343.

40. Ibid., p. 1220-1.

41. Churchill Papers 8/166.

42. Dewar G.A.B. and Lt-Col. J.H. Boraston, Sir Douglas Haig's Command V 2, London, Constable, 1922, p. 17.

43. Churchill Papers 8/166.

44. Ibid.

45. The World Crisis, p. 1260.

46. Haig-Diary 7/1/18, Blake, p. 278.

47. Churchill Papers 8/161.

48. Ibid.

49. Ibid.

50. The World Crisis, p. 1136.

51. Hankey-Diary 4/5/17, Hankey Papers 1/1.

52. Haig to Robertson 29/4/17, Blake, p. 222.

53. Haig-Diary 3/5/17, Blake, p. 226.

54. Military Effort, p. 361.

55. Haig to Churchill 15/12/26, Churchill Papers 8/204.

56. The World Crisis, p. 1230-1.

57. Churchill Papers 8/166.

58. Ibid.

59. The World Crisis, p. 1230.

60. Churchill Papers 8/166.

61. The World Crisis, p. 1229.

62. Edmonds to Churchill 20/7/26, Churchill Papers 8/203.

63. Churchill Papers 8/190.

64. Ibid 8/189. The Paragraph beginning "The retrograde movement" on p. 1126.

65. Edmonds to Churchill 2/9/26, in Ibid 8/203.

66. Edmonds to Churchill 19/10/26, in Ibid 8/190.

67. Those concerning the 59th and 36th Divisions are quoted verbatim; the accounts of the 24th and 9th Divisions are slightly changed and that of the 18th Division substantially rearranged. Edmonds to Churchill 20/7/26, Churchill Papers 8/203 and The World Crisis, p. 1254-6.

68. Edmonds to Churchill 20/7/26, Churchill Papers 8/203.

69. Churchill Papers 8/104.

70. The World Crisis, p. 1148-9. See also Appendix N.

71. Keyes to Churchill 1/12/26, Keyes Papers, 15/5.

72. Churchill Papers 8/104.

73. Churchill to Keyes 29/10/26, in Ibid 8/203.

74. Keyes to Churchill 1/12/26, in Ibid 8/174.

75. Churchill to Keyes 18/12/26, Keyes Papers, 15/5.

favours Carden's plan 63;
and Fisher 63-4
Baldwin, Brigadier-General
A.H. and August attack at
Anzac 153
Balkans (See also Bulgaria,
Greece, Roumania)
British policy in 182-183;
influenced by Russian
Front 183; inefficiency of
Balkan Armies 184-6;
communications in 186
Balzer, Lieutenant-Commander
117, 118
Barham
at Jutland 188; W/T
destroyed 192
Bartoleme, Commodore Charles
de
opinion of Carden's plan 58
Battenburg, Prince Louis of
meets with Churchill
before Coronel 10; fails
to pass Churchill's
instructions to Cradock
10; adds Defence to
Stoddart's squadron 10;
and Bacchante cruisers 18;
treatment of in The World
Crisis 13-14, 274
Battlecruisers, British
in Mediterranean 1; at
Heligoland 16; at
Scarborough Raid 20-21; at
Dogger Bank 23-4; at
Jutland 188-90; alleged
flaws in design 193
Battleship Hill
152
Bax-Ironside, Sir Henry
89
Beatty, Vice-Admiral Sir
David
at Scarborough Raid 20; at
Dogger Bank 23-4;
at Jutland
meets enemy battlecruisers
188; signal not seen by
5th B.S. 188, 189; sights
German Fleet 189; fails
to keep Jellicoe informed
190; the run north 190;

position at deployment
191; "follow-me" signal
193; treatment of in The
World Crisis 24, 181, 198,
199, 206, 208, 274
Beaverbrook, Lord
critical of Churchill's
later chapters 258;
critical of Churchill's
handling of Lloyd George
258, 259; critical of
Churchill's handling of
Bonar Law 260; critical of
Churchill's sections on
Haig and Jellicoe 262
Belgian Army
retires into Antwerp 26;
and decision to evacuate
Antwerp 31
Birdwood, Lieutenant-General
Sir William
opinion of naval attack
91; plans August attack at
Anzac 151
Birmingham
at Scarborough Raid 21
Blucher
at Dogger Bank 23
Bonar Law, Andrew
and May political crisis
130; attitude to Churchill
130, 132; and Fisher 131;
treatment of in The World
Crisis 146, 260, 278
Boraston, Lieutenant-Colonel
J.H.
on Haig's Strategy 1918,
266, 267
Borkum Operation
hazards of 46; advocated
by Churchill 51, 53, 55;
approved by War Council
55; opposed by Jellicoe
and Richmond 62
Bouvet
at Dardanelles 95
Braithwaite, Major-General
W.P.
on 29th Division
transports 120
Bratiano, Ion J.C.
policy towards Entente 183